As writer and publisher, Jon Wynne-Tyson has long been concerned to help promote a more holistic environmentalism. His own books include THE CIVILISED ALTERNATIVE, FOOD FOR A FUTURE and a novel, SO SAY BANANA BIRD, set in the Caribbean. As publisher, he has issued key works in humane education, including Porphyry's ON ABSTINENCE FROM ANIMAL FOOD, Catherine Roberts' THE SCIENTIFIC CONSCIENCE, Richard Ryder's VICTIMS OF SCIENCE and Henry Salt's classic ANIMALS' RIGHTS.

THE
EXTENDED
CIRCLE

A DICTIONARY OF HUMANE THOUGHT

COMPILED BY JON WYNNE-TYSON

*Until he extends the circle of his
compassion to all living things, man will
not himself find peace.*
Albert Schweitzer

CARDÍNAL

A Cardinal Book

First published in Great Britain by
Centaur Press Ltd, Fontwell, Sussex
Second impression, with corrections, February 1986
This edition published in Cardinal by Sphere Books Ltd 1990

Photoset in North Wales by
Derek Doyle & Associates, Mold, Clwyd.
Printed in Great Britain by
Cox & Wyman Ltd, Reading

Sphere Books Ltd
A Division of
Macdonald & Co (Publishers) Ltd
Orbit House
1 New Fetter Lane
London EC4A 1AR

A member of Maxwell Macmillan Pergamon Publishing Corporation

To my mother, Esmé Wynne–Tyson, who devoted so much of her life to affirming that no political, economic or religious system can bring lasting benefit to ourselves or to our environment unless our hearts and minds accept the paramount need for a philosophy of compassion.

Take sides. Neutrality helps the oppressor, never the victim. Silence encourages the tormentor, never the tormented.

Elie Wiesel (1928–)
on accepting the 1986 Nobel Peace Prize

CONTENTS

INTRODUCTION

Herbert Spencer said that willingness to think of oneself 'in the place of another' was 'the greatest civilizing force'. Walt Whitman, visualizing the suffering of another, declared 'I am that man.' Nearer our day, Schweitzer was convinced that 'the destiny of man is to become more and more humane'. Kenneth Clark has looked forward to our recapture of 'that feeling of kinship which will help us establish a feeling of the unity of creation'.

Voices in the wilderness, maybe, but far from being 'lone'. Indeed, the universality of the sentiment has prompted this anthology, whose aim is to present the views of some of those writers, philosophers, scientists, churchmen and less public figures who have seen – if only fitfully and with limited personal commitment – the underlying unity of life, and our obligation to extend the boundary of our compassion to the whole natural world. This awareness is as important to the humanistic as to the religious observer, for its corollary is that we cannot expect improvement in relationships between men until we have learned the lesser art of pity for those we can safely ill-treat.

This is not a dictionary of or for prophets of doom. It does not have to be. Most thinking people feel less than sanguine about the future of the human race. Any concentration of mood demands catharsis, and the logical effect of a concern over so depressing a prospect as racial annihilation must be an ambition, however despairingly held, that we may learn our lesson before it is too late. The contributors to this selection have shared a vision – whether fleetingly or steadfastly held – of an alternative to the doom-sayers' predictions.

Perhaps the most hopeful evidence of mankind's evolutionary potentialities is our capacity for selfless compassion – the deepest level of an environmental conscience. It may not be abundant, but the fact that it exists at all is conclusive evidence that we are not necessarily governed by our basest instincts; it is difficult, in fact, to dismiss the premise that its existence must inevitably bring gradual acceptance of the need to build into our educational programmes a felt sense of our obligation to identify and accept the implications of the indivisibility of cruelty and violence. That acceptance is possibly our best hope for survival.

It would be irrational for those of anthropocentric persuasion to feel antagonism toward this concept. Mankind has a self-interested obligation to show compassion toward other forms of life; for it is not, in the nature of things, feasible that hearts hardened to the suffering of creatures in subjugation to man can show genuine and sustained sympathy for their own kind.

This anthology proves that there is nothing new about the realization of the connection between our treatment of non-humans and of each other. Clear minds down the centuries have seen that the violence man shows to man is inextricably linked to the violence we have inflicted upon other species and our shared environment.

Yet despite the media's daily presentation of the sad facts of human behaviour, many still claim that concern with our treatment of other species is irrelevant and exaggerated. The nature and statistics of that treatment prove this to be, at the very least, wishful thinking. If we examine what is done to animals in the fields of vivisection and diet alone, the figures are a shocking condemnation of our indifference to others' right to life and wellbeing. Because animals lack a language we can understand, we listen only to our own thin excuses for treating them so abominably.

Yet there are those who, even today, flatly deny that non-human species are truly sentient, dismissing as anthropomorphism the suggestion that 'mere animals' should be granted rights. But the evidence that animals suffer fear and pain is as conclusive, apart from the convenient device of a shared language, as the evidence that our next-door neighbour suffers fear and pain. This alone should be good enough reason for causing the minimum suffering to other forms of life.

To sound a personal note, the first edition of this dictionary took six years to compile, and a lifetime's appalled observation of our unremitting cruelty toward non-human species. Its starting point, perhaps, was in 1929, at the death of a pig. Ten years later, war-time realization of mankind's capacity for barbarity cemented a conviction that our treatment of each other will not improve until we have learned to behave more compassionately toward all sentient life – by no means least toward the creatures that are weaker and less intelligent than ourselves, whether children, the mentally sub-normal, or non-human species.

Numerous books have been written on the specifics of our treatment of our surroundings, from pleas for a more conservative use of natural resources to stark evidence of particular examples of man's atrocious cruelties. But while such subjects as vivisection, rodeos, zoos, 'factory farming' and the many forms of contemptible bullying euphemistically known as sport, are touched on in these pages, the purpose is not to supply further evidence of specific cruelties and human failing. Such a catalogue would be vast, depressing, and perhaps self-defeating.*

The purpose is the more positive one of underlining the need for a beneficial love as an antidote to the chilling inhumanity of societies which have inherited the life-denying values of an economy deifying growth above humane and long-term considerations; whose scientific viewpoint is rooted in Descartian double-think; whose spiritual leaders have moved little beyond an anthropocentric humanism; whose vision of mankind's potential is dominated by the self-centred acquisitiveness of a consumer society.

Inevitably, the sources quoted in this book have had a higher and more promising view of our species than that held by many of the political, commercial, scientific and religious spokesmen of our day, who in their separate ways are more interested in the domination and exploitation of their own kind than in their evolutionary potentialities. But the existence of an idealistic ambition for our species is, surely, of the highest importance to our future.

In compiling this anthology, it became clear that few thinkers of stature have failed to come out in defence of the weak, the innocent and the helpless. Animals, birds, fish – that whole great nation we contemptuously designate the sub-species – are of that kind. The range and unanimity of the sentiments found in these pages indicate that too many prominent people of high creativity and imagination have spoken in defence of other sentient life for their awareness to be written off as some aberration.

Is it important that this consensus of concern should be proven? I believe it is. I feel that there are certain fundamental truths about our place in nature whose recognition is not sentimentality or neurosis, but the

* Any reader needing evidence of the callousness of which the human heart and mind are capable may refer to page 613 'Some Additional Reading'.

hallmark of a maturity. We should approach with caution the opinions of those who have failed to recognize the indivisibility of violence and man's commensurate need and obligation to bring his relationship with all living creatures into harmony if he is to contribute to building a more civilized and workable world. All that we do to other species is spiritual preparation for our interpersonal relationships.

It is a hopeful sign that much of the unease and repugnance felt by those aware of the depths to which we are prepared to sink in order to gratify the most superficial of greeds and pleasures, is to be found among young people. No longer can 'animal lovers' be dismissed as a bunch of old women wrapped up in their cats and dogs. Although the corruption of the young by their elders is still the saddest of all spectacles, the process is today being resisted not only by the idealism and empathy natural to the few whose upbringing has been spared the grossest desensitizing, but with a knowledge and articulation that are among the blessings of our media-bludgeoned times. More keenly aware of the world around them than earlier generations, many young people today accept that we cannot expect improvements in relationships between men until we have learned the lesser art of pity for those inarticulate and weaker creatures whom man exploits; that until our species has been educated into a more compassionate regard for all sentient life, tolerance between their own kind is frail and suspect.*

To my relief, there has been ample evidence that this source-book is not being overlooked by the younger activists. We live in an era of political manipulation and

---

* There is an immutable law which no amount of man's cleverness can change. As Edwin Arnold expressed it, we cannot avoid reckoning with that 'fixed arithmetic of the universe which meteth good for good and ill for ill'.

public demonstration, and many who support violence against property or person in their campaign for human or animal rights are genuinely frustrated by the seeming ineffectiveness of less dramatic methods. But danger lies in escalation. When it is apparent that violent protest can in fact bring forward legislation, the temptation is to press for further violence, especially when little else seems to arouse the interest of the media.

It is vital not to lose sight of the fact that felt compassion comes through humane education, not through violence. Legislation may be a genuine goal, but legislation to repress, rather than legislation which reflects a fundamental shift in human values, is like a drug masking a symptom. If activism is to achieve anything of lasting value, it must be fed by and employed alongside the educational process, not supplant them.

It is not easy for the young, and for those newly aware of our horrific treatment of non-humans, to accept the slower path to reform. The gut feeling is: 'Here we are, pussyfooting around with talk of humane education and considered legislation, while millions more sentient creatures are caused fear and suffering. Let's take action *now – any* action that will bring immediate change.'

Much of that action has been, and is going to be, taken; pity and idealism can overwhelm the mind, just as can fear and hatred. But however well-intentioned the reasoning, if it fosters violence and hatred toward people, it is from the same stable that makes for wars in supposedly just (or any other) causes. It ignores the inescapable fact that violence breeds violence, whatever seeming and short-term good may be achieved on the way; it fails to recognize that good ends are not justified by evil means (the very basis for any valid objection to vivisection).

What is to be, will be. Whether the commitment is to peaceful or militant measures, the need for humane education will remain. The feeling and wisdom behind the quotations in this book can never be invalidated. They can only help to create a climate in which the best answers will most rapidly be found.

In the long term, there is no real answer but to work for global agreement to build into educational systems the ethical basis for environmental responsibility. A compassionate philosophy – relating to all sentient life, not expediently allocated to ourselves but withheld from other life forms – must be our priority. Can we afford the alternative – that of continuing our horrific record as a species for whom destruction of itself and others has become endemic? I believe not. We made the future and it is not working.

Although we live in a time of growing environmental awareness, the emphasis is anthropocentric, apt to produce slogans and euphemisms which cloak the half-heartedness with which we accept our obligations. 'Conservation' is a case in point, being vaguely welcomed by many as evidence that we care about the environment. But there is a world of difference between conserving for controlled exploitation and conserving to leave alone.

The argument for an environmental ethic needs heart as much as mind. There is no great virtue or wonder in humans showing concern for other humans. Rats do it too. Most of us can identify with each other if left alone by those in the business of bringing out the worst in human nature. It is worth considering that if the slant of this anthology is markedly toward encouraging a greater compassion to lower species of animals, this is because those who have this sentiment maturely in perspective are in general against cruelty to their own as well as other species; whereas those who hold that 'the proper study of mankind is man' are usually indifferent to the creatures who share this earth with him. That balance needs to be redressed. It is the objective of this source-book to bring together the pity, the pleading and the anger of those who have had the breadth of vision not to discriminate between the objects of compassion. They are not among those responsible for the fatuous and insupportable assertion that there has to be some mysterious choice between concern for men *or* for animals.

That smug view is common among scientific humanists. To some degree, it is true, we are all humanists; but there are many levels. The most arrogant hold that man should subdue and beat nature. Such opportunists are perhaps truly 'cranks', blindly indifferent to the fate of future generations, aligned with the least responsible stratum of the scientific fraternity in being convinced of their prerogative to exploit their surroundings in whatever manner greed and curiosity dictate.

This is not to isolate humanists for criticism. Paradoxically, for all that science has enormously raised the incidence of inhumanity toward sentient life, some modern scientists and medical men have a better track record than most religious leaders for awareness of the need for a more compassionate environmentalism. Most Christian clergy have shown almost total indifference toward infliction of suffering on other species. They have gone to great lengths to create dogma, and to find biblical texts, to justify our diabolical treatment of non-human life.

Such moral blindness does not today swell their congregations, least of all from the ranks of the thoughtful young, who tend to be guided more by heart and instinct than by history and precedent. They seem little concerned whether Jesus Christ, St Paul, the Popes and other spiritual leaders, have equivocated on our responsibility to other species. What matters, in a society less bemused by doctrinal abstractions, is the conviction that cruelty is negative, evil and self-defeating, whereas pity is positive, humanizing, and life-enhancing. If it is true that Jesus or any other historical figure proved himself indifferent to the suffering of non-human life, then to that degree they proved only their own limitations.

With their great independence of thought, today's young are less impressed by the supposed wisdom of leaders and systems; more aware of the dangers inherent in total commitment to a labelled philosophy. They see the need to interpret and expand received systems, such as the current vogue for Utilitarianism (which by definition invites a conditional compassion which is less to be trusted than a heart-felt sense of kinship).

The burden of the views quoted in this anthology is that humanist and religionist alike stands in urgent need of facing the question: 'Is man an evolving species?' For if he is not, he must be regarded as a vicious and irredeemable aberration whose chosen role is to prey, plunder, torture and destroy – an absurd concept for Christians, for if mankind is immune from the process of evolution, it is clearly pointless to give credence to the gospel of Jesus Christ. Equally, for humanists to hold that man is a helpless tool of circumstance and instinct is to ascribe to him less prescience and autonomy than that enjoyed by a baboon; the mere acquisition of a more reasoning mind must be a positive handicap in a species incapable of spiritual evolution and a selfless idealism, and the sooner the world rids itself of such a dead-end, dangerous and destructive pest, the better for the balance of nature. Dismissal of the notion that man is an evolving species is the philosophy of nihilism. Its acceptance dictates the necessity for a philosophy of compassion.

By no means all whose words are quoted in these pages were as consistent as their perceptions may suggest. Schopenhauer, for instance, stressed that compassion covers all ethical necessities, for:

> In reality, what is generosity, clemency, humanity? Is it not *compassion* applied to the weak, to the guilty, or to the human race as a whole? Even benevolence and friendship are seen to result from a constant compassion directed upon a particular object; for to desire that someone should not suffer is nothing else than to desire that he should be happy ... The more closely the living spectator identifies himself with the living sufferer, the more active does pity become.

But after expressing a deep concern for animals and their sufferings, and great scorn for those who treat them as 'things' made for man's use, he could suddenly remark:

> We may observe that compassion for sentient beings is not to carry us to the length of abstaining from flesh, like the Brahmins.

As Kenneth Clark writes in his book *Animals and Men*, 'The love of animals is often spoken of by intellectuals as an example of modern sentimentality.' He quotes Vasari's well-known passage concerning Leonardo da Vinci who:

> greatly delighted in horses, and in all other animals, which he controlled with the greatest love and patience, and this he showed when, often passing by places where birds were sold, he would take them out of their cages and, having paid those who were selling them the price asked, would let them fly into the air, giving them back their lost liberty.

An earlier traveller, Corsali, writing in Leonardo's lifetime of a gentle savage tribe, says that 'they will not eat the flesh of any living thing, like our Leonardo Vinci.' As Clark wryly remarks: 'Leonardo not only loved animals, but, with a consistency rather rare among animal lovers today, was a vegetarian.'

In its more holistic perceptions, the new generation of intellectuals is nearer to Leonardo than to Schopenhauer. Young academics such as Peter Singer, Richard Ryder, Tom Regan and Stephen Clark have made respectable what earlier generations of thinking individuals have lacked the platform to express. Ecology is a tolerated specialism. It stands for a concept of life and values in which the practical, the ethical and the philosophical elements are (or, logically, should be) given equal weight. As I have suggested in an earlier book,* employed in this, its most mature if as yet nascent sense, it goes a long way toward standing for that compound of wonder, knowledge, faith and fierce inner need for a sense of direction and framework of behaviour that first prompted the notion of a supreme God.

It may be that this maturing concept of ecology is stimulating a modern yet essentially eternal philosophy for the future; a vision that may help build the bridge between science and those less material concerns which provide the main evidence that mankind is (or can become) more than a race of merely clever apes.

It has been difficult to prevent this introduction reading like an apologia, but if we think about it there are two main nightmares in our ill-conducted world – what men do to each other and what they do to other species. The connection between the two has as yet gone almost unrecognized by the public at large. But is this not what ecological morality should be about? One does not need to be a seer, a scientist, a sectarian, or even a sociologist (who ought to be a compound of all three, but seldom is) to recognize the simple but generally ignored fact that the total world situation is not going to be fundamentally improved if evolution's leading animal imagines that its only moral obligation is toward its own kind. We do not

* *The Civilized Alternative.*

need biblical endorsement to know that cruelty begets cruelty, violence breeds violence, and that the exploitation and greed of which man is so uniquely capable cannot simply be switched off like a light when he turns from his rape of the animal world to the difficulties of social relationships within his own species.

As Peter Ackroyd wrote in a review (*The Times*, 11 February 1985) of 'The Natural World' (BBC2), 'The snake sees one world and the bird sees another, emphasizing the fact that reality itself is a hall of mirrors in which each creature sees only those images which its species needs to understand.' That understanding is built into the nature of the non-human. For us, it is an awareness we have still to re-learn.

Realization of the ecological basis for kinship should be built into our educational curricula. For what have we made of education to date? We worship academic distinction — mere aptitude for absorbing facts and passing examinations. It seems we have yet to learn that it is not the power to absorb facts that makes us properly educated and superior to other apes, but the power of sympathetic imagination. The difference between a chimpanzee and an academic can be, in both senses of the phrase, no more than a matter of degree. Only insofar as our imaginations guide and enrich that sponge-like organ we too often confuse with a truly developed mind, have we any cause to hope for better things for the world and for ourselves. If all we elect to do for future generations is to make the world bloodier and beastlier and more artificial than it was when we took the first wrong turning, we would be doing ourselves and our environment a great kindness in bringing the whole episode to a rapid close.

If I had thought this inevitable I would not have bothered to compile this source-book. My hope is that it may encourage others to accept that the sane and desirable course is for our species to establish and maintain a beneficial relationship with the rest of nature. That relationship cannot be seen as beneficial unless it extends and evolves permanently into the future. It must be creative and emphatic, not predatory. Conservation, and cosmetic adjustments to the material environment, are not enough. What is required – in our behaviour, in our sense of responsibility toward each other and the rest of the world – must, as I see it, be spelt out for each one of us from our earliest years. This, surely, should be the philosophical basis for all education, and if the first rootlets can be formed in the fertile soil of a child's early home life, there is greater hope of a humane and workable future.

Such high-minded motivation has posed some problems as to whom to include in this dictionary! Many of those quoted are widely known to have been concerned with the welfare, future or evolutionary progress of their own species; their concern – rudimentary in some, clearly thought out in others – with the indivisibility of our regard for each other and for the 'lesser' forms of life, may be less familiar. But proving a point, or even proving that others have proved it, can be an unrewarding task unless heart or mind contains the 'pilot jet' needed to ignite the whole man. Putting the point more poetically, Browning wrote:

Truth is within ourselves; it takes no rise
From outward things, what'er you may believe.
There is an inmost centre in us all,
Where truth abides in fulness …

Paracelsus

The passage in this dictionary that most 'speaks to my condition' is where John Bryant says he dreams of a world 'where man is at peace, not only with himself, but also with all the other creatures of Earth,' for 'it is cruelty which dominates my every conscious moment'.

INTRODUCTION

That daily painful empathy with the predicament of all sentient life is not an easy burden to bear. But it is, perhaps, an evolutionary inevitability – at least for a significant minority of mankind – if the incidence of needless suffering in the natural world is ever to be reduced to a level consistent with the state of mind and heart of which the human race is capable, but which at present it is still reluctant to accept.

ACKNOWLEDGEMENTS

I am grateful to numerous friends who have helped me to find quotations, sources and dates, in particular to Joan Gilbert whose research talents are prodigious and whose enthusiasm for the purpose of this dictionary has been as encouraging as her suggestions have been welcome. For moral support and practical help, my special thanks also to Elizabeth Ahlston, Brigid Brophy, J.K. Bullette, Anne Campbell-Dixon, Aviva Cantor, Michael Fox, Brian Gunn, Clive Hollands, Kathleen Jannaway, Helen Jones, Clay Lancaster, Ashley Montagu, John Pontin, Tom Regan, Richard D. Ryder, Peter Singer, Keith Thomas, George Trevelyan, MaryAnn Violin and by no means least the lady librarians at the County Library, Chichester, Sussex, whose ungrudging delving has gone unrewarded except by the trim figures that their endless errands on my behalf have surely helped them to retain. I am also, of course, in debt to my wife for frequent discussions and help with detail, and for enduring what she calls 'your-not-with-me-look-again' at many a mealtime.

As the purpose of this dictionary is to reach the widest possible audience, I have shown in the Bibliography the last known publishers of key books from which I have drawn; but I now make grateful acknowledgement to (where known) the originating publishers of in-copyright material, and to the authors. In a few instances all reasonable effort to trace sources has failed, but my debt remains.

Bruce Allsopp, *Social Responsibility and the Responsible Society*, Oriel Press; Nathaniel Altman, *Ahimsa* and *Eating for Life*, Theosophical Publishing House; G.S. Arundale, *The Night Bell* and *Peace and War*, Theosophical Publishing House; Janet Barkas, *The Vegetable Passion*, Charles Scribner's Sons, Routledge Kegan Paul; Christian Barnard, *Good Life Good Death*, Prentice-Hall; Henry Beston, *The Outermost House*, Holt, Rinehart & Winston; Billy Ray Boyd, *The New Abolitionists, For the Vegetarian in You*, and from *The Nonviolent Activist*; Brigid Brophy, for passages from *Animals' Rights: a Symposium*, Centaur Press, *Hackenfeller's Ape*, Secker and Warburg, *Don't Never Forget*, Jonathan Cape, *Animals, Men and Morals*, Victor Gollancz, and from her article 'The Rights of Animals', *Sunday Times*, 10 October 1965; John Bryant, *Fettered Kingdoms*, Ferne House and *Animals' Rights: a Symposium*, Centaur Press: Michael Byrom, *Evolution for Beginners*, Linden Press; Hope Sawyer Buyukmihci by permission of *The Beaver Defenders*; Edward Carpenter, *Against Hunting*, Gollancz; Robert Churchward's Estate for extract from *A Master of Hounds Speaks*; Roger Caras, *On the Fifth Day*, Acropolis Books; Gerald Carson, *Men, Beasts, and Gods*, Scribner's; Rachel Carson, *Silent Spring*, Hamish Hamilton; Kenneth Clark, *Civilization: a Personal View*, John Murray, *Animals and Men*, Thames and Hudson; Stephen R. Clark, *The Moral Status of Animals* and *From Athens to Jerusalem*, Clarendon Press, *The Nature of the Beast*, Oxford University Press, and *Animals' Rights: a Symposium*, Centaur Press; Patrick Corbett, *Animals, Men and Morals*, Gollancz; Jacques-Yves Cousteau, *The Whale*, Cassell; the Estate of W.H. Davies for 'Sheep', 'A Child's Pet', 'The Rabbit', 'Sport', and *Autobiography of a Super Tramp*, Jonathan Cape; the Society of Authors and the Estate of Waler de la Mare for 'Hi!' and 'Tit for Tat'; Pat Derby, *The Lady and Her Tiger*, Dutton; Daniel A. Dombrowski, *The Philosophy of Vegetarianism*, University of Massachusetts Press; Maureen Duffy, for 'Both Heads Lapped Perfectly' from *Memorials of the Quick and the Dead*, Hamish Hamilton, and 'Chattel', *Men and Beasts*, Paladin Books; David Ehrenfeld, *The Arrogance of Humanism*, Oxford U.P.; Loren Eiseley, *The Star Thrower*, Wildwood House; Gavin Ewart for 'On Seeing a Priest – Eating Veal'; J. Todd Ferrier, *On Behalf of the Creatures*, Order of the Cross; Martyn Ford, *Towards Animal Rights*, Animal Aid; John Fowles, *The Tree*, Aurum Press, and extracts from *Animals*; Michael W. Fox, *One Earth, One Mind*, Coward, McCann & Geoghegan, *Returning to Eden*, Viking Press, *Between Animal and Man*, Blond and Briggs, and extracts from *Ethics and Animals*, Humana

Press; Norma Jeans and Aberdeen University Press 'The Solitaries' and 'When I shall Die' from Olive Fraser's *The Pure Account*, and Norma Jeans for Olive Fraser's 'The Other Side' and 'On a dying cygnet, stoned'; Roy Fuller, *Fellow Mortals*, Macdonald and Evans; Paul Gallico, *Honourable Cat*, Heinemann; Robert Gittings, for 'The Great Moth' from *This Tower, My Prison*, Heinemann; Stanley and Roslind Godlovitch, *Animals, Men and Morals*, Gollanca; Mark Gold, *Assault and Battery*, Pluto Press; Jane Goodall, *In the Shadow of Man*, Collins; Elizabeth Goudge, *The Joy of the Snow*, Hodder and Stoughton; J.E.P. Grigg for a passage from *Animal Guardian*; Bart Gruzalski, extract from *Ethics and Animals*, Humana Press; Rebecca Hall, *Animals are Equal*, Wildwood House, and for 'Cows'; John Harris, *Animals, Men and Morals*, Gollanca, *Animals' Rights: a Symposium*, Centaur Press; Ruth Harrison, *Animal Machines*, Vincent Stuart, *Animals, Men and Morals*, Gollancz, *Animals' Rights: a Symposium*, Centaur Press; Alice Heim, *Intelligence and Personality*, Penguin; Ronald Higgins, *The Seventh Enemy*, Hodder and Stoughton; Russell Hoban, *Turtle Diary*, Random House; the Estate of Ralph Hodgson for 'The Bells of Heaven' and 'Stupidity Street'; David Holbrook for a passage from 'Dr John Bowlby'; Clive Hollands, *Compassion is the Bugler*, Macdonald, Edinburgh, *Animals' Rights: a Symposium*, Centaur Press; C.W. Hume, *The Status of Animals*, U.F.A.W.; Christmas Humphreys, *The Buddhist Way of Life*, Allen and Unwin; Aldous Huxley, *Ends and Means* and *The Perrenial Philosophy*, chatto and Windus; W.J. Jordan, *Animals Rights: a Symposium*, Centaur Press; Philip Kapleau, *To Cherish All Life*, Zen Center, Harper & Row; Karl Kerenyi, *Evil*, Northwestern U.P.; Brian Klug for extracts from *Listening*; Jiddu Krishnamurti, *Krishnamurti to Himself*, Gollancz; the Estate of Joseph Wood Krutch, for a passage from *The Best Nature Writing of Joseph Wood Krutch, The Great Chain of Life*, Houghton Mifflin; Milan Kundera, *The Unbearable Lightness of Being*, Faber; Manfred Kyber, *Among Animals* Centaur Press; Clay Lancaster for a passage from *The Incredible World's Parliament of Religions*; Philip Larkin and Faber and Faber for 'Take One Home for the Kiddies' from *The Whitsun Weddings*; Cloris Leachman, *The Vegetarians*, ed. Rynn Berry Jr., Autumn Press; John Lewis and Bernard Towers, *Naked Ape or Homo Sapiens*, Garnstone Press; Naomi Lewis for 'The Wolf said to Francis'; Andrew Linzey, *Animal Rights*, SCM Press, *Animals' Rights: a Symposium*, Centaur Press; *Christianity and the Rights of Animals*, SPCK; Hugh Lofting, *Dr Dolittle's Post Office* and *The Voyages of Dr Dolittle*, Jonathan Capc; Alan Long, *The Vegetarians*, Autumn Press; Shena Mackay, *An Advent Calendar*, Bloodaxe Books, *A Bowl of Cherries*, Harvester Press; W. Macneile Dixon, *The Human Situation*, Edward Arnold; Norman Mailer, *Miami and the Seige of*

ACKNOWLEDGEMENTS

Chicago, Penguin; Randle Manwaring for 'Nature Reserve – Dorset'; James Michener, extract from 'Where Did the Animals Go?', Readers' Digest; Mary Midgley, *Beast and Men*, Harvester Press, *Animals and Why They Matter*, Penguin; Stanley Milgram, *Obedience to Authority*, Tavistock Publications; Spike Milligan for 'Rage in Heaven'; Ashley Montagu, *Wilderness in a Changing World*, Sierra Club, *Of Man, Animals and Morals*, Humane Society of the United States, *Growing Young*, McGraw-Hill; Victoria Moran, *Compassion: the Ultimate Ethic*, Thorsons; Musa Murataliyev, *A Man Needs a Dog*, Central Books; Iris Murdoch, *The Black Prince, Flight from the Enchanter* and *A Fairly Honourable Defeat*, Chatto and Windus, *The Sovereignty of Good*, Routledge, Kegan Paul; Gilbert Murray, *Stoic, Christian and Humanist*, Allen & Unwin; Scott Nearing, *Living the Good Life*, Schocken Books; Vaslaw Nijinsky, *Diary of Vaslav Nijinsky*, Cape; Howard L. Parsons, *Man East and West*, Gruner; David A. Paterson, *Animals' Rights: a Symposium*, Centaur Press; Marcia C. Pearson, extracts from *Washington Living* and *Agenda*; Kit Pedler, *The Quest for Gaia*, Souvenir Press; Michael Peters, *Animals, Men and Morals*, Gollancz; the Estate of Eden Phillpots for 'The Challenger' from *Brother Beast*, and 'The Cart-Horse'; Leslie G. Pine, *After Their Blood*, William Kimber; Ruth Pitter for 'The Bat', 'The Bush-Baby', the Estate of John Cowper Powys, *Autobiography*, Macdonald, *Morwyn*, Sphere Books; Tom Regan, *The Case for Animal Rights* and *All That Dwell Therein*, University of California, *In Defence of Animals*, Blackwell, *Animals' Rights: a Symposium*, Centaur Press; Lewis Regenstein, *In Defence of Animals*, Blackwell; Jeremy Rifkin, *Algeny*, Viking; Catherine Roberts, *The Scientific Conscience*, George Braziller, *Science, Animals and Evolution*, Greenwood Press; Peter Roberts, *Animals' Rights: a Symposium*, Centaur Press; Romain Rolland, *Jean Christophe*, Heinemann; Steven Rosen, *Food for the Spirit*, Bala Books; Miriam Rothschild, *The Relationship Between Animals and Man*, Oxford; Hans Ruesch, *Slaughter of the Innocent*, Bantam Books; Richard D. Ryder, *Victims of Science*, Davis-Poynter, *Animals' Rights: a Symposium*, Centaur Press, *Animals, Men and Morals*, Gollancz; Carl Sagan, *Dragons of Eden*, Hodder and Stoughton; the Estate of Henry S. Salt for poems and passages from several sources and from *Animals Rights*, International Society for Animals Rights, Centaur Press; Jack Sanderson, extract from *The Vegan*; Steve F. Sapontzis, extracts from *Morals, Reason and Animals* and *Between the Species*; Vernon Scannell for 'A Couple of Heavyweights', 'Ruminant'; Harriet Schleifer, *In Defence of Animals*, Blackwell; Bill Schul, *The Psychic Power of Animals*, Coronet Books; Vreni Schumacher for E.F. Schumacher, *Small is Beautiful*, Blond and Briggs, *A Guide for the Perplexed*, Jonathan Cape; Mrs R. Schweitzer

Miller for Albert Schweitzer, *Memories of Childhood and Youth, Out of My Life and Thought, Civilization and Ethics*, Allen and Unwin, *Reverence for Life*, Peter Owen; Richard Serjeant, *The Spectrum of Pain*, Hart-Davis; James Serpell, *In the Company of Animals*, Blackwell; Karl Shapiro for 'Interlude III'; The Society of Authors for the Estate of George Bernard Shaw, *The Doctor's Dilemma, The Devil's Disciple*, 'Killing for Sport' (from *Prefaces*), *The Revolutionist's Handbook, Back to Methuselah, The Simpleton of the Unexpected Isles* Upton Sinclair, *The Jungle*, Penguin; I.B. Singer, *Enemies, The Seance and Other Stories*, Penguin, and from Foreword to Giehl, *Vegetarianism, a Way of Life*, Harper & Row, *Lost in America*, Doubleday; Peter Singer, *Animal Liberation*, The New York Review of Books, *The Expanding Circle*, Clarendon Press, *In Defence of Animals*, Blackwell, *The Animal Liberation Movement*, Old Hammond Press; Sacheverell Sitwell, *Splendours and Miseries*, Faber and Faber; George Small, *The Blue Whale*, Columbia University Press; Alexander Solzhenitsyn, *Cancer Ward*, Bodley Head; Henry Spira, *Ethics and Animals*, Humana Press; the Estate of Margaret Stanley-Wrench for 'The Hare at Harvest' from *A Tale for the Fall of the Year*, Linden Press; Gertrude Stein, *Everybody's Autobiography*, Vintage Books; John Steinbeck, *The Sea of Cortez*, Macmillan, Toronto; the Estate of James Stephens for 'Student Taper', 'The Snare', 'The Cage', 'Little Things'; Henry Bailey Stevens, *The Recovery of Culture*, Harper Brothers, and 'The Bull Calf'; D.M. Thomas, for 'Sun Valley' from *Dreaming in Bronze*, Jonathan Cape; Keith Thomas, *Man and the Natural World*, Allen Lane; Edward Thompson, *Burmese Silver*, Gollancz; George Trevelyan, *Operation Redemption*, Turnstone Press; E.S. Turner, *All Heaven in a Rage*, Michael Joseph, and 'The Enquiring Child' by permission of *Punch*; Margaret Wheaton Tuttle, *The Crimson Cage*, Tashmoo Press; John Vyvyan, *The Dark Face of Science, In Pity and in Anger* and *Sketch for a World Picture*, Michael Joseph; J.D. Whittall, *People and Animals*, National Anti-Vivisection Society; Henry Williamson, *The Pathway*, Hamlyn; Frank Avray Wilson, *Food Fit for Humans* and *Food for the Golden Age*, C.W. Daniel, *Art as Revelation*, Centaur Press; David Wood, *Animals, Men and Morals*, Gollancz; Esmé Wynne-Tyson, *The Philosophy of Compassion*, Vincent Stuart, *Mithras*, Rider; Jon Wynne-Tyson, *The Civilised Alternative*, Centaur Press, *Food for a Future*, Davis-Poynter, *So Say Banana Bird*, Pythian Books, *Animals' Rights: a Symposium*, Centaur Press; the Estate of Francis Brett Young for 'Bête Humaine' and 'The Quails'; Marguerite Yourcenar, *Coup de Grace*, Aidan Ellis.

EDITOR'S NOTE

I hope that every quotation in this source-book may be, for someone, a starting point. Its nature makes thematic repetition inevitable, but strength lies in consensus. That people from so many walks of life have thought beyond their specialisms to a common conclusion, may surprise and encourage. If some should find the book's single-mindedness indigestible, I would be sorry, for its purpose is not to lie heavily upon the internal organs, but to offer, in the manner of chefs who know their business, good food in small quantities at the right time.

The few selections of comparable material to have been published previously have usually lacked sources and the authors' years of birth and death. Where my own source has been such selections, this has made for considerable and sometimes abortive research. Nor has it been possible to do all the reading I would have liked. I shall be indebted to readers who suggest passages for the next edition, or who make constructive criticism of this one.

J.W.-T.

GEORGE D. ABRAHAM, 1872–1965

There is no sport in the world like mountaineering. Its pleasures are not marred by the slaughter of innocent animal life, nor discomfiture to any of our fellow-beings.

The Complete Mountaineer

JOSEPH ADDISON, 1672–1719

A person who was well skilled in dissection opened a bitch, and as she lay in most exquisite tortures offered her one of her young puppies, which she immediately fell a-licking; and for the time seemed insensible to her own pain; on the removal she kept her eye fixed on it and began a wailing sort of cry which seemed to proceed rather from the loss of her young one than the sense of her own torment.

Spectator, No. 120, 1711

True benevolence, or compassion, extends itself through the whole of existence and sympathises with the distress of every creature capable of sensation.

Maxims, Observations and Reflections

LOUISA MAY ALCOTT, 1832–1888

Vegetable diet and sweet repose. Animal food and nightmare. Pluck your body from the orchard; do not snatch it from the shambles. Without flesh diet there could be no bloodshedding war.

Life, Letters and Journals

SVETLANA ALLILUYEVA, 1926–

Nobody has a right to destroy or stop life, either his own life or the life of another man, or the life of any animals, because it is not we who gave this life, and so then it is not we who are allowed to take it. 'Thou shalt not kill' is the principal law of human conduct on earth.

Life is eternal, generous, immense – like this rainbow, like this rain, like this springtime! The attempt to destroy this life is a great crime. To secure life by all means is the biggest joy of all happiness.

Those who are able to feel the miniscule particle of this great life from the earth, from the farthest stars; those who deeply rejoice in this life, and who bless it, and who are full of thankfulness toward life, possess a true religious sense.

... Violence over men, over animals, over life under all forms, cannot be justified or accepted.

One Year Later

NATHANIEL ALTMAN, 1948–

As our society has become more standardized, superficial and mechanized, many of us, through years of conditioning, have grown apart from Nature and her living creatures which share this planet with us.

This conditioning has helped produce a strong feeling of callousness on our part in our dealings with other members of the animal kingdom. This is evidenced by the prevailing belief that we as human beings are literally in charge of the earth, and everything on this planet was created for our benefit; so we may do anything we wish with it.

Eating for Life

... As a so-called 'civilized' people and as members of a society in search of lasting peace in the world, we cannot remain callous to our responsibility toward nature and insensitive to the inherent rights of the animals.

Ibid.

The pathway to Ahimsa involves the most exciting journey a person can experience. It helps us tap our deepest sources of inspiration, truth and compassion. It helps us understand the essence of patience, of humour and of sharing the best we have to offer. The pathway helps us become integrated, aware and dynamic human beings who care about the world and want to make it a better place for all its citizens. Most of all, Ahimsa involves a unique process of creativity and enjoyment in living which will be reflected in everything we do.

Ahimsa

Although other animals cannot reason or speak the way humans do, this does not give us the right to do with them as we like. Even though our supposed possession of a soul and superior intelligence are used to create an arbitrary dividing line over rights, the fact remains that all animals have the capacity to experience pain and suffering, and in suffering they are our equals.

Ibid.

BRUCE ALLSOPP, 1912–

The American Indian concept of The Great Spirit pervading all things in the natural world and relating them to each other was more mature that the European attempt to represent that spirit as a superhuman father or king of heaven whose primary object in being was to look after Man, often at the expense of all the rest of the natural world, seen in western mythology as 'His Creation'.

Social Responsibility and the Responsible Society

There is a simple answer implicit in many religions, but best expressed by Jesus, 'Love thy neighbour'. We often hear the phrase 'they behaved like animals' when men have done something particularly disgusting. In fact animals behave very well. Species preys upon species, as we do ourselves, but in nature and even among domesticated animals, standards of courtesy and respect are evident. Love is Man's birthright, but not his exclusive prerogative. There is much love in nature and Man should learn more about it.

Ibid.

Whatever the social-political system, scientists and technologists flock to the source for 'funds for research' like scavenger birds to an outfall of sewage. There is a good deal of humbug in the scientific ethos of the advancement of knowledge. In fact scientists are ten-a-penny and many of them will do anything, so long as it is called research, regardless of consequences.

Ibid.

[Man] has reached a spawning stage and is rapidly becoming a horrifying infestation ... it becomes a moral imperative, overriding all other considerations, to re-establish the balance of the human species in nature ... Man must establish and maintain a beneficial relationship with the rest of nature. It cannot be called beneficial unless it can be seen to extend permanently into the future. It must therefore be creative, not predatory. Conservation is not enough.

The Garden Earth

HENRI-FRÉDÉRIC AMIEL, 1821–1881

Small animals, small children, young lives – they are all the same as far as the need of protection and of gentleness is concerned ... If man was what he ought to be he would be adored by the animals, of whom he is too often the capricious and sanguinary tyrant ... How many other species are there, by thousands and tons of thousands, who ask peace from us and with whom we persist in waging a brutal war? Our race is by far the most destructive, the most hurtful and the most formidable, of all the species of the planet. It has even invented for its own use the right of the strongest – a divine right which quiets its conscience in the face of the conquered and the oppressed; we have outlawed all that lives except ourselves ...

Journal intime

GEORGE T. ANGELL, 1823–1909

Standing before you as the advocate of the lower races, I declare what I believe cannot be gainsaid ... that just so soon and so far as we pour into all our schools the songs, the poems and literature of mercy toward these lower creatures, just so soon and so far shall we reach the roots not only of cruelty, but of crime.

From a speech on 14 February 1884

I am sometimes asked: 'Why do you spend so much of your time and money talking about kindness to animals when there is so much cruelty to men?' I answer: 'I am working at the roots.'

Ibid.

ANON

A Dog's Epitaph

Soft lies the turf on one who finds his rest
Here on our common mother's ample breast.
Unstained by meanness, avarice and pride,

5

He never flattered and he never lied;
No gluttonous excess his slumber broke,
No burning alcohol, no stifling smoke;
He ne'er intrigued a rival to displace;
He ran, but never betted on, a race;
Content with harmless sports and moderate food,
Boundless in love, in faith, in gratitude;
Happy the man – if there be such? –
Of whom his epitaph can say as much.

Beneath this stone are deposited the remains of one who
possessed Beauty without Vanity, Strength without
Insolence, Courage without Ferocity, and all the Virtues
of a man without his Vices.

> From a stone in an Aberdeenshire churchyard in memory of
> Pompey, born 1891, died 1902 at Balguholly, remembered
> by V. and C. Tweedale.

On a Woman Lecturing a Man for Shooting Grouse

She quoted Burns's 'Wounded Hare',
    And certain stirring lines of Blake's,
And Ruskin on the fowls of air,
    And Coleridge on the water snakes.
At Emerson's 'Forbearance' he
    Began to feel his will benumbed,
At Browning's 'Donald' utterly
    His soul surrendered and succumbed.

She smiled to find her point was gained,
    And went with happy parting words
(He subsequently ascertained)
    To trim her hat with humming-birds.

> Quoted by Florence Suckling in her *Humane Educator*

Tailpiece

Tigers don't eat lettuce,
Men weren't meant for meat;

Monkeys, men or tigers –
We are what we eat.

The animals you call domestic need freedom too. You chain them up, day and night; you put them in narrow stalls, in dark and dirty stables. You kill their intelligence and soul-life by making them stare all their life at a wall, or a manger – and then, filled with contempt, you call them stupid!

SIR EDWIN ARNOLD, 1832–1904

From *The Sacrifice*

But Buddha softly said,
'Let him not strike, great King,' and therewith loosed
The victim's bonds, none staying him, so great
His presence was. Then, craving leave, he spake
Of life, which all can take but none can give,
Life, which all creatures love and strive to keep,
Wonderful, dear and pleasant unto each,
Even to the meanest; yes, a boon to all
Where pity is, for pity makes the world
Soft to the weak and noble for the strong.
Unto the dumb lips of his flock he lent
Sad pleading words, showing how man, who prays
For mercy to the gods, is merciless,
Being as god to those; albeit all life
Is linked and kin, and what we slay have given
Meek tribute of the milk and wool, and set
Fast trust upon the hands which murder them.
Nor, spake he, shall one wash his spirit clean
By blood; nor gladden gods, being good, with blood,
Nor bribe them, being evil; nay, nor lay
Upon the brow of innocent bound beasts
One hair's weight of that answer each must give

7

For all things done amiss or wrongfully,
Alone, each for himself, reckoning with
The fixed arithmetic of the universe
Which meteth good for good and ill for ill.

The Light of Asia

GEORGE S. ARUNDALE, 1878–1945

The world stands at a parting of the ways and those who suffer know this with deeply anxious hearts. One way leads to destruction. It is the way of the tolerance of cruelty, if not the active engagement in it. It is the way of hunting for sport, the way of vivisection, the way of killing for self-adornment, the way of killing animals for food, the way of making slaves of animals without thought for their happiness and wellbeing. This is the way the world has been treading.

The other way leads to salvation. It is the way of harmlessness, the way of the recognition of brotherhood with all creatures, the way of tenderness and compassion, the way of service and not of selfishness.

The Night Bell

The world as a whole is at war with the animal kingdom, as witness flesh-eating, hunting and so forth. The aftermath of inter-kingdom war is inter-human war; and let us clearly realize that war never ends war, that no League of Nations can ever end war, no treaties, no pacts, no agreements, still less force of any kind. The only way to end war is to determine that there shall be no war *anywhere*, for war anywhere means, sooner or later, war everywhere.

Peace and War

FRANCIS OF ASSISI, 1181–1226

Not to hurt our humble brethren is our first duty to them, but to stop there is not enough. We have a higher mission – to be of service to them wherever they require it.

Quoted in the *Life* by St Bonaventura

If you have men who will exclude any of God's creatures from the shelter of compassion and pity, you will have men who will deal likewise with their fellow men.

Ibid.

MARCUS AURELIUS (Antoninus), 121–180

One man is proud when he has caught a poor hare, and another when he has taken a little fish in a net, and another when he has taken wild boars, and another when he has taken bears ... Are not these robbers?

Meditations

MEHER BABA, 1894–1969

To love God in the most practical way is to love our fellow beings. If we feel for others in the same way as we feel for our own dear ones, we love God.

If we suffer in the sufferings of others and feel happy in the happiness of others, we are loving God.

If we understand and feel that the greatest act of

9

devotion and worship to God is not to hurt or harm any of His beings, we are loving God.

The Theme of Creation and Its Purposes

FRANCIS BACON, 1561–1626

Nature has endowed man with a noble and excellent principle of compassion, which extends itself also to the dumb animals – whence this compassion has some resemblance to that of a prince towards his subjects. And it is certain that the noblest souls are the most extensively compassionate, for narrow and degenerate minds think that compassion belongs not to them; but a great soul, the noblest part of creation, is ever compassionate.

Advancement of Learning

PHILIP J. BAILEY, 1816–1902

From *Festus*

All animals are living hieroglyphs.
The dashing dog, and stealthy-stepping cat,
Hawk, bull and all that breathe mean something more
To the true eye than their shapes show; for all
Were made in love and made to be beloved.
Thus must he think as to earth's lower life,
Who seeks to win the world to thought and love.

REVD F.C. BAKER, 1889–1961

To derive pleasure in being cruel is a very debasing matter. It shows a person to be unmindful of the sanctity of life and the meaning of life. There is something very foul and evil in the lives of men and women who delight in destroying helpless life, especially in what is known as 'blood sports'.

Quoted in *The Clergy Speak for Animals*

JOHN AUSTIN BAKER (Bishop of Salisbury), 1928–

In the very first chapter of the Bible it is said that in the beginning, when things were as God meant them to be, animals were not created to be food for humans. The animals were to eat grass, foliage and cereals; human beings, fruit and nuts. Only later, when sin was rampant in the world, were animals granted to humankind for food, with the sinister words: 'The fear of you and the dread of you shall fall upon all wild animals ... and birds ... and fish ...; they are given into your hands.'

Speech given at the Christian Consultative Council for the Welfare of Animals Conference in Westminster on 25 January 1986

To shut your mind, heart, imagination to the sufferings of others is to begin slowly but inexorably to die. It is to cease by inches from being human, to become in the end capable of nothing, generous or unselfish – or sometimes capable of anything, however terrible.

Sermon in Salisbury Cathedral, 4 October 1986,
World Day of Prayer for Animals

Christians, then, who close their minds and hearts to the cause of animal welfare and the evils it seeks to combat are ignoring the fundamental spiritual teaching of Christ himself. They are also refusing the role in the world for which God gave us our brains and our moral sense, to be God's agents to look after the world in the divine Spirit of wisdom and love. As we know, Christians like others are apt to justify leaving animal welfare aside on the ground that human needs are more urgent. We must hammer home that love is indivisible. It is not 'either-or', it is 'both-and', because a society that cannot find the moral energy to care and act about gross animal suffering and exploitation will do little better about human need.

Ibid.

11

WILLIAM BALLANTYNE, 1812–1886

It is said that [vivisection] promotes knowledge which is serviceable to the human race, and those who practise it defend it upon that ground. If this assertion were conclusively proved, which certainly is not the case, I should still protest against its use, and denounce it as a disgrace to a Christian land. The hypothesis upon which it is defended must be that the brain, muscles, and nerves of an animal are analogous to those of a human being, and therefore will, under certain conditions, exhibit similar results. If so, vivisectionists apply to creatures formed like themselves tortures which the ingenuity of science has rendered more terrible than any invented by the savage.

There can be no doubt that some of their victims do possess thought and memory, affection and gratitude, that might shame their persecutors, but whether these qualities are developed in the same way or are dependent upon the same causes must be matter of speculation. How can the vivisectionist know that when he touches some nerve which makes the unhappy creature writhe in unspeakable agony, the same effect would be produced upon the human frame? Some slight difference may create a complete error in the conclusion arrived at, and a human patient may be treated upon an erroneous assumption that his brain is worked upon by the same influences as that of a dog. If, on the other hand, the assumption is that animals are differently formed from ourselves, it is difficult to embrace the idea that their torture can produce beneficial consequences. I believe that speculation of a kind created by vivisection is more likely to lead to blundering than to benefit, and the report which I have read of the inquiry before the Royal Commission by no means removes the impression; but as I have already said, if it were proved to demonstration that some benefit might be obtained by it, the practice is not the less abominable and unholy. I believe that the true instincts of every pure heart will throb in sympathy with this feeling. As I write, my old collie, friend and companion for the last ten years, is looking at me with his earnest brown eyes, as if thanking me for this humble protest against the torture of dumb life.

Some Experiences of a Barrister's Life

ANNA LETITIA BARBAULD, 1743–1825

From *The Mouse's Petition*

The well-taught philosophic mind
  To all compassion gives;
Casts round the world an equal eye,
  And feels for all that lives.

BRIGITTE BARDOT, 1934–

I gave my beauty and my youth to men. Now I am giving my wisdom and experience – the best of me – to animals.

Quoted during auction of her property in aid of animal protection

JANET BARKAS, 1949–

A vegetarian régime is basically an ethical, anthropological, sociological and psychological phenomenon. At the highest level is the humane vegetarian, who supplements his ingratiating attitude toward animals with a comparable kindness toward his fellow men by avoiding their deaths as well. The lowest type of vegetarian is the psychologically motivated zealot who simultaneously practices hatred and violence toward mankind.

To become a vegetarian involves both a psychological predisposition and a distinct philosophical outlook. The recruiting efforts of religious and dietary fanatics are therefore contradictory to their desired end, for unless vegetarianism comes from the soul, it will be just another passing fad. Of course the idea must be exposed, but it cannot be indoctrinated. The basic issues involved are much too intricate and far-reaching to be overlooked or brushed aside. Just as war has been debated for centuries, so will the fleshless diet. Its appearance in contemporary societies is an indication of a positive questioning of traditional and age-old habits – a microcosm of the ideological conflicts facing thinking people of today.

The Vegetable Passion

JOHN BARLAS (Evelyn Douglas), 1860–1914

Love Sonnet

The poor dumb creatures of the field, that call
So sadly to their young; whose narrow mind,
Consciously helpless, looks up to mankind
Through piteous pleading eyes; that live in thrall,
Or, stricken in the shambles, groaning fall –
Thinking of these, how little grace they find,
And then of thee who never wast unkind,
And of our love, I could weep for them all.
This is the gift of Love, that we, so blest,
Should feel for the afflicted; that we twain
Should be united against wrong and pain,
The slaughtered lamb, the wild bird's rifled nest,
And, most of all, the fraud and force that stain
Homes of the human poor and the oppressed.

DR CHRISTIAN BARNARD, 1922–

… I had bought two male chimps from a primate colony in Holland. They lived next to each other in separate cages for several months before I used one as a donor.

When we put him to sleep in his cage in preparation for the operation, he chattered and cried incessantly. We attached no significance to this, but it must have made a great impression on his companion, for when we removed the body to the operating room, the other chimp wept bitterly and was inconsolable for days.

The incident made a deep impression on me. I vowed never again to experiment with such sensitive creatures.

Good Life Good Death

GWENDOLEN BARTER, 1904–

If father kicks the cat, then cat-kicking becomes the right thing to do in the eyes of the toddler. He is wide open to influences of every kind and will see no inconsistency in the fact that father is kind – let us say – to dogs.

I do not suggest that all hunting people are hard-hearted in their dealings with their fellow-men, but the danger is that when once we have excluded a group of human beings or animals as being undeserving of sympathy we have started 'compartmental thinking', by which one set of values can be walled off from the criticism applied to another by personal conscience and community opinion.

From 'Children and Hunting', in
Against Hunting, a Symposium, edited by Patrick Moore

ST BASIL (Bishop of Caesarea), 330–379

Petition

The earth is the Lord's and the fullness
Thereof. Oh, God, enlarge within us the
Sense of fellowship with all living
Things, our brothers the animals to
Whom Thou gavest the earth as
Their home in common with us.

We remember with shame that
In the past we have exercised the
High dominion of man with ruthless
Cruelty so that the voice of the earth,
Which should have gone up to Thee in
Song, has been a groan of travail.
May we realize that they live not
For us alone but for themselves and
For Thee and that they love the sweetness
Of life even as we, and serve Thee in their
Place better than we in others.

EVA V. BATT, 1908–1989

Of course it would not be good for business if too many people realised that milk is *not* essential to optimum health. Coupled with some of the disadvantages of relying on this product of the over-worked, sex-hormoned, antibiotic-filled, semi-invalid cow, with her proneness to udder complaints, umbilical sepsis, mastitis and chronic catarrh, etc., it might well bring about a new and refreshing outlook on food habits.

The vegan genuinely believes that 'Thou Shalt Not Kill' means exactly what it says; no more, no less. It certainly does *not* mean 'Thou Shalt Not Kill, except for the pleasure of eating the bodies of the slain, or drinking the milk intended by nature for the slaughtered calf; the vain desire to adorn the human body with the fur, feathers or skin of another animal; or because it is a very profitable business to breed or catch animals for the experimental laboratory where they will be starved, burned, gassed, poisoned, mutilated and otherwise tortured and then killed.'

World Forum, October 1961

DR M. BEDDOW BAYLY, MRCS, LRCP, 1887–1961

The question of vivisection, which may be defined as the subjection of animals to experiments in the pursuit of scientific knowledge or commercial manufacture, is primarily a moral one, and it is upon this ground that I oppose it; for I refuse to believe that the pathway of true progress in human knowledge for the attainment of health can demand for its treading the infliction of pain and suffering upon beings weaker than ourselves, but sharing with us that One Life which animates all creatures.

Indeed, man only shows his superiority to the so-called brute creation in so far as he manifests the truly human attributes of compassion for the helpless, courage in the face of personal suffering, and heroism that even prefers death to dishonourable action.

Vivisection is founded on the selfish principle that might is right, that the end justifies the means, and that the material benefit should take precedence of moral obligation. It appeals to the basest instincts of fear and cowardice and excuses any cruelty on the tyrant's plea of necessity. Before the bar of justice vivisection stands condemned on three main counts – cruelty to animals, uselessness to man, and obstruction on the path of real knowledge.

Spotlights on Vivisection

… in a universe based upon and maintained by spiritual and moral laws, nothing which is cruel – that is, which involves the infliction of pain or suffering upon a sentient creature for any purpose whatsoever save for its own benefit – can be essential for the search for and attainment of knowledge which will enhance man's material and spiritual welfare.

The Futility of Experiments on Animals

… on account of the dissimilarity between animals and human beings, it is worse than useless to attempt to base any methods of treatment or prevention of human disease on animal experimentation.

Ibid.

In a universe which embraces all types of life and consciousness and all material forms through which these manifest, nothing which is ethically wrong can ever be scientifically right; in an integrated cosmos of spirit and matter, one law must pervade all levels and all planes. This is the basic principle upon which the whole case against vivisection rests. Cicero summed it up in the four words: 'No cruelty is useful.'

Members of the Theosophical Society and Vivisection

HENRY WARD BEECHER, 1813–1887

For fidelity, devotion, love, many a two-legged animal is below the dog and the horse. Happy would it be for thousands of people if they could stand at last before the Judgement Seat and say 'I have loved as truly and I have lived as decently as my dog.' And yet we call them 'only brutes'!

Quoted in *The Clergy Speak for Animals*

ERNEST BELL, 1851–1933

That highly organized animals, capable of some of the highest moral sentiments and with a distinct personality, should be habitually spoken of as 'it', or 'which', like inanimate objects, gives the key to the position. The use of the word 'brutal' or 'brutish', for anyone specially coarse and stupid; and 'beast', or 'beastly', for anything specially disgusting, are gratuitous and undeserved insults to the sub-human animals, born of man's own conceit and want of discernment. The man who is described as behaving 'like a beast' would often in his behaviour be a disgrace to any known animal.

Summer School Papers

The old assumption that animals acted exclusively by instinct, while man had a monopoly of reason, is, we think, maintained by few people nowadays who have any knowledge at all about animals. We can only wonder that so absurd a theory could have been held for so long a time as it was, when on all sides the evidence of animals' power of reasoning is crushing.

Ibid.

Let us admit that intellect gives power. It is through it that we have command over the animals, and the ability to misuse them for our own purposes; but power without sympathy is a danger and a curse. It is this consciousness of power divorced from purer intuition that is at the root of most human ills. The animals in their personal lives and in their social behaviour, where they are gregarious, are vastly purer in their aims and conduct than we are, and it is open to doubt whether the additional power without the feeling necessary to regulate it, is to be considered better than the simple nature.

Ibid.

Vegetarianism is not a fad. It is a great and essential part of the religion of humanity. It is a step into a higher, because a less selfish, plane of life. It makes progress possible, and both individual and social development is at present seriously blocked by the meat habit and all that it implies and involves.

As long as we treat other living, sensitive creatures with like feelings as ours only as carcasses for the market and meat to be consumed, we must shut our eyes to the real kinship of all living things, and thus lose an essential factor in learning to understand, even in some degree, this mysterious world in which we find ourselves. Social progress is blocked no less than individual development. In a dozen ways this barbarous habit, inherited from savage ancestors, stands in the way of practical reforms which are much needed.

Ibid.

We cannot by any stretch of amiability say, or feel, that the meat-eater is actuated by any lofty motive in his choice. He has no unselfish ideal to work out in the matter. His whole effort is to defend or excuse that which his *feelings* all the time tell him is a selfish and cruel practice. He has to shut his eyes to much that he dares not face, to try to invent so-called scientific reasons to excuse that which in itself is obviously very undesirable and discreditable – 'a painful necessity', as he sometimes calls it.

Ibid.

Let us not think that [vegetarianism] is the end in itself. It is a means only to the end, and we must not be content to be vegetarians only. The end is the cultivation of the universal feeling of brotherhood, on which it rests, not towards animals only, but towards all men ... our treatment of our fellow-humans is largely reflected from our behaviour towards the sub-human races.

As long as our ethics in this matter are based on barbaric cruelty and selfish tyranny it will forever be well-nigh impossible to attain a high and just social morality.

Ibid.

Can we expect that war against our fellow-men, with all its carnage, injustice and barbarity, will ever strike people with the same horror that it would if we were not accustomed to daily bloodshed and murder in the shambles?

Hitherto, education has aimed almost exclusively at educating the head, while the heart has been almost entirely forgotten.

The essential point of education should not be mathematics, science or languages – all good things in their way – but the development of character, the working out of the savage still in us, and the evolution of the qualities which make for sympathy and justice.

To attain this end, nothing is better in the case of children, than the awakening in them of a feeling of interest and love for animals. To most children it comes naturally with a little encouragement and guidance – but many fall into the opposite mental habit more readily when they are left uninstructed, or are deliberately encouraged in it.

Ibid.

People who have undeveloped imaginations have no ideas beyond their material wants. Wars would be impossible had we more imagination. The sight of a street accident or a mutilated dead body lying in our own road would fill one with horror and be a lasting and painful remembrance for years, but the account of 3000 killed and mangled on the battlefield is, with many people, little more than an interesting item of news at the breakfast table – because the imaginative faculty does not and cannot picture the reality.

And so with all kinds of cruelty and injustice. Vivisection would be impossible had people in general the power to see it in imagination as it really is. Who could stand by and see an animal writhing in pain in the public streets without making practical protests against the cruel torment, but when it is in a laboratory away from sight it is practically impossible to make people realize it …

The growth of altruism in the world has been largely contemporaneous with the growth of the power of sympathy, the emotion which a being has when by means of his *imagination* he puts himself in the place of another so that his own feelings duplicate more or less the feelings of that other. It is the ability or the impulse to weep with those who weep and rejoice with those who are glad. Now sympathy is the substance and only sure basis of morality – the only tie of sincere and lasting mutualism …

True altruism and solidarity – true expansion and universalisation of the self – are found in sympathy …

In one's own individual moral or spiritual development the imagination is an indispensable factor. To keep a high ideal before one in any matter is the first step towards attaining that ideal, just as keeping a low ideal will quickly result in our gravitating down to it …

As Emile Coué says: 'It is the imagination which is the most important faculty of man … it is the training of the imagination which men ought to set about.'

Ibid.

Man is an almost hopelessly conceited animal. He thinks that not only the earth with all that it contains was created for his essential benefit, but also the sky, the sun, and indeed, the whole universe, as far as he has any knowledge of it, were designed for his purposes and welfare.

The sun shines to warm *him*; the earth brings forth fruits to feed *him*; the mountains contain metals that *he* may use them; the mines produce coal that *he* may work his machinery and cook his dinners. *He* is the standard by which everything must be measured. What he does not care for has no value. The flowers which he does not see are said, in practical language, 'to *waste* their sweetness on the desert air'.

When this is his view of inanimate nature, the world of life by which he is surrounded, of course, meets with no more respectful treatment. The animals whom he can use were, according to his view, *created for that purpose* by a beneficent Creator – the horse to draw his burdens, the cow to give her milk, the cat to kill mice for him. Even those animals whom he cannot use directly are held to be connected in some mysterious way with his welfare, as otherwise, he says, why should they exist? The Eton boy who wrote in defence of the Eton beagles that 'the hare is a useless animal, you must own, and the only use to be made of it is for the exercise of human beings', is typical of many others.

Man is the head, the apex of creation, towards whom God has been working from the beginning of time, and when he leaves this world he will find a special heaven prepared for him where no one else may enter except angels, and they, even, will not be superior to him, for he will be one himself then.

Truly a conceited being is this pigmy, whose knowledge of the universe is limited to what he can learn from or guess at by his five very imperfect senses, and a paltry undeveloped intellect which is ever palpably leading him astray.

Superiority in the Lower Animals

ARTHUR C. BENSON, 1862–1925

... Then, too, he never seems quite at home in his deplorably filthy surroundings; he looks at you, up to the knees in ooze, out of his little eyes, as if he would live in a

23

more cleanly way, if he were permitted. Pigs always remind me of the mariners of Homer, who were transformed by Circe; there is a dreadful humanity about them, as if they were trying to endure their base conditions philosophically by waiting for their release.

The Thread of Gold

JEREMY BENTHAM, 1748–1832

The day may come when the rest of the animal creation may acquire those rights which never could have been withheld from them but by the hand of tyranny ... a full-grown horse or dog is beyond comparison a more rational, as well as a more conversable animal, than an infant of a day, or a week or even a month old. But suppose the case were otherwise, what would it avail? The question is not, can they reason? Nor, can they talk? But *can they suffer*? Why should the law refuse its protection to any sensitive being? The time will come when humanity will extend its mantle over everything which breathes ...

Principles of Morals and Legislation

HENRY BERGH, 1811–1888

Now it is against all these devilish abominations, inflicted on the defenseless brute, and the unfortunate members of our own race – deeds done in the outraged name of Science, and which challenge the iniquities of hell itself to surpass – that this appeal is made to public opinion, for the exercise of its sovereign power to suppress. Is it not time that universal sentiment should put a stop to these horrid operations, which tend to harden the heart, extinguish those instincts which give man confidence in man, and make the physician more dreaded than disease itself?

It is maintained by the most eminent physiologists of the world that vivisection is not only a cruelty but a scientific failure, since the information sought to be obtained thereby is no more attainable while the body is writhing in agony than the correct hour of the day can be recorded while the clock's machinery is disordered ...

While reading these frightful atrocities, perpetrated on innocent, unoffending animals, the inquiry springs to the lips: can the perpetrators of them be human beings? Can the brain that conceives them, the heart that tolerates, and the hand that executes them belong to the being who, it is said, was made in God's own image?

Address given as founder of The American Society for the Prevention of Cruelty to Animals

CLAUDE BERNARD, 1813–1878

The physiologist is not an ordinary man: he is a scientist, possessed and absorbed by the scientific idea that he pursues. He does not hear the cries of animals, he does not see their flowing blood, he sees nothing but an organism that conceals from him the problem he is seeking to solve.

Introduction to the Study of Experimental Medicine

RYNN BERRY, 1945–

Twenty-two years ago, on August 15, 1966, I became a vegetarian. Thenceforth no fish, no meat, no eggs or dairy products would ever pass my lips. No animal would be forced to give up its life that I might sustain mine. So every year I mark the occasion, and celebrate it as though it were a birthday; for truly it was a day of liberation, joy and rebirth!

Talk given to the New York Vegan Society, 15 May 1988

ANNIE BESANT, 1847–1933

When we recognize that unity of all living things, then at once arises the question – how can we support this life of ours with least injury to the lives around us; how can we prevent our own life adding to the suffering of the world in which we live?

We find amongst animals, as amongst men, power of feeling pleasure, power of feeling pain; we see them moved by love and by hate; we see them feeling terror and attraction; we recognize in them powers of sensation closely akin to our own, and while we transcend them immensely in intellect, yet, in mere passional characteristics our natures and the animals' are closely allied. We know that when they feel terror, that terror means suffering. We know that when a wound is inflicted, that wound means pain to them. We know that threats bring to them suffering; they have a feeling of shrinking, of fear, of absence of friendly relations, and at once we begin to see that in our relations to the animal kingdom a duty arises which all thoughtful and compassionate minds should recognize – the duty that because we are stronger in mind than the animals, we are or ought to be their guardians and helpers, not their tyrants and oppressors, and we have no right to cause them suffering and terror merely for the gratification of the palate, merely for an added luxury to our own lives.

… there is one other thought closely allied to this. What of our duties to our fellow men? And here I appeal particularly to my own sex, because women are supposed to be rather the *standard* in the community of refinement, of gentleness, of compassion, of tenderness, of purity. But no one can eat the flesh of a slaughtered animal without having used the hand of a man as slaughterer. Suppose that we had to kill for ourselves the creatures whose bodies we would fain have upon our table, is there one woman in a hundred who would go to the slaughter-house to slay the bullock, the calf, the sheep or the pig? ... But if we could not do it, nor see it done; if we are so refined that we cannot allow close contact between ourselves and the butchers who furnish this food; if we feel that they are so coarsened by their trade that their very bodies are made repulsive by the constant contact with the blood with which they must be continually besmirched; if we recognize the physical coarseness which results inevitably from such contact, dare we call ourselves refined if we purchase our refinement by the brutalization of others, and demand that some should be brutal in order that we may eat the results of their brutality? We are not free from the brutalizing results of that trade simply because we take no direct part in it.

From a speech given at Manchester, 18 October 1897

HENRY BESTON, 1888–1968

We need another and a wiser and perhaps a more mystical concept of animals ... We patronize them for their incompleteness, for their tragic fate of having taken form so far below ourselves. And therein we err and err greatly. For the animal shall not be measured by man. In a world older and more complete than ours, they move finished and complete, gifted with extensions of the senses we have lost or never attained, living by voices we shall never hear. They are not brethren; they are not underlings; they are other nations, caught with ourselves in the net of life and time, fellow prisoners of the splendour and travail of the earth.

The Outermost House

KAVI YOGI MAHARSHI SHUDDHANANDA
BHARAT, 1919–

From grass to Godmen all are equal souls sensitive to joy and grief. A plant fades in the hot sun and smiles in the cool breezy evening. It cheers up when watered well. It weeps when the bud is violently plucked. Animals have five senses and man six senses. The intelligent mental man must treat plants and animals with tender love and compassion. Man as the most evolved soul, as the paragon of living beings, is obliged to practise non-violence in thought, word and deed. Soft mercy marks the human from the beast. The lion and tiger are carnivorous by instinct. Man is not a human tiger. The man who kills screaming life for food is dead to mercy and compassion. The cow and goat give milk. The oxen draw carts and plough fields. The horse carries man. The faithless man whips and rips them and gluts his stomach with their flesh. A cut animal is dead; its flesh stinks. Man eats it and makes his stomach the graveyard for poor dumb creatures. Nature gives man clean sweet vegetables; but unrefined man cuts the throat of crying animals and gluts his stomach. His heart becomes hard and the hand that cuts animals cuts tomorrow the throats of brother men in the battlefield. If war must stop in the world, blood-soaked food must stop and men must become vegetarians.

The Vegetarian Way, XXIV World Vegetarian Congress, 1977

THE HOLY BIBLE

All things whatsoever ye would that men should do to you, do ye even so to them; for this is the law and the prophets.

St. Matthew 7.12

And God said, Behold, I have given you every herb bearing seed, which is upon the face of all the earth, and every tree, in which is the fruit of a tree yielding seed; to you it shall be for meat.

And to every beast of the earth, and to every fowl of the air, and to every thing that creepeth upon the earth, wherein there is life, I have given every green herb for meat; and it was so.

Genesis 1:29, 30

To what purpose is the multitude of your sacrifices unto me? saith the Lord: I am full of the burnt offerings of rams, and the fat of fed beasts; and I delight not in the blood of bullocks, or of lambs, or of he goats ... Bring no more vain oblations ... Your new moons and your appointed feasts my soul hateth: they are a trouble unto me; I am weary to bear them. And when ye spread forth your hands, I will hide mine eyes from you: yea, when ye make many prayers, I will not hear: your hands are full of blood.

Isaiah 1:11–15

The wolf also shall dwell with the lamb, and the leopard shall lie down with the kid; and the calf and the young lion and the fatling together, and a little child shall lead them ... They shall not hurt nor destroy in all my holy mountain; for the earth shall be full of the knowledge of the Lord, as the waters cover the sea.

Isaiah 11:6–9

He that killeth an ox is as if he slew a man; he that sacrificeth a lamb, as if he cut off a dog's neck; he that offereth an oblation, as if he offered swine's blood; he that burneth incense, as if he blessed an idol. Yea, they have chosen their own ways, and their soul delighteth in their abominations.

Isaiah 66.3

Blessed are the merciful, for they shall receive mercy.

Matthew 5:7

Hurt not the earth, neither the sea, nor the trees.

Revelation 7:3

Let us therefore follow after the things which make for peace, and things wherewith one may edify another.

For meat destroy not the work of God. All things indeed are pure; but it is evil for that man who eateth with offence.

It is good neither to eat flesh, nor to drink wine, nor any thing whereby thy brother stumbleth, or is offended, or is made weak.

Romans 14:19–21

A righteous man regardeth the life of his beast: but the tender mercies of the wicked are cruel.

Proverbs 12:10

Open thy mouth for the dumb, in the cause of all such as are appointed to destruction.

Proverbs 31:8

Speak to the Earth, and it shall teach thee.

Job 12:8

HENRY J. BIGELOW, MD, 1818–1890

Watch the students at a vivisection. It is the blood and suffering, not the science, that rivets their breathless attention. If hospital service makes young students less tender to suffering, vivisection deadens their humanity and begets indifference to it.

Quoted by Albert Leffingwell, *An Ethical Problem*

The torture of helpless animals – more terrible by reason of its refinement and the effort to prolong it than burning at the stake, which is brief – is now being carried on in all civilized nations, not in the name of religion, but of science. There is little in the literature of what is called the horrors of vivisection which is not well grounded on truth. For a description of the pain inflicted I refer to that literature, only reiterating that what it recounts is largely and simply fact, selected it may be, but rarely exaggerated. Vivisection is not an innocent study. We may usefully popularize chemistry and electricity, their teaching and their experimentation, even if only as one way of cultivating human powers. But not so with painful vivisection. We may not move as freely in this direction, for there are distinct reasons against it. It can be indiscriminately pursued only by torturing animals, and the word *torture* is here intentionally used to convey the idea of very severe pain – sometimes the severest conceivable pain, of indefinite duration, often terminating, fortunately for the animal, with its life, but as often only after hours or days of refined infliction, continuously or at intervals.... Scientific vivisection has all the engrossing fascination of other physical sciences, but the transcendent torture sometimes inflicted has no parallel in any one of them.... The law should interfere. There can be no doubt that in this relation there exists a case of cruelty to animals far transcending in its refinement and in its horror anything that has been known in the history of nations.

There will come a time when the world will look back to modern vivisection in the name of Science, as they do now to burning at the stake in the name of religion.

Surgical Anaesthesia

LLOYD BIGGLE Jr, 1923–

Life is life's greatest gift. Guard the life of another creature as you would your own because it *is* your own. On life's scale of values, the smallest is no less precious to the creature who owns it than the largest ...

The Light That Never Was

L.C. BIRCH, 1918–

[The animal rights movement] should be supported by all Christians. In an ecological universe, every created entity has intrinsic value because all are subjects as well as objects. As we cover more and more of the earth with our factories, highways, towns and parking lots, we annihilate more and more plants and animals, but the only argument Western ethics has for conserving nature is that we should take care of the habitat because it takes care of us.

From address given before 450 scientists and religious leaders at the World Council of Churches Conference on Faith, Science and the Future, quoted in *Animals* (October 1979), journal of the S.P.C.A.

RICHARD DODDRIDGE BLACKMORE, 1825–1900

A long way down that limpid water – chill and bright as an iceberg – went my little self that day on a man's own errand – destruction. All the young fish seemed to know that I was one who had taken out God's certificate, and meant to have the value of it. Every one of them was aware that we desolate more than replenish the earth. For a cow might come and look at the water and put her yellow lips down; a kingfisher, like a blue arrow, might shoot through the dark alleys over the channel, or sit on a dipping withy bough with his beak sunk into his breast feathers; even an otter might float down stream, likening himself to a log of wood, with his head flush with the water top, and his oily eyes peering quietly; and yet no panic would seize other life as it does when a sample of man comes.

Lorna Doone

ELIZABETH BLACKWELL, 1821–1910

The excuse or toleration of cruelty upon any living creature by a woman is a deadly sin against the grandest force in nature – maternal love ... In not a single instance known to science has the cure of any human disease resulted necessarily from this fallacious method of research.

Erroneous Method in Medical Education

WILLIAM BLAKE, 1757–1827

The Fly

Little Fly,
Thy summer's play
My thoughtless hand
Has brush'd away.

Am not I
A fly like thee?
Or art not thou
A man like me?

For I dance,
And drink, and sing,
Till some blind hand
Shall brush my wing.

If thought is life
And strength and breath;

And the want
Of thought is death;

Then am I
A happy fly,
If I live
Or if I die.

How do you know but ev'ry bird that cuts the airy way,
Is an immense world of delight, clos'd by your senses five?

The Marriage of Heaven and Hell

HELENA PETROVNA BLAVATSKY, 1831–1891

We Europeans are nations of civilized barbarians with but a few milleniums between ourselves and our cave-dwelling forefathers who sucked the blood and marrow from uncooked bones. Thus, it is only natural that those who hold human life so cheaply in their frequent and often iniquitous wars, should entirely disregard the death-agonies of the brute creation, and daily sacrifice millions of innocent, harmless lives. For we are too epicurean to devour tiger steaks or crocodile cutlets, but must have tender lambs and golden-feathered pheasants. All this is only as it should be in our era of Krupp cannons and scientific vivisectors. Nor is it a matter of great wonder that the hardy European should laugh at the mild Hindu, who shudders at the bare thought of killing a cow, or that he should refuse to sympathize with the Buddhist and Jain, in their respect for the life of every sentient creature – from the elephant to the gnat.

'Have Animals Souls?' *Theosophist*, January/March 1886

... in civilized Europe – rapidly progressing in all things save Christian virtues – *might* remains unto this day the synonym of *right*. The entirely useless, cruel practice of shooting for mere sport countless hosts of birds and animals is nowhere carried on with more fervour than in Protestant England, where the merciful teachings of Christ have hardly made human hearts softer than they were in the days of Nimrod ...

Ibid.

The blame for this universal suffering falls entirely upon our Western religion and early education. Every philosophical Eastern system, every religion and sect in antiquity – the Brahmanical, Egyptian, Chinese and finally, the purest as the noblest of all the existing systems of ethics, Buddhism – inculcates kindness and protection to every living creature, from animal and bird down to the creeping thing and even the reptile. Alone, our Western religion stands in its isolation, as a monument of the most gigantic *human* selfishness ever evolved by human brain, without one word in favour of, or for the protection of the poor animal. Quite the reverse. For theology, underlining a sentence in the Jehovistic chapter of 'Creation', interprets it as a proof that animals, as all the rest, were created for man! *Ergo* – sport has become one of the *noblest* amusements of the upper ten. Hence – poor innocent birds wounded, tortured and killed every autumn by the million all over the Christian countries, for man's recreation ... In whatever country the European steps in, there begins the slaughter of the animals and their useless decimation ...

Is Christianity or even the Christian layman to be blamed for it? Neither. It is the pernicious system of theology, long centuries of theocracy, and the ferocious, ever-increasing selfishness in the Western civilized countries.

Why Do Animals Suffer? *Lucifer*, May 1888

WILFRID SCAWEN BLUNT, 1840–1922

... the atrocious doctrine that beasts and birds were made solely for man's use and pleasure, and that he has no duties towards them.

My Diaries

LORD (Henry) BOLINGBROKE, 1678–1751

As these animal systems come to be more and more sensible to us, and as our means and opportunities of observing them increase, we discover in them ... the same appearances, that denote a power of thinking in us ... I think it indisputable that the distance between the intellectual faculties of different men is greater than that between the same faculties in some men and some other animals ... There is in the whole animal kingdom one intellectual spring common to every species, but vastly distinguished in its effects ... though it seems to be the same spring in all, yet it seems to be differently tempered, and to have more elasticity and force in some and less in others.

Essays on Human Knowledge

ROSA BONHEUR, 1822–1899

The horse is, like man, the most beautiful and the most miserable of creatures, only, in the case of man, it is vice or property that makes him ugly. He is responsible for his own decadence, while the horse is only a slave that the Creator has given to man, who abuses it out of his ingratitude and his worldly and egoistic poverty, until he becomes lower than the animal itself.

Rose Bonheur, a Life and a Legend

JAMES BOSWELL, 1740–1795

DR JOHNSON

There is much talk of the misery which we cause to the brute creation; but they are recompensed by existence. If they were not useful to man, and therefore protected by him, they would not be nearly so numerous.

BOSWELL

But the question is, whether the animals who endure such sufferings of various kinds, for the service and entertainment of man, would accept existence upon the terms on which they have it.

Life of Dr Johnson

JOANNE BOWER, 1912–

When we consider how science is taught for the most part in schools, we realize how the natural wonder and awe of children faced with the miracles of nature are debased to a matter of dissection and diagrams. An American biologist says that if biology were taught in a manner that developed a sense of wonder and of reverence for life, and if students felt inwardly enriched from their study of life, these students would formulate as a lifelong goal the steadfast determination to protect and preserve all life and would bring healing to a world desperately in need of it.

That must surely be the goal of human beings if they are to reach their full potential. We were not sent into the world as despoilers and destroyers, and yet it is already too late to save much of beauty and glory which has already fallen to man's depredation, greed, cruelty and thoughtlessness. Unless the new consciousness can overcome these propensities, this wonderful earth is doomed, and the spirit of man with it.

Conference address September 1986:
'Quakerism and the New Consciousness'

Are we as a Society fully committed to living in loving harmony with the earth and all its creatures? Are we perhaps too much involved with our own species to acknowledge that all life is one, and to extend our concerns accordingly? Some years ago at a Quaker conference someone said words to the effect that 'I would not mind how many animals were sacrificed if the life of one Indian were saved as a result.' A voice from the floor asked 'Why?' The question was not answered. It is very difficult to answer in the light of the new consciousness. Is concentration on our own species hindering our spiritual development?

It does seem that the spiritual as well as the physical health of mankind depends on the wellbeing of the whole natural world.

Ibid.

BILLY RAY BOYD, 1945–

While non-human animals are far more than the hunting targets, research tools, and food machines that we treat them as, neither are they Bambi and Donald Duck caricatures. They are neither unfeeling brutes nor noble savages, but complex, highly sentient beings in their own right.

The New Abolitionists

Most of us would be horrified if a neighbour did to her companion animal what is routinely – and in most cases, legally – inflicted on literally millions of animals daily, not only in laboratories and in the wild, but in factory farms, transport and slaughterhouses. Most of us view ourselves as reasonably humane. While we of course act out of self-interest as well, a good deal of our politics comes from an altruistic desire for a more just and humane society; our natural kindness is repelled by the plethora of horrors we see in the world, directly or through the media.

We probably picture an idyllic traditional farm, not the instrument of intensive confinement agricultures and mechanized slaughter, when we think of where our animal foods come from – if we think about it at all. And so we fall easy prey to the propaganda of the interconnected meat, milk and egg industries. We *want* to believe that our cheese omelettes and sausages come from contented cows, pigs and chickens, who willingly give of themselves that we may continue to satisfy our culturally (and commercially) conditioned tastes. We have been blinded by speciesism to the suffering of non-human animals, just as racism, sexism, etc., prevent 'non-target' dominant groups from seeing and feeling the agonized realities of subjugated human classes.

Ibid.

The history of intra-human violence and exploitation is marked by a trail of blood and tears that shows little sign of fading away. Indeed, technological advances have made possible violence on a scale previously unimaginable. Even many of the low-technology civilizations lauded in our history books were built on the labour of countless human slaves whose rights and needs, whose agonies and shattered dreams, have been greatly downplayed or ignored altogether. Non-human animals, if anything, have fared even worse and today their exploitation by humans has escalated far beyond traditional levels.

To ignore or trivialize such massive and largely avoidable suffering of highly sentient fellow beings at human hands, to objectify them as no more than food or fur machines or tools of research is, I suggest, to make a mockery of the ideals of justice and *ahimsa* [harmlessness to all – not just human – life, a Hindu concept]. If we continue to separate ourselves off into an ivory tower of solely human-centred concerns, we will betray not only our fellow beings, but our own deeper selves. Such separation will also bring – is bringing – our physical destruction as well, whether in a nuclear holocaust or an ecological collapse. Animal rights is deep ecology, a truth expressed in diverse idioms from the religious – 'As you do unto others, so do you also unto me' – to the political – 'An injury to one is an injury to all.'

The Nonviolent Activist, January/February 1986

Guns, hunting dogs primed for blood, the crisp air of autumn mornings, the camaraderie of all-male companions ... these constituted a rite of passage from boyhood into manhood in my native Ozark mountains. I loved the smell of the trees, the feel of the ridges and valleys. The excitement of the hunt – 'buck fever' – was a welcome relief from a life lived within walls and towns.

Yet the actual killing disturbed me. The hardest part was 'finishing off' a downed animal, bleeding from bullet wounds, exhausted from the chase, facing death. Try as I might, I could neither ignore nor forget the fearful look in those pleading eyes. In this way I learned that every creature values her or his life just as much as I value mine. Although I continued to hunt for a time, I was already a dormant, would-be vegetarian, lacking sufficient moral courage – and nutritional information – to act on my most fundamental feelings and intuitions.

For the Vegetarian in You

LORD (John) BOYD ORR, CH, FRS, LL D, 1880–1971

Knowledge acquired in biological research is seldom directly applicable to human beings ... The results of scientific research, obtained under these conditions, cannot be applied directly to human beings who vary widely in their hereditary make-up, in their environment, and in their past health record.

From foreword to Davidson, *A Test Book of Dietetics*

LORD (Walter Russell) BRAIN, 1895–1966

I personally can see no reason for conceding mind to my fellow men and denying it to animals ... I at least cannot doubt that the interests and activities of animals are correlated with awareness and feeling in the same way as my own, and which may be, for ought I know, just as vivid.

From presidential address quoted Keele & Smith,
The Assessment of Pain in Men and Animals

ANNA HEMPSTEAD BRANCH, 1875–1937

To a Dog

If there is no God for thee,
Then there is no God for me.

T. CASEY BRENNAN, 1935–

Poor animals! How jealously they guard their pathetic bodies ... that which to us is merely an evening's meal, but to them is life itself.

Vegetarian Times, March 1977

PAUL BROCA, 1824–1880

Like the Roman emperors, who, intoxicated by their power, at length regarded themselves as demigods, so the ruler of the earth believes that the animals subjected to his will have nothing in common with his own nature. Man is not content to be the king of animals. He insists on

41

having it that an impassable gulf separates him from his subjects. The affinity of the ape disturbs and humbles him. And, turning his back upon the earth, he flies, with his threatened majesty, into the cloudy sphere of a special 'human kingdom'. But Anatomy, like those slaves who followed the conqueror's car crying 'Thou art a man', disturbs him in his self-admiration, and reminds him of those plain and tangible realities which unite him with the animal world.

Memoirs of Anthropology

DR JOSEPH BRONOWSKI, 1908–1974

Why do we object to experiments of a certain kind whether on human beings or on animals? We object to them because they debase the man who does them so that he does not remain capable of making an objective judgment. Some of the people from whom I got a sense of science were men of enormous humanity – they were men in whom the knowledge of nature was a sense of love, a sense of devotion, a sense of dedication.

Science and Human Values

It is not the business of science to inherit the earth, but to inherit the moral imagination; because without that, man and belief and science will perish together.

Ibid.

BRIGID BROPHY, 1929–

So far as I can tell, the original class distinction (original, that is, in each individual's experience) is the tremendous gulf between Me and All the Rest of You; any difference I see between You and You is tiny compared with the enormous difference between Me and All Others, a difference I experience in the fact that if I bump you on the head, whether You are in this case animate or a lump of stone, I merely observe the result, whereas if I get bumped on the head the universe, my universe, is totally occupied by an actual, vivid, and very unpleasant sensation.

Presently, however, there arises in most of us (perhaps not in psychopaths) a faculty of imagination (I can only label, not describe it), which informs Me that to you, You are a Me. It is this faculty, with its ability to inhabit the other side of the barrier, that knocks the class barrier down. It can never rid me of my egocentric vision. But it persuades me that if I want to make a just appraisal of reality (and I do want to; it's not a virtue; I can't help it) then I must perform a series of intellectual adjustments to discount the distorting effect of the particular point of view from which I am obliged to observe reality.

My pain in the head remains more vivid to me than your pain in the head, but if I adjust for this I have to perceive that your hitting me and my hitting you are acts in exactly the same class; I can't deplore the one without deploring the other; I have weighed them in a balance as accurate as I can make it, found them equally bad, and have thereby set irreversibly out towards social justice.

To my mind, therefore, there was both a logical and a psychological inevitability in basing the claim for the other animals' rights on social justice.

Animals' Rights: a Symposium

Once my imagination has embarked me (and it has, and I can't go back on it) on a course of thoughts making for social justice, it inevitably carries me crashing through the class barriers, including speciesism, which may be the last barrier to fall, or at least one of the last. What the movement against speciesism asks, in the light of the theory of Evolution, is that the present high barrier between the human and the other animal species should be displaced and re-erected between the animal kingdom and the vegetable kingdom (though evolutionists will expect there to be a no-man's-land at the border). A millennium from now, there may well be a symposium on the rights of plants. Humans may be working out techniques whereby we could, for instance, derive our food exclusively from fruits, which display as it were a biological acquiescence about falling off into the hands of grasping animals like ourselves. Plants are individuals, they are sensitive, and they certainly demonstrate an instinctual will to live – that is, they assert in instinctual terms a right to live. But their sensibility and individuality are not carried on by means of a central nervous system, and at the moment there is a place where our knowledge stops and seems to be an intellectually respectable place for our imaginations (at least in practice) to stop.

Ibid.

The fact that there are bigger injustices and wrongs doesn't make it right to sacrifice an innocent monkey. It doesn't alter the case at all.

… Possibly man rose by exploiting the weak. That's how he came up. But now, now he *is* up. The very thing that marks his progress is that he knows better.

… If someone had offered to bump you off at thirty, would you be reconciled to him on condition he did it humanely?

… It's not the consciousness of man that distinguishes him, it's his imagination. If you can imagine what it feels like to be an animal and you must kill it, you kill it humanely.

Hackenfeller's Ape

In point of fact, I am the very opposite of an anthropomorphiser. I don't hold animals superior or even equal to humans. The whole case for behaving decently to animals rests on the fact that we are the superior species. We are the species uniquely capable of imagination, rationality and moral choice – and that is precisely why we are under the obligation to recognize and respect the rights of animals.

Don't Never Forget

I don't myself believe that, even when we fulfil our minimum obligations not to cause pain, we have the right to kill animals. I know I would not have the right to kill you, however painlessly, just because I liked your flavour, and I am not in a position to judge that your life is worth more to you than the animal's to it.

Ibid.

Whenever people say 'We mustn't be sentimental', you can take it they are about to do something cruel. And if they add 'We must be realistic', they mean they are going to make money out of it. These slogans have a long history. After being used to justify slave traders, ruthless industrialists, and contractors who had found that the most economically 'realistic' method of cleaning a chimney was to force a small child to climb it, they have now been passed on, like an heirloom, to the factory farmers.

'We mustn't be sentimental' tries to persuade us that factory farming isn't, in fact, cruel. It implies that the whole problem has been invented by our sloppy imaginations. The factory farmers dare not quite claim that animals are incapable of feeling. The public can't be relied on to be quite so ignorant. After all, anyone who is personally acquainted with a dog, cat or canary has as much evidence that mammals and birds can feel pain,

BROPHY

terror or misery as he has in the case of his fellow citizens. Sometimes, therefore, the factory farmers maintain that factory-farmed animals are different from other animals: they don't mind being maimed, stunted and jam-packed because they have never known anything else. The argument is about as impressive as the old one that the poor didn't mind squalor and hardship because *they* had never known anything else. At other times, what the factory farmers emphasise is that animals are different from humans: we can't, we are told, judge their reactions by our own, because they don't have human feelings. But no one in his senses ever supposed they did. Anyone acquainted with animals can guess pretty well that they have less intellect and memory than humans, and live closer to their instincts. But the reasonable conclusion to draw from this is the very opposite of the one the factory farmers try to force upon us. In all probability, animals feel *more* sharply than we do any restriction on such instinctual promptings as the need, which we share with them, to wander around and stretch one's legs every now and then; and terror or distress suffered by an animal is never, as sometimes in us, softened by intellectual comprehension of the circumstances.

'We must be realistic', on the other hand, tacitly admits that factory farming is cruel but seeks to make us believe it is economically necessary. Sometimes we are even told we mustn't resist it because it is an 'advanced' method – a theory on which we ought to have welcomed Auschwitz as a great step forward in gas technology. It used to be said, of course, that slavery was economically necessary. Since we've dared to put it to the test, we've discovered that it isn't, and that we are quite ingenious enough to manage without it. But of course, even if slavery were a hundred times more economically advantageous than freedom, we couldn't, as moral and imaginative beings, tolerate it. *No more can we tolerate factory farming. It is as indefensible as the slave trade, and it is our business to make it as unthinkable.*

Unlived Life – A Manifesto Against Factory Farming

To us it seems incredible that the Greek philosophers should have scanned so deeply into right and wrong and yet never noticed the immorality of slavery. Perhaps 3000 years from now it will seem equally incredible that we do not notice the immorality of our own oppression of animals.

'The Rights of Animals', *Sunday Times*, 10 October 1965

The relationship of *Homo sapiens* to the other animals is one of unremitting exploitation. We employ their work: we eat and wear them. We exploit them to serve our superstitions: whereas we used to sacrifice them to our gods and tear out their entrails in order to foresee the future, we now sacrifice them to science, and experiment on their entrails in the hope – or on the mere offchance – that we might thereby see a little more clearly into the present. When we can think of no pretext for causing their death and no profit to turn it to, we often cause it none the less, wantonly, the only gain being a brief pleasure for ourselves, which is usually only marginally bigger than the pleasure we could have had without killing anything; we could quite well enjoy marksmanship or cross-country galloping without requiring a real dead wild animal to show for it at the end.

Ibid.

To hold vivisection never justified is a hard belief. But so is its opposite. I believe it is never justified because I can see nothing (except our being able to get away with it) which lets us pick on animals that would not equally let us pick on idiot humans (who would be more useful) or, for

47

the matter of that, on a few humans of any sort whom we might sacrifice for the good of the many.

Ibid.

Once we acknowledge life and sentiency in the other animals, we are bound to acknowledge what follows, the right to life, liberty and the pursuit of happiness. (This is not to deny that we owe them, as to our fellow-humans, a duty to end their life when the pursuit of pleasure and the shunning of pain have become impossible for them. And we have the right or duty to limit their populations by contraceptives, as we must our own.) That I like the flavour of mutton no more entitles me to kill a sheep than a taste for roast leg of human would entitle me to kill you. To argue that we humans are capable of complex, multifarious thought and feeling, whereas the sheep's experience is probably limited by lowly sheepish perceptions, is no more to the point than if I were to slaughter and eat you on the grounds that I am a sophisticated personality able to enjoy Mozart, formal logic and cannibalism, whereas your imaginative world seems confined to *True Romances* and tinned spaghetti. For the point is what your life and perceptions are worth to you, not to me, and what the sheep's life and sheepish perceptions are worth to the sheep.

Animals, Men and Morals

A medical profession founded on callousness to the pain of the other animals may eventually destroy its own sensibility to the pain of humans.

Ibid.

'Sentimentalist' is the abuse with which people counter the accusation that they are cruel, thereby implying that to be sentimental is worse than to be cruel, which it isn't.

Ibid.

H.E. MINGWAY

A culture that should have learnt better from Ambrose Bierce, Henry James, Edith Wharton, Scott Fitzgerald and Dashiell Hammet let itself be conned by Ernest Hemingway.

He took up slushy romances and he re-wrote their content in baby syntax like this and he pretended that tormenting and killing animals who are no threat to you was a brave and somehow a mystical thing to do and he perhaps supposed that pretending was the same as imagination and he also pretended that it was laudable to read with your finger running along beneath the line and after a while that pretence became true of him and he misread the first three letters of his own surname and he thought that his name said 'he-man'.

His chum Gertrude Stein was three times the writer as well as twice the man.

Symposium contributed to *Dictionary of*
Literary Biography Yearbook, 1985

In the search for the cause of multiple sclerosis and other mysterious diseases, and for a means of curing them, it is vital that no animal, human or non-human, be tortured or killed.

That, which I have given a good chunk of my life to saying in print, I now say with the authority of a person with a personal stake in the matter. It is not my personal stake that makes my anti-vivisectionist argument correct, but unless you can cite it you are open to emotional challenge by the emotionalists who support vivisection.

Human society has consistently asked itself the not-to-the-point question, 'What is the life of this rat or the freedom from terror and agony of that monkey worth to us?' The pertinent question is what they are worth to that monkey or this rat. His life is the only one that is open to him. His awareness, which you so easily suffuse with torment, is the only one he can experience.

The vivisectionist fallacy is a wilful and anti-scientific denial of the unique singularity of each individual sentient animal. To persist in asking the wrong question is fascism. You convince yourself that the life and happiness of this socialist, homosexual Gypsy-Jew, whatever it may be worth to him as a unique possession, is worth nothing to you.

Vivisection would still be a fascist atrocity even did abandonment of it, as its advocates pretend, place on you the responsibility of abandoning the hope of solving puzzles and discovering cures. In reality, however, the method, in which society has invested not only millions of lives but millions of pounds and man-hours, has produced results far from commensurate with the investment. Adherence to an expensive, luridly impressive and old-fashioned orthodoxy inhibits scientific imagination.

Baroque-'n'-Roll

ROBERT BROWNING, 1812–1899

I despise and abhor the pleas on behalf of that infamous practice, vivisection.

I would rather submit to the worst of deaths, so far as pain goes, than have a single dog or cat tortured on the pretence of sparing me a twinge or two.

From a letter

SIR ARTHUR (Wynne Morgan) BRYANT, 1899–1985

But of one thing I am convinced; that to take a dog – the most loving and trusting of creatures – and submit it, for whatever high-sounding end, to torture, physical and mental, must be vile and base. To the argument that such torture to a sentient and defenseless creature helps to preserve human life and alleviate human pain, I can only reply by saying that if my life could only be preserved on the condition of having such torture inflicted on a dog, I hope I should be man enough to refuse to keep it on such terms. And if I did not, I know I should feel utterly ashamed of myself. If we were put into the world to exist on such a basis, all our talk about humanitarianism has no real meaning.

... So long as there is any danger of such treatment being meted out to a creature who has placed himself in man's dependence and made himself man's faithful and trusting ally, I should feel that I was being party to a crime if I did not say what I thought about it.

... The capacity for nobility can be present in a dog as in a man or woman and to ignore this capacity and behave as if it was non-existent is as great a blindness or sin against the light as it is to ignore it in a man or woman.

Quoted in *Reverence for Life*

JOHN BRYANT, 1942–

I dream of a world where Man is at peace, not only with himself, but also with all the other creatures of Earth. I long for a day when Man rejects the exploitation of other species for food, clothing, health, entertainment or even companionship – for such a day will mean that cruelty no longer exists, and it is cruelty which dominates my every conscious moment.

Fettered Kingdoms

What we are saying if we support experimentation on animals is this: 'I would like to eat, wash in, inhale, drink, wear, or in some other way use a certain substance (which the human race has survived without, or with, for millions of years), but I am frightened what nasty effect that substance may have on me. Therefore, I will try it out on something weaker than myself who cannot refuse or object, so that if that someone screams, becomes ill, or dies, then I know not to use that substance.' That is cowardice!

Ibid.

There are three prerequisites for angling,
A hook, a line, and a stinker.

Ibid.

The animal welfare and rights movement must extend its influence into the area of conservation. For too long we have allowed the conservation bodies to exist without the ethic of 'rights for the individual', with the result that many blood-sportsmen have been allowed to mask their cruel activities by wearing the respectable mantles of 'conservation' simply because they take action to preserve their victims and their habitats.

Ibid.

I submit that when the whole morale of a nation can depend on the success (or lack of it) of its national team in some game; when thousands jeer at the agony of an injured rival team member; when dogs are awarded points for the manner in which they attack hares; when wild deer are driven into the sea by hounds and left to drown; when tourists applaud the torture and death of bulls; and when horses are ridden and jumped to their death in the cause of human pleasure – then we are indeed approaching the depths of depravity exhibited during the fall of the Roman empire.

I further believe that such things are not only symptomatic of our spiritual decline, but actually accelerate it, because by deriving pleasures from events which involve suffering, we allow ourselves to sink back to the subliminal instincts of 'the pack', retarding our evolution from a higher, spiritual and more noble plane.

Animals' Rights: a Symposium

ROBERT BUCHANAN, 1841–1901

God Evolving

Where'er great pity is and piteousness,
    Where'er great Love and Love's strange sorrow stay,
Where'er men cause to curse, but bend to bless
    Frail brethren fashion'd like themselves of clay;

Where'er the lamb and lion side by side
    Lie down in peace, where'er on land or sea
Infinite Love and Mercy heavenly-eyed
    Emerge, there stirs the God that is to be!

His light is round the slaughter'd bird and beast,
    As round the forehead of Man crucified –
All things that live, the greatest and the least,
    Await the coming of this Lord and Guide;

And every gentle deed by mortals done,
    Yea every holy thought and loving breath,
Lighten poor Nature's travail with this Son
    Who shall be Lord and God of Life and Death!

No God behind us in the empty Vast,
    No God enthroned on yonder heights above,
But God emerging, and evolved at last
    Out of the inmost heart of human Love!

E.D. BUCKNER, MD, AM, PhD, 1843–1907

It is a deplorable fact that many Christians are so accustomed to a certain creed and dogma of their own that they will adhere to it even at the sacrifice of the great moral laws of love and mercy.

…Physiologists have been making unnecessary and cruel experiments on man and animals for the last two or three centuries to satisfy their morbid curiosities. They have dissected every part of the body which can be dissected while living, and every part of the body after death which could not be done before. They have caused every conceivable manner of torment that the devilish nature of a man could invent. They have traced every nerve, artery, muscle, fibre and vessel. They have tortured to death by mutilating, cutting, burning, hanging, and drowning by a gradual process; they have roasted, frozen, boiled, and skinned the poor animals while in the full possession of the faculties of their souls. They have laid bare the nerves and then burned them with currents of electricity which is the most agonizing torture that can be imagined. All this has been done to learn something of the phenomena of life, and what has been the result? They have become so accustomed to material anatomy that they imagine that a thing does not exist unless they can show it on the point of their lancet or scalpel. Now can a materialist show an idea upon the point of his lancet? Or can he show a thought on the point of his scalpel? In measuring the various parts of the body, can he measure off an inch of love, a foot of anger, or a yard of jealousy? Can he locate, in that innocent, bloody piece of flesh before him, in the form of a dog, where that true and everlasting love it has for its master is found?

…Man should regard lower animals as being in the same dependent condition as minors under his government …

54

For a man to torture an animal whose life God has put into his hands, is a disgrace to his species.

...Animals are every day perishing under the hands of barbarity, without notice, without mercy, famished as if hunger was no evil, mauled as if they had no sense of pain, and hurried about incessantly from day to day, as if excessive toil was no plague, or extreme weariness was no degree of suffering ... the obligation [to be kind and merciful to animals] remains the same whether they have souls or not. Their status as respects a future life does not annihilate suffering and pain. Pain is pain; it makes no difference whether in an animal, a man, or as endured by the Son of God.

...Whoever in any manner cuts himself off from the common sympathies of our best nature by making sport of the energies of moral action, rebutting every idea that does not minister gratification either to fancy or taste, and having recourse either to a jargon of sophistries, or to trivial evasions, when other men act upon the intuitions of good sense and right motives – such a man becomes dangerous to the welfare of any community. Moral restraint serves directly to dispel errors of opinion by presenting the sense of justice and mercy as a true guide.

The Immortality of Animals

BUDDHISM

Hurt not others with that which pains yourself.

Udanavarga

By whomsoever no evil is done in deed, or word, or thought, him I call a brahmin who is guarded in these three.

Dhammapada

The Buddha has mercy even on the meanest thing.

Vinaya, Cullavagga Khandhaka

To serve the creatures is to serve the Buddha.

Indian Proverb

All beings seek for happiness; so let your compassion extend itself to all.

Mahavamsa

The sacred eightfold path or middle way – right views, right resolve, right speech, right action, right living, right effort, right attention, right meditation ... which lead to the extinction of suffering and Nirvana.

Buddha's first sermon – 4th truth. *Vinaya, Mahavagga*

The Goddess of Mercy has a thousand hands – and needs them all.

Japanese Proverb

He who, seeking his own happiness, punishes or kills beings who also long for happiness, will not find happiness after death.

Dhammapada

Let him not destroy, or cause to be destroyed, any life at all, nor sanction the acts of those who do so. Let him refrain from even hurting any creature, both those that are strong and those that tremble in the world.

Sutta-Nipata

Because he has pity on every living creature, therefore is a man called 'holy'.

Dhammapada

Full of love for all things in the world, practising virtue, in order to benefit others, this man alone is happy.

Dhammapada

One act of pure love in saving life is greater than spending the whole of one's time in religious offerings to the gods ...

Ibid.

For the sake of love of purity, the Bodhisattva should refrain from eating flesh, which is born of semen, blood, etc. For fear of causing terror to living beings let the Bodhisattva, who is disciplining himself to attain compassion, refrain from eating flesh ...

It is not true that meat is proper food and permissible when the animal was not killed by himself, when he did not order others to kill it, when it was not specially meant for him ... Again, there may be some people in the future who ... being under the influence of the taste for meat will string together in various ways sophistic arguments to defend meat eating ...

But ... meat eating in any form, in any manner, and in any place is unconditionally and once for all prohibited ... Meat eating I have not permitted to anyone, I do not permit, I will not permit ...

Lankavatara

The reason for practising dhyana [concentration of mind] and seeking to attain Samadhi [equilibrium; tranquillity; heightened and expanded awareness] is to escape from the suffering of life, but in seeking to escape from suffering ourselves why should we inflict it upon others? Unless you can so control your minds that even the thought of brutal unkindness and killing is abhorrent, you will never be able to escape from the bondage of the world's life ... After my Parinirvana [complete extinction] in the last kalpa [the time between the start of a world cycle and its extinction] different kinds of ghosts will be encountered everywhere deceiving people and teaching them that they can eat meat and still attain enlightenment ... How can a bhikshu, who hopes to become a deliverer of others, himself be living on the flesh of other sentient beings?

Surangama

The eating of meat extinguishes the seed of great compassion.

Mahaparinirvana

I have enforced the law against killing certain animals and many others, but the greatest progress of righteousness among men comes from the exhortation in favour of non-injury to life and abstention from killing living beings.

Asoka's *Edicts*

GEORGE LOUIS LECLERC DE BUFFON, 1707–1788

Man is enabled to use, as a master, his power over animals. He has multiplied them more than Nature could have done. He has formed innumerable flocks, and by the cares which he takes in propagating them he seems to have acquired the right of sacrificing them for himself. But he extends that right much beyond his needs. For, independently of those species which he has subjected and of which he disposes at his will, he makes war also upon wild animals, upon birds, upon fishes. He does not even limit himself to those of the climate he inhabits. He seeks at a distance, even in the remotest seas, new meats, and entire Nature seems scarcely to suffice for his intemperance and the inconstant variety of his appetites.

Man alone consumes and engulfs more flesh than all other animals put together. He is, then, the greatest destroyer, and he is so more by abuse than by necessity. Instead of enjoying with moderation the resources offered him, in place of dispensing them with equity, in place of repairing in proportion as he destroys, of renewing in proportion as he annihilates, the rich man makes all his boast and glory in consuming, all his splendour in destroying, in one day, at his table, more material than would be necessary for the support of several families. He abuses equally other animals and his own species, the rest of whom live in famine, languish in misery and work only to satisfy the immoderate appetite and the still more insatiable vanity of this human being who, destroying others by want, destroys himself by excess.

And yet Man might, like other animals, live upon vegetables. Flesh is not a better nourishment than grains or bread. What constitutes true nourishment, what contributes to the nutrition, to the development, to the growth, and to the support of the body, is not that brute matter which, to our eyes, composes the texture of flesh or of vegetables, but those organic molecules which both contain; since the ox, in feeding on grass, acquires as much flesh as man or as animals who live upon flesh and blood ... The essential source is the same; it is the same matter, it is the same organic molecules which nourish the Ox, Man and all the animals ... It is proved by facts that Man could well live upon bread, vegetables and the grains of plants, since we know entire nations and classes of men to whom religion forbids to feed upon anything that has life.

L'Histoire Naturelle

LUTHER BURBANK, 1849–1926

If, as we know, the creatures with fur, feathers or fins are our brothers in a lower stage of development, then their very weakness and inability to protest demands that man should refrain from torturing them for the merc possibility of obtaining some knowledge which he believes may be to his own interest.

Letter to Mrs C.P. Farrell, 2 October 1909

ROBERT BURNS, 1759–1796

From *On Scaring Some Water-Fowl*

The eagle from the cliffy brow,
Marking you his prey below,
In his breast no pity dwells,
Strong necessity compels:
But Man, to whom alone is giv'n
A ray direct from pitying Heav'n,
Glories in his heart humane –
And creatures for his pleasure slain!

On Seeing a Wounded Hare

Inhuman man! Curse on thy barbarous art,
    And blasted be thy murder-aiming eye:
    May never pity soothe thee with a sigh,
Nor ever pleasure glad thy cruel heart!

Go, live, poor wanderer of the wood and field,
    The bitter little that of life remains;
    No more the thickening brakes and verdant plains
To thee shall home, or food, or pastime yield.

Seek, mangled wretch, some place of wonted rest,
    No more of rest, but now thy dying bed!
    The sheltering rushes whistling o'er thy head,
The cold earth with thy bloody bosom prest.

Oft as by winding Frith, I, musing, wait
    The sober eve, or hail the cheerful dawn,
    I'll miss thee sporting o'er the dewy lawn,
And curse the ruffian's aim, and mourn thy
    hapless fate.

From *A Winter's Night*

The heart benevolent and kind
The most resembles God.

From To a Mouse

Wee, sleekit, cow'rin, tim'rous beastie,
O, what a panic's in thy breastie!
Thou need na start awa sae hasty
      wi' bickering brattle!
I wad be laith to rin an' chase thee,
      wi' murdering pattle!

I'm truly sorry man's dominion
Has broken Nature's social union,
An' justifies that ill opinion
      which makes thee startle
At me, thy poor, earth-born companion
      an' fellow mortal!

HOPE SAWYER BUYUKMIHCI, 1913–

A child is inherently kind. He needs only training to develop himself in ways of kindness. He needs only to be taught *how* to be kind.

Editorial in The Beaver Defenders

Responsibility ended. Compassion stifled. Is that the lesson we want our children to learn?

Ibid.

Nearly without exception, children have a natural fondness and genuine sympathy for animals and appreciation of an animal's beauty and joy of living. To me, this confirms that man does not have an inborn urge to kill, as is often claimed by those who take a pessimistic view of such related phenomena as hunting, warfare, and wanton cruelty.

How, then, do our life-loving children turn into a race of hunters and warriors? Not by instinct, I am sure, but through persistent conditioning. Despite outward professions to the contrary, our society still places a high value on aggression and prepares our children for violence. The children's natural sympathies are thus gradually perverted and their spirits are hardened. As they grow older they learn that it is 'sissy' to feel sorry for animals (or anyone else).

In thousands of ways – through television, movies and other communications media – youngsters are constantly sold the idea that violence is fun. Why does our society tolerate and even encourage such mass brutalization? Possibly there remains, as a leftover from more primitive times, a widespread if unspoken belief that young boys must prove their manhood by killing, if not in war then by hunting.

Hunting thus fits the pattern of an aggressive, warlike society. Yet, fortunately, an increasing number of responsible people feel that such a society is as outmoded as hunting itself. If war is waged on the present technological level, the whole world will be wiped out. Warfare thus becomes meaningless.

Likewise, if hunting is continued on its present scale with modern weapons, the animal population will be wiped out. Hunting thus becomes meaningless in the same sense as war. It no longer has utility.

If mankind really has a sense of good and evil, here's a concrete problem on which to exercise that sense. It surely needs some exercise.

I believe that the growing recognition that aggressive attitudes are intolerably dangerous in the modern world will bring about a profound change in educational philosophy in the near future. Perhaps we may hope that coming generations of children will be allowed to retain their naturally humane and joyful disposition in later life, including their compassionate feeling for animals.

Unexpected Treasure

MICHAEL BYROM, 1927–

Moral growth, like all progress, proceeds through innovators who inevitably must contend with the massed opposition of their own generation. But it is because of their efforts that a general moral advance is achieved. In a sense, they teach other people how to feel. By communicating their own deeply felt convictions to others, they awake similar latent feelings which in time become customs. To us, the thought of burning a woman alive in public is a horrible abomination, but it was practised as a social necessity in the Middle Ages. A few hundred years from now, our descendants will not be able to recall our habit of raising friendly animals in order to kill them and eat their decaying bodies, without repulsion.

Evolution for Beginners

A scientist is a man with abnormal insight into the physical side of life, and in consequence, largely unconcerned with aesthetic and moral issues. To him, the questions, 'Is it possible?' and 'Is it necessary?' are the questions of importance, and 'Is it right?' of no account whatever. A laboratory is thus a moral-less, soulless place where life-saving drugs are produced dispassionately alongside poison gas or hydrogen bombs, and where the torture of defenceless animals is sanctified by the excuse that mankind is being benefited. Those who are morally sensitive enough to feel revolted at the notion of vivisection, are often confused when faced with the indisputable argument that human lives can be saved as the results of these experiments. 'Which are more valuable', it is asked, 'dogs or humans?' To which the answer, of course, is 'Dogs, if the humans are so inhuman as to torture dogs in order to save their own miserable skins.'

These experiments are not benefiting mankind, they

are degrading mankind. Human progress does not lie in finding a cure for cancer by killing ten thousand animals; it lies in realizing that the cure for cancer is not worth the life of a single animal. Human progress, in other words, lies in moral, not in scientific or medical progress.

Ibid.

The destiny of mankind lies through inner spiritual development and not outward material exploitation. Darwinian ethics, which sanction a policy of power and domination, justify the contemporary appraisal of Man as the conqueror and master of Nature ... men must learn to live in harmony with Nature and not to rape, plunder and use her for selfish ends. This is the lesson learnt by every military conqueror: to live in peaceful affiliation with his enemy once the victory parade is over.

The attitude that Nature is to be lived with and not exploited can only develop as the Darwinian attitude, which has won human security, declines. Until it declines, most of our actions will be sinful and our reward misery. Our actions will consist mostly of a reckless usage of Nature and animals for purposes of self-indulgence, or, as we complacently describe it, in order to raise the standard of living.

Ibid.

LORD (George Gordon) BYRON, 1788–1824

From *Don Juan*

And angling, too, that solitary vice,
    Whatever Izaak Walton sings or says:
The quaint, old, cruel coxcomb, in his gullet
Should have a hook, and a small trout to pull it.

Byron comments in his Notes: This sentimental savage, whom it is a mode to quote (amongst the novelists) to show their sympathy for innocent sports and old songs, teaches how to sew up frogs, and break their legs by way of experiment, in addition to the art of angling, the cruellest, the coldest, and the stupidest of pretended sports.

Inscription on the Monument of a Newfoundland Dog

When some proud son of man returns to earth,
Unknown to glory, but upheld by birth,
The sculptor's art exhausts the pomp of woe,
And storied urns record who rest below:
When all is done, upon the tomb is seen,
Not what he was, but what he should have been:
But the poor dog, in life the firmest friend,
The first to welcome, foremost to defend,
Whose honest heart is still his master's own,
Who labours, fights, lives, breathes for him alone,
Unhonour'd falls, unnoticed all his worth,
Denied in heaven the soul he held on earth:
While man, vain insect, hopes to be forgiven,
And claims himself a sole exclusive heaven!

Oh, man! Thou feeble tenant of an hour,
Debased by slavery, or corrupt by power,
Who knows thee well must quit thee with disgust,
Degraded mass of animated dust!
Thy love is lust, thy friendship all a cheat,
Thy smiles hypocrisy, thy words deceit!
By nature vile, ennobled but by name,
Each kindred brute might bid thee blush for shame.
Ye, who perchance behold this simple urn,
Pass on – it honours none you wish to mourn:
To mark a friend's remains these stones arise;
I never knew but one, and here* he lies.

* Newstead Abbey, 30 November 1808

PARKES CADMAN, 1864–1936

Life in any form is our perpetual responsibility. Its abuse degrades those who practise it. Its rightful use is a signal of genuine manhood. If there is a superintend:ng justice, surely it takes account of the suffering and injuries of the helpless. Let us be perfectly clear about the spirituality of the issue before us. We have abolished human bondage because it cursed those who imposed it. It is now our bounden duty to oppose cruelty to those creatures of our common Father which share with man the mystery of life.

The Clergy Speak for Animals

THOMAS CAMPBELL, 1777–1844

Poor Dog Tray

On the green banks of Shannon, when Sheelah was nigh,
No blithe Irish lad was so happy as I;
No harp like my own could so cheerily play,
And wherever I went was my poor dog Tray.

When at last I was forced from my Sheelah to part,
She said (while the sorrow was big at her heart),
Oh! remember your Sheelah when far, far away;
And be kind, my dear Pat, to our poor dog Tray.

Poor dog! He was faithful and kind to be sure,
And he constantly loved me, although I was poor;
When the sour-looking folk sent me heartless away,
I had always a friend in my poor dog Tray.

When the road was so dark, and the night was so cold,
And Pat and his dog were grown weary and old,
How snugly we slept in my old coat of grey,
And he lick'd me for kindness – my old dog Tray.

Though my wallet was scant, I remembered his case,
Nor refused my last crust to his pitiful face;
But he died at my feet on a cold winter day,
And I play'd a sad lament for my poor dog Tray.

Where now shall I go, poor, forsaken, and blind?
Can I find one to guide me, so faithful and kind?
To my sweet native village, so far, far away,
I can never return with my poor dog Tray.

DR LOUIS J. CAMUTI, 1893–1981

Love of animals is a universal impulse, a common ground
on which all of us may meet. By loving and
understanding animals, perhaps we humans shall come
to understand each other.

All My Patients Are Under the Bed

Never believe that animals suffer less than humans. Pain
is the same for them that it is for us. Even worse, because
they cannot help themselves.

Park Avenue Vet

CANADIAN SENATE COMMITTEE ON HEALTH, WELFARE AND SCIENCE

If we are to teach children how to respect their human
and natural environment and all its elements they must
be taught they are a part of nature: 'All life is one and all
its manifestations are ascending the ladder of evolution.'
One of the objectives of education from nursery school
onwards must be to give children a balanced sensitivity to
life – a humane education.

Report, *Child at Risk*

NOEL CANNON, 1917–

Where animals are concerned, humanity seems to have switched off its morals and aesthetics – indeed, the very imagination. Those faculties function erratically enough in our dealings with one another. But at least we recognize their faultiness. We spend an increasing number of our cooler moments trying to forestall the moral and aesthetic breakdowns which are liable, in a crisis, to precipitate us into atrocities against each other. We have bitter demarcation disputes about where the rights of one man end and those of the next man begin, but most men now acknowledge that there are such things as the rights of the next man. Only in relation to the next animal can civilized humans persuade themselves that they have absolute and arbitrary rights – that they may do anything whatever that they can get away with.

> Speech before the second annual convention of the National Cat
> Protection Society in Los Angeles, 25 October 1975

ROGER CARAS, 1924–

> Writing about the fur industry's cries of 'ruination' if boycotts continued

It is also true that lots of jobs will be lost when the drug traffic in this country dries up, and not just among pushers; lots of law enforcement people will have to look for new jobs, too. You must forgive me if I equate the two, but what the drug traffic is to the human race, the fur trade is to the animal kingdom. Happily we don't have to equate the two or choose between them. We can hate and fight both the drug racket and the fur industry. Workers in both fields will have to develop new skills.

Of the claim that rodeo is Americana

So was slavery, cannibalism in the Donner Pass, the Bad Day at Black Rock, prohibition, the slaughter of the American Indian and the wasting of their priceless culture, the slaughter of the bison and the whale, lynching blacks, the Ku Klux Klan, Father Coughlin, Joe McCarthy and the Vigilantes ... all Americana. Is that enough excuse for a cultural artefect to persist?

I have said it again and again, and I will say it on the day I die if I have time. It is wrong to cause pain. It is wrong to cause fear, and to allow preventable pain and preventable fear to exist is no less an offence than causing them. That is my credo. I will argue it in heaven and hell. I will face any man or woman alive and argue it forever. I am more sure of that than I am of my private view of God and religion. I am more sure of that than I am of anything else in my experience as a man. I believe that credo is a valid view of my responsibility on earth.

Magazine of the Humane Society of the United States

... I do know this from long association with the scientific community (not as an adversary but as a friend): about 80 per cent of what goes on in the laboratory has nothing whatsoever to do with the good of mankind. Only 20 per cent can be exalted to that level. That remaining 80 per cent is for the fun, profit, reputation, or other benefit of the experimenter. We may be a little less sure of ourselves beside the laboratory bench than we are by the rodeo chute or the slaughterhouse ramp or the leghold trap. But this I can tell you: we have enough right on our side to push on ahead, know it better and clean that mess up.

On the Fifth Day

Who can go to a rodeo and then criticize the hunter? ... an expertly placed bullet would be the best gift a rodeo horse could receive.

Death As A Way of Life

EDWARD CARPENTER, 1844–1929

Do you batten like a ghoul on the dead corpses of animals, and then expect to be of a cheerful disposition? Do you put the loving beasts to torture as a means of promoting your own health and happiness? Do you, O foolishest one, fancy to bind men together by Laws (of all ideas the most laughable) and set whole tribes of unbelievers at work year after year patching that rotten net? Do you live continually farther and farther from Nature, till you actually doubt if there be any natural life, or any avenging instinct in the dumb elements? – And then do you wonder that your own life is slowly ebbing – that you have lost all gladness and faith? ...

I saw deep in the eyes of the animals the human soul look out upon me.

I saw where it was born deep down under feathers and fur, or condemned for awhile to roam fourfooted among the brambles. I caught the clinging mute glance of the prisoner, and swore that I would be faithful,

Thee my brother and sister I see and mistake not. Do not be afraid. Dwelling thus and thus for a while, fulfilling thy appointed time – thou shalt come to thyself at last.

Thy half-warm horns and long tongue lapping round my wrist do not conceal thy humanity any more than the learned talk of the pedant conceals his – for all thou art dumb we have words and plenty between us.

Come nigh little bird with your half-stretched quivering wings – within you I behold choirs of angels, and the Lord himself in vista.

Towards Democracy

Far as custom has carried man from man, yet, when at last in the ever-branching series the complete human being is produced, it knows at once its kinship with all the other forms. More, it knows its kinship with the animals. It sees that it is only habit, an illusion of difference, that divides; and it perceives after all that it is the same human creature that flies in the air, and swims in the sea, or walks biped upon the land.

Civilization

The opinion that man can gain real advance by betraying and sacrificing an innocent fellow creature is exactly this. He may truly gain a mere point of technical information, but with regard to the true, the divine knowledge that he and the creature he torments are *one*, and that he cannot inflict injury on it without bringing injury and suffering on himself – with regard to this knowledge, which is to the other as the sun in heaven is to a farthing candle in a cellar, he is in gross and thick darkness. Every time he pins the trembling rabbit down to the operating table he draws a fresh veil between himself and the source of all Life and Light, and in the name of Knowledge confirms himself in pitiful blindness and ignorance. And the nation which tolerates and sanctions these practices does the same. It prepares for itself a long catalogue of retributory diseases and sufferings, which cannot be curtailed even till long after the iniquities which gave rise to them have ceased.

Vivisection

Let us not rail against knowledge, or be understood in any way to rail against knowledge. Progress in knowledge is man's splendid prerogative, one of his deepest instincts and greatest pleasures. Yet here, too, as in everything else, reason and good sense are concerned. To sacrifice – in the thirst for some fresh detail of information – whole hecatombs of living creatures, to carry on experiments so stultifying as I have described, is to indulge in a mere lust of knowledge (or, I should say, curiosity); and is exactly equivalent to indulging in any other lust that you can think of. To pursue knowledge in this way is to cover ourselves with darkness. It is to blind ourselves to that greatest and most health-giving of all knowledge – the sense of our common life and unity with all creatures. It is to sacrifice the greater to the less; it is to suffer loss rather than to effect a gain.

Ibid.

EDWARD CARPENTER (Dean of Westminster), 1910–

To make a sport of taking life, to do it for fun, to organize it into a form of collective enjoyment, is to fail to act responsibly and with a proper reverence for God's creation. It is to fall back into that bondage, into that predatory system of nature, from which the Christian hope has always been that not only man but the natural order itself is to be released and redeemed ... Hunting represents, in dramatic form and often in colourful dress, both man's lack of sensitivity to his real condition and his unwillingness seriously to try to lift the whole order of creation into a higher estate, closer to the pattern 'shown in the mount' – an estate more noble, more divine.

From *Against Hunting*, ed. P. Moore

It may well be that man's attitude to the animal world spills over into his attitude to his own fellows. The exploitation of the one springs from the same temper of mind that exploits the other.

Ibid.

ALEXIS CARREL, MD, 1873–1944

Scientific civilization has destroyed the soul of the world.

Man the Unknown

GERALD CARSON, 1899–

After years of strife, the careerists of science are clearly ahead, largely because they are adept in arousing fearful and self-regarding thoughts among the lay public by threatening a new Dark Age for medicine if there is any curtailment of their absolute freedom.

Central to the problem is the most thorny philosophical issue man has ever faced, the problem of evil. This mysterious and harsh dilemma arises when one contemplates the undeserved sufferings of blameless animals. Is the pursuit of knowledge the highest good? If so, what knowledge? Should animals suffer misery, stress, pain and slow death for trivial human purposes? To test a hair dye? To advance the interests of cigarette manufacturers? Should the beasts die in experiments that have already been performed countless times? Is mutilation, torment and death a price our animal companions on this planet should be required to pay so that a high school biology student may win a science-fair prize and be interviewed on television?

Men, Beasts, and Gods

RACHEL CARSON, 1907–1964

We cannot have peace among men whose hearts find delight in killing any living creature.

Silent Spring

As cruel a weapon as the cave man's club, the chemical barrage has been hurled against the fabric of life.

Ibid.

GINA CERMINARA, 1914–1984

Animals are related to us much more closely than we think. Though they lack speech, their mental processes are not very unlike our own. They are similar to us in their fears, their pains, their affections, their frustrations, their terrors, their devotions, their gratitudes, in short, in all their emotions, even though they may know them in lesser complexity and degree than we. They are, as Mohammed said, *a people like ourselves*. Regarded from the evolutionist and reincarnationist point of view, they must be a people struggling along like ourselves, on the long, difficult road to perfection.

Many Lives, Many Loves

THOMAS CHALMERS, 1780–1847

The brute animals have all the same sensations of pain as human beings, and consequently endure as much pain when their body is hurt; but in their case the cruelty of torment is greater, because they have no mind to bear them up against their sufferings, and no hope to look forward to when enduring the last extreme pain …

Quoted in *The Clergy Speak for Animals*

LORD CHESTERFIELD (Philip Dormer Stanhope), 1694–1773

… there still remain in the streets of this metropolis, more scenes of barbarity than, perhaps, are to be met with in all Europe besides. Asia (at least in the larger population of it – the Hindus) is well known for compassion to 'brutes'; and nobody who has read Busbequius will wonder at me for most heartily wishing that our common people were no crueller than the Turks …

74

... to me it appears strange that the men against whom I should be enabled to bring an action for laying a little dirt at my door, may with impunity drive by it half-a-dozen calves, with their tails lopped close to their bodies and their hinder parts covered with blood ...

... I cannot but join in opinion with Mr Hogarth, that the frequency of murders among us is greatly owing to those scenes of cruelty which the lower ranks of people are so much accustomed to; instead of multiplying such scenes, I should rather hope that some proper method might be fixed upon either for preventing them, or removing them out of sight, so that our infants might not grow up into the world in a familiarity with blood.

If we may believe the Naturalists, that a lion is a gentle animal until his tongue has been dipped in blood, what precaution ought we to use to prevent man from being inured to it, who has such superiority of power to do mischief?

The World, No. LXI, 19 August 1756

GEORGE CHEYNE, 1671–1743

To see the convulsions, agonies and tortures of a poor fellow-creature, whom they cannot restore nor recompense, dying to gratify luxury and tickle callous and rank organs, must require a rocky heart, and a great degree of cruelty and ferocity. I cannot find any great difference, on the foot of natural reason and equity only, between feeding on human flesh and feeding on [other] animal flesh, except custom and example.

Essay on Regimen

SWAMI CHIDANANDA, 1916–

The Yoga Science has classified all things into Purifying, Agitating and Stupefying in their ultimate effect upon

75

human faculties. Satvaguna is Purifying, Rajas is Agitating and Tamas is Stupefying. The food that human beings consume is also subject to this classification. Meat diet falls under the Tamasic and Rajasic category. It is inimical to the upward evolutionary ascent of the human nature. Vegetarian food has been advocated by Yoga Science as purifying and beneficial.

The essential Reality within man is an Eternal, indestructible Spiritual Principle which is Divine in essence. The true goal of human life and the destiny of man is the awakening of the unfoldment of the inner Spiritual essence and experience of Divine Illumination. Animal food is the product of slaughtering. It is unspiritual and therefore deprives man of the attainment of Spiritual destiny, namely Divine Perfection. Compassion is Divine. Cruelty is unspiritual. The human body, which is the moving temple of the Living God enshrined, is not meant to be made into the fleshy graveyard of slaughtered animals, creatures that are the dumb, harmless and innocent brethren of mankind mutely trusting man, their 'superior' keeper.

The Vegetarian Way, XXIV World Vegetarian Congress, 1977

ST JOHN CHRYSOSTOM, *c.* 347–407

The Saints are exceedingly loving and gentle to mankind, and even to brute beasts ... Surely we ought to show them [animals] great kindness and gentleness for many reasons, but, above all, because they are of the same origin as ourselves.

Homilies

NATIONAL ASSEMBLY OF THE CHURCH OF ENGLAND

We make animals work for us, carry for us, amuse us and earn money for us. We also make them die for us, sometimes in ways which would be rapidly rejected if we could readily see it done. In many fields we use them, not with gratitude and compassion, but with thoughtlessness, arrogance and complete selfishness. Man appears to be one of the few animals which inflicts pain for his own pleasure, yet humanity is an attribute applied exclusively to him ... It is also relevant to ask whether man has the right to perform any experiments which inflict pain.

Report by the Board for Social Responsibility, 1970

... the Church Assembly is of the opinion that the practices of hare coursing, deer hunting and other hunting are cruel, unjustifiable and degrading and urges Christian people in the light of their Christian profession and responsibility to make plain their opposition to activities of this sort and their determination to do all in their power to secure their speedy abolition.

Ibid.

CAPT. PAUL RYCAUT DE SHORDICHE-CHURCHWARD (ROBERT CHURCHWARD), 1907–1981

It is time everyone knew something that it took me forty years to learn – that all hunting for 'sport', and fox-hunting above all, is organized torture leading to murder.

The lesson has been a painful one to me. It was only seven years ago that I finally took it to heart. Then I was joint Master of Foxhounds with the South Shropshire Hunt. I resigned my honoured position because I could no longer bear to hunt and kill wild creatures.

A Master of Hounds Speaks

MARCUS TULLIUS CICERO, 106–43 B.C.

There remains the wild-beast hunts, two a day for five days – magnificent; there is no denying it. But what pleasure can it possibly be to a man of culture, when either a puny human being is mangled by a most powerful beast, or a splendid beast is transfixed with a hunting spear? And even if all this is something to be seen, you have seen it more than once; and I, who was a spectator, saw nothing new in it. The last day was that of the elephants, and on that day the mob and crowd was greatly impressed, but manifested no pleasure. Indeed the result was a certain compassion and a kind of feeling that that huge beast has a fellowship with the human race.

Letters to Friends 7.1, trans. W. Glyn Williams

LORD (Kenneth) CLARK, 1903–1983

I believe that order is better than chaos, creation better than destruction. I prefer gentleness to violence, forgiveness to vendetta. On the whole I think that knowledge is preferable to ignorance, and I am sure that human sympathy is more valuable than ideology ... I believe in courtesy, the ritual by which we avoid hurting other people's feelings by satisfying our own egos. And I think we should remember that we are part of a great whole, which for convenience we call nature. All living things are our brothers and sisters.

Civilization: a Personal View

We love animals, we watch them with delight, we study their habits with ever-increasing curiosity; and we destroy them. We have sacrificed them to the gods, we have killed them in arenas in order to enjoy a cruel excitement, we still hunt them, and we slaughter them by the million out of greed ... The overwhelming majority eat their kinsmen without a thought. They do not think of the stockyards and slaughterhouses which, in most places, are kept decently out of sight. They look with rapture at the new-born lambs without considering why in the end they are there. 'Little lamb, who eat thee, Dost thou know who eat thee?' Almost the only great picture of an animal being slaughtered is Jean François Millet's *Death of a Pig*. It was complementary to his touchingly beautiful *Birth of a Calf*; and we share his feelings of horror and love. But on reflection we realize that the calf in its turn will be slaughtered. In these matters we are governed solely by our feelings, and not by our reason.

Animals and Men

We must recognize that the faculty of speech, which has given us power over those fellow creatures whom we once recognized as brothers, must carry with it a proper measure of responsibility. We can never recapture the Golden Age; but we can regain that feeling of kinship which will help us establish a feeling of the unity of creation. It is a faith we all may share.

Ibid.

STEPHEN R.L. CLARK, 1945–

... enough has been said to demonstrate the desperate need for a practical and philosophical reappraisal of our standing in the world. It is no longer enough to fantasize, for example, that dolphins may prove our intellectual equals and be admitted into a new, terrestrial society; it is not enough to tell ourselves stories about those other intelligences who may inhabit other worlds of this galaxy, and speculate on how we may treat each other. There are other sentient creatures all about us, who may lack our verbalizing gifts but who have their lives to live and their own visions of reality to worship. We are not separate from them, and owe them honour. To imagine that their lesser 'intelligence' (whatever that may be) licenses our tyranny is to leave the way open for any human intellectual élite to treat the rest of us as trash. Intelligence is a great gift, certainly, but it is of value only in its service of the multimillionfold enterprise that is the biosphere, and beyond that, the world. 'There is not a beast upon the earth, nor a bird that flies, but is a nation like to you.' (*Koran* 6; *see* Khan.) Let us try the experiment, you and I, of meaning, when we say 'we', not merely 'we men', but 'we mammals' or 'we animals'. Maybe very few mammals or animals will ever join with you and me in any fully and mutually conscious enterprise: but the same is true even of human beings. And in remembering our solidarity and common ancestry with creatures not of our immediate kind we may come to be kinder to such creatures of our species as are not to our taste. Humanists sought to purchase the welfare of their fellow men by denigrating 'beasts': such antagonisms are counterproductive. In pursuing the various self-deceptions endemic to man, particularly but not exclusively to civilized man, through the labyrinth of orthodox thought and of my imagination, I have not committed myself to any particular view of the 'facts' or of the nature of 'moral enquiry'. I do not believe that there is any credible account of either which could excuse our present depredations. I am inclined, perhaps unfairly, to think that no-one has any standing in such a discussion who has not taken the simple, minimal step of abandoning flesh-foods. Honourable men may honourably disagree about some details of human treatment of the non-human, but vegetarianism is now as necessary a pledge of moral devotion as was the refusal of emperor-worship in the early Church. Those who have not made that pledge have no authority to speak against the most inanely conceived experiments, nor against hunting, nor against fur-trapping, nor bear-baiting, nor bull-fights, nor pulling the wings off flies. Flesh-eating in our present circumstances is as empty a gluttony as any of these things. Those who still eat flesh when they could do otherwise have no claim to be serious moralists.

The Moral Status of Animals

... each creature is the outward sign of an equal soul, and to be respected as such. One who sees a friend looking out of the eyes of a beaten dog can no longer think only of the ever-changing 'balance of nature'. To beat or imprison or kill is to close the eyes of one's own soul, to refuse to recognize our friends and equals through the windows of the world. It has long been understood that to keep a fellow human as a slave is to refuse to be 'human', to insist on being that lesser thing, a master, a mere element in a social nexus. In refusing to play our part as elements in the biological nexus of prey and predator we remember ourselves as friends and equals from beyond the world.

From Athens to Jerusalem

If we are to understand the animals with whom we share the world, we need to watch them, interact with them, without too much prejudice. Understanding them, we may also understand ourselves a little more. By seeing what constrains and motivates our kindred we may, perhaps, discover what the morals and manners of the human beasts might be.

The Nature of the Beast

Affection towards clan-mates, love of children, deference to authority, disinclination to kill those who have reminded us of common humanity, even some respect for property: these features of human life do not, it seems, stem from our intellectual gifts. We share them with our cousins.

Ibid.

I do not believe that chimpanzees, rats and the rest should be sacrificed, even for an acknowledged greater good: such sacrifice infringes their right to refuse. In my morality, all creatures with feelings and wishes should be thought of as ends in themselves and not merely as means.

Animals' Rights: a Symposium

CLEMENTINE HOMILIES, Second Century

The unnatural eating of flesh-meats is as polluting as the heathen worship of devils, with its sacrifices and its unpure feasts, through participation in which a man becomes a fellow-eater with devils.

FRANCES POWER COBBE, 1822–1904

I venture to record a little of my own experience in the matter, part of which was gained as an assistant in the laboratory of one of the greatest living experimental physiologists. In that laboratory we sacrificed daily from one to three dogs, besides rabbits and other animals, and after four months' experience I am of opinion that not one of those experiments on animals was justifiable or necessary. The idea of the good of humanity was simply out of the question and would be laughed at, the great aim being to keep up with, or get ahead of, one's contemporaries in science, even at the price of an incalculable amount of torture needlessly and iniquitously inflicted on the poor animals ... I think the saddest sight I ever witnessed was when the dogs were brought up from the cellar to the laboratory ... they seemed seized with horror as soon as they smelt the air of the place, divining, apparently, their approaching fate. They would make friendly advances to each of the three or four persons present, and as far as eyes, ears, and tail could make a mute appeal for mercy eloquent, they tried it in vain.

Autobiography

[It is] an *impious* doctrine – I say it deliberately, an *impious* doctrine – that God has made it any man's duty to commit the great sin of cruelty by way of obtaining a benefit for suffering humanity.

Modern Rack

SAMUEL TAYLOR COLERIDGE, 1772–1834

From *The Rime of the Ancient Mariner*

Farewell, farewell! but this I tell
To thee, thou Wedding-Guest!
He prayeth well, who loveth well
Both man and bird and beast.

He prayeth best, who loveth best
All things both great and small;
For the dear God who loveth us,
He made and loveth all.

STEPHEN COLERIDGE, 1854–1936

The law at present punishes a boy who tortures a cat, and has nothing to say against men and women who torture an otter. The law sends a carter to prison who, for his living, drives a horse with a sore neck to market, but has nothing to say against the nobility, clergy, and others who, for their amusement, hunt a stag for seven hours and more, inflicting unspeakable anguish upon it, ending in an awful death. The law directs the police to prosecute a layman for causing precisely the same suffering to an animal as it permits and encourages a man of science to inflict upon it. All these things those dumb images that sit round the table in Jermyn Street have done nothing, and will do nothing, to amend. They will continue to look at each other in silence until others have awakened the conscience of mankind to the iniquity of torturing animals for pastime, and when all is over but the final and glorious triumph, they will be heard at last mumbling a claim for the credit of the long combat.

Vivisection: A Heartless Science

I have myself been the unwilling witness of an otter hunt, and a more sickening spectacle it is difficult to conceive. That any man or woman, much less than any Christian, could be possessed with so much cruelty and cowardice, and could derive pleasure from such a pitiful scene of hopeless suffering, filled me with unutterable disgust.

Ibid.

It is manifest that the whole question of man's rights over and duties towards animals is a moral one which has no special relation to Science; and therefore distinguished men of Science have no more qualification to claim authority to dictate to us about it than have distinguished musicians, painters, or lawyers.

Ibid.

In its corporate capacity [the Church] never combats abominations that are firmly established. My father, when he was Chief Justice of England, and in a position when it was necessary for him to weigh his words, wrote:

> 'As far as I know the Church of England never raised a finger, and a very few of its bishops ever raised a voice, to put down our own slave trade, or set free our own slaves.
>
> 'Sir Arthur Helps tells us that he never heard a single sermon, out of many hundreds he attended, in which the duty of kindness to dumb animals had ever been alluded to.'

Ibid.

Physical pain is perhaps not the worst evil that can afflict mankind. To us, 'with such large discourse looking before and after', bodily pangs are less insufferable than remorse, ruin, jealousy, or a broken heart. But with animals this is not so; to them physical pain is the worst of all evils. They have no armour of the mind wherewith to summon to their aid an intellectual fortitude. They can look up to no martyr's crown, they cannot bring their miseries to the feet of a pitiful God. Therefore it is that our sympathies are so deeply moved by the spectacle of animal suffering, therefore it is that we say that to pursue knowledge through the agony of animals is an act only possible to a man whose heart is dead.

Ibid.

The knowledge that horrible mutilations may be daily and hourly executed upon the bodies of living creatures with no adequate security for their insensibility, makes very many humane people profoundly miserable; it rises day and night between them and their peace of mind; it haunts their lives waking and asleep; it deprives them of joy in this world which might otherwise be theirs.

Ibid.

The worship of Science, which has depressed this country for the last fifty years, is a very degrading episode in our history; it has ridiculed a classical education because human letters conferred mind upon mankind instead of money, and it has elevated a sterile materialism to the dignity of a religion.

Ibid.

CONFUCIANISM

Is there any one maxim which ought to be acted upon throughout one's whole life? Surely the maxim of loving kindness is such: Do not unto others what you would not they should do unto you.

Analects

The ways are two: love and want of love. That is all.

Mencius ?372–?289 B.C.

Have a compassionate heart toward all creatures.

T'ai-shang kan-ying p'ien, a Confucian-Taoist treatise written
before the 14th cent. A.D. Attr. Ko Hung, 284–363

Respect the old and cherish the young. Even insects, grass and trees you must not hurt.

Ibid.

Buy captive creatures and set them free. Hold fast to vegetarianism and abstain from taking life.

Whenever taking a step, always watch for ants and insects. Prohibit the building of fires outside (lest insects be killed) and do not set mountain woods or forests ablaze.

Help people in distress as you would help a fish in a dried-up rut. Free people from danger as you would free a sparrow from a fine net.

Benefit living creatures and human beings. Cultivate goodness and happiness.

Yin-chih-wen, a Confucian-Taoist treatise, probably
post-4th cent. A.D. Attr. Wen Ch'ang

MARIE CORELLI, 1855–1924

'A fine morning's killing, ay! All their necks wrung – all dead birds! Once they could fly – fly and swim! Fly and swim! All dead now – and sold cheap in the open market!'

The Master-Christian

PATRICK CORBETT, MA, 1916–

... we make no bones about our object in contributing to this book [*Animals, Men and Morals*]: we want to change the world. Our view as to how men should see and treat animals is at present the view of a minority, but we believe that this minority is growing and we want to make it grow faster.

Man is a moral being. This means that he not only experiences pain and pleasure, seeking to avoid the one and attain the other, but is sympathetically aware of the pains and pleasures of others, realises how the pains and pleasures of different individuals interlock, and experiences in this connection that mysterious sense of good and bad which leads him to regard some activities as not merely advantageous to himself, but intrinsically admirable, and others as not merely imprudent but wrong.

A moral being, furthermore, is one who is capable of foresight, of reflection upon the principles of obligation or goodness which his conscience suggests to him, and of seeking with more or less success to make his behaviour conform to them. Moral philosophers have long exercised themselves with questions as to what 'good' and 'ought' really mean, as to how they are related to each other and to the experiences of pain and pleasure, and as to how it is possible for men, embedded as they are in the universal causality of nature, to adopt principles and make choices. Their researches, notoriously, have not led to any settled conclusions, but for our purposes this does not matter. We take it that you will agree as a matter of common sense that we men are moral beings, and that you will therefore be prepared to reflect with us upon the facts and principles involved in the treatment of animals, and to consider what should be done next.

To take this supposed agreement a little further: we believe that almost any man, if presented with the issue as to whether another living creature should or should not continue to exist or as to whether it should or should not suffer, would agree, so long as other lives and interests are not at stake, that it *should* live and *should not* suffer. Other things being quite equal, is it not better that even a fly should be rather than not be, and a rat thrive, rather than agonize or languish? We realize that there may be people who can sincerely say that nothing concerns them but their own life and pleasure, the life and pleasure of others – whether animal or human – being quite indifferent or even objectionable to them; but we think that the great majority will, on reflection, join us in dismissing that view as morally intolerable.

For us, anyway, the respect for life – to call by that name the disinterested satisfaction in the existence and prosperity of other living things – is integral to man. To be generally indifferent to the life and welfare of others while making exceptions in favour of those who happen to be useful to us; to take positive pleasure in the suffering and death of others, as did the Moors' murderers; to be prepared, as were the Nazis, to sacrifice anyone and anything to one's own aggressive impulses: these are to turn one's back upon that model of a disinterested, loving and respectful life which we all carry with us in our hearts and which, however much we bluster, we must if we are truthful acknowledge in the end.

Animals, Men and Morals

NORMAN COUSINS, 1915–

The heart of the matter is that some people like to cause injury or death to living things. And many of those who do not are indifferent to those who do.

In Place of Folly

The individual is capable of both great compassion and great indifference. He has it within his means to nourish the former and outgrow the latter.

Nothing is more powerful than an individual acting out of his conscience, thus helping to bring the collective conscience to life.

Human Options

What is happening today is that the natural reactions of the individual against violence are being blunted. The individual is being desensitized by living history. We are developing new reflexes and new responses that tend to slow down the moral imagination and relieve us of essential indignation over impersonal hurt. We are becoming casual about brutality. We have made our peace with violence.

Ibid.

JACQUES-YVES COUSTEAU, 1910–

Perhaps the time has come to formulate a moral code which would govern our relations with the great creatures of the sea as well as with those on dry land. That this will come to pass is our dearest wish.

If human civilization is going to invade the waters of the earth, then let it be first of all to carry a message of respect – respect for all life.

The Whale: Mighty Monarch of the Sea

WILLIAM COWPER, 1731–1800

From *The Task*

Detested sport,
That owes its pleasures to another's pain;
That feeds upon the sobs and dying shrieks
Of harmless nature, dumb, but yet endued
With eloquence, that agonies inspire,
Of silent tears, and heart-distending sighs!

The heart is hard in nature, and unfit
For human fellowship, as being void
Of sympathy, and therefore dead alike
To love and friendship both, that is not pleased
With sight of animals enjoying life,
Nor feels their happiness augment his own ...

Witness the patient ox, with stripes and yells
Driven to the slaughter, goaded, as he runs,
To madness; while the savage at his heels
Laughs at the frantic sufferer's fury, spent
Upon the guiltless passenger o'erthrown.
He too is witness, noblest of the train
That wait on man, the flight-performing horse;
With unsuspecting readiness he takes
His murderer on his back, and push'd all day
With bleeding sides and flanks, that heave for life,
To the far distant goal, arrives and dies.
So little mercy shows who needs so much!
Does law, so jealous in the cause of man,
Denounce no doom on the delinquent? None.
He lives, and o'er his brimming beaker boasts
(As if barbarity were high desert)
The inglorious feat, and clamorous in praise
Of the poor brute, seems wisely to suppose
The honours of his matchless horse his own.
But many a crime deem'd innocent on earth,
Is register'd in heaven; and these no doubt

Have each their record, with a curse annex'd.
He may dismiss compassion from his heart,
But God will never ...

    I would not enter on my list of friends
(Though graced with polish'd manners and fine sense,
Yet wanting sensibility) the man
Who needlessly sets foot upon a worm.
An inadvertent step may crush the snail,
That crawls at evening in the public path;
But he that has humanity, forewarn'd,
Will tread aside, and let the reptile live.

Ye, therefore, who love mercy, teach your sons
To love it too. The springtime of our years
Is soon dishonour'd and defiled in most
By budding ills, that ask a prudent hand
To check them. But, alas! none sooner shoots,
If unrestrain'd, into luxuriant growth,
Than cruelty, most devilish of them all.
Mercy to him that shows it, is the rule
And righteous limitation of its act,
By which Heaven moves in pardoning guilty man;
And he that shows none, being ripe in years,
And conscious of the outrage he commits,
Shall seek it, and not find it in his turn.

It is no wonder that my intimate acquaintance with these specimens* of the kind has taught me to hold the sportsman's amusement in abhorrence; he little knows what amiable creatures he persecutes, of what gratitude they are capable, how cheerful they are in their spirits, what enjoyment they have of life, and that, impressed as they seem with a peculiar dread of man, it is only because man gives them a peculiar cause for it.

               *From Cowper's account of his tame hares, published
               in *The Gentleman's Magazine*, 28 May 1784

The Butterfly in Church

Butterfly, butterfly, why come you here?
    This is no bower for you;
Go, sip the honey-drop sweet and clear,
    Or bathe in the morning dew.

This is the place to think of heaven,
    This is the place to pray;
You have no sins to be forgiven –
    Butterfly – go away!

PIETRO CROCE, MD, 1920–

Let us leave the ethical aspects to the animal defenders, and let us try, as physicians, to concentrate all our energy and all our professional morality on the scientific aspect.

The first, basic question is the following: Is vivisection, or animal experimentation, a scientific method? My unhesitating answer is: No! To use the animal as an experimental model for a human being is an arbitrary and totally unscientific act. Therefore the method deriving from it is false from its premise, because *it is based on a false experimental model*.

So if we now want to define animal experimentation on a scientific level, in the language of science, how should we define it? The most accurate definition is: a *methodological error*. And a science that is based on a false methodology can only be a false science. Whoever is ready to accept this line of thought will now ask: Well, what can we do?

It seems to me that the only appropriate answer to this question is: *let's get rid of the error*, let's cancel it from the experimental methodology. And this could happen outright, if gigantic interests didn't stand in the way. This compels us to examine the strategies which must determine our future actions. But it is precisely in this

connection that the standpoints of the anti-vivisectionists, or those who profess to be anti-vivisectionists, diverge, splitting into three factions:
– The first one suggests to limit animal experiments, to reduce the number of animal victims. For this purpose its advocates want to resort to the methods wrongly called 'alternatives'.
– The second school of thought suggests controlling animal experiments by means of laws.
– The third body of opinion demands total and unconditional abolition.
Let us examine these three suggestions.

First suggestion: Reduction of Animal Experiments.
All those who support this proposal accept, perhaps without being aware of it, the standpoint of the *animal welfarists*, who reason as follows: let us try to limit the number of animals that have to suffer and die. Thereby they not only accept the path that promotes suffering and death for the animals, but also the claim that we cannot do without vivisection.

If these people are convinced that animal experiments are useful to medical science, their suggestion is certainly in keeping with their ideas. But this suggestion is in no way directed against animal experiments, even less so in a scientific sense. It only amounts to a form of *animal protection*. But a kind of protectionism that is subordinate to supposedly compelling human needs; a protectionism that accepts the principle of Man being the master of all other living beings and having the right to use them as he thinks fit.

Second suggestion: Controlling through Laws.
This, too, is a proposal of the animal welfarists or protectors. But precisely this suggestion is also advocated by our opponents, the vivisectionists, who see in it the triumphant Trojan horse: disguised as opponents of

vivisection, they act as if they were supporting our movement, while their intention is to undermine it from within.

To control animal experiments through laws means conferring a legal and moral status on this false method, awarding it a place among the truly scientific, ethically legal forms of procedure. It means giving the vivisectors the absolute right to carry on forever, undisturbed, sheltered and protected by the law.

Many of those who advocate the 'legal control' of vivisection stoop to pragmatic consequences such as proposing to ban experiments only for 'unnecessary' products like cosmetics, but retaining them for 'serious' purposes like medicine, surgery and pharmacology.

Thus, according to them, vivisection is a 'serious' matter, which must be reserved for 'serious' purposes. This is the greatest eulogy ever received by animal experimentation, a deification of vivisection.

Third suggestion: Total Abolition.
This is the only logical choice, and the only correct choice on a scientific basis: total abolition of animal experiments, this unscientific method that is responsible for old as well as new damages to human health, and for some real iatrogenic (doctor-induced) disasters. A method which impedes the advance of medicine and prevents using rational and truly scientific methods.

> Address to the first International Symposium of
> Doctors Against Animal Experimentation, held
> at the Zürich Kongresshaus, 25 April 1987

Professor, when did you start experimenting on animals?
Almost longer ago than I can remember, since I did my first experiments when I was a student. As I progressed in my career, abreast of my professional reputation and prestige, I did more and more animal experimentation. And I don't feel at all guilty about it. I did what I had

been taught. I was absolutely convinced of the scientific validity of vivisection: a conviction that has been forced on me during my university studies and has conditioned me for many years thereafter. So I now define myself 'a criminal victim'. I was the victim of a stupidity that had been imposed upon me. But I think it's more interesting to explain how I came to discover the truth. At a certain moment of my life, while meditating about what I was doing, I realized its uselessness. Actually, one doesn't have to be a genius to understand that vivisection is an aberration, a foolish practice which leads medicine astray. And this in turn means causing millions of human victims. Let's keep in mind that we are all victims of toxic drugs, of wrong medical notions and illusions.

Do you mean to say that there is no true correlation between the animal and the human organism?
Not only that. There is no correlation even between man and man. Without speaking of racial differences, although they are important, the human species is divided in four major blood groups, each one very different from the others. If there are such differences among human beings, humans are even far more different from animals. Certain apparent similarities are unimportant biologically. I keep being amazed by the incomprehension of those researchers who hope to find an animal that is similar to a human being, a model for us. The experimenters started with frogs – which belong to a different species – and progressed to mice, then to rabbits, from rabbits to cats, from cats to dogs, always deluding themselves that by climbing the zoological ladder they moved closer to the human species. Until today every vivisector's ultimate wish is to experiment on monkeys, because, with an incredible biological ignorance, he considers them close to human beings, just owing to their appearance or because they are able to

walk more or less erect. But the researchers don't stop at monkeys. Paradoxically, they themselves prove me right: by experimenting more and more on people, they admit that the results of their animal research are not reliable, they mean nothing.

So you think that vivisection is useless or even harmful for man?
Totally useless and potentially harmful. Research can't be built on fallacious bases. The answer we obtain from animal experiments is never reliable, in spite of occasional coincidences. That's why vivisection must be abolished.

Do you think it is possible to avoid the infliction of pain in the kind of experiments that are being conducted in laboratories today?
It is not possible. And I am sorry to say that the vivisectors who conduct cruel experiments are right – from their point of view, of course – when they don't even try to spare sufferances. In fact, if they did try, it would be useless to do the kind of experiments in which the animal has to survive. Sometimes the experiments consist in ascertaining the vital limitation of an organism from which, say, the pancreas has been extirpated. That's why the vivisector never respects the law, and very often the same animal is used again and again, even though the law expressly forbids it. It's a veritable hell.

From interview by *Amici Miei*, Rome, February 1988

ERNEST CROSBY, 1856–1907

A strange lot this, to be dropped down in a world of barbarians – men who see clearly enough the barbarity of all ages except their own.

The Soul of the World

WILL CUPPY, 1884–1949

If an animal does something we call it instinct; if we do the same thing for the same reason, we call it intelligence.

National Enquirer, 27 January 1981

JAMES OLIVER CURWOOD, 1879–1927

My love for nature and my fight for conservation of wild life compel me to strenuously acclaim the cause of anti-vivisection. It seems to me that man, in his monumental egoism and selfishness, has completely forgotten the fact that he himself is an animal, and that the same life and blood which run through his veins are also a part of those very creatures which he tortures with his experiments. Man, as a true animal, is the Big Brother of all other animal life; a little more fortunate, a little more advanced in the ultimate scheme of things – that is all.

Letter to Mrs C.P. Farrell, 13 September 1923

MR JUSTICE CUSACK, 1916–1978

To say that you behaved like animals is offensive to the animal creation because animals of the farmyard and field have an innate sense of decency.

At Leeds Assizes, U.K., 1971

HIS HOLINESS THE XIV DALAI LAMA OF TIBET, 1935–

I do not see any reason why animals should be slaughtered to serve as human diet when there are so many substitutes. After all, man can live without meat. It is only some carnivorous animals that have to subsist on flesh. Killing animals for sport, for pleasure, for adventures, and for hides and furs is a phenomenon which is at once disgusting and distressing. There is no justification in indulging in such acts of brutality.

The Vegetarian Way, 1967

In our approach to life, be it pragmatic or otherwise, the ultimate truth that confronts us squarely and unmistakably is the desire for peace, security and happiness. Different forms of life in different aspects of existence make up the teeming denizens of this earth of ours. And, no matter whether they belong to the higher group as human beings or to the lower group, the animals, all beings primarily seek peace, comfort and security. Life is as dear to a mute creature as it is to a man. Just as one wants happiness and fears pain, just as one wants to live and not to die, so do other creatures.

Ibid.

L.T. DANSHIELL, 1914–

Show me the enforced laws of a state for the prevention of cruelty to animals and I in turn will give you a correct estimate of the refinement, enlightenment, integrity and equity of that commonwealth's people.
　… The lack of humane education is the principal cause of crime.

From a legislative address, Texas

CLARENCE DARROW, 1857–1938

Man cares nothing for the pain of any animal when his pleasure is involved … He makes a shambles of the earth in order to satisfy his appetites and give him joy.

The Story of My Life

Man really assumes that the entire universe was made for him; that while it is run by God it is still run for man. God is just a sort of caterer whose business it is to find out what men want and then supply these wants.

Ibid.

If man would exercise such little imagination as he has, and would contemplate all the life of the universe, human and animal and plant, he would have to admit that every form of life comes and goes in the same way ... Not a single syllable can be said for the immortality of man that cannot be said for every other animal that ever roamed the plains and fields and woods.

Ibid.

When we abandon the thought of immortality we at least have cast out fear. We gain a certain dignity and self-respect. We regard our fellow-travellers as companions in the pleasures and tribulations of life. We feel an interest in them, knowing that we are all moved by common impulses and touched by mutual understanding. We gain kinship with the world. Our neighbours and friends and we ourselves are travelling the same route to a common doom. No one can feel this universal relationship without being gentler, kindlier and more humane toward all the infinite forms of beings that live with us, and must die with us.

Ibid.

CHARLES DARWIN, 1809–1882

We have seen that the senses and intuitions, the various emotions and faculties, such as love, memory, attention and curiosity, imitation, reason, etc., of which man boasts, may be found in an incipient, or even sometimes in a well-developed condition, in the lower animals.

The Descent of Man

There is no fundamental difference between man and the higher mammals in their mental faculties ... The difference in mind between man and the higher animals, great as it is, certainly is one of degree and not of kind.

Ibid.

The love for all living creatures is the most noble attribute of man.

Ibid.

Animals, whom we have made our slaves, we do not like to consider our equal.

Letters

REVD J. TYSSUL DAVIS, 1872–1944

Why is it that kindly persons, people endowed with pity and compassion, folk of quick sympathy, who have tears for the lightest ailment of their pet cat or dog, can endure this daily rottenness, this daily massacre, this sacrifice the voices of whose victims rise up to heaven in wearisome lament, in an unending stream of despairing appeal? The outstanding reasons are *an utter dearth of imagination* and *the terrific power of habit.* There is not a single person present who would or could be so heartless, or so bloodthirsty, or so barbarous as to go out and prepare a dinner by taking a lamb frolicking in the field, 'the lamb that looks you in the face', as Shelley said, and kill it. There is not one who would have the heart to stay it in its innocent play, and deprive it of its life, of its game with its companions in the pasture; not one who could descend to this unmentionable savagery.

Quoted in *It is the Privilege of Power to Protect*

W.H. DAVIES, 1871–1940

A Child's Pet

When I sailed out of Baltimore,
   With twice a thousand head of sheep,
They would not eat, they would not drink,
   But bleated o'er the deep.

Inside the pens we crawled each day
   To sort the living from the dead;
And when we reached the Mersey's mouth
   Had lost five hundred head.

Yet every night and day one sheep,
   That had no fear of man or sea,
Stuck through the bars its pleading face,
   And it was stroked by me.

And to the sheep-man standing near,
   'You see', I said, 'this one tame sheep?
It seems a child has lost her pet,
   And cried herself to sleep.'

So every time we passed it by
   Sailing to England's slaughterhouse,
Eight ragged sheep-men – tramps and thieves –
   Would stroke that sheep's black nose.

The Rabbit

Not even when the early birds
Danced on my roof with showery feet
Such music as will come from rain –
Not even then could I forget
The rabbit in his hours of pain;
Where, lying in an iron trap,
He cries all through the deafened night –
Until his smiling murderer comes,
To kill him in the morning light.

Sport

Hunters, hunters,
Follow the Chase.
I saw the Fox's eyes,
Not in his face
But on it, big with fright –
Haste, hunters, haste!

Say, hunters, say
Is it a noble sport?
As rats that bite
Babies in cradles, so,
Such rats and men
Take their delight.

Although of a quiet disposition, my fondness for animals
is likely at any time to lead me into danger. After reading
cases of vivisection I have often had dreams of boldly
entering such places [vivisection laboratories], routing
the doctors ['scientists'] with a bar of iron, cutting the
cords and freeing the animals, despite of any hurt I might
receive from bites and scratches. Perhaps I should cut a
ridiculous figure, walking through the crowded streets
with a poor meek creature under each arm, but that
would not bother me much in the performance of a
humane action.

Autobiography of a Super Tramp

From *Sheep*

They sniffed, poor things, for their green fields,
    They cried so loud I could not sleep;
For fifty thousand shillings down
    I would not sail again with sheep.

LEONARDO DA VINCI, 1452–1519

Truly man is the king of beasts, for his brutality exceeds theirs. We live by the death of others: We are burial places!

Merijkowsky, *Romance of Leonardo da Vinci*

I have from an early age abjured the use of meat, and the time will come when men such as I will look upon the murder of animals as they now look upon the murder of men.

From da Vinci's *Notes*

Nothing will be left.
Nothing in the air, nothing under the earth, nothing in
the waters.
All will be hunted down, all exterminated.

Ibid.

SIR JOHN WILLIAM DAWSON, 1820–1899

Natural science does, however, perceive a discord between man, and especially his artificial contrivances, and nature; and a cruel tyranny of man over lower beings and interference with natural harmony and symmetry. In other words, the independent will, free agency and inventive powers of man have set themselves to subvert the nice and delicate adjustments of natural things in a way to cause much evil and suffering to lower creatures, and ultimately to man himself. Science sees, moreover, a great moral need which it cannot supply, and for which it can appeal only to the religious idea of a divine redemption.

From Address given at the Chicago Columbian Exposition of 1893,
quoted in Lancaster: *The Incredible World's Parliament of Religions*

103

DORIS DAY, 1927–

Killing an animal to make a coat is a sin. It wasn't meant to be and we have no right to do it. A woman gains status when she refuses to see anything killed to be put on her back. Then she's truly beautiful!

Newspaper interview

JOHN LAME DEER, 1900–

You don't want the bird. You don't have the courage to kill honestly – cut off the chicken's head, pluck it and gut it – no, you don't want this anymore. So it all comes in a neat plastic bag, all cut up, ready to eat, with no taste and no guilt. Your mink and seal coats, you don't want to know about the blood and pain that went into making them. Your idea of war – sit in an airplane, way above the clouds, press a button, drop the bombs, and never look below the clouds – that's the odourless, guiltless, sanitized way.

… That terrible arrogance of the white man, making himself something more than God, more than nature, saying 'I will let this animal live, because it makes money'; saying 'This animal must go, it brings no income, the space it occupies can be used in a better way. The only good coyote is a dead coyote.' They are treating coyotes almost as badly as they used to treat Indians.

You are buying and selling death.

Lame Deer, Seeker of Visions

WALTER DE LA MARE, 1873–1956

Hi!

Hi! Handsome hunting man,
Fire your little gun.
Bang! Now that animal
Is dead and dumb and done.
Nevermore to peep again, creep again, leap again,
Eat or sleep or drink again, oh, what fun!

Tit for Tat

Have you been catching of fish, Tom Noddy?
Have you snared a weeping hare?
Have you whistled 'No Nunny' and gunned a poor
    bunny,
Or a blinded bird of the air?

Have you trod like a murderer through the green woods,
Through the dewy deep dingles and glooms,
While every small creature screamed shrill to Dame
    Nature
'He comes – and he comes!'?

Wonder I very much do, Tom Noddy,
If ever, when off you roam,
An Ogre from space will stoop a lean face
And lug you home:

Lug you home over his fence, Tom Noddy,
Of thorn-sticks nine yards high,
With your bent knees strung round his old iron gun
And your head dan-dangling by:

And hang you up stiff on a hook, Tom Noddy,
From a stone-cold pantry shelf,
Whence your eyes will glare in an empty stare,
Till you are cooked yourself!

PAT DERBY, 1942–

They [gorillas] are brave and loyal. They help each other. They rival elephants as parents and whales for gentleness. They play and have humour and they harm nothing. They are what we should be. I don't know if we'll ever get there.

You have to love animals for what they are or leave them alone. The best thing you can do for them if you love them is leave them alone and see that other people do too.

Wild animals are not meant to be owned, any more than human beings are. Nobody has the right to pass a cougar or a gorilla on from hand to hand.

The Lady and Her Tiger

SHRI MORARJI DESAI, 1896–

I am a vegetarian both by birth and by conviction. The tradition of vegetarianism, you will admit, is strong among several communities in this country. I happen to belong to one of them. Add to this fact that as I grew up, I bestowed a great deal of thought upon this problem and arrived at the conviction that I should continue to be a vegetarian. This was because I was persuaded that to sustain one's life at the expense of the life of another of God's creatures is not conducive to one's spiritual growth.

The philosophy of *ahimsa* or non-violence is part of all religious faiths. Buddha and Lord Mahavira preached it in times long past. Gandhiji taught us the same lesson in our own day. Its roots lie in the concept that one should abstain from doing violence to any other living being. If I am entitled to kill a living creature either for my pleasure or for my nourishment, equally would somebody else be justified in killing me for his enjoyment or sustenance.

There is an extreme sect of vegetarians who even

rcfrain from taking milk or milk products for fear of depriving certain living creatures of what is their right. Some will not use silk or skins either, for the same reason. Such people I would reckon as belonging to a plane higher than mine.

Autobiography

MADAME DE STAËL, 1766–1817

The more I see of men, the more I like dogs.

Memoirs

H. JAY DINSHAH, 1933–

Mankind cannot, I submit, save itself from destruction through mere cleverness of scientific technology selfishly applied, nor through wishful thinking. But through a deep sense of brotherhood of all life, and a willingness and eagerness on the part of each and every person to work constructively for the preservation and enhancement of life, mankind may yet be preserved and go forward into the next millennium with confidence, competence and compassion.

The Vegetarian Way, XXIV World Vegetarian Congress, 1977

... To anyone who believes that life itself has some purpose – or is even its own reason for being – one should not wantonly destroy even plants. The destruction of any life is thus an act not to be taken lightly, or presumed to be isolated in the scheme of things. It is to be preceded by careful consideration of the responsibilities and the possible alternatives involved, and accompanied by an understanding that one is indeed doing the right thing according to his present state of existence ... The ethical vegetarian is seriously interested in lessening the suffering that he may be causing in the world – even inadvertently inflicted upon relatively low forms of life.

Ahimsa, August 1971

Man must get his thoughts, words and actions out of this vast moral jungle. We are not predators. We are, hopefully, more than instinctive killers and selfish brutes. Why take such a dim view of our potentialities and capabilities?

Out of the Jungle

Man cannot pretend to be higher in ethics, spirituality, advancement, or civilization than other creatures, and at the same time live by lower standards than the vulture or hyena ...

The Pillars of Ahimsa indisputably represent the clearest, surest path out of the jungle, and toward the attainment of that highly desirable goal.

Ibid.

LADY FLORENCE DIXIE, 1857–1905

What is it but deliberate massacre when thousands and tens of thousands of tame, hand-reared creatures are every year literally driven into the jaws of death and mown down in a peculiarly brutal manner? A perfect roar of guns fills the air; louder tap and yell the beaters, while above the din can be heard the heart-rending cries of wounded hares and rabbits, some of which can be seen dragging themselves away, with legs broken, or turning round and round in their agony before they die! And the pheasants! They are on every side, some rising, some dropping; some lying dead, but the great majority fluttering on the ground wounded; some with both legs broken and a wing; some with both wings broken and a leg; others merely winged, running to hide; others mortally wounded, gasping out their last breath amidst the hellish uproar which surrounds them. And this is called 'sport'!

The Horrors of Sport

We owe much to animals, and their rights are still shamefully neglected, while wild animals are absolutely uprotected. Many women are heedlessly, and others ignorantly cruel in this particular ... Experience has taught me the cruelty and horror of much miscalled sport. Wide travel, much contact with the animal world, and a good deal of experience in a variety of sports have all combined to make me ashamed and deeply regretful for every life my hand has taken.

From interview with Charles W. Forward, 1894

C.E. DODGSON (Lewis Carroll), 1832–1898

The world has seen and tired of the worship of Nature, of Reason, of Humanity; for this nineteenth century has been reserved the development of the most refined religion of all – the worship of self ... The enslavement of his weaker brethren – 'the labour of those who do not enjoy, for the enjoyment of those who do not labour' – the degradation of women – the torture of the animal world – these are the steps of the ladder by which man is ascending to his higher civilization ... This, then, is the glorious future to which the advocate of secular education may look forward: the dawn that gilds the horizon of his hopes! An age when all forms of religious thought shall be things of the past; when chemistry and biology shall be the A B C of a State education enforced on all; when vivisection shall be practised in every college and school; and when the man of science, looking forth over a world which will then own no other sway than his, shall exult in the thought that he has made of this fair green earth, if not a heaven for man, at least a hell for animals.

In a letter to the *Pall Mall Gazette*, 12 February 1875

Is the anatomist, who can contemplate unmoved the agonies he is inflicting for no higher purpose than to gratify a scientific curiosity, or to illustrate some well-established truth, a being higher or lower in the scale of humanity, than the ignorant boor whose very soul would sicken at the horrid sight?

Ibid.

DANIEL A. DOMBROWSKI, 1953–

If my criticisms of the Christian attitude toward animals seem harsh it is because familiarity breeds annoyance, if not contempt. There is no reason why Christianity had to take the course it did regarding animals. When hearts are given over to enslavement instead of to sharing our goods with animals, or at least to acting as stewards to God's bounty, it is hard to see how one has not violated the law of *agape*.

Vegetarianism: the Philosophy Behind the Ethical Diet

If animals experience not only pain, but also the desire to avoid pain, why does the meat-eater feel justified in causing them unnecessary pain? Rather than demanding that the vegetarian supply the proof that a being has rights (assuming that sentiency might be such a condition), ... perhaps the burden of proof should be on the meat-eater to justify his position in the light of the pain he causes.

Ibid.

JOHN DONNE, 1573–1631

Is any kind subject to rape like fish?
Ill unto man, thay neither doe, nor wish;
Fishers they kill not, nor with noise awake,
They doe not hunt, nor strive to make a prey
Of beasts, nor their yong sonnes to beare away;
Foules they pursue not, nor do undertake
To spoile the nests industrious birds do make;
Yet them all these unkinde kinds feed upon,
To kill them is an occupation.
    And lawes make Fasts, and Lents for their destruction.

The Progress of the Soule

FYODOR MIKHAILOVICH DOSTOEVSKY, 1821–1881

Love animals: God has given them the rudiments of thought and joy untroubled. Do not trouble their joy, do not harass them, do not deprive them of their happiness, do not work against God's intent. Man, do not pride yourself on your superiority to animals: they are without sin, and you, with your greatness, defile the earth by your appearance on it, and leave the traces of your foulness after you.

The Brothers Karamazov

Love all God's creatures, the animals, the plants,
Love everything to perceive the divine mystery in all.

Ibid.

The roots of our thoughts and our feelings are not here but in other worlds, and when the sense of oneness with those worlds grows weak or is destroyed in you, the heavenly growth will die in you. Then you will be indifferent to life, and even grow to hate it.

Ibid.

AIR CHIEF MARSHAL LORD DOWDING, 1882–1970

Even should it be conclusively proved that human beings benefit directly from the suffering of animals, its infliction would nevertheless be unethical and wrong …

Address to the House of Lords, 1952

Failure to recognize our responsibilities to the animal kingdom is the cause of many of the calamities which now beset the nations of the world … Nearly all of us have a deep rooted wish for peace – peace on earth; but we shall never attain the true peace – the peace of love, and not the uneasy equilibrium of fear – until we recognize the place of animals in the scheme of things and treat them accordingly.

House of Lords, 18 July 1957

I have come to realize that the dominion which we have been given over the animals is a serious responsibility. It does not mean that we are justified in exploiting the animals, and taking their lives and causing them pain and terror, and treating them as chattels for our profit or sport or amusement. The animals are our younger brothers and sisters on the same ladder of evolution as we, and we are responsible for helping them up the ladder instead of retarding their development by cruel and callous and greedy exploitation.

The British Vegetarian, March/April 1959

MURIEL THE LADY DOWDING, 1908–

Do we deserve health and freedom from accidents when in the name of research we deliberately bring disease and agony on millions of animals by vivisection? I think we do not and, by the great law of cause and effect, 'As you sow, so shall you reap,' we must reverse this dreadful state of affairs. Man must start to put right the world he is destroying and, of the many disasters he has brought about, probably the most evil is that of imprisoning a living, feeling and, in many cases, terrified animal, infecting it with painful illness, mutilating it, and eventually, after its suffering, taking its life.

Public lecture

ARTHUR CONAN DOYLE, 1859–1930

'At least,' said I, 'you must allow me to send you over some fish and some meat from our larder.'

'We are not Christians,' he answered, 'but Buddhists of the higher school. We do not recognize that man has a moral right to slay an ox or a fish for the gross use of his body. He has not put life into them, and has assuredly no mandate from the Almighty to take life from them save under most pressing need. We could not, therefore, use your gift if you were to send it.'

The Mystery of Cloomber

MAUREEN DUFFY, 1933–

Both Heads Lapped Perfectly

I am you brother
who share our body.
At one time
they would have
put us on sideshow
with the bearded lady

113

the mermaid
the hermaphrodite
nature's prodigies
except that they made us
double tongued
four eyed.

If they urge me
I will twitch our paw
or thump our tail
to show we are
still alive.
I was a good dog
jumped through hoops to please.
Don't snap at me
try to bite me off
we have only ourself
and I'm afraid
of what goes on
inside your head.

At the moment our human world is based upon the suffering and destruction of millions of non-humans. To perceive this and to begin to do something to change it in personal and public ways is to undergo a change of perception akin to religious or political conversion. Nothing can ever be seen in quite the same way again because once you have admitted the terror and pain of other species you will, unless you resist conversion, be always aware of the endless permutations of suffering that support our society.

Men and Beasts

Chattel

Driving back from the literature festival
through Otley handsome in black stone
with white revers of painted windows and doors

I follow behind a tin truck
gaping an open vent high up at the back.
Stopped at the lights the gap is filled
with broad snout, a wet black sponge for sucking up
sweetness from deep in summer grass.
You crane your head in the hole sideways to let
each eye in turn roll up at the sky.
Deep in the tumbril shock you don't speak.
I know where you're going this summer's morning
and feel you know it too though how
when no one has ever come back with tell-tale
smell of blood and fear on staring hide?
I imagine though I can't see the shrunken dug
flat as a perished rubber glove.
The street is called Wharfedale View. It looks across
to where the moors throw a green quilt
for miles under a high sky. Why can't I just
draw the steel bolt on the tailgate
and let you run and run up there till you drop?
But the lights change. You turn Left; I go Right
for Leeds and perhaps I'm quite wrong
and you're just being moved on to new pasture.
Then why can't I safe home sleep
but see still your face laid along the tailgate
with one moist eye turned up questioning
whether I would have drawn that bolt
if you'd been able to ask me in a tongue
I couldn't kid myself I misunderstood?

ISADORA DUNCAN, 1878–1927

Who loves this terrible thing called War? Probably the
meat-eaters, who having killed, feel the need to kill …
The butcher with his bloody apron incites bloodshed,
murder. Why not? From cutting the throat of a calf to

cutting the throats of our brothers and sisters is but a step. While we are ourselves the living graves of murdered animals, how can we expect any ideal conditions on the Earth?

Quoted in 'The Inedible Complex' by Carol Adams

LAWRENCE EASTERBROOK, 1902–1965

… of one thing I am certain, keeping hens in batteries is a cruel system of which any civilized country ought to be ashamed. Every natural instinct of the hen is thwarted by the cages. I have seen these prisoners thrusting their necks out, at the top, then at the sides, in a vain attempt at freedom. When they are removed, their bones are as brittle as matchsticks, and some are unable to walk. This condition has been described by the Ministry of Agriculture as 'thriving'. The Ministry also says that calves in pens so narrow that they cannot get their heads round, to drive away the flies, are 'thriving'. They would not put on weight unless they were contented. Yet my doctor tells me that a man living on nothing but water in a confined space would put on weight. I don't think that this is the kind of thriving the Ministry officials would welcome.

News Chronicle article, 1959

PRINCE PHILIP, DUKE OF EDINBURGH, 1921–

In the end we must, I think, somehow conclude that they [the animals] have as much right to this planet as we have.

Speech, New York, 1971

We may have discovered the existence of radio sources several million light years away with an immensely clever piece of equipment, but we continue to treat each other and all the other living things on our planet in a way which is only a bare improvement on primitive man ... I want to suggest that scientific and technological progress is not only valueless, it is actively harmful, unless it is modified or directed by a social and humanitarian outlook.

Men, Machines and Sacred Cows

There must be an optimum size [of population] which would ensure that all future generations had a fair share of the planet's limited resources. If we assume that child mortality can be reduced further, and the expectations of life can be stretched a bit more, this puts an absolute limit on the average number of children that women can produce in order to maintain a balance between births and deaths.

... The inescapable conclusion is that the economics of growth have ensured that man cannot win the contest with nature. [That so-called conquest] is actively and effectively contributing to the decline and ultimate extinction of the human species ... Whatever happens to the human species, nature will continue on its way without a backward glance at the self-imposed fate of its most successful and intelligent production.

The ultimate irony is that the growth of human knowledge and understanding, the obsession with economic growth and the conflict between rival social and economic ideologies, have destroyed what pretension man ever had to being a special creation with special responsibilities for the rest of creation.

Rational economics and blind science have blunted all sense of the ethical and moral factors which might have been capable of exercising a restraining influence on human behaviour.

Presidential address 'Man's conquest of nature', Royal Society of
Arts, 23 March 1988

If the world (human) population continues to expand at its present rate, there is absolutely no hope whatsoever that wildlife is going to survive.

Radio 4, 'It's Your World', 20 April 1986

THOMAS A. EDISON, 1847–1931

Non-violence leads to the highest ethics, which is the goal of all evolution. Until we stop harming all other living beings, we are still savages.

Harper's Magazine, 1890

DAVID EHRENFELD, 1938–

It is my impression that personal ego is increasing in the world, and I ascribe this to a humanist influence, which has left us with no alternative but to love ourselves best of all. This is exactly the opposite of what was predicted not long ago by Father Teilhard de Chardin, who believed that the discoveries of science would help humanity achieve a single world consciousness, a 'noosphere', in which mind and spirit would flow around the planet like a magnetic field.

... on the one hand [the humanists] promise a future that will be good for everybody, and on the other they criticize (as I have recently heard done) the anti-humanist insistence upon a gentle and humble approach to the environment as a personal religious belief which should not be inflicted on the rest of society.

The Arrogance of Humanism

ALBERT EINSTEIN, 1879–1955

It is my view that the vegetarian manner of living by its purely physical effect on the human temperament would most beneficially influence the lot of mankind.

Letter to *Vegetarian Watch-Tower*, 27 December 1930

A human being is a part of the whole, called by us the 'Universe', a part limited in time and space. He experiences himself, his thoughts and feelings, as something separate from the rest – a kind of optical delusion of his consciousness. This delusion is a kind of prison for us, restricting us to our personal desires and to affection for a few persons nearest to us. Our task must be to free ourselves from this prison by widening our circle of compassion to embrace all living creatures and the whole of nature in its beauty. Nobody is able to achieve this completely, but the striving for such achievement is in itself a part of the liberation and a foundation for inner security.

New York Post, 28 November 1972

LOREN EISELEY, 1907–1977

Man has the capacity to love, not just his own species, but life in all its shapes and forms. This empathy with all the interknit web of life is the highest spiritual expression I know of. 'Love not the world,' the Biblical injunction runs, 'neither the things that are in the world' ... But I *do* love the world ... I love its small ones, the things beaten into the strangling surf; the bird, singing, which falls and is not seen again ... I love the lost ones, the failures of the world.

The Star Thrower

Let men beat men, if they will, but why do they have to beat and starve small things? Why? Why? I will never forget that dog's eyes, nor the eyes of every starved mongrel I have fed from Curacao to Cuernavaca. Nor the drowning one I once fished out of an irrigation ditch in California, only to see him limp away with his ribs showing ... This is why I am a wanderer forever in the

119

streets of men, a wanderer in mind, and, in these matters, a creature of desperate impulse.

All the Strange Hours

One does not meet oneself until one catches the reflection from an eye other than human.

The Unexpected Universe

GEORGE ELIOT, 1819–1880

Women should be protected from anyone's exercise of unrighteous power ... but then, so should every other living creature.

From a letter

JOHN ELLIOTSON, MD, FRS, 1791–1868

A course of experimental physiology in which brutes are agonized to exhibit facts already established, is a disgrace to the country that permits it.

Human Physiology

RALPH WALDO EMERSON, 1803–1882

You have just dined, and however scrupulously the slaughterhouse is concealed in the graceful distance of miles, there is complicity.

Fate

EMPEDOCLES OF AGRIGENTUM, *fl.* 460 B.C.

... but this was the greatest pollution among men, to devour the goodly limbs [of animals] whose life they had reft from them.

Katharmoi (Purifications)

LORD (Thomas) ERSKINE, 1750–1823

Animals are considered *as property only*. To destroy or to abuse them, from malice to the proprietor, or with an intention injurious to his interest in them, is criminal. *But the animals themselves are without protection.* The law regards them not *substantively*. They have no RIGHTS!

... I am to ask your Lordships, in the name of that God who gave to Man his dominion over the lower world, to acknowledge and recognize that dominion to be A MORAL TRUST.

... For every animal which comes in contact with Man, and whose powers, and qualities, and instincts, are obviously constructed for his use, Nature has taken the same care to provide, and as carefully and bountifully as for man himself, organs and feelings for its own enjoyment and happiness. Almost every sense bestowed upon Man is equally bestowed upon them – seeing, hearing, feeling, thinking, the sense of pain and pleasure, and passions of love and anger, sensibility to kindness, and pangs from unkindness and neglect, are inseparable characteristics of *their* natures as much as of *our own*.

Cruelty to Animals, the speech of Lord Erskine in the House of Peers on the second reading of the Bill for preventing malicious and wanton cruelty to animals, 1809

DR ALFRED G. ETTER, 1919–

Animals are the ultimate art of the universe. They are at once functional, appealing, mysterious and inspiring. In caves and sanctuaries of the past, great unknown artists demonstrated their admiration for the creatures with which they once shared daily life. The tragedy of today is that we not only have to forgo this kind of association, but are embarked upon a campaign to destroy these masterpieces of creation. One by one we crowd them toward extinction with gun, spray, saw, match, bulldozer, bomb, markets, indifference and procrastination. And the greatest of these is procrastination.

Testament before a Senate sub-committee, 1976

JON EVANS, 1917–

Vivisection is wrong because it is an abuse of man's power over the helpless, involving pain and suffering. The name for this is cruelty, and cruelty is immoral, no matter what the reason for its introduction.

Address to International Association Against
Painful Experiments on Animals, 1971

To inflict cruelties on defenceless creatures, or condone such acts, is to abuse one of the cardinal tenets of a civilized society – reverence for life.

Editorial, *Animals' Defender*

GAVIN EWART, 1916–

On Seeing a Priest – Eating Veal

Put down that calf, thou Man of Flesh,
Put down that veal, thou Bloody Man,
God's creatures are the wheels that mesh,
And He will eat *you*, when He Can.

Unfrock thyself, thou Man of Blood,
Thou art but meat, and so are these,
And have been since before the Flood:
Go down on thy unbasted knees,

And ponder on Eternal Fires
And battered fish and slaughtered lambs.
Restrain thy animal desires,
Be cured – or God will smoke thy hams!

New Statesman, 14 August 1964

GEORGE R. FARNUM, 1885–1973

Tenderness and pity should never be taken as weakness. Men who have been great in the true sense have never been indifferent to the rights, nor blind to the needs, of the helpless.

The education of the heart should ever go hand in hand with the cultivation of the mind. Kindness toward all sentient creatures and compassion for suffering in all its forms are the hallmarks of the enlightened community and the badge of the cultural individual.

Reverence for Life

The persistence of vivisection constitutes a grave indictment of our fundamental humanity and a terrible wrong in the sight of a just and merciful God ... the tragic implications of a situation which permits members of a civilized society to be successfully led by false and highly organized propaganda into the belief that the practice of vivisection by callous instructors, clumsy students, and morally indifferent 'scientists' is designed to promote the happiness and welfare of humanity.

Ideals and Aspirations

J. TODD FERRIER, 1855–1943

Western Christianity, in seeking to conquer the east, has too often only materialized the faith. And the failure of missionaries to win over the cultured of the east is through our gross western habits in living. For the man whose religion teaches him to hold all life sacred, is not likely to be converted to a faith that deems no life sacred but man's.

On Behalf of the Creatures

And I might go on to speak of earlier times and later times, of how the Egyptian Dynasty came to grief, and in later days proud, boastful Israel; how nations early and late have died out as a result of the closing of the Intuition through gross habits of life and inhumane conduct; how Greece and Rome in the height of their glory were practically frugivorous; how the finest intellects throve on simple earth-fare, and Caesar's armies conquered the western world on maize and oil; and also, how the decline and fall of Greece and Rome may be traced back to the gross life that grew up as the result of voluptuous living.

There is no limit to the testimony of history on the physical, moral and religious advantages of non-flesh diet. Whether we listen to Greece or to Rome, to Egypt or to Israel, to the Historian, the Philosopher, or to the Theologian, the message is the same.

They have all discovered in every land that Higher Law of God written in the human heart and in nature, disobedience to which brings physical pain and corruption, moral dullness and inertia, spiritual blindness and impotence – the very things which now lie upon society like a nightmare.

And having discovered that law in themselves, and recognizing the solidarity of the whole world of life, they lived and toiled to better the Earth by saving men from degrading habits, and redeeming them unto a life of full-rounded virtue, in which tenderness and compassion, mercy and fellow-feeling should not be wanting even towards the sub-human creatures.

Ibid.

As behind all effects there are causes, so it is true of our commercial and social conditions. The lack of true reverence for human life has had its origin in our failure to apprehend the sacredness of all life ... Nor will they fail to see that most of the cankerous evils which are eating up the richest life of the nation may be traced back to the barbaric customs and habits of the people, past and present.

Ibid.

Much of the indifference, apathy, and even cruelty which we see has its origin in the false education given the young concerning the rights of animals, and their duty towards them.

Ibid.

It ought to make all who profess evangelical Christianity ashamed that the finest and most compassionate souls have not been within their own borders, but rather amongst those whose deepest thoughts have aroused the suspicion of heresy. Evangelical Christianity, as people understand it, has absolutely failed to kindle the Divine Compassion and to realize itself in a great fire of sacred devotion to all life.

Ibid.

It is difficult to understand how anyone who has studied animals could come to the conclusion that they do not *feel*; and more difficult still to understand how any man who professes to have been moved by the compassion of God could believe and teach that we need not consider the feelings of the other species, as they are only *things* – 'mere chattels'. Yet men do believe such things, and teach them. And when we realize how much the doctrine is held in 'high places', it is not to be wondered at that cruelty abounds, and our fellow-creatures are made to pass through the fire of unspeakable suffering as sacrifices to the Moloch of human lust and scientific insanity.

Ibid.

We are what we think; as we desire so do we become! By our thoughts, desires, and habits, we either ascend to the full divine dignity of our nature, or we descend to suffer and learn.

Ibid.

JULIA ALLEN FIELD, 1937–

We cannot glimpse the essential life of a caged animal, only the shadow of its former beauty.

'Reflections on the Death of an Elephant',
Defenders, **42**, Spring 1967

G.W. FOOTE, 1850–1915

Morality itself eventually broadens into Humanity, and then we hear of 'Natural Rights'. It is all a question of development. Moral Rights are widespread new sentiments, demanding incorporation into Legal Rights; and Natural Rights are still newer sentiments, aspiring to recognition as Moral Rights, with a view to ultimate incorporation as Legal Rights. Legal Rights represent the wisdom and power of the present, and Natural Rights represent the wisdom and power of the future. They are, respectively, a solid fact, a general demand and a growing aspiration. As the aspiration ripens it becomes a demand, and as the demand gathers power it passes into a fact.

Evidently, therefore, the word 'Rights' requires a qualifying adjective before it can be admitted as a term in our discussion. And I fancy the point of wisdom lies in the golden mean. We need not discuss the Legal Rights of animals, since these can be decided by an appeal to the Statute Book; nor need we discuss the Natural Rights of animals, as this involves too many grave differences of opinion and sentiment; but I think we may profitably discuss the Moral Rights of animals, for this simply means – Are they, or are they not, participators in the beneficence of our ethical progress? Or, in other words, Is our treatment of animals consistent with the moral ideas we should blush to repudiate? For, after all, animals can never have enforceable rights against us; they must take their fate from our hands; at the best they can only be sharers in the fruits of our wisdom and humanity.

... I regard [vivisection] as the ultimate horror of man's unjust dealing with the animals. I believe that Secularists are prepared to support legislation for its entire prohibition. We are not in favour of any priesthood. The old ecclesiastical priesthood burnt men for the good of mankind; the new medical priesthood tortures animals for the same object. But bad means never lead to a good end. I suspect salvation that has to be promoted by murder. I am not in love with health that has to be promoted by torture. Personally I do not want to find a little gold dust in the polluted troughs of cruelty. I would rather keep poor and clean. Nor will I be misled by cheap talk about the great principle of sacrifice. When an Anarchist told me, soon after the assassination of President Carnot, that new ideas always had their baptism of blood, I told him that I did not object to their shedding blood; they might shed all they had; what I objected to was their shedding the blood of others. If some person, full of scientific zeal, and burning with the enthusiasm of humanity, will offer himself to be vivisected, I shall respect his generosity, whatever I may think of his intelligence. But I object to his offering me. He must wait till I offer myself. And I object to his offering any other man – or any other animal.

... it seems to me that the true guarantee for the eventual better treatment of animals is the cultivation of humanity – the greatest word in the world. This is far safer ground for our hopes than any abstract theory of 'rights'. It is in the gradual extension of the sympathetic instinct, from the individual to the family, from the family to the tribe, from the tribe to the nation, from the nation to the race, and from our own race to that of the animals, that we find the surest promise for the future of humanitarianism. Above all things, let us cultivate sympathy and imagination. Imagination brings near to us the distant in time and space; and all cruelty, short of positive malignity, would be restrained by a realization of future consequences.

Children should be taught to be humane. Mere cleverness may make a clever rogue; it is *humane* education that is most needed, and, alas, that is most neglected. The scientific side of life is better able than the poetic to take care of itself. True culture involves the training of the emotions as well as the intellect, otherwise we shall never realize the fine ideal of Renan, who 'could not be discourteous even to a dog'. When we have cultivated humanity in children, and afforded later opportunity for its practice by men and women, the problem before us will be solved ... Let us be humane to each other, and the spirit of humanity will naturally extend itself to the whole kinship of life.

From a lecture given before the Humanitarian League,
published 6 and 18 March, 1904 in *The Freethinker*

MARTYN FORD, 1954–

That animals should be the subject of serious moral concern may seem a rather strange idea. After all, the gulf between us and them is so enormous – so the theory goes – that we can't possibly think of them in the same way as ourselves. We eat them, hunt them, laugh at them, wear them, inflict pain upon them. Our language itself reflects the bias. 'Animal' or 'pig' are just two of many terms of abuse commonly used. Intelligence, co-operation and altruism are all allegedly human characteristics, whilst territoriality, aggression and dominance are considered to belong to the realm of animal nature.

But the myth has to be sustained, for some deeply rooted practices may be threatened. Animal experimentation and factory farming are the two greatest examples of 'speciesism' at work. We have chosen to deny other animals fundamental consideration purely because they happen to belong to other species of animal. Like racism, speciesism is arbitrary and irrational. And it explains why otherwise decent people can condone suffering on a vast scale, pay for it with their taxes, and bestow titles and honours on those who carry out the atrocities.

Towards Animal Rights

DIAN FOSSEY, 1940–1985

I feel more comfortable with gorillas than people. I can anticipate what a gorilla's going to do, and they're purely motivated.

St. Louis Post Dispatch, 1980

JOHN FOWLES, 1926–

Only fools think our attitude to our fellow men is a thing distinct from our attitude to 'lesser' life on this planet.

The Trees

But I think the most harmful change brought about by Victorian science in our attitude to nature lies in the demand that our relation with it must be purposive, industrious, always seeking greater knowledge.

Ibid.

Then I went through a shooting and fishing phase, a black period in my relations to nature, and one which now, taught by Clare and Thoreau, I look back on with an angry shame. That phase ended dramatically one dusk when I was wildfowling in the Essex marshes. I winged a curlew. It fell in the mud beside the Thames, and I ran to pick it up. Curlew scream like children when they are wounded, and in too much haste I reversed my gun in order to snap the bird's head against the stock. The curlew flapped, the gun slipped, I grabbed for it. There was a violent explosion. And I was left staring down at a hole blasted in the mud not six inches from my left foot. The next day I sold my gun. I have not intentionally killed a bird or an animal since.

Now, when I observe myself, a specimen of that vicious parasitical predator *Homo sapiens*, I see that I fell into all the great heresies of man's attitude to nature.

First of all, I was a collector. One of the reasons I wrote – and named – my novel *The Collector* was to express my hatred of that whole perversion: because all natural history collectors in the end collect the same thing: the death of the living. And in this age of 'environmental control' (so often a barefaced euphemism for the annihilation of any species of life that threatens profit margins) collecting animate objects such as birds' eggs or insects for pleasure *must* be evil. No moral choice of our time is clearer.

Animals (US), Vol.13, Part 9, 1971

We know quite enough facts now; where we are still miserably retarded is in our emotional and aesthetic relationship to wildlife. Nature is a sort of art sans art; and the right human attitude to it ought to be, unashamedly, poetic rather than scientific.

Ibid.

GEORGE FOX, 1624–1691

What wages doth the Lord desire of you for his earth that he giveth to you ... but that you give him the praises and honour, and the thanks, and the glory; and not that you should spend the creatures upon your lusts, but to do good with them; you that have much to them that have little; and so to honour God with your substance, for nothing brought you into the world, nor nothing you shall take out of the world, but leave all creatures behind you as you found them.

Works, vol. IV

DR MICHAEL W. FOX, 1937–

The ultimate expression of being fully human is to be open to the world within and without and to embrace all of life equally with reverence, humility and compassion.

The missing link between animals and a truly humane mankind is man himself, who does not yet see himself as a part of the world, claiming it instead for himself.

Men who bring nations to war for 'just causes' are no less blind than those who enjoy blood sports, using live animals as bait and injuring them both physically and psychologically. It is this blindness that leads to so much human misery, oppression, conflict and suffering, as well as destruction of nature and cruelty to animals. How can people begin to be aware of their inhumanity and end the hell on earth that their values and actions create ... to see through and beyond themselves and their self-limiting reality?

The way, surely, is through an overreaching moral and ethical system of values (metavalues) that transcends the values within and differences between various groups, be they hunters, conservationists, corporations or ethnic groups. By metavalues I mean those values that arise after seeing and appreciating another being, be it a tree, a wolf, or a man, for itself, independent of one's own personal priorities, interests or expectations.

...We know from the truths of evolution and ecology that we are all related and interdependent. Anthropomorphism (crediting animals with human emotions and traits) is, however, outdated. Rather we know that we are like animals. This is objective zoomorphism or scientific animism. We feel as they do and we have similar basic needs and emotions. One should not confuse the outdated anthropomorphic view with true empathy. Empathy is understanding the emotions of another without projections, without anthropomorphic thinking.

One Earth, One Mind

Human liberation will begin when we understand that our evolution and fulfilment are contingent on the recognition of animal rights and on a compassionate and responsible stewardship of nature.

... The weakness of humanity is our blindness, a cultural blind spot which some call ignorance, in which a selfish and immature ego claims the world as ours and prevents us from seeing ourselves as a part of the world. Kinship with all life is a biological (evolutionary) fact, but our culture, our ways of doing, perceiving and relating, blind us to this reality.

Returning to Eden

An act of violence against nature should be judged as severely as that against society or another person. The turning over of a stone, the unnecessary felling of a tree, or the slaughter of an animal is a crime to be weighed in judgment against the wants and needs of the person and the values of his society.

Between Animal and Man

Kinship with all life must be expressed in *action* since belief alone is no longer enough. Above and beyond our own immediate needs we all have a responsibility as stewards of this small planet since we have a reflective consciousness unlike any other animal, so far as is known. With this consciousness we can control our own evolution and we must assume this responsibility fully, since we stepped out of the constraining laws of nature when we first domesticated plants and animals and developed a technology. Nature can no longer direct us – we must guide ourselves and cherish our heritage in all that is wild and natural.

By virtue of this consciousness there is a god within us; man *is* both animal and god. Man must integrate both these sides of his nature if he is to be truly human. Kinship with all life and responsibility would then be expressed above and beyond the self-limiting and often destructive motives and priorities of the culture. These would ultimately change through consensus. But the change must first come from within us. Faith alone is not enough. It must be expressed in action and motivated by a sense of commitment to others as well as to oneself.

Ibid.

Humans should not create disharmony for their own short-term 'good' because ultimately it will not be in their best interests, for what is good for humankind is, by virtue of the law of ecosystems, good for all life.

For example, the acceptance of, or indifference towards, unjustified pain or suffering in animals may lead to or be associated with a more generalized inhumane indifference, a growing, dehumanizing lack of compassion in society as a whole. Cruelty towards animals has been linked with sociopathic behaviour and child abuse. Such correlations warrant our concern and illustrate the point of similarity in relationships between

one human and another and between humans and
animals.

'Philosophy, Ecology, Animal Welfare, and the "Rights" Question',
from *Ethics and Animals*, eds. Miller and Williams

OLIVE FRASER, 1909–1977

The Solitaries

The merry badger keeps his way
Nocturnally,
And I go merry to my play
Even as he.

Minding our own business,
Tending our own,
We are no more than this.
Leave us alone.

The Otter Slide

Here did the pads skid and slide
Here did the bead-bright eyes gleam.
Here in blood and torment died
The happy genius of this stream.

On a dying cygnet, stoned

O king, dream not upon the fabulous air
And, dreaming, beat, and beating, wounded wake.
I have a passion that my heart must bear
And thou has one that thine will break.

I weep for thee on thy last pool's last brink,
The royal ruin'd head, bewrayèd wing,
But in thy death 'tis of my kin I think
With horror, grief past uttering.

'When I shall die'

When I shall die, let there be mountains near,
The milk-white ptarmigan, the wand'ring deer.
When I shall die, let the poor dipper call
Out of her foothills by the waterfall.

O let no human, festering, hating heart
Come in that place with ignorance or art.
Let there be none to mock my life with words
But the bare mountains and the calling birds.

EDWARD AUGUSTUS FREEMAN, 1823–1892

The awful wrongs and sufferings forced upon the
innocent, helpless, faithful animal race, form the blackest
chapter in the whole world's history.

History of Europe

CURTIS FRESHEL, 1886–1968

Most experts agree that animal testing today is virtually
pointless. As one clinical director puts it: 'You cannot
really rely on tests with any other animal or combination
of animals to predict drug or surgical action in man.'

But if the animal vivisectionist gains little from his
experiments, he will acquire one talent which will stay
with him for life: a capacity for indifference to the
sufferings of any living creature. This ability to shrug off
pain-wracked spasms and tortured moans will serve him
in good stead when he moves up to experiment on his
human guinea pigs.

When knowledge is worshipped and understanding is

ignored; when sympathy and pity are sneered at as weaknesses; when what is morally right becomes less important than what is expedient; and when conscience is quieted by ambition – the budding surgeon has then completed his transformation from healer to 'scientist.'

World Forum, July/September 1967

In the West, the fear that cruelty to animals might poison the outlook of today's teenagers is being voiced ever more frequently. Such thoughful people as the late Dorothy Thompson and Eleanor Roosevelt have questioned the spreading practice of classroom dissection. Why not build in a child the habit of good rather than evil? they asked.

Many have called for a return to faith in God as the answer to juvenile delinquency. Yet as Gandhi once put it, 'It ill becomes us to invoke in our daily prayers the blessings of God the compassionate, if we in turn will not practise elementary compassion toward our fellow creatures.'

Ibid.

M.R.L. ('EMAREL') FRESHEL, 1864–1949

The demand for butcher's meat may not seem materially lessened because I do not eat it, but it is lessened notwithstanding, and I rejoice to know that in the past seven years my abstinence from flesh must have resulted in a little less slaughter, and I am glad to have reduced by even one drop the depth of that ocean of blood. I have heard the Biblical statement that man was to have dominion over all the earth quoted as a justification for the eating of the lower animals. We will some day be so civilized that we will recognize the great truth that dominion implies care and guardianship and protection, rather than the right to destroy.

Golden Rule Cook-Book

RELIGIOUS SOCIETY OF FRIENDS (Quakers)

Let the law of kindness show no limits. Show a loving consideration for all God's creatures.

General Advices, 1928

We shall respect that of God in all creations. We shall live in loving harmony with the earth. Humankind shall be a joyful gardener of the world given us by God, and shall use its fruits wisely and moderately.

Position reached at a Peaceable Kingdom workshop of American Quakers at the University of Southern Maine, August 1979

JAMES ANTHONY FROUDE, 1818–1894

Wild animals never kill for sport. Man is the only one to whom the torture and death of his fellow-creatures is amusing in itself.

Oceana

ROY FULLER, 1912–

It is man who has fallen, not the beasts: that is the message even for the irreligious, and to some extent salvation can be measured by his very treatment of them.

Fellow Mortals

THOMAS FULLER, 1608–1661

He that will not be merciful to his beast is a beast himself.

The Holy State

PAUL GALLICO, 1897–1976

And yet somehow it is the homeless cat that has become the byword for misery and wretchedness and which daily holds up the mirror to human conscienceless neglect of all that suffer.

And so this derelict impinges upon my awareness, because it is there. I see it daily, gaunt, bedraggled, dirty, its ribs showing through matted fur, sores on its body and eyes, hungry, frightened, defeated, and its breaks my heart.

It is cold and I am warm, starving when I am sated, wet and shivering in the rain and hail when I am dry and safe, abandoned when I am afforded love and companionship. Nothing softens or ameliorates its life of hardship and squalor; its birthplace and burial ground a refuse heap.

It is, I think, the fall from high estate that makes its plight so vivid and painful. For by nature it is fastidious, gregarious, clean, neat, dignified and proud.

Honourable Cat

JOHN GALSWORTHY, 1867–1933

Once admit that we have the right to inflict unnecessary suffering and you destroy the very basis of human society.

Much Cry – Little Wool

You are not living in a private world all your own. Everything you say and do and think has its effect on everybody around you. For example, if you feel and say loudly enough that it is an infernal shame to keep larks and other wild song-birds in cages, you will infallibly infect a number of other people with that sentiment, and in course of time those people who feel as you do will become so numerous that larks, thrushes, blackbirds and linnets will no longer be caught and kept in cages.

How do you imagine it ever came about that bears and bulls and badgers are no longer baited; cocks no longer openly encouraged to tear each other to pieces; donkeys no longer beaten to a pulp?

Only by people going about and shouting out that these things made them uncomfortable.

When a thing exists which you really abhor, I wish you would remember a little whether in letting it strictly alone you are minding your own business on principle, or simply because it is comfortable to do so.

Ibid.

If you know anything of politics, you will realize the enormous difficulty there always is in getting Parliament to pass a law which does away with, or seriously curtails, a vested interest, or even a time-honoured fashion. The moment it comes to trying to save beasts suffering at the expense of a definite class of men or women, the reformer is right up against it …

We simply have to recognize that the whole movement towards decent treatment of animals and birds is a terribly slow one, and that its only chance of real progress lies in gradual educational infection.

A Sheaf

MOHANDAS KARAMCHAND GANDHI, 1869–1948

The greatness of a nation and its moral progress can be judged by the way its animals are treated.

Vivisection is the blackest of all the black crimes that man is at present committing against God and His fair creation. It ill becomes us to invoke in our daily prayers the blessings of God, the Compassionate, if we in turn will not practise elementary compassion towards our fellow creatures.

The Moral Basis of Vegetarianism

I do not regard flesh-food as necessary for us at any stage and under any clime in which it is possible for human beings ordinarily to live. I hold flesh-food to be unsuited to our species. We err in copying the lower animal world – if we are superior to it.

Mahatma Gandhi, his Mission and Message

I want to realize brotherhood or identity not merely with the beings called human, but I want to realize identity with all life, even with such things as crawl upon earth.

Quoted in *Words of Gandhi*

… the basis of my vegetarianism is not physical, but moral. If anybody said that I should die if I did not take beef-tea or mutton, even under medical advice, I would prefer death. That is the basis of my vegetarianism. I would love to think that all of us who called ourselves vegetarians should have that basis. There were thousands of meat-eaters who did not stay meat-eaters. There must be a definite reason for our making that change in our lives, for our adopting habits and customs different from society, even though sometimes that change may offend those nearest and dearest to us. Not for the world should you sacrifice a moral principle. Therefore the only basis for having a vegetarian society and proclaiming a vegetarian principle is, and must be, a moral one.

Address to London Vegetarian Society, 20 November 1931

I hold today the same opinion as I held then. To my mind the life of a lamb is no less precious than that of a human being. I should be unwilling to take the life of a lamb for the sake of the human body. I hold that, the more helpless a creature, the more entitled it is to protection by man from the cruelty of man.

An Autobiography, the Story of My Experiments

PIERRE GASSENDI, 1592–1655

As for flesh, true, indeed, is it that man is sustained on flesh. But how many things, let me ask, does man do every day which are contrary to, or beside, his nature? So great, and so general, is the perversion of his mode of life, which has, as it were, eaten into his flesh by a sort of deadly contagion, that he appears to have put on another disposition. Hence, the whole care and concern of philosophy and moral instruction ought to consist in leading men back to the paths of Nature.

Man lives very well upon flesh, you say, but if he thinks this food to be natural to him, why does he not use it as it is, as furnished to him by Nature? But, in fact, he shrinks in horror from seizing and rending living or even raw flesh with his teeth, and lights a fire to change its natural and proper condition ... What is clearer than that man is not furnished for hunting, much less for eating, other animals? In one word, we seem to be admirably admonished by Cicero that man was destined for other things than for seizing and cutting the throats of other animals. If you answer, 'that may be said to be an industry ordered by Nature, by which such weapons are invented,' then, behold, it is by the very same artificial instrument that men make weapons for mutual slaughter. Do they this at the instigation of Nature? Can a use so noxious be called *natural*? Faculty is given by Nature, but it is our own fault that we make a perverse use of it.

Letter to Van Helmont

JEAN GAUTIER, 1875–1964

I wrote this book because I wished to fix the memory of my dog Yuni, whose qualities were great and whose death caused and still causes me much sorrow; I wished also to call people's attention to unfortunate dogs; and my final object has been to show the clergy of my country, who have little understanding of things that concern animals, that man is not a centre but that all creation – man, animals, plants – is oriented towards God and that, in fact, we are all of a piece [*solidaires*].

A Priest and His Dog

JOHN GAY, 1685–1732

The Wild Boar and the Ram

Against an elm a sheep was ty'd;
The butcher's knife in blood was dy'd;
The patient flock, in silent fright,
From far beheld the horrid sight;
A savage Boar, who near them stood,
Thus mock'd to scorn the fleecy brood.
    All cowards should be serv'd like you.
See, see, your murd'rer is in view;
With purple hands and reeking knife
He strips the skin yet warm with life:
Your quarter'd sires, your bleeding dams,
The dying bleat of harmless lambs
Call for revenge. O stupid race!
The heart that wants revenge is base.
    I grant, an ancient Ram replys,
We bear no terror in our eyes,
Yet think us not of soul so tame,
Which no repeated wrongs inflame;
Insensible of ev'ry ill,
Because we want thy tusks to kill.
Know, Those who violence pursue
Give to themselves the vengeance due,
For in these massacres they find
The two chief plagues that waste mankind.
Our skin supplys the wrangling bar,
It wakes their slumbering sons to war,

142

And well revenge may rest contented,
Since drums and parchment were invented.

STEVEN J. GELBERG, 1951–

Because he cannot really sense his own soul, the mundane religionist cannot sense it in other creatures and so thinks nothing of feasting on their slaughtered remains. Insisting that some living creatures have life but no soul, he inadvertently assumes the ideologic posture of the materialist, who reduces life to a mere biologic function. Under the sway of this contradiction, he fondles one lesser creature and slaughters another, pampering one as his pet and cannibalizing the other as his dinner. Devoid of even rudimentary consciousness of spirit, he remains blissfully unaware of his sin.

Belief in souls in animals aside, the mundane religionist lacks the moral keenness and simple compassion to be sickened by the bloody cruelty which he tacitly endorses as a human carnivore. Due to dullness, he remains unaware that the creature he blithely eats had to endure unspeakable suffering in the slaughterhouse – suffering for which he himself, as its chief beneficiary, is responsible. His scriptures enjoin 'Thou shalt not kill,' but he kills with blind, grinding routine. 'As you did it to one of the least of these my brethren,' says Jesus, 'you did it to me.'

The Transcendental Imperative; the Case for 'Otherworldly' Religion,
presented at Assembly of the World's Religions I, 1985

EDWARD GIBBON, 1737–1794

The thrones of Asia have been repeatedly overturned by the shepherds of the North [the Tartars], and their arms have spread terror and devastation over the most fertile

143

and warlike countries of Europe. On this occasion as well as on many others, the sober historian is forcibly awakened from a pleasing vision, and is compelled, with some reluctance, to confess that the *pastoral* manners, which have been adorned with the fairest attributes of peace and innocence, are much better adapted to the fierce and cruel habits of military life.

To illustrate this observation, I shall now proceed to consider a nation of shepherds and of warriors in the three important articles of (1) their diet, (2) their habitations, and (3) their exercises. The corn, or even the rice, which constitutes the ordinary and wholesome food of a civilized people, can be obtained only by the patient toil of the husbandman. Some of the happy savages who dwell between the tropics are plentifully nourished by the liberality of Nature; but in the climates of the North a nation of shepherds is reduced to their flocks and herds. The skilful practitioners of the medical art will determine (if they are able to determine) how far the temper of the human mind may be affected by the use of animal or of vegetable food; and whether the common association of carnivorous and cruel deserves to be considered in any other light than that of an innocent, *perhaps a salutary*, prejudice of humanity. Yet, if it be true that the sentiment of compassion is imperceptibly weakened by the sight and practice of domestic cruelty, we may observe that the horrid objects which are disguised by the arts of European refinement are exhibited in their naked and most disgusting simplicity in the tent of a Tartar shepherd. The Oxen or the Sheep are slaughtered by the same hand from which they were accustomed to receive their daily food, and the bleeding limbs are served, with very little preparation, on the tables of their unfeeling murderers.

History of the Decline and Fall of the Roman Empire

JOAN GILBERT, 1931–

Every civilizing step in history has been ridiculed as 'sentimental', 'impractical', 'womanish', etc., by those whose fun, profit or convenience was at stake.

We are all fortunate that contempt has never been able to squelch the more admirable human qualities … sensitivity to injustice, sympathy with suffering, protectiveness toward the helpless, recognition of wider and wider kinships. These feelings have been behind every compassionate crusade the world has ever seen. Mankind continues to become gradually less cruel because a few people in every generation keep saying, 'This just isn't right. It hurts me to see it.'

Letter in American Horseman

… if it is worse to eat your parents than strangers, and worse to eat people than animals, then logic would also give higher status to those animals who have known a one-to-one relationship with man. We owe something extra to animals who have given up their natural life for us, endured misfortune because of our ignorance or indifference, learned to trust to us for everything and, in spite of it all, often developed affection for us.

Ibid.

THOMAS GISBORNE, 1758–1846

From *The Worm*

Let them enjoy their little day,
Their humble bliss receive;
O, do not lightly take away
The life thou canst not give.

GEORGE GISSING, 1857–1903

I remember once, when I let fall a remark on the subject of horse-racing among friends chatting together, I was voted 'morose'. Is it really morose to object to public gatherings which their own promoters declare to be dangerous for all decent folk? Everyone knows that horse-racing is carried on mainly for the delight and profit of fools, ruffians and thieves. That intelligent men allow themselves to take part in the affair, and defend their conduct by declaring that their presence 'maintains the character of a sport essentially noble', merely shows that intelligence can easily enough divest itself of sense and decency.

The Private Papers of Henry Ryecroft

I hate and fear Science because of my conviction that, for long to come if not for ever, it will be the remorseless enemy of mankind. I see it destroying all simplicity and gentleness of life, all the beauty of the world; I see it restoring barbarism under the mask of civilization; I see it darkening men's minds and hardening their hearts; I see it bringing a time of vast conflicts, which will pale into insignificance 'the thousand wars of old', and as likely as not, will whelm the laborious advances of mankind in bloodstained chaos.

Ibid.

ROBERT GITTINGS, 1911–

The Great Moth

Visitant to our dumbly human home,
Dull coal or shrivelled leaf, the great moth lay,
Out of storm-wet October come,
The window's lashing spray.

Strange confidant, the legs that crooked my finger
Settled like truth, though little I had to give,
Knowing how short such breath-spans linger,
How brief the creatures live.

Yet wishing to offer the slightest goodwill gesture,
Placed with free hand a bowl of honeysuckle near,
And sudden as a charm, the charred vesture
Was shed: a tremble like a tear

Shook the rose-barred body and vibrant wings,
Delight stood quivering in violent, delicate spread.
Above the sweetly-scented springs
Of life, it arose from the dead

Triumphant: and not one of us, bending over,
But felt the catch of hope and courage of heart,
As if with plumes of grace to hover
A spirit took our part.

ELLEN GLASGOW, 1874–1945

Then in the midst of my earnest play, I hear a scream of pain, a sound of stones flung and falling, the heavy tread of feet running. Down the middle of the street, coming toward me through the sun and dust, a large black dog flees in terror. The dog passes me; he hesitates. He turns his head and looks at me, and he flees on. The men and boys shout. I rush into the street. My mammy and the strange nurse rush after me. Mammy reaches me first. She swoops down and gathers me up into her arms. But I have seen what it means to be hunted. I run on with the black dog. I am chased … I am beaten with clubs and caught in a net. I am seized and dragged away to something unseen and frightful. 'Hush, Baby,' Mammy pleads with me. 'Hush, my baby.' But I cannot hush. I have felt cruelty, and I shall never forget. Something deep down in me has, for the first time, awakened, something with a passionate, tormented hatred of merciless strength, with a heartbreaking pity for the abused and inarticulate, for all the helpless victims of life, everywhere …

... every tree near our house had a name of its own and a special identity. This was the beginning of my love for natural things, for earth and sky, for roads and fields and woods, for trees and grass and flowers; a love which has been second only to my sense of enduring kinship with birds and animals, and all inarticulate creatures.

The things I feared were not in the sky, but in the nature and in the touch of humanity. The cruelty of children ... the blindness of the unpitiful – these were my terrors. But not the crash of thunder overhead, not the bolts of fire from the clouds.

... this rage – I have never forgotten it – contained every anger, every revolt I had ever felt in my life – the way I felt when I saw the black dog hunted, the way I felt when I watched old Uncle Henry taken away to the almshouse, the way I felt whenever I had seen people or animals hurt for the pleasure or profit of others ...

I hated the things they believed in, the things they so innocently and charmingly pretended. I hated the sanctimonious piety that let people hurt helpless creatures. I hated the prayers and the hymns – the fountains and the red images that coloured their drab music, the fountains filled with blood, the sacrifice of the lamb.

... there is never a time when God or man, or the god invented by man, requires a libation of cruelty.

The Woman Within

A Creed

In fellowship of living things,
    In kindred claims of Man and Beast,
In common courtesy that brings
    Help from the greater to the least,
In love that all life shall receive,
    Lord, I believe.

JEAN ANTOINE GLEÏZÈS, 1773–1843

What most strikes the observer when he throws an attentive glance over the earth, is the *relative* inferiority of man, considered as what he is, in regard to what he ought to be: it is the feebleness of the work compared with the aptitude of the workman. Many of his inspirations are good, and most of his actions bad; and it is to this strange fact that must be attributed, without doubt, the universal contempt that man exhibits towards his fellows ... We must remount to the source, and see if there is not in man's existence some essential act which, reflecting itself on all the rest, would communicate to them its fatal influence. Let us consider, above everything, the *distinctive* quality of man – that which raises him above all other beings. It is clear that it is Pity. His utter failure to exhibit this feeling of pity towards his humble fellow-being, as well as to his own kind, engages us to inquire what is the *permanent* cause of such failure; and we find it, at first, in that unhappy facility with which man receives his *impressions* of the beings by whom he is surrounded. These impressions, transmitted with life and cemented by habit, have formed a creation apart and separate from himself, which is consequently beyond the domain of his conscience, or, if you prefer it, of the ordinary jurisprudence of men. Thus men continue to accuse themselves of being unjust, violent, cruel and treacherous to one another, but they do not accuse themselves of cutting the throats of other animals and of feeding upon their mangled limbs, which, nevertheless, is the chief cause of that injustice, of that violence, of that cruelty, and of that treachery ...

It is thus that many Europeans, whom their destiny conducts to the cannibal countries, after some months of sojourn with the natives, make no difficulty in seating themselves at their banquet, and of sharing their horrible repast, which at first had excited their horror and disgust. They begin with devouring a dog: from the dog to the man the space is soon cleared.

Men believe themselves to be just provided that they fulfil, in regard to their fellows, the duties which have been prescribed to them. But it is goodness which is the justice of man; and it is impossible, I repeat it, to be good towards one's fellows without being so towards other beings. Let us not be the dupes of appearances. Seneca, who lived only on the herbs of his garden, to which he owed those last gleams of philosophy which enlightened, so to speak, the fall of the Roman Empire, holds that crime cannot be circumscribed; *Nullum intra se manet vitium*. And if, as Ovid affirms, the sword struck men only after having first been dyed in the blood of the lower animals, what interest have we not in respecting such a barrier? Like Aeolus, who held in his hands the bag in which the winds were confined, we may at our will, according as we live upon plants or upon animals, tranquillize the earth or excite terrible tempests upon it.

Thalysie: ou La Nouvelle Existence

It is essentially that lightness of mind, or, rather, that sort of stupidity, which makes all reflection upon anything which is opposed to their habits, painful to the generality of mankind. They would turn their head aside with horror, if they saw what a single one of their repasts costs Nature. They eat animals as some amongst them launch a bomb into the midst of a besieged town, without thinking of the evils which it must bring into a crowd of individuals, strangers to war – women, children, and old men – evils the near spectacle of which they could not support, in spite of the hardness of their hearts … Today, when everything is calculated with so much precision, there will not be wanting persons with sufficient assurance to attempt to prove that there is more of advantage for the domesticated animals to be born and live, on condition of having their throats cut, than if they had remained in 'nothingness', or in the natural state. As for the word 'nothingness', I confess that I do not understand it, but I understand the other very well; and I have never conceived how man could have had the barbarity to accumulate every torture upon his helpless victims. But if he thinks himself to escape from the influence of actions so dastardly and so infamous, he is in a very great error …

I have known a large number of good souls who offered up the most sincere wishes for the establishment of this doctrine of humaneness, who thought it just and true in all its aspects, who believed in all that it announces; but who, in spite of so praiseworthy a disposition, dared not be the first to give the example. They awaited this movement from minds stronger than their own. Doubtless such are the minds which give the impulse to the world; but is it necessary to await this movement when one is convinced of one's self? Is it permissible to temporize in a question of agony and torture for innocent beings whose sole crime is *to have been born*? No! Well-doing is not so difficult. Ah! What is your excuse, besides, pusillanimous souls? I blush for you at the miserable pretexts which keep you back. It would be necessary, say you, to separate one's self from the world; to renounce one's friends and neighbours. I see no such necessity, and I think, on the contrary, that if you truly loved the world and your neighbours, you would hasten to give them an example which must have so powerful an influence upon their present happiness and upon their future destiny.

Ibid.

151

ROSLIND GODLOVITCH, 1944–

If we hold genuine moral principles about animals, these will not differ in substance from those we hold about human beings ... If humans have natural rights, then so do animals.

Animals, Men and Morals

STANLEY GODLOVITCH, 1947–

Once one accepts that there is something essentially different between a dog chasing after a stick and a stone plummeting to earth, then one will have a hard time in morally justifying, for example, why a healthy dog is given lung cancer with tobacco smoke in order to prove something to a suicidal human who smokes forty cigarettes a day.

Animals, Men and Morals

MARK GOLD, 1952–

There is no prospect of reversing current trends until it is acknowledged that animals are primarily sensitive creatures with individual needs rather than products on a plate, statistics on a graph, tools for research, or cogs in a machine for converting grain to flesh.

Assault and Battery

When taken to extremes, such as attributing human moral values or appreciation of beauty to animals, [anthropomorphism] can obviously become as ridiculous as the scientific experts would have us believe. On the other hand, many of what we like to think of as human characteristics clearly do exist in farm animals. Observation of a group of calves or young pigs in a field cannot fail to show behaviour comparable to that of young children – boundless energy one moment, fast asleep the next, a sense of fun and adventure, curiosity in what goes on around them, mischievousness, a close bond with their parents and enjoyment in the companionship of their own species. None of these qualities can be proved by scientific experiments, but they are still facts. While anthropomorphism admittedly cannot give us an exact assessment of the needs and experiences of animals, it is, nevertheless, basically the best method available to us. As we are human beings and not pigs, cows or chickens, we have only human feelings and thoughts on which to base our decisions. To try and exclude these or to imagine that through some completely objective scientific discovery we can produce 'conclusive evidence', is to deny all the qualities by which we create any worthwhile human values. In a real sense it is to become subhuman.

Ibid.

OLIVER GOLDSMITH, 1728–1774

The Hermit

Then turn to-night, and freely share
　　Whate'er my cell bestows,
My rushy couch and frugal fare,
　　My blessing and repose.

No flocks that range the valley free,
　　To slaughter I condemn;
Taught by the power that pities me,
　　I learn to pity them.

But from the mountain's grassy side,
　　A guiltless feast I bring,
A scrip with herbs and fruit supplied,
　　And water from the spring.

> Then, pilgrim, turn, thy cares forego,
>   All earth-born cares are wrong;
> Man wants but little here below,
>   Nor wants that little long.

The better sort here pretend to the utmost compassion for animals of every kind; to hear them speak, a stranger would be apt to imagine they could hardly hurt the gnat that stung them. They seem so tender, and so full of pity, that one would take them for the harmless friends of the whole creation, the protectors of the meanest insect or reptile that was privileged with existence. And yet (would you believe it?) I have seen the very men who have thus boasted of their tenderness, at the same time devour the flesh of six different animals, tossed up in a fricassee. Strange contrariety of conduct. They pity, and they eat the objects of their compassion ...

Man was born to live with innocence and simplicity, but he has deviated from nature; he was born to share the bounties of heaven, but he has monopolized them; he was born to govern the 'brute creation', but he has become their tyrant. Hail, O ye simple, honest Brahmins of the East! Ye inoffensive friends of all that were born to happiness as well as you! You never sought a short-lived pleasure from the miseries of other creatures! You never studied the tormenting arts of ingenious refinement; you never surfeited upon a guilty meal! How much more purified and refined are all your sensations than ours!

Letter to the Public Ledger, No. xv

SIR VICTOR GOLLANCZ, 1893–1967

I think the rapidly growing tendency to regard animals as born for nothing except slavery to so-called humanity absolutely disgusting.

The Unlived Life

LEWIS GOMPERTZ, 1779–1861

The dreadful situation of the brute creation, particularly of those which have been domesticated, claims our strictest attention ...

Who can dispute the inhumanity of the sport of hunting – of pursuing a poor defenceless creature for mere amusement, till it becomes exhausted by terror and fatigue, and of then causing it to be torn to pieces by a pack of dogs? From what kind of instruction can men, and even women, imbibe such principles as these? How is it possible they can justify it? And what can their pleasure in it consist of? Is it not solely in the agony they produce to the animal? They will pretend that it is not and try to make us believe so too – that it is merely in the pursuit. But what is the object of their pursuit? Is there any other than to torment and destroy?

Moral Inquiries on the Situation of Man and of Brutes

It seems that the crime of cruelty proceeds greatly from improper education. Subjects of moral inquiry are too often chased from the attention of youth, from a false idea that they are mere chimeras too difficult to enter into, that they only serve to confound us and to lead us into disputes, which never come to a conclusion; that they cause us to fall into eccentricities, and unfit us for all the offices of life, and at last drive us into downright madness.

Forbid it that we should give assent to such tenets as these! That we should suffer for one moment our reason to be veiled by such delusions! But on the contrary let us hold fast every idea, and cherish every glimmering of such kind of knowledge, as that which shall enable us to distinguish between *right* and *wrong*, what is due to one individual – what to another.

Ibid.

JANE (Van Lawick-) GOODALL, 1934–

The zoo chimp has none of the calm dignity, the serenity of gaze or the purposeful individuality of his wild counterpart. Typically, he develops odd stereotypes in his behaviour – as he walks he may give one hand a slight rotation to the side, always the same hand, always the same side ... Most people are only familiar with the zoo or the laboratory chimpanzee. This means that even those who work closely with chimpanzees, such as zoo-keepers or research scientists, can have no concept or appreciation of what a chimpanzee really *is*. Which is, perhaps, why so many scientific laboratories maintain chimpanzees in conditions which are appalling, housed singly for the most part in small concrete cells with nothing to do day in and day out except to await some new – and often terrifying or painful – experiment.

In the Shadow of Man

EVA GORE-BOOTH, 1870–1926

Life

For God's sake, kill not: Spirit that is breath
With Life the earth's gray dust irradiates;
That which has neither part nor lot with death
Deep in the smallest rabbit's heart vibrates.
Of God we know naught, save three acts of will:
Love that vibrates in every breathing form,
Truth that looks out over the window sill,
And Love that is calling us home out of the storm.

ELIZABETH GOUDGE, 1900–1984

Nothing living should ever be treated with contempt. Whatever it is that lives, a man, a tree, or a bird, should be touched gently, because the time is short.

Civilization is another word for respect for life ...

The Joy of the Snow

JAMES GRAHAME, 1765–1811

The Bleeding Hand

When snowdrops die, and the green primrose leaves
Announce the coming flower, the *Merles* note,
Mellifluous, rich, deep-toned, fills all the vale,
And charms the ravished air. The hawthorn bush
New-budded is his perch; there the gray dawn
He hails; and there, with parting light, concludes
His melody. There, when the buds begin
To break, he lays the fibrous roots; the clay
His jetty breast has soiled ...

        The nest complete
His partner, and his helper in his work,
Happy, assumes possession of her home;
While he upon a neighbouring tree, his lay
More richly full melodiously renews ...

Alas! Not long the parents' partial eye
Shall view the fledgling wing; ne'er shall they see
The timorous pinion's first essay at flight.
The truant school-boy's eager, bleeding hand,
Their house, their all, tears from the tending bush;
A shower of blossoms mourns the ruthless deed!

REVD JAMES GRANGER, 1723–1776

How often is [the horse] whipped, spurred, battered and starved to death? What a piteous spectacle is his lean, hide-bound, scarred and maimed carcass, thus miserably disfigured by man, before he is dismembered and devoured by dogs ... It hath been observed that there is no country upon the face of the earth that is not totally sunk in barbarism where this beast is so ill-treated as it is in our own; hence England is proverbially 'the Hell of Horses'. Our humanity hath also with great appearance of reason been called in question by foreigners on account of our barbarous customs of baiting and worrying animals and especially that cruel and infamous sport still practised among us on Shrove Tuesday. But this character of cruelty, which is hardly to be equalled among savages ... is only applicable to the most stupid, ignorant and uncivilized of our countrymen. Those of higher rank and knowledge are far more humane and benevolent than those that endeavour to fix so ignominious a reproach upon the body of the people.

Sermon at Shiplake, Oxon, 18 October 1772

GEORGE GRANVILLE (Lord Lansdowne), 1667–1735

The Boar

A boar who had enjoyed a happy span
For many a year and fed on many a man,
Called to account, softening his savage eyes,
Thus suppliant pleads his cause before he dies:
'For what am I condemned? My crimes no more
To eat a man than yours to eat a boar.
We seek not you, but take what chance provides,
Nature and mere necessity our guides:
You murder us in sport, then dish us up
For drunken feats, a relish for the cup.
We lengthen not our meals: but you much feast;
Gorge till your bellies burst – pray, who's the beast?
With your humanity you keep a fuss,
But are in truth worse brutes than all of us.'

THE GREENPEACE PHILOSOPHY

... the simple word 'ecology' embodies a concept that is as revolutionary as the Copernican breakthrough. As suddenly as Copernicus taught us that the earth was not the centre of the universe, ecology teaches us that mankind is not the centre of life on this planet. Ecology has taught us that the entire earth is part of our body and that we must learn to respect it as we respect ourselves. As we feel for ourselves, we must feel for all forms of life ... the whales, the seals, the forests, the seas ... The tremendous beauty of ecological thought is that it shows us a pathway back to an understanding and an appreciation of life itself.

Newsletter

SIR WILFRED GRENFELL, 1865–1940

Kindness to all God's creatures is an absolute rock-bottom necessity if peace and righteousness are to prevail.

The Adventure of Life

GREY OWL (Archibald Belaney), 1888–1938

[The keeper] remembered that a beaver may live more than twenty years – twenty years in that prison of iron and concrete! In twenty years his own family would be grown up and away from there; he himself might be gone. The town would have become a great city (it was not really a very big place); people would come and go – free people, happy people – and through it all, this unhappy little beast, who had done no harm to anyone, and seemed only to want someone to be kind to him, would, for twenty long and lonely years, look out through the bars of that wretched pen as though he had

159

been some violent criminal; waiting for the freedom that would never be his, waiting only to die at last. And, thought the keeper, for no good reason at all, except that a few thoughtless people, who never really cared if they ever saw a beaver, might stare for a minute or two at the disconsolate little prisoner, and then go away and forget they had ever seen him.

The Adventures of Sajo and her Beaver People

JOHN EDWARD POYNDER GRIGG (Lord Altrincham), 1924–

The various Christian orthodoxies attribute a 'soul' to the human animal which separates him fundamentally from the brute creation. There is some evidence, however, that English Christians are embarrassed by a doctrine of Apartheid which excludes dumb friends from the grace and the hope of glory.

There is no doubt whatever that many persons are not being taken in by all those who say that the animals have not a soul. Anyone looking into the soulful eyes of a dog should be in no doubt that if a human has one, then other animals cannot be placed as soulless.

The alleged dumbness of animals is much exaggerated. What we mean when we call them dumb is that their utterances are less articulate than ours. Their language is purely intuitive, whereas ours is apparently the expression, as well as the product, of reason. In fact, most human beings 'think' with their instincts, and their words are no more rational in essence than a dog's bark or a bird's cheep.

Animal Guardian, April/May 1962

BART GRUZALSKI, 1942–

Everything we have learned about animals suggests that in terms of experiencing terror, pain, grief, anxiety and stress these sentient beings are relevantly similar to humans. It is reasonable to believe that our knowledge of the quality of human dying will also tell us something about the dying process of other animals. For humans, the most horrible deaths involve terror. When this factor is not present, and especially when the process of dying is not unexpected for the dying person, dying can be peaceful. From this minimal observation about human dying and the observation that domestic animals are typically slaughtered in circumstances that are unfamiliar and terrifying for the animals, it follows that the experience of being slaughtered is no worse for these animals than the worst deaths experienced in the wild and significantly worse than the deaths of wild animals that die from disease or old age in familiar and unterrifying surroundings. In addition, because the life of an adult animal raised for food is much shorter than the life of a similar animal in the wild, there will be more dyings per total adult population among these animals than among wild animals of similar species. Hence, both in quantity and quality of deaths, rearing animals for food produces a great deal of death-related anguish and terror that is directly a consequence of humans using them for food.

'The Case Against Raising And Killing Animals For Food' from *Ethics and Animals*, eds. Miller and Williams

EDGAR A. GUEST, 1881–1959

Obligation

They cannot ask for kindness
Or for mercy plead,
Yet cruel is our blindness

> Which does not see their need.
> World-over, town or city,
> God trusts us with this task:
> To give our love and pity
> To those who cannot ask.

JOSEPH JOHN GURNEY, 1788–1847

We clearly rank the practice of hunting and shooting for diversion, with vain sports; and we believe the awakened mind may see that even the leisure of those whom Providence hath permitted to have a competence for worldly goods, is but ill filled up with these amusements. Therefore, being not only accountable for our substance, but also for our time, let our leisure be employed in serving our neighbour and not in distressing the creatures of God for our amusement.

Observations (quoting from an earlier
Quaker book, *Book of Extracts*)

WALTER ROBERT HADWEN, JP, MD, LRCP, MRCS, LSA, 1854–1932

The practice of the vivisection of living animals stands condemned by its very inhumanity. It is impossible for a thoughtful mind to conceive that a well-ordered universe demands the infliction of physical pain and suffering upon one portion of its sentient inhabitants in order to bring blessing upon another portion. Such a claim implies an idea of justice that is foreign to a religious conception of its meaning. The fact that intellectual and educated men are engaged in this pursuit is no evidence of its rightfulness and value. Intellectual and educated men have been guilty of the greatest crimes in history. The iniquity of the procedure is aggravated by the fact that expedience has demonstrated its inutility, inasmuch as, conclusions derived from the torture of the one have invariably failed to solve problems in relation to the other. The anatomical and physiological differences in the two classes have proved fatal to scientific deductions. Hence, failure and disaster, disease and death, due to misleading results from vivisection have strewn the whole course of this horrible practice during its long, black history of twenty centuries.

Letter to Mrs C.P. Farrell, 28 January 1923

H. FIELDING HALL, 1859–1917

To him [the Burmese] men are men, and animals are animals, and men are far the higher. But he does not deduce from this that man's superiority gives him permission to ill-treat or kill animals. It is just the reverse. It is because man is so much higher than the animals that he can and must observe towards animals the very greatest care, feel for them the very greatest compassion, be good to them in every way he can. The Burmese's motto should be *noblesse oblige*. He knows the meaning, if he knows not the words.

The Soul of a People

REBECCA HALL, 1947–

Cows

The cows graze in the field beside this house.
Gentle friends, I wish them the right to a natural death
In dignified old age.

Yesterday I saw a farmer who looked just like a cow,
But ugly for being human;
His poor, thick, red head stood out fatly,
His slow movements bespoke ponderous thoughts.

Later we talked of cows' heads offered by butchers:
I wonder if dogs would tear at his boiled head?
Or if fussy English people would relish
His nicely boiled and compressed pink tongue
Between slices of white bread
For tea on the lawn?

And if they did, would they know the difference?
And if they did, would they, finally, care?

We cannot talk with [animals] as we can with human
beings, yet we can communicate with them on mental and
emotional levels. They should, however, be accorded
equality in that they should receive both compassion and
respect; it is unworthy of us to exploit them in any way.

Animals are Equal

TOM T. HALL, 1936–

My major concern is to get the point across that kindness
to animals isn't just a one-week affair. Kindness is a
day-in and day-out thing. It's a year-round thing. And
for me, it's part of a greater concern, namely a concern
with what's happening to the whole environment.
Kindness itself is part and parcel of dealing right with the
earth we are on. We must do everything possible to
maintain our environment and to rid it of cruelties of all
kinds. I want to get this message across, especially to the
kids; we must be responsible for this earth and for the life
we find on it.

Syndicated newspaper interview

HAMBURG ORDINANCE

Cruelty to animals undermines the foundations of morality and should be restrained by a definite law. Unfortunately, it cannot be denied that this evil is abroad among us. We see it daily before our eyes in various forms: in the nefarious and heartless mistreatment of horses, and of cattle for slaughter; in coarse viciousness towards domestic animals; in the cruelties which children are permitted to inflict upon all sorts of creatures without reprimand from their criminally indifferent parents – and indeed even in many truly inhuman experiments upon living animals made in connection with scientific investigations in themselves of no importance.

Issued by the Town Council in 1825

RUDOLPH HAMMER, MD, LLD, 1886–1949

Vivisection has done little for the art of the doctor at the bedside, but it has done immeasurable harm to the character and mind of the rising generation of doctors. The physician should be a man of kindness; sometimes his position may even have to be almost that of a priest; therefore, his hands should remain clean from all the unspeakable horrors which are allowed to be practised in the name of science. Culture and humanity can never be furthered by barbarism.

Vienna, 5 October 1909, quoted in
The Anti-Vivisection Review, January/March 1914

OTOMAN ZAR-ADUSHT HA'NISH,
MD, DD, 1844–1936

It is strange to hear people talk of Humanitarianism, who are members of societies for the prevention of cruelty to children and animals, and who claim to be God-loving

165

men and women, but who, nevertheless, encourage by their patronage the killing of animals merely to gratify the cravings of appetite.

Mazdaznan Science of Dietetics

Because certain animals live upon their prey, it does not prove that one has a right to eat them in turn, any more than a man has a right to prey upon his neighbours. The animal kingdom must be redeemed by the life of the higher and nobler species, not by eating the animals, but by loving them and recognizing in them the reflection of our own ideas and ideals, which in their case have not yet been completely developed.

Ibid.

SIR ALISTER HARDY, 1896–1985

I heretically think it likely that love, joy and beauty are not only generated but felt (who knows) far down in the animal world and that man alone has come to discuss and express them in words.

Darwin and the Spirit of Man

THOMAS HARDY, 1840–1928

... the cruelty that goes on under the barbarous régime we call civilization.

Letter to Florence Henneker on man's treatment of animals

The establishment of the common origin of all species logically involves a readjustment of altruistic morals, by enlarging the application of what has been called the Golden Rule from the area of mere mankind to that of the whole animal kingdom.

From a letter to *The Humanitarian*, 1910

The discovery of the law of evolution, which revealed that all organic creatures are of one family, shifted the centre of altruism from humanity to the whole conscious world collectively. Therefore, the practice of vivisection has been left by that discovery without any logical argument in its favour.

Ibid.

The Darkling Thrush

I leant upon a coppice gate
    When frost was spectre-gray,
And winter's dregs made desolate
    The weakening eye of day.
The tangled bine-stems scored the sky
    Like strings of broken lyres,
And all mankind that haunted nigh
    Had sought their household fires ...

At once a voice arose among
    The bleak twigs overhead
In a full-hearted evensong
    Of joy illimited;
An aged thrush, frail, gaunt, and small,
    In blast-beruffled plume,
Had chosen thus to fling his soul
    Upon the growing gloom.

So little cause for carollings
    Of such ecstatic sound
Was written on terrestrial things
    Afar or nigh around,
That I could think there trembled through
    His happy goodnight air
Some blessed Hope, whereof he knew
    And I was unaware.

The Blinded Bird

So zestfully canst thou sing?
And all this indignity,
With God's consent, on thee!
Blinded ere yet a-wing
By the red-hot needle thou,
I stand and wonder how
So zestfully thou canst sing!

Resenting not such wrong,
Thy grievous pain forgot,
Eternal dark thy lot,
Groping thy whole life long,
After that stab of fire!
Enjailed in pitiless wire;
Resenting not such wrong!

Who hath charity? This bird.
Who suffereth long and is kind,
Is not provoked, though blind
And alive ensepulchred?
Who hopeth, endureth all things?
Who thinketh no evil, but sings?
Who is divine? This bird.

JOHN HARRIS, 1946–

Suppose that tomorrow a group of beings from another planet were to land on Earth, beings who considered themselves as superior to you as you feel yourself to be to other animals. Would they have the right to treat you as you treat the animals you breed, keep and kill for food?

Animals, Men and Morals

The vast majority of those who eat meat never consider its rights and wrongs; society condones it, and that is sufficient reason to think no further. So it is the vegetarian who is called upon to explain his odd behaviour, and not those who support the unnecessary slaughter that meat-eating requires. It requires very little moral sense to realize that the taking of life is an important matter, yet for most people the choice between a nut cutlet and a beefsteak is about as important as that between chipped and boiled potatoes; a matter of taste, not morality.

Ibid.

... philosophizing and campaigning still have an important place in guiding public opinion, and you will not be very successful if you do not practise what you preach. No one can claim to have a genuine interest in the welfare of animals if they continue to condone their unnecessary slaughter – not, at any rate, without being accused of hypocrisy. To continue to eat the object of your concern is a stunning piece of self-deception.

Animals' Rights: a Symposium

RUTH HARRISON, 1920–

That animals are sensitive to pain and discomfort is obvious from the fact that in the higher animals the sensory and nervous systems are similar to those of man. An animal of higher intelligence would have a greater span of memory and sense of anticipation and therefore suffer more acutely than less highly developed species, but the initial pain felt would be experienced equally by both.

Animal Machines

It is worth noticing [in the *Protection of Animals Act* 1911] that cruelty is never defined as an absolute quality; there is plenty of scope for interpretation in the Act. What strikes one forcibly is also the reluctance to define cruelty in relation to animals reared and killed for meat. In fact if one person is unkind to an animal it is considered to be cruelty, but where a lot of people are unkind to animals, especially in the name of commerce, the cruelty is condoned and, once large sums of money are at stake, will be defended to the last by otherwise intelligent people.

Ibid.

The first instinct the farmer frustrates in all animals except pigs, is that of the new born animal turning to its mother for protection and comfort and, in some cases, for food. The chick comes out of the incubator and never sees a hen; the calf which is to be fattened for veal or beef is taken from the cow at birth, or very soon after; and even the piglet is weaned far earlier now than it used to be. The factors controlling this are mainly economic.

Ibid.

It is time we faced the facts and acknowledged the more subtle and insidious forms of suffering now being inflicted on our animals and carried to a degree which could not possibly have been envisaged by the enactors of the 1911 Act. It would seem to me to be taking our domination of the animal world beyond moral limits to cause ill health to an animal simply to produce pale flesh, the only attribute of which is the fulfilment of a snob requirement. Veal calf producers talk readily enough of cruelty, even admit that some of their methods are inhumane, but offer you flimsy excuse that they are only producing *what the public wants*. We must cease to pander to an unenlightened public. We have laws to punish perverted and ignorant children who torture animals because it gives them pleasure; it is time we applied these laws to causing suffering to animals because their carcasses then are said to tickle our palates.

Ibid.

It is a sobering thought that animals could do without man, yet man would find it almost impossible to do without animals.

Animals, Men and Morals

Most people accept the position of eating meat only on condition that the animal has pleasure in life while it lives and is then humanely slaughtered. In no instance can these two criteria be guaranteed today. Many people have become so repulsed by the situation that they have taken the first step towards opting out of it by becoming vegetarians. I use the phrase 'first step' because much suffering is involved in the supply of dairy produce. The vegan, who attempts to eschew all animal products and by-products, takes the most logical step towards elimination of cruelty, a step to which only a very small but gallant minority have so far devoted their lives.

Ibid.

Family organization is broken and young animals are increasingly being denied a mother to turn to for comfort and for grooming. One of the saddest and most pathetic of farm practices – inevitable at the present time for the supply of dairy produce – is the separation of the calf from the cow at birth or soon after.

> Separating the calf from its mother shortly after birth undoubtedly inflicts anguish on both. Maternal care for the young is highly developed in cattle, and it is only necessary to observe the behaviour of the cow and the calf when they are separated to appreciate this. *Brambell Report.*

Ibid.

We must do all in our power to educate the public, for I believe that in the end only a change of heart is really effective.

Animals' Rights: a Symposium

BRET HARTE, 1836–1902

A bird in the hand is a certainty. But a bird in the bush may sing.

Quoted in Reader's Digest

DAVID HARTLEY, 1705–1757

With respect to animal diet, let it be considered that taking away the lives of animals, in order to convert them into food, does great violence to the principles of benevolence and compassion. This appears from the frequent hard-heartedness and cruelty found among those persons whose occupations engage them in destroying animal life, as well as from the uneasiness which others feel in beholding the butchery of animals. It is most evident in respect to the larger animals and those with whom we have a familiar intercourse – such as oxen, sheep, and domestic fowls, etc. – so as to distinguish, love and compassionate individuals. They resemble us greatly in the make of the body, in general, and in that of the particular organs of circulation, respiration, digestion, etc.; also in the formation of their intellects, memories and passions, and in the signs of distress, fear, pain and death. They often, likewise, win our affections by the marks of peculiar sagacity, by their instincts, helplessness, innocence, nascent benevolence, etc., and, if there be any glimmering hope of an 'hereafter' for them – if they should prove to be our brethren and sisters in this higher sense – in immortality as well as mortality, in the permanent principle of our minds as well as in the frail dust of our bodies – this ought to be still further reason for tenderness for them.

Observations on Man

PAUL HARVEY, 1918–

Ever occur to you why some of us can be this much concerned with animals suffering? Because government is not. Why not? Animals don't vote.

From his syndicated column, January 1981

Many hunters talk about their mutuality of respect for wildlife. That's always sounded to me like phoney-baloney, else they would take on the big game hand-to-hand instead of with huge guns with scope sights ... As to the argument that nature in the raw is cruel – of course it is! Animals can indeed be cruel to one another. *But we are supposed to be something more than they!* Dickensian compassion rescued children from sweat shops. Lincolnian empathy rescued slaves from being 'things'. Civilization weeps while it awaits one more emancipation.

Ibid., November 1981

NATHANIEL HAWTHORNE, 1804–1864

A ride to Brighton yesterday morning, it being the day of the weekly cattle fair. William Allen and myself went in a wagon, carrying a calf, to be sold at the fair. The calf had not had his breakfast, as his mother had preceded him to Brighton; and he kept expressing his hunger and discomfort by loud, sonorous baas, especially when we passed any cattle in the fields or on the road. The cows grazing within hearing expressed great interest, and some of them came galloping to the roadside to behold the calf ... He was a prettily behaved urchin and kept thrusting his hairy muzzle between William and myself, apparently wishing to be stroked and petted. It was an ugly thought, that his confidence in human nature, and Nature in general, was to be so ill rewarded as by cutting his throat and selling him in quarters. This, I suppose, has been his fate before now.

The American Notebooks

... and we have so far improved upon the custom of Adam and Eve, that we generally furnish forth our feasts with a portion of some delicate calf or lamb, whose unspotted innocence entitles them to the happiness of becoming our sustenance.

Ibid.

PHILIPPE HECQUET, 1661–1737

It is incredible how much prejudice has been allowed to operate in favour of [flesh] meat, while so many facts are opposed to the pretended necessity of its use.

Treatise on Dispensations

CARDINAL HEENAN, 1905–1975

When I was young I often heard quoted a piece of Christian philosophy which was taken as self-evidently true. It was the proposition that animals have no rights. This, of course, is true only in one sense. They are not human persons and therefore they have no rights, so to speak, in their own right. But they have very positive rights because they are God's creatures. If we have to speak with absolute accuracy we must say that God has the right to have all his creatures treated with proper respect.

Nobody should therefore carelessly repeat the old saying that animals have no rights. This could easily lead to wanton cruelty. I speak of wanton cruelty because only the perverted are guilty of deliberate cruelty to animals or, indeed, to children. The difficulty is that many people

174

do not realise the extent to which cruelty to animals is practised as a matter of business ... It was once pointed out to me that the catechism had no question about cruelty to animals. This was true, but in giving lessons on Christian doctrine teachers now include the subject of cruelty to animals. The best and most experienced teachers do not, of course, talk of cruelty to animals. They talk of kindness to animals. Christians have a duty not only to refrain from doing harm, but also to do positive good.

Foreword to Ambrose Agius, *God's Animals*

ALICE HEIM, 1913–

The work on 'animal behaviour' is always expressed in scientific sounding terminology, which enables the indoctrination of the normal, non-sadistic young psychology student to proceed without his anxiety being aroused. Thus techniques of 'extinction' are used for what is in fact torturing by thirst or near-starvation or electric-shocking; 'partial reinforcement' is the term for frustrating an animal by only occasionally fulfilling the expectations which the experimenter has aroused in the animal by previous training, 'negative stimulus' is the term used for subjecting an animal to a stimulus which he avoids, if possible. The term 'avoidance' is O.K. because it is an observable activity. The terms 'painful' or 'frightening' stimulus are less O.K. since they are anthropomorphic, they imply that the animal has feelings – and that these may be similar to human feelings. This is not allowable because it is non-behaviouristic and unscientific (and also because this might deter the younger and less hard-boiled researcher from pursuing certain ingenious experiments. He might allow a little play to his imagination). The cardinal sin for the experimental psychologist working in the field of 'animal behaviour' is anthropomorphism. Yet if he did not believe in the analogue of the human being and the lower animal even he, presumably, would find his work largely unjustified.

Intelligence and Personality

JAMES HERRIOT, 1916–

I hope to make people realize how totally helpless animals are, how dependent on us, trusting as a child must that we will be kind and take care of their needs ... [They] are an obligation put on us, a responsibility we have no right to neglect, nor to violate by cruelty.

In a television interview

I have no patience with people who get angry with animals ... it's stupid to see a man lose his temper with an animal ... they know things we don't know, that's for sure ... I wish people would realize that animals are totally dependent on us, helpless, like children, a trust that is put upon us ... I could do terrible things to people who dump unwanted animals by the roadside.

From a television interview on 'Today', 1978

HESIOD, *c*. 8th century B.C.

Strong with the ashen spear, and fierce and bold,
Their thoughts were bent on violence alone.
The deed of battle, and the dying groan.
Bloody their feasts, with wheaten food unblessed.

Works and Days

RONALD HIGGINS, 1929–

Science operates with spotlight, knife, needle and forceps. Its characteristic focus is sharp; its techniques are division, separation, dissection, simplification, reduction, measurement. Its manner is fearless, intrusive, icily objective. The dedication to the disciplines of empirical evidence and the hunger for discovery are so intense that the purposes served are often overlooked. How else can scientists bring themselves to rot the eyes of rabbits with poison gases; force beagles to chainsmoke; reverse the eyes of kittens or graft additional limbs or heads on to dogs? How else could a (woman) scientist get a prize for a chemical to destroy rice crops? It is all for truth of a kind, just as it is for efficiency of a kind that technologists devise anti-personnel weapons that will implant metal fragments too deep for surgery.

Such scandals ... illustrate not only how science cannot in practice be morally neutral, but how easily its disinterested objectivity can destroy a more reverent awareness of the observed. As a tool, objective reason is essential. As a disguised metaphysic, often unconscious and always illegitimate, it ignores or denies every level of reality that it cannot itself pin down and manipulate. It sees nothing in a rainbow that is not applied optics, and little in Helen of Troy that cannot be dissected on the anatomist's slab.

In contrast there is the subjective mode of knowing, visionary awareness, the mode of the poet, artist, composer and mystic. This is intuitive rather than calculating; synoptic rather than analytic. It transcends rather than reduces. It seeks the mysterious, rich and encompassing symbol rather than the barren precision of the sign. It offers what science can never offer – knowledge *of*, not just *about*, persons. This is something which comes through direct and intimate communication between being and being; through communion, not detached observation.

The relation of being to being is the root of art, of human fellowship and of communication between man and nature. It reveals itself in the incandescence of an old boot painted by Van Gogh, in the mutual absorption of lovers, and not least in the ways of 'primitive' animists who still know the spirit of the beast, the tree, the stream and the place.

The Seventh Enemy

HINDUISM

This is the sum of duty: do naught to others which if done to thee, would cause thee pain.

Mahabharata

Non-injury, truthfulness, freedom from theft, lust, anger and greed, and an effort to do what is agreeable and beneficial to all creatures – this is the common duty of all castes.

Srimad-Bhagavatam

Good men extend their pity, even unto the most despicable animals. The moon doth not withhold the light, even from the cottage of a Chandala [outcast].

Hitopadesa

True happiness consists in making happy.

Bharavi's Kiratarjuniya

Those who have forsaken the killing of all; those who are helpmates to all; those who are a sanctuary to all; those men are in the way of heaven.

Hitopadesa

Not to kill is a supreme duty.

Ibid.

What is religion? Compassion for all things which have life. What is happiness? To animals in this world, health. What is kindness? A principle in the good. What is philosophy? An entire separation from the world.

Ibid.

Truth, self-control, asceticism, generosity, non-injury, constancy in virtue – these are the means of success, not caste or family.

Mahabharata

We bow to all beings with great reverence in the thought and knowledge that God enters into them through fractioning Himself as living creatures.

Ibid.

He who injures harmless beings from a wish to give himself pleasure, never finds happiness, neither living nor dead.

He who does not seek to cause the sufferings of bonds and death to living creatures, but desires the good of all, obtains endless bliss.

He who does not injure any creature, obtains without an effort what he thinks of, what he undertakes, and what he fixes his mind on.

Meat cannot be obtained without injury to animals, and the slaughter of animals obstructs the way to Heaven; let him therefore shun the use of meat.

Having well considered … the cruelty of fettering and slaying living beings, let him entirely abstain from eating flesh.

He who does not eat meat becomes dear to men, and will not be tormented by diseases.

He who permits the slaughter of an animal, he who kills it, he who cuts it up, he who buys or sells meat, he who cooks it, he who serves it up, and he who eats it, are all slayers.

There is no greater sinner than that man who seeks to increase the bulk of his own flesh by the flesh of other beings.

The Laws of Manu V, 45-52

CARDINAL HINSLEY, 1865–1943

Cruelty to animals is the degrading attitude of paganism.

From a sermon

RUSSELL HOBAN, 1925–

They won't stop killing the whales. They make dog- and cat-food out of them, face creams, lipstick. They kill the whales to feed the dogs so the dogs can shit on the pavement and the people can walk in it. A kind of natural cycle. Whales can navigate, echo-locate, sing, talk to one another but they can't get away from the harpoon guns. The International Whaling Commission is meeting here in London right now but they won't stop the killing of whales.

Turtle Diary

The zoo is a prison for animals who have been sentenced without trial and I feel guilty because I do nothing about it. I wanted to see an oyster-catcher, so I was no better than the people who caged the oyster-catcher for me to see.

There's nothing to be done, really, about animals. The answer isn't in us. It's almost as if we were put here on earth to show how silly they aren't. I don't mind. I just like being around them.

Ibid.

RALPH HODGSON, 1871–1962

The Bells of Heaven

'Twould ring the bells of Heaven
The wildest peals for years,
If Parson lost his senses
And people came to theirs,
And he and they together
Knelt down with angry prayers
For tamed and shabby tigers,
And dancing dogs and bears,
And wretched, blind pit-ponies
And little hunted hares.

Stupidity Street

I saw with open eyes
Singing birds sweet
Sold in the shops
For the people to eat,
Sold in the shops of
Stupidity Street.

I saw in vision
The worm in the wheat,
And in the shops nothing
For people to eat;
Nothing for sale in
Stupidity Street.

WILLIAM HOGARTH, 1697–1764

I had rather, if cruelty has been prevented by the four
prints [*The Four Stages of Cruelty*], be maker of them than
of the [Raphael] cartoons.

Apology for Painters

DAVID HOLBROOK, 1923–

What biologists like Buytendijk are trying to restore to biology is the concept of 'intrinsic worth' in the object of attention. (It is perhaps worth suggesting that this principle is hideously violated, in British education, when thousands of 'O' Level candidates are sent the dead body of a dogfish to cut up for an examination: what possible respect for life can such a biology inculcate, as the plastic bags are passed round the schools, containing creatures sacrificed for certificates?) All living creatures have an individuality, and biology must study the type in the individual.

From: *Dr John Bowlby: No need to nod to positivist dogma*

CLIVE HOLLANDS, 1929–

The Government must now act in a responsible manner to discharge the promises made to the animal welfare lobby. Legislation must offer real protection and safeguards for the welfare of animals. The price of implementing such legislation will on occasion take the form of loss of commercial profit or of higher prices. Even so, this and future governments must be bold and fearless in demonstrating that the rights of animals (and not weak and unenforceable regulations) will form the basis for legislation.

Compassion is the Bugler

I am not basically a conservationist. When the last great whale is slaughtered, as it surely will be, the whales' suffering will be over. This is not the whales' loss, but man's. I am not concerned about the wiping out of a species – this is man's folly – I have only one concern, the suffering which we deliberately inflict upon animals whilst they live.

Animals' Rights: a Symposium

182

REVD V.A. HOLMES-GORE, MA, 1909–1952

The saints who loved the creatures were not typical of Christians as a whole, and we have seen that they had no influence on Church teaching or Christian practice. In more recent times the really humanitarian movements have been unorthodox and have encountered opposition from the Church authorities. It is true that the efforts of a London vicar [the Revd Arthur Brooms] to prohibit cruel sports led to the establishment of the R.S.P.C.A., but the greatest work on behalf of anti-vivisection and vegetarianism was done by those who were considered very unorthodox. It is significant that those who championed the creatures most wholeheartedly were those who understood their real nature. The Church, on the other hand, cannot tell us who the creatures really are. The Roman Catholic Church flatly contradicts Genesis i, 24–5, by asserting that they were not created by God. Thus we read in the *Catholic Dictionary* of 1897: 'As their [the animals'] souls operate through matter so they spring from matter and perish with it. They are not created by God, but are derived with their bodies from their parents by natural operation ... Hence their soul is extinguished with the dissolution of the body.'

Such reasoning (apart from resting upon false premises) is hard to follow and is clearly prompted by the desire to 'justify' man's ill-treatment of the creatures. This is seen clearly in the words of Joseph Rickaby: 'There is no shadow of evil resting on the practice of causing pain to "brutes" in sport, where the pain is not in the sport itself, but an incidental concomitant of it. Much more, in all that conduces to the sustenance of man, may we give pain to "brutes", as also in the pursuit of Science. Nor are we bound to any anxious care to make this pain as little as may be. "Brutes" are things in our regard.'

[*Moral Philosophy*].

It would be difficult to find a more striking example of callousness towards animal suffering. The above quotation would justify any amount of torture inflicted on creatures, whether it is in the hunting field, the slaughterhouse, or the vivisector's laboratory. And this torture is said to be permissible because brutes are merely things.

Thus it becomes abundantly clear that man's cruelty to the creatures is largely due to his failure to realize who they are. That the creatures are not things should be obvious to the lowest intelligence. They are highly sensitive organisms – organisms capable of intense feeling and affection, and what is more, they are (like ourselves) creatures, i.e. creatures of our Heavenly Father.

If we consider the testimony of those who have tried to understand them from a higher standpoint than the merely scientific one, we shall find that they all agree that they have souls and that these survive physical death. If it is objected that it is impossible to prove this, we would reply that it is equally difficult to prove that human beings have immortal souls. And yet in each case we can point to things which support such a belief. Just as there are desires implanted by God in man that can only be satisfied in a future existence, so there are traits in the character of the creatures which by their very nature must be eternal. Thus the self-sacrificing love and trust that a dog has for its master and the sorrow that it feels over the loss of a friend are qualities that are not only human, but divine.

The belief in a soul for the creatures has been held by the Egyptians, the Hindus and the Buddhists. It was once to be found in Persia, in Greece and Italy. The Druids, the Welsh bards, the Norsemen and the Germans all had the same belief. It can be traced among the natives of Mexico, the tribes of Africa and America. The idea may take strange forms, but it is found throughout almost the whole world except where Christianity holds sway. It is a terrible tragedy that those who claim to follow the Master should have done so much to dispel a belief that should have helped to ameliorate the lot of the creatures. Not that they have ever been able to bring any evidence against it apart from their own false traditions and prejudices. The remark of Voltaire that 'If it were true that they [the creatures] had no souls, it would be necessary to invent souls for them,' is highly significant, for (as Anna Kingsford says) 'Earth has become a hell for want of this doctrine.' It is largely because the creatures are popularly believed to be soulless that they are treated so callously, for if it were admitted that they had souls it would become obvious that they had rights. But this is just what both Catholic and Anglican theologians deny.

These We Have Not Loved

There is no escape from the law that we reap what we sow. The result of cruelty is always the same. It brings its own nemesis. There is no such thing as necessary cruelty, any more than necessary sin. The nation that allows men to torture animals, in the vain hope of wresting scientific secrets from their quivering bodies and alleviating our own sufferings at such a price, can reap nothing but sorrow.

Ibid.

THOMAS HOOD, 1799–1845

A Butcher

Whoe'er has gone thro' London street
Has seen a butcher gazing at his meat,
    And how he keeps
      Gloating upon a sheep's
Or bullock's personals, as if his own;

How he admires his halves
   And quarters, and his calves
As if in truth upon his own legs grown –
   His fat, *his* suet,
His kidneys peeping elegantly thro'it,
   His thick flank, and *his* thin,
   His shank, *his* shin,
Skin of his skin, and bone too of his bone!

   With what an air
He stands aloof across the thoroughfare
Gazing, and will not let a body by,
Tho' *buy, buy, buy*! be constantly his cry.
Meanwhile with arms akimbo, and a pair
Of Rhodian legs, he revels in a stare
At his Joint Stock – for one may call it so,
   Howbeit with a *Co*.
The dotage of self-love was never fonder
Than he of his brute bodies all a-row;
Narcissus in the wave did never ponder,
   With love so strong,
   On his *portrait charmant*,
As our vain Butcher on his carcass yonder.

   Look at his sleek round skull!
How bright his cheek, how rubicund his nose is!
   His visage seems to be
   Ripe for beef-tea;
Of brutal juices the whole man is full.
In fact, fulfilling the metempsychosis,
   The Butcher is already half a Bull.

ALICE HOPF, 1904–

If an animal's not equipped to make sounds like talking,
it doesn't mean it can't think. All we have to do is to
figure out how to make it convey its thoughts.

Star Circus

LORD (Douglas) HOUGHTON (of Sowerby), CH,
1898–

I ask upon what pinnacle do we base human life and wellbeing that denies all rights whatsoever to every species but our own?

... Those who refuse to help erect the milestones are not on the march.

House of Commons debate, 11.May.1973

I do not equate animals with children, nor do I make them alternatives in my affections, my concern, or my work. They are different species, each with their rights and claims upon the living world. It is not a matter of priorities ... of 'either-or', it is a matter of the moral standards of human beings, and those to me are all embracing and all pervasive. They are all that justifies the continued existence of mankind. I am not called upon to apportion my deepest feelings between children and animals. I care about all living things – and for the weak and helpless most of all.

... I reject the proposition that fondness for animals implies some lack of concern for human beings. Do I have to prove a love of children by being cruel to animals? Is the person who is cruel to animals likely to love children all the more? Is that the proposition, or is cruelty an evil streak in the nature of some humans which makes a selfless love, whether for humans or animals, impossible?

House of Lords, 19.June.1978

... if we are to make any advance at all we must move forward into a territory which is heavily defended by those of noble birth and lofty purpose, by the cheap food brigade, the men of science and of medicine, and sundry merchants and mercenaries. This is where we move from the land of the sadist, the fiend and the half-wit, to assault the vested interests, the fashion and beauty specialists, the cattle men, the hunting men, the hare coursers and the rest. While public opinion is pretty clear on what may be thought to be wanton, avoidable, or unnecessary cruelty, it is by no means so positive about cruelty inflicted on animals in the course of satisfying human needs: in attitudes towards killing for food, or even for sport, towards painful experiments in our laboratories, or even to the merciless trapping of wild animals for their skins or furs – areas where the moral issues are blurred by material gains or by the pleasures involved.

Animals' Rights: a Symposium

JOHN HOYT, 1932–

For too long we have occupied ourselves with responding to the consequences of cruelty and abuse and have neglected the important task of building up an ethical system in which justice for animals is regarded as the norm rather than the exception. Our only hope is to put our focus on the education of the young.

Lecture, Humane Society of the United States

I have no argument with those who tell me that there is great pleasure in experiencing the out-of-doors associated with hunting. Nor do I protest that it takes skill, fortitude and perhaps a bit of daring to track and stalk animals. My argument with those who hunt begins at the point where the animal is victimized for no meaningful or useful purpose, save one of personal pleasure and satisfaction, which is quite beyond my comprehension. It hardly seems a very enhancing moment when by use of some sort of weapon, I am able to cause injury or death to a living creature that has been reduced to little more than an animate target.

Ibid.

ELBERT HUBBARD, 1856–1915

Thou shalt love the stars, the ocean, the forest, and reverence all living things, recognizing that the source of life is one.

Note Book of Elbert Hubbard

W.H. HUDSON, 1841–1922

After leaving the cowkeeper I had that feeling of revulsion very strongly which all who know and love cows occasionally experience at the very thought of beef. I was for the moment more than tolerant of vegetarianism and devoutly hoped that for many days to come I should not be sickened with the sight of a sirloin on some hateful board, cold, or smoking hot, bleeding its red juices into the dish when gashed with a knife, as if undergoing a second death ... even monkey's flesh is abhorrent to us, merely because we fancy that creature in its ugliness resembles some old men and some women and children that we know. But the gentle, large-brained, social cow that caresses our hands and faces with her rough blue tongue, and is more like man's sister than any other non-human being – the majestic, beautiful creature with the Juno eyes, sweeter of breath than the rosiest virgin – we slaughter and feed on her flesh – monsters and cannibals that we are!

Afoot in England

Bear in mind that the children of life are the children of joy; that the lower animals are only unhappy when made so by man; that man alone, of all the creatures, has 'found out many inventions', the chief of which appears to be the art of making himself miserable, and of seeing all Nature stained with that dark and hateful colour.

Far Away and Long Ago

A lifelong intimacy with animals has got me out of the common notion that they are automata with a slight infusion of intelligence in their composition. The mind in beast and bird, as in man, is the main thing.

A Hind in Richmond Park

EMRYS HUGHES, MP, 1894–1969

Terror, agony, and abominable cruelty are inseparable from the experiments on animals at the Government Microbiological Research Establishment at Porton Down – an Animal Belsen.

Hansard

VICTOR HUGO, 1802–1885

It was first of all necessary to civilize man in relation to his fellow men. That task is already well advanced and makes progress daily. But it is also necessary to civilize man in relation to nature. There, everything remains to be done … Philosophy has concerned itself but little with man beyond man, and has examined only superficially, almost with a smile of disdain, man's relationship with things, and with animals, which in his eyes are merely things. But are there not depths here for the thinker? Must one suppose oneself mad because one has the sentiment of universal pity in one's heart? Are there not certain laws of mysterious equity that pertain to the whole sum of things, and that are transgressed by the thoughtless, useless behaviour of man to animals? … For myself, I believe that pity is a law like justice, and that kindness is a duty like uprightness. That which is weak has the right to the kindness and pity of that which is strong. Animals are weak because they are less intelligent. Let us therefore be kind and compassionate towards them. In the relations of man with the animals, with the flowers, with all the objects of creation, there is a whole great ethic [*toute une grande morale*] scarcely seen as yet, but which will eventually break through into the light and be the corollary and the complement to human ethics.

Alpes et Pyrénées

C.W. HUME, 1886–1981

In neither the Old nor the New Testament ... is there to be found that contemptuous attitude towards sub-human creatures which went with the humanism of the Renaissance. If man's superior capacities confer on him a privileged position, privilege does not exempt him from responsibility: 'A righteous man regardeth the life of his beast, but the tender mercies of the wicked are cruel' (Prov. 12:10) ... The rationalist approach has been unfavourable not only to Christianity and to physical science but also to the spirit of neighbourliness towards animals, notably in the case of the Cartesian philosophy ...

Victorian England was deeply shocked when Darwin suggested that the brutes are in fact man's poor relations. Some valuable animal, such as a thoroughbred racehorse, might be held in esteem, but those which are classed as vermin because they share man's food-preferences and diseases are even now treated with callous contempt ...

Charity is indivisible. If a man resents practical sympathy being bestowed on animals on the ground that all ought to be reserved for the species to which he himself happens to belong, he must have a mind the size of a pin's head.

The Status of Animals

The major cruelties practised on animals in civilized countries today arise out of commercial exploitation, and the fear of losing profits is the chief obstacle to reform.

Ibid.

The Renaissance proper, which may be dated from the fifteenth century and which, as the price of its bestowal of literary and artistic gifts, exacted a decline of spiritual religion, an eruption of superstition, and all the horrors of witch-burning and heresy-hunting, also created a new religion of humanism which tended to dethrone God and to put man in God's place. In humanism man became the centre of the universe and the object of his own worship; animals did not count except in so far as they provided man with food, labour and entertainment; they had no rights against his supreme dominance, and were not entitled to any consideration except in so far as they were useful property. Obviously, not everybody became a narrow-minded anthropocentric humanist; more sensible views survived and have never wholly perished. But the humanism of the fifteenth-century Renaissance, combined with the thirteenth-century impact of the neoplatonized Aristotle, and combined also with the effect of urban life on the climate of lay opinion, helped to dechristianize the Church's relations with God's sub-human creatures.

Ibid.

To this day the more conventional biologists suffer from an obsessional fear of anthropomorphism, and even put such words as 'hunger' and 'fear' between quotes (a literary solecism in any case) when writing about animals.

The quotes are a way of saying 'I cannot get on without Anthropomorphism, but I am ashamed to be seen with her in public.'

Ibid.

BRONWEN HUMPHREYS, 1947–

Very few people question that it is an act of kindness to put an animal painlessly to death if it is injured beyond hope of a pain-free future; or that it is better to neuter our pets than to allow thousands of unwanted litters to be born. But mention that it might be better for a breeding sow in a farrowing crate if she had never been born, and you will be met with chants of 'Any life is better than no life.' Humans have an odd way of finding justification for activities that bring them pleasure, or profit, or both.

Editorial, *The Vegetarian*, May/June 1984

CHRISTMAS HUMPHREYS, 1901–1983

Life is one, said the Buddha, and the Middle Way to the end of suffering in all its forms is that which leads to the end of the illusion of separation, which enables man to see, as a fact as clear as sunlight, that all mankind, and all other forms in manifestation, are one unit, the infinitely variable appearance of an indivisible Whole.

The Buddhist Way of Life

As we increasingly become aware of the One Life breathing in each brother form of life, we learn the meaning of compassion, which literally means to 'suffer with' ... How does [the] self cause the desire which causes suffering? ... by the illusion of separateness, the unawareness of One.

Ibid.

JAMES HENRY LEIGH HUNT, 1784–1859

The Horse Wounded in Battle

O friend of Man! O noble creature,
Patient and brave and mild by nature,
Mild by nature and mute as mild,
Why brings he to these passes wild
Thee, gentle Horse, thou shape of beauty?
Could he not do his dreadful duty
(If duty it be, which seems mad folly),
Nor link thee to his melancholy?

To the Grasshopper and the Cricket

Green little vaulter in the sunny grass,
Catching your heart up at the feel of June,
Sole voice that's heard amidst the lazy noon,
When even the bees lag at the summoning brass,
And you, warm little housekeeper, who class
With those who think the candles come too soon,
Loving the fire, and with your tricksome tune
Nick the glad silent moments as they pass:
Oh sweet and tiny cousins, that belong,
One to the fields, the other to the hearth,
Both have your sunshine; both, though small, are strong
At your clear hearts; and both seem given to earth
To ring in thoughtful ears this natural song –
In doors and out, summer and winter, mirth.

FANNIE HURST, 1889–1968

I am against vivisection because I see no reason to believe
that its benefits to humanity justify the cruel practice.
The scientific results of all the years of the practice are
nebulous. The ethical results are concrete. So long as
vivisection exists it means there are still men and women
who can crucify dumb animals and betray their trust and

friendship. Let the vivisectionists cure that moral sore by ceasing the fiendish practice.

Letter to Mrs C.P. Farrell, 1922

ALDOUS HUXLEY, 1894–1963

Compared with that of the Taoists and Far Eastern Buddhists, the Christian attitude toward Nature has been curiously insensitive and often downright domineering and violent. Taking their cue from an unfortunate remark in Genesis, Catholic moralists have regarded animals as mere things which men do right to exploit for their own ends ...

Modern man no longer regards Nature as being in any sense divine and feels perfectly free to behave toward her as an overweening conquerer and tyrant.

The Perennial Philosophy

Real progress is progress in charity, all other advances being secondary thereto.

Ends and Means

... I see this problem of man's relation to Nature as not only an immediate practical problem, but also as a problem in ethics and religion. It is significant that neither Christianity nor Judaism has ever thought of Nature as having rights in relation to man, or as being in some way intrinsically divine. You will find orthodox Catholic moralists asserting (on the basis of those extremely unfortunate remarks in Genesis) that animals may be treated as things. (As though things didn't deserve to be treated ethically!) The vulgar boast of the modern technologist to the effect that man has conquered Nature has roots in the Western religious tradition, which affirms that God installed man as the boss, to whom Nature was to bring tribute. The Greeks knew better than the Jews and Christians. They knew that hubris towards Nature was as much of a sin as hubris towards fellow men. Xerxes is punished, not only for having attacked the Greeks, but also for having outraged Nature in the affair of bridging the Hellespont. But for an ethical system that includes animate and inanimate Nature as well as man, one must go to Chinese Taoism, with its concept of an Order of Things, whose state of wu-wei, or balance, must be preserved; of an in-dwelling Lagos or Tao, which is immanent on every level of existence from the physical, through the physiological, up to the mental and the spiritual. In many passages, particularly of the *Specimen Days in America*, Whitman comes very close to the Taoist position. And because of Whitman and Wordsworth and the other 'Nature mystics' of the West, I feel that it might not be too difficult for modern Europeans and Americans to accept some kind of Taoist philosophy of life, with an ethical system comprehensive enough to take in Nature as well as man. People have got to understand that the commandment, 'Do unto others as you would that they should do unto you' applies to animals, plants and things, as well as to people; and that if it is regarded as applying only to people (as it has been in the Christian West), then the animals, plants and things will, in one way or another, do as badly by man as man has done by them. It seems to me that, if we are to have a better policy towards Nature, we must also have a better philosophy.

From a letter to Fairfield Osborn, 16 January 1948
quoted *Letters of Aldous Huxley*, ed. Grover Smith

It was not until the nineteenth century, when orthodox Christianity had lost much of its power over European minds, that the idea that it might be a good thing to behave humanely towards animals began to make headway.

The Perennial Philosophy

ELSPETH HUXLEY, 1907–

Sir, Could we have a moratorium on the use of the phrase 'they behaved like animals' to describe any especially nasty form of human brutality? Carnivores certainly kill when they need their dinners, but do so as quickly as they can. Herbivores just eat vegetation and do not interfere with others.

Do we hear of dolphins torturing other dolphins, gorillas cutting, or biting, bits off other gorillas, elephants inflicting prolonged periods of terror on other elephants, or indeed on any other animal?

Rather should dolphins left to die in nets, gorillas killed in order that their dried heads should be sold to tourists, elephants dying in agony from poisons for the sake of their tusks, exclaim in condemnation of acts of savagery (should these ever occur) committed by members of their own species: 'They behaved like humans.' – Yours faithfully, etc.

Letter in *The Times*, 14 December 1984

THOMAS HENRY HUXLEY, 1825–1895

– was examined and if what I hear is a correct account of the evidence he gave, I may as well throw up my brief!

I am told that he openly proposed the most entire indifference to animal suffering and said he only gave anaesthetics to animals to keep them quiet.

I declare to you that I did not believe the man lived who was such an unmitigated, cynical brute as to profess and act upon such principles, and I would willingly agree to any law which would send him to the treadmill.

Life of Thomas Huxley

REVD J.R. HYLAND, 1943–

Not only did the prophets point out that sacrifices and ceremonies were man-made substitutes for the true worship of God, they also faced their people with the fact that the violence done to sacrificial animals was reflected in the violence that human beings were willing to inflict on each other. And slaughtering animals, as an act of worship among the Hebrews, was eventually reflected in the practice of human sacrifice.

The Slaughter of Terrified Beasts

A people who remained insensitive to the travesty of a worship that called for the terrorizing and slaughter of other creatures was a people whose spiritual development was being retarded; a people who had not yet taken their first step toward a millenial world.

Amazingly, though the Latter Prophets called for the reform or abolition of many of the institutions and practices that had been sanctified by the Hebrews, their message survived in the scriptures of their people. Their words were preserved because they spoke to Judaism's deepest roots. These men of God had not introduced new concepts into Israel; they had *reintroduced* themes that went back to the very beginning – back to the time of Genesis. And their great age of prophecy was a sign that it was time for the human race to recover its spiritual heritage. Speaking in the name of God, the prophets let the people know that it was time for the world to once again reflect the qualities that God had ordained at the Creation – love, compassion, and mercy for all creatures.

Ibid.

CHRISSIE HYNDE, 1951–

The way I feel about [eating meat] is, if you're going to kill someone's child and eat it, you might as well kill your own child and eat it. I mean, I'm a mother. I know. I have a pretty good idea of the kind of emotions that it would put me through to have somebody take my baby away from me. Now why, as even a remotely sensitive creature, would I wish to inflict that kind of suffering on any other creature – be it human or whatever? It's completely inhumane. There's no way you can justify it. There's no way anyone who has humanity or any compassion can stand here and take a calf away from its mother and think that that's all right.

Interview reported in *Vegetarian Times*, September 1987

IAMBLICHUS, *c*. 250–*c*.325

Pythagoras enjoined abstinence from the flesh of animals because this was conducive to Peace. Those who are accustomed to abominate the slaughter of other animals, as iniquitous and unnatural, will think it still more unlawful and unjust to kill a man or to engage in war. Especially he exhorted the politicians and legislators to abstain, for if they were willing to act justly, in the highest degree, it was indubitably incumbent upon them to not injure any of the lower animals, since how could they persuade others to act justly, if they themselves proved to be indulging an insatiable avidity by devouring those animals allied to us, since through the communion of life and the same elements, and the sympathy existing, they are as it were conjoined to us by a fraternal alliance.

De Vita Pythagorica

WILLIAM RALPH INGE (Dean Inge), 1860–1954

We have enslaved the rest of the animal creation, and have treated our distant cousins in fur and feathers so badly that beyond doubt, if they were able to formulate a religion, they would depict the Devil in human form.

Outspoken Essays

The great discovery of the nineteenth century, that we are of one blood with the lower animals, has created new ethical obligations which have not yet penetrated the public conscience. The clerical profession has been lamentably remiss in preaching this obvious duty.

From a sermon

It is unhappily true that (in the words of A. Jameson in 1854) 'the primitive Christians by laying so much stress upon a future life, and placing the lower creatures out of the pale of hope, placed them at the same time out of the pale of sympathy, and thus laid the foundation for an utter disregard of animals'.

Christian Ethics and Modern Problems

ROBERT GREEN INGERSOLL, 1833–1899

Of what possible use is it to know just how long an animal can live without food, without water; at what time he becomes insane from thirst, or blind, or deaf? Who but a fiend would try such experiments? And, if they have been tried, why should not all the fiends be satisfied with the report of the fiends who have made them? Must there be countless repetitions of the same horror?

Let us do what we can to do away with this infamous practice – a practice that degrades and demoralizes and hardens, without adding in the slightest to the sum of useful knowledge.

Without using profane words, words of the most blasphemous kind, it is impossible to express my loathing, horror and hatred of vivisection.

From his appendix to *Personal Experiences* by Philip G. Peabody, one-time President of the New England Anti-Vivisection Society

Vivisection is the inquisition – the hell – of science. All cruelty which the human – or, rather, the inhuman – heart is capable of inflicting is in this one word. Below this there is no depth. This word lies like a coiled serpent at the bottom of the abyss ... Those who are incapable of pitying animals are, as a matter of fact, incapable of pitying man.

It is not necessary for a man to be a specialist in order to have and express his opinion as to the right or wrong of vivisection. It is not necessary to be a scientist or a naturalist to detest cruelty and to love mercy. Above all the discoveries of the thinkers, above all the inventions of the ingenious, above all the victories won on fields of intellectual conflict, rise human sympathy and a sense of justice.

Letter to Philip G. Peabody, 27 May 1890

ISLAM

Treat others as thou wouldst be treated. What thou likest not for thyself, dispense not to others.

Sufism – Abdullah Ansari

An adultress was forgiven, who passed by a dog at a well, and the dog was holding out his tongue from thirst, which was near killing him. The woman drew off her boot and tied it to the end of her veil, and drew water for the dog, and gave him to drink, and for this she was forgiven.

Mishkat-el-Masabih

There is not an animal on the earth, nor a flying creature on two wings, but they are people like unto you.

Qur'an

DR L.P. JACKS, 1860–1955

Morality is much more than an affair between man and man; the scope of right and wrong extends far beyond the bounds of human society ... Man is much more than a social being in the human sense; he is a cosmic being, and it is only by understanding himself as a cosmic being – or a child of the universe – that he can understand himself as a social being, or son of man, and learn to behave himself rightly towards sons of men in general ... The society to which man belongs includes not only all other members of the human race, but the animals, the plants, the sun, moon and stars, and the whole realm of inorganic matter.

My Neighbour the Universe

GLENDA JACKSON, 1936–

No one really needs a mink coat in this world ... except minks.

From a syndicated newspaper interview

JAINISM

(Ahimsa-paramo-dharmah – non-injury to living beings is the highest religion)

In happiness and suffering, in joy and grief, we should regard all creatures as we regard our own self, and should therefore refrain from inflicting upon others such injury as would appear undesirable to us if inflicted upon ourselves.

Yogashastra

Jain monks have compassion to all beings; avoid what is sinful; abstain from food especially prepared for them; abstain from wicked deeds and from injuring living beings.

Maxim of the Monks

A man should wander about treating all creatures as he himself would be treated.

Sutrakritanga

Harmlessness is the only religion.

Jain maxim

Gambling, eating meat, wine-bibbing, adultery, hunting, thieving, debauchery – these seven things in this world lead to the hells.

Sanskrit Shloka

Flesh cannot be procured without causing destruction of life; one who uses flesh, therefore, commits *himsa* [injury] unavoidably.

Purushartha Siddhyupaya

With the three means of punishment, words, thoughts and acts, ye shall not injure living things.

Jaina Sutras

Beings which kill others should not be killed in the belief that the destruction of one of them leads to the protection of many others.

Purushartha Siddhyupaya

All beings hate pains; therefore one should not kill them. This is the quintessence of wisdom: not to kill anything.

Sutrakritanga

Viler than unbelievers are those cruel ones who make the law that teaches killing.

Yogashastra

Mercy to living beings, self-restraint, truth, honesty, chastity and contentment, right faith and knowledge, and austerity are but the entourage of morality.

Sila-prabhrita

Unless we live with non-violence and reverence for all living beings in our hearts, all our humaneness and acts of goodness, all our vows, virtues, and knowledge, all our practices to give up greed and acquisitiveness are meaningless and useless.

Mahavira (599–527 BC) in the *Agamas*

Propagate the religion which is a blessing to all creatures in the world.

Acharanga Sutra

In this world of misery, disease, old age and death, there is no other protection, refuge or help than our own practice of the truth. Others are powerless; as we sow we reap.

Quoted by Warren in *Jainism*

He who harms animals has not understood or renounced deeds of sin ... Those whose minds are at peace and who are free from passions do not desire to live at the expense of others.

Acharanga Sutra

All breathing, existing, living, sentient creatures should not be slain nor treated with violence, nor abused, nor tormented, nor driven away. This is the pure unchangeable Law.

Sutrakritanga

WILLIAM JAMES, MD, LLD, 1842–1910

The rights of the helpless, even though they be brutes, must be protected by those who have superior power. The individual vivisector must be held responsible to some authority which he fears. The medical and scientific men who time and again have raised their voices in opposition to all legal projects of regulation, know, as well as anyone else does, the unspeakable possibilities of callousness, wantonness and meanness of human nature; and their unanimity is the best example I know of the power of club opinion to quell independence of mind. No well organized sect or corporation of men can ever be trusted to be truthful or moral when under fire from the outside. In this case the watch-word is to deny alleged fact stoutly, to concede no point of principle, and to stand firmly on the right of the individual experimenter. His being 'scientific' must, in the eye of the law, be a sufficient guarantee that he can do no wrong.

From a letter in the *New York Evening Post*, 22 May 1909

We divert our attention from disease and death as much as we can; and the slaughterhouses and indecencies without end on which our life is founded are huddled out of sight and never mentioned, so that the world we recognize officially in literature and in society is a poetic fiction far handsomer and cleaner and better than the world that really is.

Varieties of Religious Experience

ANNA BROWNELL JAMESON, 1794–1860

… the primitive Christians, by laying so much stress upon a future life in contradistinction to this life and placing the lower creatures out of the pale of hope, placed them at the same time out of the pale of sympathy, and thus laid the foundation for this utter disregard of animals in the light of our fellow creatures.

Commonplace Book of Thoughts, Memories and Fancies

FRANCIS JAMMES, 1868–1938

Going to Paradise with the Asses

O God, when You send for me, let it be
Upon some festival day of dusty roads.
I wish, as I did ever here below,
By any road that pleases me to go
To Paradise, where stars shine all day long.
Taking my stick out on the great highway,
To my dear friends the asses I shall say:
I am Francis Jammes going to Paradise,
For there is no hell where the Lord God dwells.
Come with me, my sweet friends of azure skies,
You poor, dear beasts who whisk off with your ears
Mosquitoes, peevish blows, and buzzing bees.

Let me appear before You with these beasts,
Whom I so love because they bow their head
Sweetly, and halting join their little feet
So gently that it makes you pity them.
Let me come followed by their million ears,
By those that dragged the car of acrobats,
Those that had battered cans upon their backs,
She-asses, limping, full as leather bottles,
And those, too, that they breech because of blue
And oozing wounds, round which the stubborn flies
Gather in swarms. God, let me come to You
With all these asses into Paradise.

Let angels lead us where Your rivers soothe
Their tufted banks, and cherries tremble, smooth
As in the laughing flesh of tender maids.
And let me where Your perfect peace pervades
Be like Your asses, bending down above
The heavenly waters through eternity,
To mirror their sweet, humble poverty
In the clear waters of eternal love.

KATHLEEN JANNAWAY, 1915–

Anthropologists may well have exaggerated the importance of the carnivorous path to dominance. Human intelligence must have been developed still more by the need of plant selection and preparation and by agriculture than by hunting animals. Golden periods of harmony may well have existed in various human societies of the past. Echoes of them remain to inspire us with hope. Just as the adoption of the vegan diet is made easy for most people because it accords with basic frugivorous functioning, so the move to a worldwide peaceful culture may not seem so strange once we wake from our present nightmare of carnivorous living.

The Vegan, Winter 1976

We must not be ashamed of our sensitivity and active imaginations. So many of us have felt that we were odd because while others could enjoy watching lambs skipping in the fields, running to their mothers for protection at the least alarm, we experienced in imagination the coming of the slaughterhouse lorries and the lambs bleating in vain as they were herded for the throat cutting.

All humans, in common with all vertebrates, demonstrate to a greater or lesser degree the ability to sacrifice themselves for their young. We have to fan the glimmer of that primitive love until it becomes a consuming fire that will burn away all our weaknesses, indulgencies, hesitancies – our very selves. We can only do this if we give full rein to the imaginative sensitivity and the compassion for helpless creatures that are the hallmark of ethical vegetarianism.

Ibid., Autumn 1984

JOHN RICHARD JEFFERIES, 1848–1887

I have observed that almost all those whose labour lies in the field, and who go down to their business in the green meadows, admit the animal world to a share in the faculty of reason. It is the cabinet-makers who construct a universe of automatons.

The Open Air

ROBINSON JEFFERS, 1887–1962

From *The Inhumanist*

The sun blazed from the west; the old man saw his
    shadow on his horse's shadow
Wending beside him along the cloud-wall. 'Well, it is very
    curious', he said,
'That Worse always rides Better. I have seen in my life
    time many horsemen and some equestrian statues.
I have observed the people and their rulers; and a circus
    monkey on a Great Dane; and man on the earth.'

SOAME JENYNS, 1704–1787

The butcher knocks down the stately ox with no more compassion than the blacksmith hammers a horse-shoe, and plunges his knife into the throat of an innocent lamb with as little reluctance as the tailor sticks his needle into the collar of a coat.

Disquisitions on Several Subjects

JEROME K. JEROME, 1859–1927

He is very imprudent, a dog is; he never makes it his business to inquire whether you are in the right or the wrong, never asks whether you are rich or poor, silly or wise, sinner or saint. You are his pal. That is enough for him.

The Idle Thoughts of an Idle Fellow

Ah! Old staunch friend, with your deep, clear eyes and bright quick glances that take in all one has to say before one has time to speak it, do you know you are only an animal and have no mind? Do you know that dull-eyed, gin-sodden lout leaning against the post out there is immeasurably your intellectual superior? Do you know that every little-minded, selfish scoundrel, who never did a gentle deed or said a kind word, who never had a thought that was not mean or low, or a desire that was not mean and base, whose every action is a fraud, and whose every utterance is a lie – do you know that these crawling skulks are as much superior to you as a sun is to a rush light, you honourable, brave-hearted, unselfish brute? They are men, you know, and men are the greatest, noblest and wisest and best beings in the whole, vast, eternal universe! Any man will tell you that.

Ibid.

F. TENNYSON JESSE (Mrs H.M. Harwood), 1889–1958

The religions of the world are responsible for much of the pain of the dumb creation. It is a bad business for an animal in Catholic countries, because he has no 'soul', and soullessness, by some curious form of logic, has no rights. The Christian religion has unfortunately always taught that man is the lord of creation, and that all other living things were created for his pleasure. This curious and monstrous egoism developed, it is imagined, because man can talk and thus lay down the law, and animals cannot.

Sabi Pas

It seems to a simple soul that cruelty is especially terrible because it hurts the animal, and whatever the author of *Moral Philosophy* [Father Rickaby] may say, reflex consciousness is exactly what an animal does possess. Whether or not it has a soul it certainly has a body. The whole attitude of Christianity would be laughable if it were not so tragic, and for man to imagine that the spots on a butterfly's wing, the cunning imitation of a twig and leaf by certain insects, the blaze of colour at the mating season, the call of the birds, were all made for his benefit, cannot but be ridiculous.

Ibid.

WILLIAM STANLEY JEVONS, 1835–1882

From my own observation I can affirm that many sportsmen acquire a taste for the simple wanton destruction of life apart from all ulterior purposes. Provided an animal will only make a good moving target they want to shoot it. They will do this at sea, in woods and inaccessible places where there is no possibility of recovering the animals, or of putting them out of pain if badly wounded. In Norway and Australia I have frequently seen the sporting instinct of the English develop itself in freedom, and I can only conclude that 'sport' is synonymous with the love of the clever destruction of living things.

Fortnightly Review, May 1876

SAMUEL JOHNSON, 1709–1784

Among the inferior professors of medical knowledge is a race of wretches whose lives are only varied by varieties of cruelty; whose favourite amusement is to nail dogs to tables and open them alive; to try how long life may be continued in various degrees of mutilation, or with the excision or laceration of the vital parts; to examine whether burning irons are felt more acutely by the bone or tendon; and whether the more lasting agonies are produced by poison forced into the mouth, or injected into the veins.

It is not without reluctance that I offend the sensibility of the tender mind with images like these. If such cruelties were not practised it were to be desired that they should not be conceived, but since they are published every day with ostentation, let me be allowed once to mention them, since I mention them with abhorrence ...

The anatomical novice tears out the living bowels of an animal and styles himself physician; prepares himself by familiar cruelty for that profession which he is to exercise upon the tender and the helpless, upon feeble bodies and broken minds, and by which he has opportunities to extend his arts and torture; and continues those experiments upon infancy and age, which he has hitherto tried upon cats and dogs. What is alleged in defence of these hateful practices everyone knows, but the truth is that by knives, fire and poisons, knowledge is not always sought, and is very seldom attained. I know not that by living dissections any disovery has been made by which a single malady is more easily cured. And if the knowledge

JONES

of physiology has been somewhat increased, he surely buys knowledge dear who learns the use of the lacteals at the expense of his own humanity. It is time that a universal resentment should rise against those horrid operations, which tend to harden the heart and make the physicians more dreadful than the gout or the stone.

The Idler, 5 August 1758

An infallible characteristic of meanness is cruelty.
Men who have practised tortures on animals without pity, relating them without shame, how can they still hold their heads among human beings?

Ibid.

HELEN JONES, 1925–

Regulation of exploitation [of animals] reinforces the exploitation while offering a salve for the human conscience at the expense of the victims. Regulation no more addresses the real issue of the exploitation and suffering of animals than do larger shanties, fewer beatings and slightly reduced hours of labour for slaves.

'Animal Rights: A View and Comment', 1981 Report by the International Society for Animal Rights

WILLIAM JONES ('of Nayland'), 1726–1800

Cruelty to dumb animals is one of the distinguishing vices of low and base minds. Wherever it is found, it is a certain mark of ignorance and meannesss; a mark which all the external advantages of wealth, splendour and nobility cannot obliterate. It is consistent neither with learning nor true civility.

Zoologia Ethicae

DR DAVID STARR JORDAN, 1851–1931

Our treatment of animals will someday be considered barbarous. There cannot be perfect civilization until man realizes that the rights of every living creature are as sacred as his own.

The Days of a Man

W.J. JORDAN, 1925–

… man has been able to alter the slow process of evolution by his ability to learn. Guided by culture rather than his genes, he is changing the environment faster than he can cope with it and he is losing his reverence for life. He is captivated by ideas which increase his rate of learning, though they are not necessarily correct. He has become dazzled by knowledge – the fallibility of Science is never questioned. Indeed, if anyone wants to praise anything one calls it 'scientific' and one can denigrate ideas or theories simply by calling them 'unscientific'. The use of the word 'unscientific' is taken by most people to mean 'unworthy'. Indeed, Science has become the new religion, scientists the high priests and their ritual attire the white laboratory coat …

We must not rely wholly on ideas, whether they be scientific or otherwise; rather we must 'listen' to our own inner natures.

Animals' Rights: a Symposium

Nature is necessary for mankind, his survival depends on it: that is the continual message of ecology. His growth and understanding depend on it too, and we have seen his genes demand that he does what they dictate for peace of mind and contentment. Man is motivated by basic needs such as hunger and thirst, and when these are satisfied he becomes aware of other needs; for example, to love and belong. Then other needs, such as to know and to learn, enter his awareness. Maslow describes this as a pyramid of self-realization. A basic component is reverence for life.

Ibid.

NIYAMA JOY, 1943–

The frightening and sad thing is that such people run our country, our everyday lives. Our lives are in the hands of insensitive people, and they pass their insensitivity on to their children. So it continues, generation after generation.

We are a doomed world unless mothers everywhere start showing their young children, especially the boys, how to have a respect and love for the smallest of creatures that share this beautiful planet.

Surely it follows that if they can respect even an ant, then they will respect and show kindness to human beings. I am often horrified at children's cruelty to insects, unchecked by parents.

My children and I will stop and watch everything we see on our walks and get great enjoyment from it. We have to teach our children sensitivity and a great love for animals everywhere. They need it and our world needs it to survive.

From a letter on hunting deer, West Somerset Free Press,
26 August 1988

C.G. JUNG, 1875–1961

During my medical education at the University of Basle I found vivisection horrible, barbarous and above all unnecessary.

Collected Works

FRANZ KAFKA, 1883–1924

Now I can look at you in peace; I don't eat you any more.

Reported remark made while admiring fish in an aquarium

IMMANUEL KANT, 1724–1804

The more we come in contact with animals and observe their behaviour, the more we love them, for we see how great is their care of their young.

Lectures on Ethics

If [man] is not to stifle his human feelings, he must practise kindness towards animals, for he who is cruel to animals becomes hard also in his dealings with men. We can judge the heart of a man by his treatment of animals.

Ibid.

PHILIP KAPLEAU, 1912–

While in Japan [Kapleau became a Buddhist monk in 1956] I wrestled with my conscience, trying to reconcile the first Buddhist vow to refrain from taking life with my obvious complicity in the slaughter of innocent creatures whose flesh I consumed. I pretended to love animals while at the same time regularly eating them.

This struggle, I now realize, generated the headaches and stomach upsets that had plagued me in Japan. But once I stopped indulging in animal flesh, to my surprise and delight the headaches disappeared and the digestive difficulties evaporated. There were other dividends, too. Now that I was no longer swallowing dead cows, pigs,

215

chickens and fish, I could gaze upon live ones with innocent delight. And I knew Anatole France was only half right when he said, 'Until one has loved an animal a part of one's soul remains unawakened.' What he also needed to say was that until one has stopped *eating* animals true peace of soul is impossible.

To Cherish All Life

Ultimately the case for shunning animal flesh does not rest on what the Buddha allegedly said or didn't say. What it does rest on is our innate moral goodness, compassion, and pity which, when liberated, lead us to value all forms of life. It is obvious, then, that wilfully to take life, or through the eating of meat indirectly to cause others to kill, runs counter to the deepest instincts of human beings.

Ibid.

Meat-eaters often argue that in devouring other creatures man, also an animal, is only doing what animals in the wild themselves do, that the survival of one creature demands the death of another. What this argument ignores is that carnivores can survive only by eating other animals – they have no choice, their stomachs compel them to – but human beings can survive, and survive well, without devouring other creatures. That man is a predator, and the deadliest of all, no unprejudiced person will deny, for to the extent that he destroys his own kind and other species – the latter as much for sport and profit as for food – no other creature is his equal. Even so, human beings are distinguished from other animals by their powers of reasoning and self-transcendence, their sense of justice and compassion. We pride ourselves on our uniquely human ability to make ethical judgments and take moral responsibility for our actions. To protect the weak and gentle from the homicide aggressions of the strong and ruthless, we establish laws decreeing that one who wantonly murders another (except in self-defence or in defence of his country) be severely punished for his evil deed, and this often involves the sacrifice of his own life. In our human relationships we disavow, or like to believe we disavow, the morality of might makes right. But where non-humans are concerned, especially those whose flesh or skins we covet, or on whose bodies we wish to conduct lethal experiments, we oppress and exploit them freely, justifying our harsh treatment on the ground that since they are beings of inferior intelligence, with no sense of right or wrong, they have no rights. If the value of a life, human or non-human, is to be judged by the quality of that being's intelligence, then, like the Nazis, we ought to put to death senile and mentally retarded human beings, for many animals are more intelligent and better able to interact with their own species than, say, a mentally retarded adult. Analogously, suppose extraterrestrial beings of a higher intelligence than ours were to invade our planet. Would they be morally justified in destroying and eating us simply because we did not measure up to their levels of intelligence and they like the taste of our flesh?

From an ethical standpoint, however, the criterion is not a being's intelligence or its ability to make moral judgments, but its capacity for suffering pain, physical and emotional. And animals do experience pain – they are not things. They can be lonely, sad and frightened; they suffer greatly when deprived of their young; and they cling to life as much as human beings do. It is idle to speak, as some do, of destroying livestock painlessly, for there will always be the terror and anguish they experience in the slaughterhouse and in the cattle trucks on the way to their execution, not to mention branding, dehorning and castration, the most common cruelties

217

they undergo in their rearing for slaughter. Let us ask ourselves, would we consent to being killed, while in good physical and mental health, just because it could be done painlessly? Do we, ultimately, have the right to deprive other species of their lives when no greater social good is being served, and where compassion does not demand it? How dare we pretend to love justice when for the pleasure of our tongues and palates we murder hundreds of thousands of defenceless animals in cold blood every day without a 'shadow of remorse' and without anyone suffering the slightest punishment. What an evil karma we human beings continue to store up for ourselves, what a legacy of violence and terror we bequeath future generations!

Ibid.

JOHN KEATS, 1795–1821

Isabella

With her two brothers this fair lady dwelt,
    Enriched from ancestral merchandize,
And for them many a weary hand did swelt
    In torched mines and noisy factories,
And many once proud-quiver'd loins did melt
    In blood from stinging whip – with hollow eyes
Many all day in dazzling river stood,
To take the rich-ored driftings of the flood.

For them the Ceylon diver held his breath,
    And went all naked to the hungry shark;
For them his ears gush'd blood; for them in death
    The seal on the cold ice with piteous bark
Lay full of darts; for them alone did seethe
    A thousand men in troubles wide and dark;

Half-ignorant, they turn'd an easy wheel,
That set sharp racks at work, to pinch and peel.

JOHN HARVEY KELLOGG, MD, LLD, FACS, 1852–1943

The basis for the ethical argument against flesh-eating is to be found in the fact that lower animals are, in common with man, sentient creatures. We have somehow become accustomed to think of our inferior brethren, the members of the lower orders of the animal kingdom, as things; we treat them as sticks or stones, as trees and other non-sentient things that are not possessed of organs of sense and feeling. We are wrong in this; they are not things, but *beings*. We forget the wonderful likeness that exists between us and these lower creatures. We neglect the fact that their brains are much like our brains, their muscles like our muscles, their bones like our bones, that they digest as we digest, that they have hearts that beat as ours beat, nerves that thrill as ours thrill, that they possess to a wonderful degree the same faculties, the same appetites, and are subject to the same impulses as we. An ox, a sheep, can hear, see, feel, smell, taste and even think, if not as well as man, at least to some degree after the same fashion. The lamb gambolling in the pasture enjoys life much in the same way as the little child chasing butterflies across the meadow. A horse or a cow can learn, remember, love, hate, mourn, rejoice and suffer, as human beings do. Its sphere of life is much restricted, but life is not the less real and not the less precious to it; and the fact that the quadruped has little is not a good and sufficient reason why the biped, who has much, should deprive his brother of the little that he hath. For the most part it must be admitted that the lower animals have adhered more closely to the divine order than has man, and hence are worthy to live.

The Natural Diet of Man

Must we not confess that our readiness to take the lives of animals and to eat them for food is largely based upon the fact, as Plutarch suggested hundreds of years ago, that they do not possess the faculty of human speech? If a butcher about to cut the throat of a lamb should be suddenly addressed by the innocent creature with a pathetic appeal for its life, it would doubtless be necessary for him to take a few more steps downward in the degradation of his manhood before he would be able to bring himself to the accomplishment of his cruel purpose.

Ibid.

THOMAS À KEMPIS, 1379–1471

And if thy heart be straight with God, then every creature shall be to thee a mirror of life and a book of holy doctrine, for there is no creature so little or so vile, but that sheweth and representeth the goodness of God.

Imitation of Christ

BRUCE KENT, 1929–

For long enough, and quite rightly, speakers from the peace organizations have stressed the terrible present price of war. There have been perhaps twenty million deaths, the direct result of war, since 1945. There have been millions more who could have lived decent human lives had not the world turned its resources to war. As many deaths from starvation and malnutrition as from the Hiroshima bomb every three days, we are told!

Now here, under our eyes, in photograph and print, comes another whole area of human wickedness ... the torture and awful deaths of so many animals who are sacrificed in country after country to keep the 'defence'

220

machine going. These victims are the absolute innocents. What is done to them is yet another example of the ruthlessness of the strong and the exploitation of the weak.

Shock, however, is not enough. New organizations are not needed. A new understanding of the connections which ought to draw the peace and animal rights organizations together in partnership and sometimes joint campaigning, is.

From foreword to *The Military Abuse of Animals*

KARL KERENYI, 1897–1973

We must strive for a kind of education that will teach men not to kill and to cause as little suffering as possible. It should be the first task of philosophy, theology, psychology, indeed, of all the disciplines concerned with the study of men ... to find out why there are men who desire to kill and are capable of killing. We should not hesitate to search for the primal cause of evil. Once we see it clearly, we may be less evil than we are now.

Evil

AGA KHAN (Prince Sadruddin), 1933–

The philosophy behind vivisection, the sacrifice of creatures we regard as 'inferior' beings, differs little from that behind the concentration camp or the slave-trader.

Observer newspaper, 16 August 1981

WILLIAM KING, 1663–1712

From *Mully of Mountown*

How fleet is air! how many things have breath
Which in a moment they resign to death,
Depriv'd of light and all their happiest state

Not by their fault but some o'erruling Fate!
Although fair flow'rs, that justly might invite,
Are cropt, nay, torn away, for man's delight,
Yet still those flow'rs, alas! can make no moan,
Nor has Narcissus now a pow'r to groan;
But all those things which breathe in diff'rent frame,
By tie of common breath, man's pity claim.
A gentle lamb has rhetoric to plead,
And when she sees the butcher's knife decreed,
Her voice entreats him not to make her bleed:
But, cruel gain and luxury of taste
With pride, still lays man's fellow-mortals waste.
What earth and waters breed, or air inspires,
Man, for his palate fits, by tort'ring fires.

ANNA KINGSFORD, MD, 1846–1888

As to the second contention, that Nature's law is the law
of prey, and that therefore man has *a priori* a natural
right to rend and torment, it should be answered that the
term 'Nature' implies neither individuality nor responsibility, but simply *condition*. All that Nature does is to
permit the manifestation of acquired qualities *in
individuals*. In such sense we must understand the phrase
'habit is Nature'. This fact does not justify responsible
humanity in the manifestation of cruelties which put to
shame the worst of the carnivora. It is by dint of
following what Mr Matthew Arnold calls 'the stream of
tendency which makes for righteousness' that man has
risen out of the baser elements of his nature to the
recognition of the standard known as the 'golden rule'.
And it is precisely in proportion as he has set himself, on
every plane of his activity, to

> 'Move upward, working out the beast,
> And let the wolf and tiger die'

within him, that he has become higher, nobler – in a word, more manly. The modern advocates of flesh-eating and vivisection, on the contrary, would reverse the sentiment of the lines just quoted, and would have us

'Move down, returning to the beast,
And letting heart and conscience die',

making thereby the practice of the lowest in the scale of Nature the rule of the highest, and abasing the moral standard of mankind to the level of the habits of the most dangerous or noxious orders of brutes.

Our opponents are fond of calling arguments such as these 'sentimental', and seem to imagine that the word completely disposes of their value. But that this should be the case serves but to reveal more clearly their own position. For it shows either that they are ignorant of what the word 'sentiment' means – ignorant that honour is a sentiment, that courage, truthfulness, love, sympathy, friendship and every moral quality, the possession of which constitutes the superiority of civilized man over the savage and the brute, are sentiments; or else that they deliberately intend to obliterate these qualities from the curriculum of future generations of mankind and to exclude them from their definition of humanity. The pretence of modern civilization is to aim only at the acquirement of intellectual knowledge and physical gratification, with but scant, if any, regard to moral limits. In the creed of the nineteenth century, man is man, not because he has it in him to love justice and to refrain from doing wrong, but because, being a pre-eminently clever beast, he is the strongest and most successful of all beasts.

But the disciple of Buddha and of Pythagoras, the preacher of the Pure Life and of the Perfect Way, cries to humanity, 'Be men, not in mere physical form only – for form is worth nothing – but in spirit, by virtue of those qualities which exalt you above tigers, swine or jackals! Under all your pseudo-civilization lies a foul and festering sore, a moral blemish, staining your lives and making social amenities unlovely. For the sake of ministering to your depraved and unnatural appetites, there exists a whole class of men, deprived of human rights, whose daily work is to kill, and who pass all their years in shedding blood and in superintending violent death. Away, then, with the slaughterhouses! Make to yourselves a nobler ideal of life and of human destiny!'

From lecture given at Girton College, Cambridge, 24 April 1882

The ordinary flesh-eater, if he be a man of any perception, is always fain to acknowledge, on being pressed, that there is something in the usual mode of feeding which clashes with his finer sense of what ought to be. He would rather not talk about the slaughterhouse, he feels that the whole subject is, somehow, unsavoury, and more or less frankly admits that he cannot associate the idea of slaughter with what are called 'Utopian' theories of existence. But, in most cases, he is not ready to sacrifice the least of his appetites to his conscience. He likes the taste of flesh-meat, he will tell you, and does not wish to deprive himself of the pleasures it gives him. It is the custom of Society to eat it and he has no desire to make himself conspicuous by refusing to partake of the dishes set before him by his friends. Such an attitude of mind, of course, can only be dealt with effectually by an effort of will on the part of the individual himself. The excuses thus formulated are precisely those which every transgressor of every moral law turns to bay on the man who seeks to reform or convict him. The reason of such a man may be amply convinced that flesh-eating is neither scientific nor civilized and yet he lacks the courage to carry these convictions into practice. No logic is able to influence a person of this kind. His affair is with his

Conscience rather than with his reason.

But sometimes we meet opponents who tell us that the plea for purer and more merciful living rests on mere 'sentiment' ... Sentiment is but another name for that moral feeling which alone has made man the best that he is now ...

... it is precisely the power to recognize and exercise the sentiments which makes man to differ from the beasts ... And our system of living is pre-eminently a sentimental system, founded in the nature of Humanity, and made for true Men.

The Theosophist, February/March 1884

The great need of the popular form of the Christian religion is precisely a belief in the solidarity of all living things ... Who can doubt it who visits Rome – the city of the Pontiff – where now I am, and witnesses the black-hearted cruelty of these 'Christians' to the animals which toil and slave for them? ... Today I saw a great, thick-shod peasant kick his mule in the mouth out of pure wantonness. Argue with these ruffians, or with their priests, and they will tell you 'Christians have no duties to the beasts that perish.' Their Pope has told them so. So that everywhere in Catholic Christendom the poor, patient, dumb creatures endure every species of torment without a single word being uttered on their behalf by the teachers of religion. It is horrible – damnable. And the true reason of it all is because the beasts are popularly believed to be soulless.

The Credo of Christendom

CHARLES KINGSLEY, 1819–1875

He was not only, I soon discovered, a water drinker, but a strict vegetarian, to which, perhaps, he owed a great deal of the almost preternatural clearness, volubility and sensitiveness of mind.

Alton Locke

RUDYARD KIPLING, 1865–1936

The Beasts Are Very Wise

The beasts are very wise,
Their mouths are clean of lies,
They talk one to the other,
Bullock to bullock's brother
Resting after their labours,
Each in stall with his neighbours.
But man with goad and whip
Breaks up their fellowship,
Shouts in their silky ears,
Filling their soul with fears.
When he has ploughed the land,
He says: 'They understand.'
But the beasts in stall together,
Freed from the yoke and tether
Say as the torn flanks smoke:
'Nay, 'twas the whip that spoke.'

Horses

And some are sulky, while some will plunge.
(*So ho! Steady! Stand still, you!*)
Some you must gentle, and some you must lunge.
(*There! There! Who wants to kill you?*)
Some – there are losses in every trade –
Will break their hearts ere bitted and made,
Will fight like fiends as the rope cuts hard,
And die dumb-mad in the breaking yard.

BRIAN KLUG, 1949–

The world by which we are actually surrounded contains animals – animals with lives to lead – and not mere 'organisms' that 'vocalize' or 'emit behavioral responses' to 'stimuli'. A so-called theory that obscures this fact is no theory at all, but a form of tyranny exercised over ordinary language so as to impose a particular interest or will.

From address given to the 100th anniversary symposium of the American Anti-Vivisection Society, 1983

As one Professor of Biology and director of a laboratory at Yale University was recently quoted as saying, 'these animals have no rights at all, and those people who think they do are ... grossly deficient'. His animals, he says, are 'the raw materials of the lab'.

These are not the words of a *callous* man, but of a *cultured* man – a man who speaks from and within the culture of science. And because this is our culture too, we, who are no more callous than he is, are disposed to hear him. Our ears are attuned to what the doctors of science have to say. None of them advocates using animals frivolously or gratuitously. They tell us that it is 'necessary' to paralyse monkeys or rear them in isolation chambers; to immerse rats in boiling water or stun them with electric shock; to expose dogs to radiation and to burn the eyes of rabbits with sodium hydroxide. We are good listeners. When they use this word 'necessary' we understand tacitly that they are alluding to the wellbeing of the human race. We might still have queries and reservations. But this word 'necessary' stills our tongue and strikes a chord deep within us. We soon shake our heads and say, 'Well, if it's necessary, it's necessary.' We are good at repeating our lessons, and this is a lesson we learn repeatedly, whether it is from textbooks or from popular books, magazines or commercials. Wherever we look, this 'necessary' is written between the lines; it is written into our culture and we learned it – like science itself learned it – in our formative years. We are educated readers. Therefore we are easy to persuade.

The conviction that we *must* use lab animals – that it is

necessary to use them – is overlaid with connotations that pervade our education at its core. At the core of our education is a way of orientating ourselves towards the natural world around us. It is this orientation which primes us to see lab animals as pieces of equipment, as tools of the scientist's trade. Animals are not simply the raw materials of the lab; they are part of the 'deep structure' of the dream of science – *our* dream of conquest, of remaking nature in our image and extending our reach so as to encompass all things within our grasp. There is romance and hope and challenge in this dream.

Furthermore, it is no mere fantasy: every day our grasp grows wider, our grip becomes stronger. That is why it is so hard for us to broach and to think about and to discuss the questions that underlie laboratory animal use. How does one take issue with a dream – especially when one is caught up with it oneself? On the other hand, what kind of people are we if our dream requires, every year, tens of millions of animals to be put to the question? We do not pause to reflect. The inquisition of nature and of animals proceeds apace; and we have ways of making them talk.

Listening, Vol.18, No.1

JIDDU KRISHNAMURTI, 1895–1986

It is odd that we have so little relationship with nature, with the insects and the leaping frog and the owl that hoots among the hills calling for its mate. We never seem to have a feeling for all living things on the earth. If we could establish a deep abiding relationship with nature we would never kill an animal for our appetite, we would never harm, vivisect, a monkey, a dog, a guinea pig for our benefit. We would find other ways to heal our wounds, heal our bodies. But the healing of the mind is something totally different. That healing gradually takes place if you are with nature, with that orange on the tree, and the blade of grass that pushes through the cement, and the hills covered, hidden, by the clouds.

This is not sentiment or romantic imagination but a reality of a relationship with everything that lives and moves on the earth. Man has killed millions of whales and is still killing them. All that we derive from their slaughter can be had through other means. But apparently man loves to kill things, the fleeting deer, the marvellous gazelle and the great elephant. We love to kill each other. This killing of other human beings has never stopped through the history of man's life on this earth. If we could, and we must, establish a deep long-abiding relationship with nature, with the actual trees, the bushes, the flowers, the grass and the fast moving clouds, then we could never slaughter another human being for any reason whatsoever. Organized murder is war, and though we demonstrate against a particular war, the nuclear, or any other kind of war, we have never demonstrated against war. We have never said that to kill another human being is the greatest sin on earth.

Krishnamurti to Himself: His Last Journal

JOSEPH WOOD KRUTCH, 1893–1970

When a man wantonly destroys one of the works of man, we call him a vandal. When he wantonly destroys one of the works of God, we call him a sportsman.

The Great Chain of Life

How anyone can profess to find animal life interesting and yet take delight in reducing the wonder of any animal to a bloody mass of fur and feathers is beyond my comprehension.

Ibid.

A few mornings ago I rescued a bat from a swimming pool. The man who owned the pool – but did not own the bat – asked me why. That question I do not expect ever to be able to answer, but it involves a good deal. If even I myself could understand it, I would know what it is that seems to distinguish man from the rest of nature and why, despite all she has to teach him, there is also something he would like to teach her if he could.

Nature books always explain – for the benefit of utilitarians – that bats are economically important because they destroy many insects. For the benefit of those more interested in the marvellous than in the profitable, they also usually say something about the bat's wonderful invention of a kind of sonar by the aid of which he can fly in the blackest night without colliding with even so artificial an obstruction as a piano wire strung across his path. But before lifting my particular bat out of the swimming pool, I did not calculate his economic importance and I did not rapidly review in my mind the question whether or not his scientific achievement entitled him to life.

Still less could I pretend that he was a rare specimen or that one bat more or less would have any perceptible effect on the balance of nature. There were plenty of others just like him, right here where I live and throughout this whole area. Almost every night I have seen several of his fellows swooping down to the swimming pool for a drink before starting off for an evening of economically useful activity. A few weeks before I had, as a matter of fact, seen near Carlsbad, New Mexico, several hundred thousand of this very species in a single flight. That had seemed like enough bats to satisfy one for a normal lifetime. Yet here I was, not only fishing a single individual from the water, but tending him anxiously to see whether or not he could recover from an ordeal which had obviously been almost too much for him.

Probably he had fallen in because he had miscalculated in the course of the difficult maneuver involved in getting a drink on the wing. Probably, therefore, he had been in the water a good many hours and would not have lasted much longer. But he looked as though he wanted to live and I, inexplicably, also hoped that he would. And that would seem to imply some sort of kindliness more detached, more irrational, and more completely gratuitous than any nature herself is capable of. 'So careful of the type she seems, so careless of the single life.'

At Carlsbad, so it seemed to me, I had seen bats as nature sees them. Here by the swimming pool, I had seen an individual bat as only man can see him. It was a neat coincidence which arranged the two experiences so close together, and I shall always think of them in that way.

Even I find it difficult to love, in my special human way, as many bats as I saw at Carlsbad. Nature is content to love them in her way and makes no attempt here to love them in the way that even I would fail at. She loves bats in general and as a species. For that reason she can never get enough of them. But as long as there are plenty in the world, she is unconcerned with any particular bat. She gives him his chance (or sometimes his lack of it) and if he does not, or cannot, take it, others will. A margin of failure is to be expected. The greatest good of the greatest number is a ruling principle so absolute that it is not even tempered with regret over those who happen not to be included within the greatest number.

Thus nature discovered, long before the sociologists did, the statistical criterion. Bureaucratic states which accept averages and curves of distribution as realities against which there is no appeal represent a sort of 'return to nature' very different from what that phrase is ordinarily taken to imply. Insofar as the great dictators can be assumed to be in any sense sincere when they profess a concern with the welfare of their people or even with that of mankind, their concern is like nature's — indifferent to everything except the statistically measurable result. If they really love men, then they love them only as nature loves bats. She never devised anything so prompt and effective as the gas chamber, but her methods are sometimes almost equally unscrupulous. For she also has her methods — not always pretty ones — of getting rid of what she considers the superfluous. She seems to agree, in principle, with those who maintain that any decisive concern with a mere individual is unscientific, sentimental and ultimately incompatible with the greatest good of the greatest number.

But one bat in a swimming pool is not the same thing as two or three hundred thousand at Carlsbad. Because there is only one of him and only one of me, some sort of relationship, impossible in the presence of myriads, springs up between us. I no longer take toward him the attitude of nature or the dictator. I become a man again, aware of feelings which are commonly called humane but for which I prefer the stronger word, human.

The Best Nature Writing of Joseph Wood Krutch

MILAN KUNDERA, 1929–

The very beginning of Genesis tells us that God created man in order to give him dominion over fish and fowl and all creatures. Of course, Genesis was written by a man, not a horse. There is no certainty that God actually did grant man dominion over other creatures. What seems more likely, in fact, is that man invented God to sanctify the dominion that he had usurped for himself over the cow and the horse. Yes, the right to kill a deer or a cow is the only thing all of mankind can agree upon, even during the bloodiest of wars.

The reason we take that right for granted is that we

stand at the top of the hierarchy. But let a third party enter the game — a visitor from another planet, for example, someone to whom God says, 'Thou shalt have dominion over creatures of all other stars' — and all at once taking Genesis for granted becomes problematical. Perhaps a man hitched to the cart of a Martian or roasted on the spit by inhabitants of the Milky Way will recall the veal cutlet he used to slice on his dinner plate and apologize (belatedly!) to the cow ...

Be that as it may, Tereza continued on her path, and, watching her heifers rub against one another, she thought what nice animals they were. Calm, guileless and sometimes childishly animated, they looked like fat fifty-year-olds pretending they were fourteen. There was nothing more touching than cows at play. Tereza took pleasure in their antics and could not help thinking (it is an idea that kept coming back to her during her two years in the country) that man is as much a parasite on the cow as the tapeworm is on man: We have sucked their udders like leeches. 'Man the cow parasite' is probably how non-man defines man in his zoology books.

Now, we may treat this definition as a joke and dismiss it with a condescending laugh. But since Tereza took it seriously, she found herself in a precarious position: her ideas were dangerous and distanced her from the rest of mankind. Even though Genesis says that God gave man dominion over all animals, we can also construe it to mean that He merely entrusted them to man's care. Man was not the planet's master, merely its administrator, and therefore eventually responsible for his administration. Descartes took a decisive step forward: he made man '*maître et propriétaire de la nature*'. And surely there is a deep connection between that step and the fact that he was also the one who point-blank denied animals a soul. Man is master and proprietor, says Descartes, whereas the beast is merely an automaton, an animated machine, a *machina animata*. When an animal laments, it is not a lament; it is merely the rasp of a poorly functioning mechanism. When a wagon wheel grates, the wagon is not in pain; it simply needs oiling. Thus, we have no reason to grieve for a dog being carved up alive in the laboratory.

True human goodness, in all its purity and freedom, can come to the fore only when its recipient has no power. Mankind's true moral test, its fundamental test (which lies deeply buried from view), consists of its attitude towards those who are at its mercy: animals. And in this respect mankind has suffered a fundamental debacle, a debacle so fundamental that all others stem from it.

The Unbearable Lightness of Being

MANFRED KYBER, 1880–1933

Animals have their tragic and their comic side, and resemble us in many ways. They, too, have their distinctions and individualities. Many people believe that there is a huge gap separating them from the animals, but it is only really a step in the Wheel of Life, for we are all children of the One. To understand a fellow creature, we must regard him as a brother.

Among Animals (trans. O. Fishwick)

ALPHONSE MARIE LOUIS DE LAMARTINE, 1790– 1869

We cannot have two hearts, one for the animals, the other for man. In cruelty toward the former and cruelty toward the latter there is no difference but in the victim.

Physically, [my early education] was derived in a large measure from Pythagoras and from the *Emile*. Thus it was based upon the greatest simplicity of dress, and the most rigorous frugality with regard to food. My mother was convinced, as I myself am, that killing animals, for the sake of nourishment from their flesh and blood, is one of the infirmities of our human condition; that it is one of those curses imposed upon man either by his 'fault' or by the obduracy of his own perversity. She believed, as I do still, that the habit of hardening the heart towards the most gentle animals, our companions, our helpmates, our brothers in toil, and even in affection, on this earth; that the slaughtering, the appetite for blood, the sight of quivering flesh, are the very things to have the effect to brutalize and harden the instincts of the heart. She believed, as I do still, that such nourishment, although, apparently, much more succulent and active, contains within itself irritating and putrid principles, which embitter the food and shorten the days of man.

To support these ideas she would instance the numberless refined and pious people of India, who abstain from everything that has life, and the hardy, robust, pastoral race, and even the labouring population of our fields, who work the hardest, live the longest and most simply, and who do not eat flesh ten times in their lives. She never allowed me to eat it until I was thrown into the rough-and-tumble life of the public school. To wean me from the liking for it she used no arguments, but availed herself of that instinct in us which reasons better than logic. I had a lamb, whom a peasant of Milly had given me, and whom I had trained to follow me everywhere, like the most attached and faithful dog. We loved each other with that first love which children and young animals naturally have for each other. One day the cook said to my mother in my presence, 'Madame, the lamb is fat, and the butcher has come for it, must I give it him?' I screamed, and threw myself on the lamb, asking what the butcher would do with it, and what was a butcher? The cook replied that he was a man who gained his living by killing lambs, sheep, calves, and cows. I could not believe it. I besought my mother and readily obtained mercy for my favourite. A few days afterwards my mother took me with her to the town and led me, as by chance, through the Shambles. There I saw men with blood-stained arms felling a bullock. Others were killing calves and sheep and cutting off their still palpitating limbs. Streams of blood smoked here and there upon the pavement. I was seized with a profound pity, mingled with horror, and asked to be taken away. The idea of these horrible and repulsive scenes, the necessary preliminaries of the dinner I saw served at table, made me hold animal food in disgust, and butchers in horror.

Les Confidences

CLAY LANCASTER, 1917–

Dharmapala commented that Aśoka's 'glory was to spread the teachings of the Buddha throughout the world by the force of love, and indeed nobody could say that he had failed.... When Buddhism flourished in India, the arts, sciences and civilization reached their zenith, ... Wherever Buddhism has gone, the nations have imbibed its spirit, and the people have become gentler and milder.' For high cultural attainments, prolonged periods of peace and prosperity, and the amenities of a humane society, no civilization elsewhere can compare with those under the aegis of Buddhism in Asia: the Gupta period in India, the T'ang and Sung in China, when the Emperors resided at Nara and Kyoto in Japan, the Sailendra in Java, the great cities of Anuradapura and Polonnaruwa in Ceylon, and Pagan in Burma. Nor should we overlook that most splendid of medieval capitals, Angkor Thom, in Cambodia, whose builder, Jayavarman VII, emulated Aśoka in establishing laws and instituting shelters to promote the wellbeing of humanity and fauna.

The busy Occidental has no time for such irrelevancies. For quiet recreation he takes the children to the zoo, to be amused by the jungle giants restlessly pacing up and down the concrete floor in their iron-bar cages, the comical antics of elephants begging peanuts and the wry expressions on the faces of the monkeys, imprisoned for crimes not they but men have committed against them. Or, for more strenuous recreation, he takes his gun and goes hunting, to track and kill the forest denizens, which he calls 'sport'. He may bring home a trophy of his skill, a deer's head, to mount and hang on his wall to attest to what a brute he is. His women folk patronize the trapper, the mutilators of baby seals, the skinner, the furrier – all of those immoral people who make a living murdering and robbing innocent quadrupeds of their natural apparel to become secondhand garments for pitiless bipeds. His contributions support heartless vivisectors, those who conduct caustic experiments on living animals, wherein – Mark Twain once described it – the victims are 'boiled, baked, scalded, burnt with turpentine, frozen, cauterized; they have been partly drowned and brought back to consciousness to have the process repeated; they have been cut open and mangled in every part of the body, and have been kept alive in a mutilated state for experiments lasting days or weeks'. Much of this is student 'training'. Martyrs include dogs, cats, guinea pigs, apes and so on; mute rabbits have been heard to shriek from excruciating pain during vivisection practices. Mostly such atrocities are performed behind closed doors and in soundproof laboratories, and the public may be excused for its indolence regarding them. But elsewhere the results of such malevolence are exposed to plain view. In the modern supermarket are long rows of shelves stacked high with dismembered carcasses of lambs, calves, cows, and pigs, packaged in transparent plastic, revealing bones, muscles, fat, oozing blood and lymph, with eager shoppers selecting these products of agony, suffering and death to feed to equally calloused diners. All of these people would be horrified at the thought of their house pets being so killed, maimed, and processed for dining-room consumption as the remains of the less fortunate beings they have purchased; but a more general view of the matter has not entered their heads. At best they offer the excuse that humans are so far above the other animals that it is quite appropriate for the one to be doomed to become the other's food. By the same reasoning, hominoids from outer space, equally superior to man, would be entirely justified in condemning humans to the slaughterhouse and packing plant for their feasts. If this planet is ever invaded by galaxy foreigners with weapons so efficient that they become absolute masters within a matter of minutes, it will be unlucky for man if their recreational and sporting practices, delight in experimentation and taste in clothing as well as food have no more regard for universal ethics than have the prevailing Western religions.

The Incredible World's Parliament of Religions:
A Comparative and Critical Study

As has been seen, many of the Christian speakers made little attempt to heed the exact wording and meaning of the scriptures, but interpreted (actually falsified) them according to what suited their purpose at the moment. Some admitted that assurance of immortality was a tenuous matter as stated, and that it was limited to Jews in both the Old and New Testaments. Others pointed out how unreliable the book was due to its dubious authorship, questionable translations, haphazard arrangement, erroneous grammar and poor choice of terms. There might have been some justification for acclaiming Jesus the unparalleled prophet if his character as presented in *The Gospel of the Holy Twelve* had been accepted. Here his kindness is consonant, extending to all manner of creatures; he speaks against officials who defile the temple, but he does not resort to savage violence against them as in standard versions of the episode. However, this greater Christ requires the observance of universal ethics, which Christians do not want. They prefer a carnivorous, wine-bibbing Jesus of righteous wrath, so that they can act the same way themselves yet remain among the 'elect' without the additional burden of having to practice goodness.

Ibid.

WALTER SAVAGE LANDOR, 1775–1864

Cruelty is the chief, if not the only sin.

From *A Satire on Satirists*
For eaters of goose liver there is drest
This part alone; the cats divide the rest;
The fire that plumps it, leaves the creature dry,
So too with poets does the poetry;
This is their liver, truffled, tender, sweet,
And all beside is sad unchristian meat.*

* Landor added: '*And all beside is sad unchristian meat* – He who could partake of such an abominable luxury, knowing its process, ought not even to be buried where men are buried, but (in strict retributive justice) given to the kites and crows.'

WILLIAM LANGLAND, c.1332–c.1400

A View from Middle-Earth

This was my dream: Nature stood nigh me,
Said, 'Come with me, William, and view the world's
   wonders.'
To a mountain we moved – Middle-Earth its name is –
To learn by looking. With new sight I witnessed
The sun and the sea and the sand beside it,
And the secret places of grove and grassland
Where birds and beasts could mate unmolested –
The wildwood creatures, a blaze of beauty!
The wings of the wildfowl, so flecked with colours.
I saw man and his mate too, now poor, now with plenty,
In war and in peace – but where was their wisdom?
Grasping and greedy, they gave away nothing.
But the creatures followed the rule of Reason
Wise in their feeding and in their engendering.
No hound, nor horse, not one kind of creature,
Meddled with mate that was carrying young ones.
I watched the birds build nests in the bushes;
No human hand could have worked such weaving.
Where could we match the magpie's mastery
In twining twigs for the nest she'll breed in?
No carpenter could contrive such craftwork
No builder build it, whatever the blueprint.
Other birds were as much a marvel.
Some hid their homes from harm and hunters
In moor and marshes where men could not mark them,
Their eggs close hidden from foraging fingers.
Some in the tree-tops met and mated,
High out of harm when they hatched their young ones.
How did they know? What teacher taught them?
Then I stared at the sea, at the sky full of starlight,
At the flowers in the forest, their fresh fair colours,
At the grasses, even their green so varied,

Some grasses sweet, some sour to the tasting –
Too many the mysteries; but what most moved me
Was how Reason guided the whole of nature,
All creation, save one kind only –
Man and his mate.

From The Vision of Piers Plowman translated into
modern English by Naomi Lewis

GILL LANGLEY, MA, PhD, MIBiol., 1952 –

To date our understanding of the natures and capacities of other animals has most often been limited not by their 'differentness' from us, but by the simplicity of our preconceptions and assumptions about them. Animals may differ in degree but not radically in kind from us. We demean ourselves by ignoring the evidence of our similarities and continuing with our prejudices against the rest of the animal kingdom.

Cambridge University debate October 1987

TOM LANTOS, 1928 –

The issue of animal experimentation has a profound moral dimension to it. In this area, more than in any other, we speak and act for those who have no means of defending themselves. Not just their welfare, but their lives, are in our hands.

Public disillusionment with science in general is increasing year by year. Never before has there been such a tide of moral outrage over what we have seen and heard is happening in our Nation's animal laboratories. However, what we face today is not a crusade against science per se. Rather, it is a movement set on defining our needs and determining how best to fill them without resorting to inhumane and uncivilized means. It is a sign that we are entering a new age of social and ethical considerations, for we now seek knowledge and benefit uncontaminated by brutality.

> From a speech in the House of Representatives, 22 March 1983, quoted in the *Congressional Record*, Washington, Vol.129, No.37

PHILIP LARKIN, 1922–1986

Take One Home for the Kiddies

On shallow straw, in shadeless glass,
Huddled by empty bowls, they sleep:
No dark, no dam, no earth, nor grass –
Mam, get us one of them to keep.

Living toys are something novel,
But it soon wears off somehow.
Fetch the shoebox, fetch the shovel –
Mam, we're playing funerals now.

DR DOUGLAS LATTO, 1913 –

To live in harmony with one another, we need to live in harmony also with the animals, on a balanced vegetarian diet without vivisection, which has no bearing on human health. Vegetarianism is natural, and the only defence for flesh-eating is the acquired taste.

Like the higher apes, we are fruit-and-nut-eating, as proved by our teeth, saliva, tongue, biting-and-chewing muscles, skin, nails, alimentary tract and so on. To eat flesh, Man must forget the gambolling lamb. No longer to want to eat it means he is more at peace with his surroundings. It is not true that we have to kill out of self-preservation. Animals that are killed reproduce faster, and creatures that are not killed do not overrun the earth.

A pest is some creature that takes more out of the

world than it puts into it, and that is Man alone. It is Man who has upset the balance of Nature, killing off certain predators, moving animals to where they don't belong and have no natural enemies, all this for his own misconceived purposes. Man considers a pest any animal that doesn't put money into his pocket. So war is launched upon the animals with disease viruses, chemicals and guns, all to remedy Man's own blunders.

Steps Unto Him, September/December 1959

DR GORDON LATTO, 1911 –

In a lunch session in a slaughterhouse, a lamb jumped out of its pen and came unnoticed up to some slaughtermen who were sitting in a circle eating their sandwiches; the lamb approached and nibbled a small piece of lettuce that a man was holding in his hand. The men gave the lamb some more lettuce and when the lunch period was over they were so affected by the action of the lamb that not one of them was prepared to kill this creature, and it had to be sent away elsewhere – showing that within each human soul there is an element of pity, compassion and love in varying degrees. It is our duty to encourage the higher qualities in each individual to bloom and blossom wherever possible.

If Britain adopted a vegetarian way of life, many of her problems would recede and dissolve ... If this way of living were adopted, a great deal of cruelty would cease; compassion, pity and consideration for others would grow and there would be happier and healthier conditions in the world and on this island. It is change not of legislation that is wanted, but a change of heart of the peoples.

The Vegetarian Way, XXIV World Vegetarian Congress, 1977

Apart from the value of the frugivorous diet to man himself, it also brings great benefit to our younger brothers, the sub-human creatures. When we lose our sense of pity and compassion for the creatures, we harden our hearts to them and also to our brother man.

The Vegetarian Way, 1967

D.H. LAWRENCE, 1885–1930

Middleton, Thursday

My dear Katherine,

… It is snow, snow, snow here – white, white. Yesterday was the endless silence of softly falling snow. I thought the world had come to an end – that I was like a last inhabitant of the moon when the moon shed all its snow and went into a white dream for ever, slowly breathing its last in a soft, dim snowfall, silent beyond silence. Nobody comes, the snow is white on the shrubs, the tuft of larches above the road have each a white line up the trunk.

Lord! Lord! Only the rabbit feet and the bird feet are all over the paths and across the yard …

There is a pheasant comes and lies by the wall under the gooseberry bushes, for shelter. He is so cold, he hardly notices us. We plan to catch him by throwing over him the netted hammock. But for the sake of his green head and his long pointed feathers, I cannot. We thought we would catch him and send him you to eat. But when I look at him, so clear as he is and formal on the snow, I am bound to respect a thing which attains to so much perfection of grace and bearing.

From a letter to Katherine Mansfield

Lobo

… Men!
Two men!
Men! The only animal in the world to fear!

… Two Mexicans, strangers, emerging out of the dark
and snow and inwardness of the Lobo valley.
What are they doing here on this vanishing trail?

What is he carrying?
Something yellow.
A deer?

Qué tiene, amigo?
Leon —

He smiles, foolishly, as if he were caught doing wrong.
And we smile, foolishly, as if we didn't know.
He is quite gentle and dark-faced.

It is a mountain lion,
A long, long slim cat, yellow like a lioness.
Dead.

He trapped her this morning, he says, smiling foolishly.

Lift up her face,
Her round, bright face, bright as frost.
Her round, fine-fashioned head, with two dead ears;
And stripes in the brilliant frost of her face, sharp, fine
dark rays,
Dark, keen, fine rays in the brilliant frost of her face.
Beautiful dead eyes.

Hermoso es!

They go out towards the open;
We go on into the gloom of Lobo.
And above the trees I found her lair,

A hole in the blood-orange brilliant rocks that stick up,
a little cave.
And bones, and twigs, and a perilous ascent.

So, she will never leap up that way again, with the yellow
flash of a mountain-lion's long shoot!
And her bright striped frost face will never watch any
more, out of the shadow of the cave in the
blood-orange rock,
Above the trees of the Lobo dark valley-mouth!

Instead, I look out.
And out to the dim of the desert, like a dream, never real;
To the snow of the Sangre de Cristo mountains, the ice of
the mountains of Picoris,
And near across at the opposite steep of snow, green
trees motionless standing in snow, like a Christmas toy.
And I think in this empty world there was room for me
and a mountain lion.
And I think in the world beyond, how easily we might
spare a million or two of humans
And never miss them.
Yet what a gap in the world, the missing white frost face
of the slim yellow mountain lion!

Birds, Beasts and Flowers

An inkpot ... is a polyp, a little octopus which, alas,
frequents the Mediterranean and squirts ink if offended
... Alessandro caught inkpots: and like this. He tied up a
female by a string ... through a convenient hole in her
end ... When Alessandro went a-fishing, he towed her,
like a poodle, behind. And thus, like a poodly-bitch, she
attracted hangers-on in the briny seas. And these poor
polyp inamorati were the victims. They were lifted as
prey onboard, where I looked with horror on their grey,
translucent tentacles and large, cold, stony eyes. The

she-polyp was towed behind again. But after a few days she died.

And I think, even for creatures so awful-looking, this method is indescribably base, and shows how much lower than an octopus even is lordly man.

Sea and Sardinia

Lizard

A lizard ran out on a rock and looked up, listening no
 doubt to the sounding of the spheres.
And what a dandy fellow! The right toss of a chin for you
 and swirl of a tail!

If men were as much men as lizards are lizards
 they'd be worth looking at.

Snake

... Someone was before me at my water-trough,
And I, like a second comer, waiting.

He lifted his head from his drinking, as cattle do,
And looked at me vaguely, as drinking cattle do,
And flickered his two-forked tongue from his lips, and
 mused a moment,
And stooped and drank a little more,
Being earth-brown, earth-golden from the burning
 bowels of the earth
On the day of Sicilian July, with Etna smoking.

The voice of my education said to me
He must be killed.
For in Sicily the black, black snakes are innocent, the gold
 are venomous.

And voices in me said, If you were a man
You would take a stick, and break him now, and finish
 him off.

But must I confess how I liked him,
How glad I was he had come like a guest in quiet, to drink
    at my water-trough
And depart peaceful, pacified, and thankless,
Into the burning bowels of this earth?

Was it cowardice, that I dared not kill him?
Was it humility, to feel so honoured?
I felt so honoured.

    And yet those voices:
If you were not afraid, you would kill him!

    And truly I was afraid, I was most afraid,
But even so, honoured still more
That he should seek my hospitality
From out of the dark door of the secret earth.

    He drank enough
And lifted his head, dreamily, as one who has drunken,
And flickered his tongue like a forked night on the air, so
    black,
Seeming to lick his lips,
And looked around like a god, unseeing, into the air,
And slowly turned his head,
And slowly, very slowly, as if thrice adream,
Proceeded to draw his slow length curving round
And climb again the broken bank of my wall-face.

    And as he puts his head into that dreadful hole,
And as he slowly drew up, snake-easing his shoulders,
    and entered farther,
A sort of horror, a sort of protest against his withdrawing
    into that horrid black hole,
Deliberately going into the blackness, and slowly drawing
    himself after,
Overcame me now his back was turned.

I looked around, I put down my pitcher,
I picked up a clumsy log
And threw it at the water-trough with a clatter.

I think it did not hit him,
But suddenly that part of him that was left behind
   convulsed in undignified haste,
Writhed like lightning, and was gone
Into the black hole, the earth-lipped fissure in the
   wall-front,
At which, in the intense still noon, I stared with
   fascination ...

And immediately I regretted it.
I thought how paltry, how vulgar, what a mean act!
I despised myself and the voices of my accursed human
   education.
And I thought of the albatross,
And I wished he could come back, my snake.
For he seemed to me again like a king,
Like a king in exile, uncrowned in the underworld.
Now due to be crowned again.

And so, I missed my chance with one of the lords
Of life.
And I have something to expiate;
A pettiness.

JOHN LAWRENCE, 1753–1839

Can there be one kind of justice for men and another for
brutes? Is feeling in them a different thing to what it is in
ourselves? Is not a beast produced by the same rule and
in the same way as we ourselves? Is not his body
nourished by the same food, hurt by the same injuries,
his mind actuated by the same passions and affections
which animate the human breast and does not he, also, at

last, mingle his dust with ours and in like manner surrender up the vital spark? Is this spark or soul to perish because it chanced to belong to a beast? Is it to become annihilate? Tell me, learned philosophers, how that may possibly happen.

On the Rights of Beasts

CLORIS LEACHMAN, 1926 –

As soon as I realized that I didn't need meat to survive or to be in good health, I began to see how forlorn it all is. If only we had a different mentality about the drama of the cowboy and the range and all the rest of it. It's a very romantic notion, an entrenched part of American culture, but I've seen, for example, pigs waiting to be slaughtered, and their hysteria and panic was something I shall never forget for the rest of my life.

The Vegetarians

C.W. LEADBEATER, 1854–1934

Every religion has taught that man should put himself on the side of the will of God in the world, on the side of good as against evil, of evolution as against retrogression. The man who ranges himself on the side of evolution realizes the wickedness of destroying life; for he knows that, just as he is here in this physical body in order that he may learn the lessons of this plane, so is the animal occupying his body for the same reason, that through it he may gain experience at his lower stage. He knows that the life behind the animal is the Divine Life, that all life in the world is Divine; the animals therefore are truly our brothers, even though they may be younger brothers, and we can have no sort of right to take their lives for the gratification of our perverted tastes – no right to cause them untold agony and suffering merely to satisfy our degraded and detestable lusts.

We have brought these things to such a pass with our mis-called 'sport' and our wholesale slaughtering, that all wild creatures fly from the sight of us. Does that seem like the universal brotherhood of God's creatures? Is that your idea of the golden age of worldwide kindliness that is to come – a condition when every living thing flees from the face of man because of his murderous instincts? There is an influence flowing back upon us from all this – an effect which you can hardly realize unless you are able to see how it looks when regarded with the sight of the higher plane. Every one of these creatures which you so ruthlessly murder in this way has its own thoughts and feelings with regard to all this; it has horror, pain and indignation, and an intense but unexpressed feeling of the hideous injustice of it all. The whole atmosphere about us is full of it. Twice lately I have heard from psychic people that they felt the awful aura or surroundings of Chigaco even many miles away from it. Mrs Besant herself told me the same thing twenty years ago in England – that long before she came in sight of Chicago she felt the horror of it and the deadly pall of depression descending upon her, and asked: 'Where are we and what is the reason that there should be this terrible feeling in the air?' To sense the effect as clearly as this, is beyond the reach of the person who is not developed; but, though all the inhabitants may not be directly conscious of it and recognize it as Mrs Besant did, they may be sure that they are suffering from it unconsciously, and that that terrible vibration of horror and fear and injustice is acting upon every one of them, even though they do not know it.

Vegetarianism and Occultism

251

The destruction of life is always a crime. There may be certain cases in which it is the lesser of two evils: but here [in eating the flesh of animals] it is needless and without a shadow of justification, for it happens only because of the selfish unscrupulous greed of those who coin money out of the agonies of the animal kingdom in order to pander to the perverted taste of those who are sufficiently depraved to desire such loathsome aliment. Remember, it is not only those who do the obscene work, but those who by feeding upon this dead flesh encourage them and make their crime remunerative, who are guilty before God of this awful thing. Every person who partakes of this unclean food has his share of the indescribable guilt and suffering by which it has been obtained. It is universally recognized in law that *qui facit per alium facit per se* – whatsoever a man does through another he does himself.

A man will often say: 'But it would make no difference to all this horror if I alone ceased to eat meat.' That is untrue and disingenuous. First it would make a difference, for although you may consume only a pound or two each day, that would in time amount to the weight of an animal. Secondly, it is not a question of amount but of complicity in a crime, and if you partake of the result of a crime, you are helping to make it remunerative, and so you share in the guilt. No honest man can fail to see that this is so. But when men's lower lusts are concerned they are usually dishonest in their view, and decline to face the plain facts. There surely can be no difference of opinion as to the proposition that all this horrible unnecessary slaughter is indeed a terrible crime.

Ibid.

I read an article only the other day in which it was explained that the nauseating stench which rises from those Chicago slaughterhouses, and settles like a fatal miasma over the city, is by no means the most deadly influence that comes up from that Christian hell for animals, though it is the breath of certain death to many a mother's darling. The slaughterhouses make not only a pest-hole for the bodies of children, but for their souls as well. Not only are the children employed in the most revolting and cruel work, but the whole trend of their thoughts is directed towards killing. Occasionally one is found too sensitive to endure the sights and sounds of that ceaseless awful battle between man's cruel lust and the right of every creature to its own life. I read how one boy, for whom a minister had secured a place in the slaughterhouse, returned home day after day pale and sick and unable to eat or sleep, and finally came to that minister of the gospel of the compassionate Christ and told him that he was willing to starve if necessary, but that he could not wade in blood another day. The horrors of slaughter had so affected him that he could no longer sleep. Yet this is what many a boy is doing and seeing from day to day until he becomes hardened to the taking of life; and then some day, instead of cutting the throat of a lamb or a pig, he kills a man, and straightway we turn our lust for slaughter upon him in turn, and think that we have done justice.

I read that a young woman who does much philanthropic work in the neighbourhood of these pest-houses declares that what most impresses her about the children is that they seem to have no games except the relation of slaughterer to the victim. This is the education which so-called Christians are giving to the children of the slaughterhouse – a daily education in murder; and then they express surprise at the number and brutality of the murders in that district. Yet your Christian public goes on serenely saying its prayers and singing its psalms and listening to its sermons, as if no such outrage were being perpetrated against God's children in that sink-hole of pestilence and crime. Surely the habit of eating dead flesh has produced a moral apathy among us.

Are you doing well, do you think, in rearing your future citizens among surroundings of such utter brutality as this? Even on the physical plane this is a terribly serious matter, and from the occult point of view it is unfortunately far more serious still; for the occultist sees the psychic result of all this, sees how these forces are acting upon the people and how they intensify brutality and unscrupulousness. He sees what a centre of vice and of crime you have created; and how from it the infection is gradually spreading until it affects the whole country, and even the whole of what is called civilized humanity.

The average man is not after all a brute, but means to be kind if he only knew how. He does not think; he goes on from day to day, and does not realize that he is taking part all the time in an awful crime. But facts are facts, and there is no escape from them; every one who is partaking of this abomination is helping to make this appalling thing a possibility, and undoubtedly shares the responsibility for it. You know that this is so, and you can see what a terrible thing it is; but you will say: 'What can we do to improve matters – we who are only tiny units in this mighty, seething mass of humanity? It is only by units rising above the rest and becoming more civilized that we shall finally arrive at a higher civilization of the race as a whole. There is a Golden Age to come, not only for man but for the lower kingdoms, a time when humanity will realize its duty to its younger brothers – not to destroy them, but to help them and train them, so that we may receive from them, not terror and hatred, but love and devotion and friendship, and reasonable co-operation. A time will come when all the forces of Nature shall be intelligently working together towards the final end, not with constant suspicion and hostility, but with universal recognition of the Brotherhood which is ours because we are all children of the same Almighty Father.

Let us at least make the experiment; let us free ourselves from complicity in these awful crimes; let us set ourselves to try, each in our own small circle, to bring nearer that bright time of peace and love which is the dream and the earnest desire of every true-hearted and thinking man. At least we ought surely to be willing to do so small a thing as this to help the world onward towards that glorious future; we ought to make ourselves pure, our thoughts and our actions as well as our food, so that by example as well as by precept we may be doing all that in us lies to spread the gospel of love and of compassion, to put an end to the reign of brutality and terror, and to bring nearer the dawn of the great kingdom of righteousness and love when the will of our Father shall be done upon earth as it is in heaven.

Ibid.

W.E.H. LECKY, 1838–1903

I venture to maintain that there are multitudes to whom the necessity of discharging the duties of a butcher would be so inexpressibly painful and revolting, that if they could obtain a flesh diet on no other condition, they would relinquish it for ever.

History of European Morals

The animal world being altogether external to the scheme of redemption, was regarded as beyond the range of duty, and the belief that we have any kind of obligation to its members has never been inculcated – has never, I believe, been even admitted – by Catholic theologians.

Ibid.

Spain and southern Italy, in which Catholicism has most deeply implanted its roots, are even now, probably beyond all other countries in Europe, those in which inhumanity to animals is most wanton and unrebuked.

Ibid.

The moral duty to be expected in different ages is not a unity of standard, or of acts, but a unity of tendency ... At one time the benevolent affections embrace merely the family, soon the circle expanding includes first a class, then a nation, then all humanity, and finally, its influence is felt in the dealings of man with the animal world.

Ibid.

DR HENRY LEE, FRCS, 1817–1898

The hands of the vivisector, by the repeated use of morally unlawful things, gradually become hardened, and a kind of creeping paralysis finally extends to the vital parts. We have it on evidence before the Royal Commission that, while interested in his experiments, he thinks nothing of the animals' sufferings, but, which is of far more importance, common experience shows that, as a rule, he is quite indifferent to the mental and sometimes bodily sufferings which the records of his experiments produce upon a large section of the public.

Found among his papers after his death

RONNIE LEE, 1951–

We have been at war with the other creatures of this earth ever since the first human hunter set forth with spear into the primeval forest. Human imperialism has everywhere enslaved, oppressed, murdered and mutilated the animal peoples. All around us lie the slave camps we have built for our fellow creatures, factory farms and vivisection laboratories, Dachaus and Buchenwalds for the conquered species. We slaughter animals for our food, force them to perform silly tricks for our delectation, gun them down and stick hooks in them in the name of sport. We have torn up the wild places where once they made their homes. The million-year Reich of the master-species continues. Speciesism is more deeply entrenched within us even than sexism, and that is deep enough.

'How Long Shall These Things Be?' *Peace News*, 4 April 1975

An individual animal doesn't care if its species is facing extinction – it cares if it is feeling pain.

Interview in *Agenda*, September/October 1982

ALBERT LEFFINGWELL, MD, 1845–1916

Say what we will, there is a kind of moral deterioration inseparable from the act of killing anything which is doing us no harm. To put out of existence a noxious animal or insect is to obey the instinct of self-preservation; but to take a perfectly harmless creature, kin to the pet of many a child, and to deprive it of whatever joys come from living ... simply that children may see how curiously Nature has constructed it ... can hardly fail to give them a sense of wrongful complicity with deprivation of another's rights.

Is it wise to blunt this sensibility regarding the sacredness of life? I am not referring to the psychopathic child, but to all children alike. There will come a time when as young men and women they should know how to prevent pain, by causing the painless termination of life; but for childhood that lesson should be *unlearned* and as far as possible delayed. The beauty, the grace, the excellence of all harmless living things is the lesson for children, rather than precocious intimacy with the mystery of death.

Then, too, there is yet another danger. The desire, the ambition to imitate is one of the first instincts of conscious life. I question whether ever there was an experiment in a classroom that some child did not try to imitate in private ... then you have initiated childhood into private vivisection. Is that advisable? Admit that you caution your class against such repetitions. But you cannot easily convince an inquiring mind that what is right for the teacher to do in public may not also be copied in the privacy of his own room and in the presence of his classmates.

Editorial on vivisection for *Voice of the Voiceless*

ROBERT LEIGHTON, 1611–1684

The Bunch of Larks

Portly he was, in carriage somewhat grand;
    Of gentleman he wore the accepted marks:
He trod the busy street, and in his hand
    He bore a bunch of larks!

I met him in the street, and turn'd about,
    And mused long after he had flaunted by.
A bunch of larks! and his intent, no doubt.
    To have them in a pie.

Yes, four-and-twenty larks baked in a pie!
    O, what a feast of melody is there!
The ringing chorus of a summer sky!
    A dish of warbling air!

How many dusty wanderers of the earth
    Have those still'd voices lifted from the dust!

And now to end their almost heavenly mirth
 Beneath a gourmand's crust!

But as he pricks their thin ambrosial throats,
 Will no accusing memories arise,
Of grassy glebes, and heaven-descending notes,
 And soul-engulfing skies?

'Give me', cries he, 'the *substance* of a thing –
 Something that I can eat, or drink, or feel –
A poem for the money it will bring –
 Larks for the dainty meal.'

Well, he may have his substance, and I mine.
 Deep in my soul the throbbing lark-notes lie.
My substance lasts, and takes a life divine –
 His passes with the pie.

FRIEDA LE PLA, 1892–1978

Once admit that a good end justifies the use of any methods, no matter how diabolical in their cruelty, there could very easily be hell let loose on earth, with morality and human feeling exterminated. For the human mind is ingenious enough to produce endless excuses about 'good objects' to justify the perpetration of any crime under the sun – from the assassination of some distinguished human being to the torture of an innocent animal – as it always has done times without number throughout its history. Normal human beings would agree that such things as cruelty, meanness, injustice, etc., are evil in themselves, definite sins which defile the moral nature; so how can any number of 'good ends' make them otherwise than what they are in themselves, having adverse effects on the characters of those individuals and groups stooping to employ them? Sin, evil, always brings about evil results sooner or later, whether in material consequences or in the moral and spiritual nature of the wrongdoer – or in both. The present chaos in medical theories, and the failure to discover the cause and cure of such diseases as cancer, and the large number and variety of diseases now rampant in the world, are in themselves proof that what is morally wrong can never be scientifically right.

Vivisection Right or Wrong?

Vivisection is an adverse reflection on the character of God. If it were *really* a law of the universe (that is, a law of the Creator's) that humans could only gain and keep their health by the vivisection of fellow-beings weaker and smaller than themselves, what sort of a law-maker and creator would this imply? Surely not a God of love, compassion, and justice, Who is Father of these His sub-human children just as He is Father of all humans, and in Whom, as in His human children, there is something of His very own self? Rather, the maker of such a law would need to be one devoid of the aforesaid qualities, devoid of tenderness and chivalry, who would ruthlessly and pitilessly sacrifice his weaker creatures to the strong, and who would unfairly exploit the innocent for the guilty who themselves bring about their own ailments by defiance of the laws of health. The existence of such atrocities as vivisection has contributed to drive a number of ardent, sensitive-souled humanitarians into agnosticism because all their highest idealism and spirit of chivalry revolts passionately against the idea of a God who would countenance such cruelties as vivisection, let alone *ordain* them as the sole and necessary means whereby humans could derive desired benefits. Such humanitarianism could not possibly accept and adore as a perfect, an ideal God, such a law-maker as he must be who could ordain that only cruel methods are effective to attain a good and worthy end.

Ibid.

It is not the human person's *physical* body that renders him 'more valuable' than an animal. It is the quality of his soul-life, his moral life. A race of physically healthy humans, perfectly formed, immune to disease, but minus the God-bestowed virtues of chivalry, compassion and justice towards their weaker sub-human kinsfolk, taking mean advantage of their helplessness to exploit them ruthlessly for human ends (whether for 'sport' or for 'scientific' research), living complacently on the bad old maxim that a good end justifies any means, even of diabolical cruelty – such a race, spiritually deformed and scarred by the ugliness of selfish ruthlessness, would not be morally above the lower animals and would be a degraded people compared with such noble, chivalrous souls as Jesus of Nazareth, Buddha, and St Francis of Assisi.

Ibid.

C.S. LEWIS, 1898–1963

Vivisection can only be defended by showing it to be right that one species should suffer in order that another species be happier ... If we cut up beasts simply because they cannot prevent us and because we are backing our own side in the struggle for existence, it is only logical to cut up imbeciles, criminals, enemies, or capitalists for the same reasons.

The Problem of Pain

A rational discussion of this subject [vivisection] begins by enquiring whether pain is, or is not, an evil. If it is not, then the case against vivisection falls. But then so does the case for vivisection. If it is not defended on the ground that it reduces human suffering, on what ground can it be defended? And if pain is not an evil, why should human suffering be reduced? We must therefore assume as a basis for the whole discussion that pain is an evil, otherwise there is nothing to be discussed.

Vivisection

The Christian defender, especially in the Latin countries, is very apt to say that we are entitled to do anything we please to animals because they 'have no souls'. But what does this mean? If it means that animals have no consciousness, then how is this known? They certainly behave as if they had, or at least the higher animals do. I myself am inclined to think that far fewer animals than is supposed have what we should recognize as consciousness. But that is only an opinion. Unless we know on other grounds that vivisection is right we must not take the moral risk of tormenting them on a mere opinion. On the other hand, the statement that they 'have no souls' may mean that they have no moral responsibilities and are not immortal. But the absence of 'soul' in that sense makes the infliction of pain upon them not easier but harder to justify. For it means that animals cannot deserve pain, nor profit morally by the discipline of pain, nor be recompensed by happiness in another life for suffering in this. Thus all the factors which render pain more tolerable or make it less totally evil in the case of human beings will be lacking in the beasts. 'Soullessness', in so far as it is relevant to the question at all, is an argument against vivisection.

Ibid.

Most [vivisectors are] naturalistic and Darwinian. Now here, surely, we come up against a very alarming fact. The very same people who will most contemptuously brush aside any consideration of animal suffering if it stands in the way of 'research' will also, in another context, most vehemently deny that there is any radical difference between man and the other animals. On the naturalistic view the beasts are at bottom just the same *sort* of thing as ourselves. Man is simply the cleverest of the anthropoids. All the grounds on which a Christian might defend vivisection are thus cut from under our feet. We sacrifice other species to our own not because our own has any objective metaphysical privilege over others, but simply because it is ours. It may be very natural to have this loyalty to our own species, but let us hear no more from the naturalists about the 'sentimentality' of anti-vivisectionists. If loyalty to our own species, preference for men simply because we are men, is not a sentiment, then what is it? It may be a good sentiment or a bad one. But a sentiment it certainly is. Try to base it on logic and see what happens!

Ibid.

And though cruelty even to beasts is an important matter, [the vivisectors'] victory is symptomatic of matters more important still. The victory of vivisection marks a great advance in the triumph of ruthless, non-moral utilitarianism over the old world of ethical law; a triumph in which we, as well as animals, are already the victims, and of which Dachau and Hiroshima mark the more recent achievements. In justifying cruelty to animals we put ourselves also on the animal level. We choose the jungle and must abide by our choice.

First and Second Things

DRS JOHN LEWIS, 1889–1972, and
BERNARD TOWERS, 1922 –

Animals are not ferocious just because they are animals. We do them an injustice by blaming them for our crimes. Most animals live very peaceably together, and intra-specific aggression is rare except under abnormal conditions of overcrowding. Carnivores act as predators when requiring food, but this does not mean that they are continuously angry, irascible, quarrelsome and dangerous. In their domestic lives, and in relation to the animals they do not feed on, carnivores are as without malice as other animals. And, moreover, man is not a carnivore.

This tradition [of belief in early man as having been an aggressive, hostile, belligerent cannibal] is a myth, but many of us believe in it as if it were a universally established truth. Hence the further myth of our social evolution from bestial, savage, prehistoric ancestors who were in a continuous state of warfare. Contrary to this view the evidence indicates that prehistoric man was, on the whole, a more peaceful, co-operative, unwarlike, unaggressive creature than we are, and that we of the civilized world have in historical time become more aggressive in many ways.

Naked Ape or Homo Sapiens?

NAOMI LEWIS, 1920–

The Wolfe said to Francis

The wolf said to Francis
'You have more sense than some.
I will not spoil the legend;
Call me, and I shall come.

But in the matter of taming
Should you not look more near?
Those howlings come from humans.
Their hatred is their fear.

We are an orderly people.
Though great our pain and need,
We do not kill for torture;
We do not hoard for greed.

But the victim has the vision —
A gift of sorts that's given
As some might say, by history
And you, perhaps, by heaven.

Tomorrow or soon after
(Count centuries for days)
I see (and you may also
If you will turn your gaze) —

How the sons of man have taken
A hundredfold their share.
But the child of God, the creature,
Can rest his head nowhere.

See, sky and ocean empty,
The earth scorched to the bone;
By poison, gun, starvation
The last free creature gone.
But the swollen tide of humans
Sweeps on and on and on.

No tree, no bird, no grassland
Only increasing man,
And the prisoned beasts he feeds on —
Was *this* the heavenly plan?'

Francis stood there silent.
Francis bowed his head.
Clearly passed before him
All that the wolf had said.

Francis looked at his brother
He looked at the forest floor.
The vision pierced his thinking,
And with it, something more
That humans are stony listeners.

The legend stands as before.

Assumptions, mindless acceptances, the notion that you have to think or behave in a certain way because of custom, fashion, tradition – these are the cause of most of the world's evils. 'You can't change people', 'It has always been done, so it must be right.' A bad or cruel thing does not become un-bad or un-cruel just by crossing a frontier, an ocean or a private wall.

Books for your Children, Spring 1985

RONALD M. LIGHTOWLER, 1905 –

To make a religion of Vegetarianism, or any other 'ism', would be a dangerous form of idolatry, and it is a tendency to which the human mind is prone, and which needs to be watched. But are we not following the call of the best of the prophets and sages of the past and of the great Christian Manifestor when we believe that the following of true vision and the application of true principles results in concrete benefits to the life upon earth?

Editorial, *The British Vegetarian*, November/December 1961

The fact that many, probably most, children would, if left to their inner promptings, be natural vegetarians, gives a strong bias to the belief that as creatures of a God of Love, the impulse of compassion is implanted deep within the human soul. At the intellectual and conceptual level, however, mankind has been 'conditioned' or 'brainwashed' for centuries, and practically compelled to conform to the pattern of that 'Establishment' which is, basically, anything but the Kingdom of God on earth, with its system of privilege; its doctrines of the 'just war' along with the 'blessing' of guns, and now, no doubt, atomic bombs; its indulgence in blood-sports and its pathetic belief in the ultimate omnipotence of the black magic of vivisection to provide knowledge leading to health.

Life without cruelty to, or exploitation of, Man and the lesser creatures, is the full-rounded vision that catches, upholds and inspires us to continue to make such sacrifices as may be necessary towards the establishment of this finer Kingdom of Health, Happiness and true, spiritually based Progress, here on earth. For it is *here* that the pattern of life is so desperately needing changing. It is *here* that life has to be lived at this stage, character formed, and Man's power over the elements of the earth, through his discovery of his own in-dwelling divine powers, to be realized, righteously used and demonstrated in a triumphant life.

We believe that the day is fast approaching when the knowledge which, as vegetarians, we have, and the testimony we shall be called upon to bear, will prove to be a supremely vital factor in the future history of mankind. So, while all around us moral and ethical standards are falling and people are perishing, because 'they have no vision', let us hold together and encourage one another in following the path of true compassion in action.

Ibid.

ABRAHAM LINCOLN, 1809–1865

I could not have slept tonight if I had left that helpless little creature to perish on the ground.

> Reply to friends who chided him for delaying them by stopping
> to return a fledgling to its nest. (attr.)

I am in favour of animal rights as well as human rights. That is the way of a whole human being.

Complete Works

I care not much for a man's religion whose dog and cat are not the better for it.

Ibid.

EMILIA AUGUSTA LOUISE LIND-AF-HAGEBY, 1878–1963

To fight against vivisection is to fight against the principal fortress of the foe of idealism and spiritual evolution. Not until this fortress be shattered, and even its ruins removed from the face of this earth, can we justly claim to possess civilization.

The Shambles of Science

The Shambles of Science was inspired by moral indignation, and written as a protest against the cruelties of vivisection, the callousness of vivisectors, and the demoralizing effect of vivisectional demonstrations before students. Before I proceed to lay before the Commission facts which corroborate the accusations made in the book, I wish to plead the priority and the ultimate persistence of the moral objection and revolt against experiments upon living animals. There can be no doubt that the vivisection of human beings would at present be of the utmost scientific value to the same section of scientists who claim the right to vivisect animals, but the majority of vivisectors shrink from expressing such desires, though there are exceptions. We have advanced so far in our moral conceptions that a general clamour for human beings for vivisectional purposes would meet with disapproval and resentment. The question of utility or uselessness is here rightly deemed to be immaterial in comparison with the moral issue, and in the same way a further moral development will prohibit the vivisection of animals. The history of the evolution of morals affords repeated proofs of such moral victories ...

From the purely physical point of view, it might be advantageous to kill off a few thousands of our incurable lunatics, imbecile children, incorrigible paupers, worst criminals. But we refrain from acting in accordance with such a view because we are restrained by a moral consciousness, which was non-existent in our savage state. Moral evolution has forced us to include the sub-human races in the circle of our compassion and our sympathy. Kindness to animals, gradually passing into a conscious acknowledgment of their rights and our duties towards them, is the last and finest product of our developing altruism ...

In the light of progressive morals, anti-vivisection is not an isolated fad, or the expression of uncurbed sentiment – it is part of a great whole, of a humanitarianism which includes every sentient creature in its protective embrace, and which condemns every form of cruelty to man or beast. The abolition of vivisection, then, becomes an unavoidable moral necessity of the future; for the growth of sympathy and the demand for justice cannot permanently be stopped by any appeals to our cowardly fears, or to purely egotistical considerations.

In evidence before the Second Royal Commission
on Vivisection appointed in 1906

I declare that I am opposed to the practice of vivisection because it is inseparable from cruelty to animals.

I believe cruelty to animals to be an evil, not only to the victims but to those who practise it, an obstacle to social progress, and contrary to the highest instincts of humanity.

I decline to accept the vivisectors' plea that cruelty is justifiable provided it is 'useful'.

I am confident that a practice which is morally wrong cannot be scientifically right.

I justify the movement to protect animals from cruelty and injustice by knowledge of the kinship between them and the human race, and I repudiate the assertions made by some vivisectors that animals are incapable of feeling pain or suffering distress.

I know from the published writings of vivisectors, and the accumulated evidence of pain, caused by experiments on living animals, that the use of anaesthetics cannot, and does not, protect the animals from suffering.

I desire completely to dissociate myself from scientific research and medical practice tainted with cruelty, and from all participation in the use of the alleged benefits of vivisection. I shall not knowingly consult any member of the medical profession who supports and defends vivisection.

> *An Anti-vivisection Declaration* (signed by anti-vivisectionists
> world-wide, it was submitted as 'a statement of principle
> and a bond of unity, with the object of forming a strong
> international fellowship'. It was translated into other
> languages and served as an international
> register of antivivisectionists)

VACHEL LINDSAY, 1879–1931

I want live things in their pride to remain.
I will not kill one grasshopper vain
Though he eats a hole in my shirt like a door.
I let him out, give him one chance more.
Perhaps while he gnaws my hat in his whim,
Grasshopper lyrics occur to him.

> From *The Sante Fe Trail*

WILLIAM JAMES LINTON, 1812–1898

A Nature so Ungentle

I know not that we have this absolute right
Over all animal life for human use;
But this I know, the slaying in mere sport,

Without skill or danger, without need,
Moves my abhorrence. I were shamed to own
A nature so ungentle, yes, so base.
A gentle and a manly game, forsooth,
Your amateur butcher's!

ANDREW LINZEY, 1952–

Moral education, as I understand it, is not about inculcating obedience to law or cultivating self-virtue, it is rather about finding within us an ever-increasing sense of the worth of creation. It is about how we can develop and deepen our intuitive sense of beauty and creativity.

From the Proceedings of the Symposium held by the
Humane Education Council at Sussex University, 1980

Despite one or two minority appeals our society is not outraged at man's unremitting use of the animal world. Ecologists and environmentalists may talk of 'ecological consciousness', or 'environmental responsibility' but seldom, if ever, is this responsibility articulated towards other non-human species in particular.

Animal Rights

It has, I think, to be sadly recognized that Christians, Catholic or otherwise, have failed to construct a satisfactory moral theology of animal treatment, and neither are Christians to be marked out by their special regard for animal life. Indeed the traditional Roman Catholic view expressed by Joseph Rickaby, S.J., that 'Brute beasts, not having understanding, and therefore not being persons, cannot have any rights,' precludes any discussion. It is also, I think, significant that when Robert Mortimer, formerly Anglican Bishop of Exeter, was asked to defend fox-hunting pursuits, he went on record as judging that they reinforced 'man's high place in the hierarchy of being'.

Ibid.

It is an unfortunate fact that those people who are most eloquent in their demand for the conservation of animals are often those most eager to violate animal life at the first opportunity.

Ibid.

Sophistry, however, is part of a long literary tradition in which we have been encouraged to look upon animals in a particular way. From the *Tales of Beatrix Potter*, *Wind in the Willows*, *Animal Farm*, to the present-day best-seller of Richard Adams, *Watership Down*, man has sought to humanize animals in attributing to them human emotions and characteristics. It is true, of course, that some animals do possess, or rather appear to display, certain similar emotions and characteristics. But the case for animal rights does not depend upon the exhibition of these characteristics (except upon the need for sentiency). Animals do not have to display human characteristics or emotions to possess moral rights.

We have become so anthropomorphic in our approach to animals that we have supposed that for animals to possess moral rights they must become, or evolve to be, more 'human' ... the animal's right to live is to live within the characteristics and situation of life that is part of its animality. Whether animals display human emotions is immaterial to the issue. Actually supposing that animals possess the full range of emotions and needs which humans do (allowing the Beatrix Potter dream world to influence our behaviour), which may include the reading of books or voting for a particular political party, is a kind of fantasy (bad anthropomorphism) which generates an attitude exactly opposed to animal welfare.

Ibid.

Western culture is inextricably bound up with man's exploitation of millions of animals as food, as research tools, for entertainment, and for clothing, and for enjoyment and company. The sheer scope and complexity of our exploitation is, I contend, an indication of how far we have accepted the dictum that animals exist for man's use and pleasure. It is sheer folly to suppose that we can completely extricate ourselves from this complexity of exploitation with minimal disturbance to Western society as we now know it. Nevertheless, having begun the slow and often tedious task of challenging traditional assumptions, new fields of sensitivity have already begun to emerge, and it is this task of hastening the moral evolution of the consciousness of our fellow humans that we must undertake. The Christian tradition with its vast influence on Western culture has a unique role to play in showing its ability to change perspectives and challenge even its most cherished assumptions.

Animals' Rights: a Symposium

The point to be grasped from the saintly tradition is that to love animals is not sentimentality (as we now know it) but true spirituality. Of course there can be vain, self-seeking loving, but to go (sometimes literally) out of our way to help animals, to expend effort to secure their protection and to feel with them their suffering and to be moved by it – these are surely signs of spiritual greatness.

Christianity and the Rights of Animals

The creation waits with eager longing for the revealing of the sons of God. And who are these? They are, simply put, Spirit-led individuals who will make possible a new order of existence; who will show by their life the possibility of newness of life. Quite practically, the task required of us is to recognize God's rights in his creation, rights for animals to be themselves as God intends: to live; to be free; and to live without suffering, distress and injury.

Ibid.

... why precisely then do we hold animal experimentation to be sinful? The straightforward answer is that the philosophy which justifies it inevitably justifies other evils. Once our moral thinking becomes dominated by crude utilitarian calculations, then there is no right, value or good that cannot be bargained away, animal or human.

Ibid.

There was a time after *Animal Rights* when I held for a while that some form of experimentation might be justified. It seemed to me inevitable that some appeals to benefit have moral claim upon us. But the intervening years have also confirmed my earlier view that the institutionalization of experimentation presents us with nothing less than the massive subjugation of millions of animal lives who are bred, sold, confined and used on the presupposition that they have *only* utilitarian value. 'Evil' is the only appropriate moral category I can find which expresses the enormity of the immorality that this involves.

Ibid.

JOHN LOCKE, 1632–1704

This tendency [to cruelty] should be watched in them [children], and, if they incline to any such cruelty, they should be taught the contrary usage. For the custom of *tormenting and killing* other animals will, by degrees, harden their hearts even towards men ... And they, who delight in the suffering and destruction of inferior creatures, will not be apt to be very compassionate or benign to those of their own kind. Children should from the beginning be brought up in an abhorrence of killing or tormenting living beings ... And indeed, I think people from their cradles should be tender to all sensible creatures ... All the entertainment and talk of History is of nothing but fighting and killing; and the honour and renown that is bestowed on conquerors, who, for the most part, are but the *great butchers* of mankind, further mislead youth.

Thoughts on Education

HUGH LOFTING, 1886–1947

In fact, every kind of creature that does not eat meat was there, living peaceably and happily with the others in this land where vegetable food abounded and the disturbing tread of Man was never heard.

Dr Dolittle's Post Office

'If I had my way, Stubbins, there wouldn't be a single lion or tiger in captivity anywhere in the world. They never take to it. They're never happy. They never settle down. They are always thinking of the big countries they have left behind. You can see it in their eyes, dreaming – dreaming always of the great open spaces where they were born; dreaming of the deep, dark jungles where their mothers first taught them how to scent and track the deer. And what are they given in exchange for all this?' asked the Doctor, stopping in his walk and growing all red and angry – 'What are they given in exchange for the glory of an African sunrise, for the twilight breeze whispering through the palms, for the green shade of the matted, tangled vines, for the cool, big-starred nights of the desert, for the patter of the waterfall after a hard day's hunt? What, I ask you, are they given in exchange for *these*? Why, a bare cage with iron bars; an ugly piece of dead meat thrust in to them once a day, and a crowd of fools to come and stare at them with open mouths!'

The Voyages of Dr Dolittle

ALAN LONG, PhD, 1925–

Toward the end of their [veal calves] life, when they are about three months old, they are unable to turn around; they are kept in crates. Also they go to slaughter almost as babies; they're very young. These are very cruel circumstances even for a grown-up animal, and for a very young animal it is even worse; so it's about the cruellest part of the whole business. Many slaughtermen detest it. 'They should ban it; it's sheer bloody murder,' they told me at the last abattoir I visited. It's a poignant moment when a bewildered little calf, just torn from its dam, sucks the slaughterman's fingers in the hope of drawing milk and gets the milk of human kindness. It is a relentless, merciless, remorseless business.

The Vegetarians

[Slaughtermen] have a defensive attitude toward their work and I have found that usually they will tell you – particularly as they get older and they can pick and choose a bit – that they are disturbed about the slaughter of lambs and calves. They will say, 'Well, they're just babies; I feel a bit of a bugger doing it, because it nuzzles up and it licks my fingers before I stick the knife in.' Slaughtermen don't like slaughtering horses, and a lot of slaughtermen have told me that they don't like ritual slaughter.

They have various sentimental quirks. For instance, sometimes a ewe will give birth in the slaughterhouse, and they won't slaughter the lamb; they'll feed it, make a pet of it. But then, there isn't much point in slaughtering a lamb that size because there's hardly any meat on it; it's nearly all bone. So what the slaughtermen do is make a pet of it and then ultimately they give it to a farmer. It comes back a bit later on, unrecognized, and it is slaughtered just like all the others.

Ibid.

The fate of the cow and her calf must diminish us. We are too proud, too arrogant, and too cruel. We shrink too easily from emotion and resort all too sparingly – as if it were a sign of decadence – to the language of kindness and mercy. We indulge our cleverness and convenience ignobly. We have the wit and resource to become friendlier denizens of this world.

From a radio interview, 1985

HENRY WADSWORTH LONGFELLOW, 1807–1882

From *The Birds of Killingworth*

You slay them all! And wherefore? For the gain
   Of a scant handful more or less of wheat,
Or rye, or barley, or some other grain,
   Scratched up at random by industrious feet,
Searching for worm or weevil after rain!
   Or a few cherries that are not so sweet
As are the songs these uninvited guests
Sing at their feast with comfortable breasts.

Think every morning, when the sun peeps through
   The dim, leaf-latticed windows of the grove,
How jubilant the happy birds renew
   Their old melodious madrigals of love!
And when you think of this, remember, too,
   'Tis always morning somewhere, and above
The awakening continents, from shore to shore,
Somewhere the birds are singing evermore.

Think of your woods and orchards without birds!
   Of empty nests that cling to boughs and beams,
As in an idiot's brain remembered words
   Hang empty 'mid the cobwebs of his dreams!
Will bleat of flocks or bellowing of herds
   Make up for the lost music, when your teams
Drag home the stingy harvest, and no more
The feathered gleaners follow to your door?

How can I teach your children gentleness and mercy to the weak and reverence for life, which in its nakedness and excess, is still a gleam of God's omnipotence, when by your laws, your actions and your speech, you contradict the very things I teach?

Letters

KONRAD LORENZ, 1903–1989

The fidelity of a dog is a precious gift demanding no less binding moral responsibilities than the friendship of a human being.

... Even today man's heart is still the same as that of the higher social animals, no matter how far the achievements of his reason and his rational moral sense transcend theirs. The plain fact that my dog loves me more than I love him is undeniable and always fills me with a certain feeling of shame.

Man Meets Dog

MARGARET LUCAS (Duchess of Newcastle), 1624–1674

The Hunting of the Hare

......
Men hooping Loud, such Acclamations made,
As if the Devil they Imprisoned had,
When they but did a shiftless Creature Kill;
To Hunt, there needs no Valiant Souldiers Skill:
But Men do think that Exercise and Toil,
To keep their Health, is best, which makes most Spoil,
Thinking that Food and Nourishment so good,
Which doth proceed from others Flesh and Blood.
When they do Lions, Wolves, Bears, Tigres see
Kill silly Sheep, they say, they Cruel be,

But for themselves all Creatures think too few,
For Luxury, wish God would make more New;
As if God did make Creatures for Mans meat,
And gave them Life and Sense for Man to Eat,
Or else for Sport or Recreations sake
For to Destroy those Lives that God did make,
Making their Stomacks Graves, which full they fill
With Murthered'd Bodies, which in Sport they Kill;
Yet Man doth think himself so Gentle and Mild,
When of all Creatures he's most Cruel, Wild,
Nay, so Proud, that he only thinks to Live,
That God a God-like Nature him did give,
And that all Creatures for his Sake alone
Were made, for him to Tyrannize upon.

CLARE BOOTHE LUCE, 1903–

It is difficult to entertain a warm feeling for a 'medical man' who can strap an unanaesthetized dog on a table, cut its vocal cords and spend an interesting day – or week – slowly eviscerating or dismembering it. The researchers do not deny this themselves. They claim that, despite the wholesale bloody experimentation on animals, the only real proof of the drugs found by the chemists or the operating techniques suggested by the experimentation on animals, must be, in the end, verified by trying them on human subjects.

Address to Congress

LUCRETIUS, *c*. 99–55 B.C.

Many a time by the gods' comely shrines the calf falls in death, murdered close by the altars smoking with incense, while the blood's warm tide wells up from the heart. The mother, bereft of her offspring, wanders through the green glades; on the ground she sees its cloven hoofprints; she haunts every spot if perchance she might gain sight of her lost young one; she goes apart and utters her complaint to the leafy wood, and payeth many a visit to the stall, full of longing for her child. Nor tender willows, nor dew besprent grass, nor the streams that glide between their deep banks, can avail to give her joy or shake off her load of care, nor can the sight of the other calves scattered o'er the joyous pasture, suffice to turn her thoughts aside, or lighten her of her care.

De Rerum Naturae

EDGAR LUSTGARTEN, 1907–1978

We have a special duty to all animals, and we must fight against the merchants of animal suffering who subordinate compassion to the heartless demands of so-called scientific progress.

ATV television programme 'Free Speech'

MA'ARRI, 973–1058

The Flea

To let go from my hand a flea that I have caught is a kinder act than to bestow a dirhem on a man in need.

There is no difference between the black earless creature which I release and the Black Prince of Kinda who bound the tiara [on his head].

Both of them take precaution [against death]; and life is dear to it [the flea], and it passionately desires the means of living.

Trans. R.A. Nicholson

Give a drink of water as alms to the birds which go forth at morning, and deem that they have a better right than men [to thy charity].

For their race brings not harm upon thee in any wise,
   when thou fearest it from thine own race.

Ibid.

PAUL McCARTNEY, 1942–

We don't eat anything that has to be killed for us. We've
been through a lot and we've reached a stage where we
really value life.

Interview in McCall's Magazine, August 1984

JAMES EUSTACE RADCLYFFE McDONAGH, FRCS,
1881–1965

Vivisection is mostly undertaken in the expectation that
the goal which has been mentally erected is attainable.
The results never justify the means as erecting goals is an
idle pursuit, as evidenced by research conducted on these
lines retarding instead of advancing progress.

The Universe Through Medicine

FRED A. MCGRAND, 1895–

Cruelty has cursed the human family for countless ages.
It is almost impossible for one to be cruel to animals and
kind to humans. If children are permitted to be cruel to
their pets and other animals, they easily learn to get the
same pleasure from the misery of fellow-humans. Such
tendencies can easily lead to crime.

Parliamentary address, Ottawa

JOHN MACGREGOR, 1825–1892

Oh, the roast beef of old England! the sad twinges borne
by that undercut before we eat the sirloin in London –

the Slesvig thumps to drive it to a pen on the Weser, the German whacks to force it up a gangway on board, the haulings and shoves, the wrenchings of horns and screwing of tails to pack it in the hold of the steamer, the hot, thirsty days and cold hungry nights of the passage, the filth, the odour, the feverish bellowing and the low dying moan at each lurch of the sea – who can sum up these for one bullock's miseries? And there are thousands every day. If a poor bullock becomes at all seasick, he speedily dies. If he is even weaker than his unhappy companions, and lies down after two days and nights of balancing on sloppy, slippery boards, he is trampled under the others' hoofs and squeezed by their huge bodies, and suffocated by the pressure and foulness. Through the livelong night while we Christians on board are sleeping in our berths, these horrid scenes are enacted. Morning comes, and the dead must be taken from the living. A great boom is rigged up and a chain is let down, and the steam winch winds and winds it tight and straining with some strong weight below far, far down in the lowest of the three tiers, where no light enters, and whence a Stygian reeking comes. Slowly there comes up, first the black frowning, murdered head and horns, and dull blue eyes and ghastly grinning face of a poor dead bullock, and then his pendant legs and his huge long carcass. To see the owner's mark on his back they scrape away the slush and grime, then he is swung over the sea and a stroke of the axe cuts the rope round his horns. Down with a splash falls the heavy carcass; £20 worth of meat floats on a wave or two, and then is engulfed. Another, and another, and twenty-two are thus hauled up and cast into the sea, and this, too, *on the first day* of a *very calm passage*. What in a storm? Oh, the roast beef of old England!

Rob Roy Canoe Cruise on the Baltic

SHENA MACKAY, 1944–

… and the last building visible against the white sky before the road bent to the north, a square red-brick building blazing electric light on to the lawns in front where seagulls walked on the glassy grass. Inside, white sparkling pillars rose to a glass ceiling; the entrance was at the back and was flanked on one side by a ceramic sheep deep in daisies and on the other by a red and white cow ruminating over gutters running with blood. Three young mothers swung by their feet from hooks, blood and viscera slopped from their cut throats and were hosed away by a man in white wellingtons. A new arrival came up the ramp and through a gate, looked round uncertainly, a mallet thudded on its skull, throat was cut, skin peeled off to reveal a red and white silk undergarment, edible parts tossed on one pile, hooves and horns clattered to the floor, to end eventually as jellies, like the glossy blackcurrant castle that shivered beneath the spoon at the party …

An Advent Calendar

She rammed the hoover into the corner to get a recalcitrant piece of fluff, an instinct made her pull it back, too late. A wounded green lace-wing insect rolled there in whatever agony such broken filigree legs and wings could feel. She switched off and picked it up and carried it, weightless and heavy as lead, to the garden and left it there. 'That's what comes of hoovering' she told herself … She plunged a cabbage into cold water and started to remove its outer leaves to tempt the tortoise. She stared into the basin, or sink, in the manner of the poem, and a tiny grey drowned slug floated from under a leaf. That's what comes of cooking.

A Bowl of Cherries

W. MACNEILE DIXON, 1866–1946

And there is a similar silence [in the Christian documents] in respect of the animal world. Their status in God's creation is overlooked. They are not thought of as concerned in the Fall, as sinful, as in need of grace or redemption, or as having any share in a future life. Presumably in heaven we shall never meet with them, and some of us will miss our favourites, birds, or dogs and horses. If animals were not, like ourselves, sufferers, condemned like us to death, that silence might somehow be explained. But death, we are told, entered the world through sin, and though not partakers in sin they partake of death in consequence. Nor does it appear that they have rights of any kind, nor do we have duties in respect of them. We may, it seems, treat them according to our good pleasure.

It must, indeed, be allowed that for the most part the philosophers regard them with a like indifference. Many could find no better reason for the kind treatment of animals than the fear that lack of sympathy with them might blunt our human sympathies. How much nobler were Plutarch's sentiments! See the admirable passage in his *Life of Marcus Cato*. The poets without exception stand by them.

> If aught of blameless life on earth may claim
> Life higher than death, though death's dark
>   wave rise high,
> Such life as this amongst us never came,
> To die.
>
> (Swinburne, 'At a Dog's Grave') The Human Situation

It has dawned upon men that there is no escape from the conclusion that they are simply animals, one species among thousands, and with no claim to any royal or divine prerogative: lords of creation, if you will, but certainly not heirs of heaven.

I cannot accept the view of some theologians that man's animal ancestry may be set aside without anxiety as of no serious import, that their predecessors of the last century had no cause for alarm when Darwinism received the imprimatur of science and that they needlessly exaggerated its bearing upon faith and doctrine. If man could be proved a separate and unique being, how eased were the situation for theologians. The old belief in the human species as a special creation, altogether peculiar and outstanding, laid a firm foundation for the great cathedral of religious thought. Regard man as a creature among other creatures, of the same lineage, and you are involved in a very delicate and difficult operation. You are immediately driven to the question: How then is he to be distinguished from the rest? You cannot make light of the query: it is crucial for religion and ethics. No doubt he has by virtue of superior intelligence placed all the other tribes under his feet. The distinction is not sufficient. Too much hangs in the balance. Is this difference one of kind, or merely of degree? Such a difference as anyone can see between the octopus and the camel, the caterpillar and the eagle, or something far deeper? The churches have built high upon the difference, whatever it be, but have they built on quicksand or eternal granite?

Ibid.

It has been the habit of theologians and moralists to overlook the lower creation. These unpretentious beings are left out of account as spiritually and ethically negligible. They have had their revenge. To treat the whole animal kingdom, as most religions have done, with calm disdain, is no longer possible. Personally I am not at ease with a theology which has forgotten them, as Christianity appears to have done. And when you are asked, 'Where yawns the impassable gulf between us and them?'; when you are requested to produce the title deeds for man's unique status, you must make some answer. A supreme dignity and a grave responsibility attach to the rank you claim for him. You base it upon the assertion that he stands in a peculiar relation to God, has need of religion, and is responsible for his actions. To these matters the other creatures appear to be indifferent, and to do without them well enough. What need have we of religion, if they have none, or of morals, if they have none? 'They do not lie awake in the dark, and weep for their sins', as Whitman wrote. 'They do not make me sick discussing their duty to God.' They are not expected to display virtuous habits, exercise self-discipline, or respond to calls of conscience. They adapt themselves to nature with the most perfect composure, appear, indeed, to know all about it, and without much thinking, and with far less hubbub and noise seemingly to manage their affairs rather better than we, with all our elaborate machinery of talk and thought. I have a great respect for them. To conclude curtly with Bacon that 'men are not animals erect, but immortal gods', however agreeable a proposition, and turn your attention elsewhere, will no longer serve.

Ibid.

CHARLES R. MAGEL, 1920–

Ask the experimenters why they experiment on animals, and the answer is: 'Because the animals are like us.' Ask the experimenters why it is morally O.K. to experiment on animals, and the answer is: 'Because the animals are not like us.' Animal experimentation rests on a logical contradiction.

From a speech given at the Animal Liberation from
Laboratories Rally, Los Angeles, 26 October 1980

PROFESSOR T.M.P. MAHADEVAN, 1911–

Why is it wrong to kill? Because the action makes the killer descend to the level of the brute and corrupts his character. Why is it good to save any being in distress? Because a man's character becomes noble if he renders help to those who need it, and he realizes his true Self by the exercise of virtues like generosity and compassion. Spirituality must express itself as universal love.

The Vegetarian Way, XXIV World Vegetarian Congress, 1977

NORMAN MAILER, 1923–

The stockyards were like this, the famous stockyards of Chicago were at night as empty as the railroad sidings of the moon. Long before the Democratic Convention of 1968 came to the Chicago Amphithcatre, indeed eighteen years ago when the reporter had paid his only previous visit, the area was even then deserted at night, empty as the mudholes on a battlefield after a war has passed. West of the Amphitheatre, railroad sidings seemed to continue on for miles, accompanied by those same massive low sheds larger than armouries, with pens for tens of thousands of frantic beasts, cattle, sheep and pigs, animals in an orgy of gorging and dropping and waiting and smelling blood.

In the slaughterhouses, during the day, a carnage worthy of the Disasters of War took place each morning and afternoon. Endless files of animals were led through pens to be stunned on the head by hammers and then, hind legs trussed, be hoisted up on hooks to hang head down, and ride along head down on an overhead trolley which brought them to Negroes or whites, usually huge, the whites most often Polish or Hunkies (hence the etymology of Honkie – a Chicago word), the Negroes up from the South, huge men built for the shock of the work, slash of a knife on the neck of the beast and gouts of blood to bathe their torso (stripped of necessity to the waist) and blood to splash their legs. The animals passed a psychic current back along the overhead trolley – each cut throat released its scream of death into the throat not yet cut and just behind, and that penultimate throat would push the voltage up, drive the current back and further back into the screams of every animal upside down and hanging from that clanking overhead trolley, bare electric bulbs screaming into the animal eye and brain, gurglings and awesome hollows of sound coming back from the open plumbing ahead of the cut jugular as if death were indeed a rapids along some underground river, and the fear and absolute anguish of beasts dying upside down further ahead passed back along the line, back all the way to the corrals and the pens, back even to the siding with the animals still in boxcars, back, who knew – so high might be the psychic voltage of the beast – back to the farm where first they were pushed into the truck which would take them into the train. What an awful odour the fear of absolute and unavoidable death gave to the stool and stuffing and pure vomitous shit of the beasts waiting in the pens in the stockyard, what a sweat of hell-leather, and yet the odour, no, the titanic stench, which rose from the yards was not so simple as the collective diarrhetics of an hysterical army of beasts, no, for after the throats were cut and the blood ran in rich gutters, red light on the sweating back of the red throat-cutters, the dying and some just-dead animals clanked along the overhead, arterial blood spurting like the nip-ups of a little boy urinating in public, the red-hot carcass quickly encountered another Black or Hunkie with a long knife on a long stick who would cut the belly from chest to groin and a stew and a stink of two hundred pounds of stomach, lungs, intestines, mucosities, spleen, exploded cowflop and pigshit, blood, silver lining, liver, mother-of-pearl tissue, and general gag-all would flop and slither over the floor, the man with the knife getting a good blood-splatting as he dug and twisted with his blade to liberate the roots of the organ, intestine and impedimenta still integrated into the meat and bone of the excavated existence he was working on.

Well, the smell of the entrails and that agonized blood electrified by all the outer neons of ultimate fear got right into the grit of the stockyard stench. Let us pass over into the carving and the slicing, the boiling and scraping, annealing and curing of the flesh in sugars and honeys and smoke, the cooking of the cow carcass, stamp of the inspector, singeing of the hair, boiling of hooves, grinding of gristle, the wax-papering and the packaging, the foiling and the canning, the burning of the residue, and the last slobber of the last unusable guts as it went into the stockyard furnace, and up as stockyard smoke, burnt blood and burnt bone and burnt hair to add their properties of specific stench to fresh blood, fresh entrails, fresh fecalities already all over the air. It is the smell of the stockyards, all of it taken together, a smell so bad one must go down to visit the killing of the animals or never eat meat again. Watching the animals be slaughtered, one knows the human case – no matter how close to angel we may come, the butcher is equally there. So be it. Chicago makes for hard minds. On any given night, the smell may go anywhere – down to Gary to fight with the smog and the coke, out to Cicero to quiet the gangs with their dreams of gung ho and mop-up, North to Evanston to remind the polite that *inter faeces et urinam* are we born, and East on out to Lake Michigan where the super felicities in the stench of such earth-bound miseries and corruptions might cheer the fish with the clean spermy deep waters of their fate.

Yes, Chicago was a town where nobody could ever forget how the money was made. It was picked up from floors still slippery with blood, and if one did not protest and take a vow of vegetables, one knew at least that life was hard, life was in the flesh and in the massacre of the flesh – one breathed the last agonies of beasts.

Miami and the Siege of Chicago

MAIMONIDES (Rabbi Moses ben Maimon), 1135–1204

It should not be believed that all beings exist for the sake of the existence of man. On the contrary, all the other beings too have been intended for their own sakes and not for the sake of anything else.

[Regarding animals and their offspring], there is no difference between the pain of humans and the pain of other living beings, since the love and tenderness of the mother for the young are not produced by reasoning, but by feeling, and this faculty exists not only in humans but in most living beings.

Guide for the Perplexed

EDWARD MAITLAND, MA, 1824–1907

Being thus whole men themselves, our teachers and exemplars were beyond the danger of committing the stupendous and disastrous blunder which marks the immaturity of those who have dictated the philosophy of the present age and who form the chief obstacle to our movement. This is the blunder which consists in confounding form with substance and mistaking the exterior and phenomenal part of man for man himself, and fancying that to gratify this is necessarily to benefit the man. No, for those whom we follow, the human form, in order to be valid, required, like any other form, to be *filled up*. It must have the *man* inside it. It was not the form, but the qualities, or character, that makes, and that *is*, the man. And hence their prime care was to perfect this inside and real man, knowing that the rest would duly follow.

The Higher Aspects of Vegetarianism

BERNARD MANDEVILLE, 1670–1733

I have often thought, if it was not for this tyranny which Custom usurps over us, that men of any tolerable good nature could never be reconciled to the killing of so many animals for their daily food, as long as the bountiful Earth so splendidly provides them with varieties of vegetable dainties. I know that reason excites our compassion but faintly, and therefore I would not wonder how men should so little commiserate such imperfect creatures as crayfish, oysters, cockles and indeed all fish in general. As they are mute, and their inward formation, as well as outward figure, vastly differ from ours, they express themselves unintelligibly to us, and therefore it is not strange that their grief should not affect our understanding, which it cannot reach. For nothing stirs us to pity so effectually as when the symptoms of misery strike immediately upon our sense, and I have seen people moved at the noise a live lobster makes upon the spit, that could have killed half a dozen fowls with pleasure.

But in such perfect animals as sheep and oxen, in whom the heart, the brain and nerves differ so little from ours, and in whom the separation of the spirits from the blood, the organs of sense, and consequently feeling itself, are the same as they are in human creatures, I cannot imagine how a man not hardened in blood and massacre is able to see a violent death, and the pangs of it, without concern.

In answer to this, most people will think it sufficient to say that all things being allowed to be made for the service of man, there can be no cruelty in putting creatures to the use they were designed for. But I have heard men make this reply while their nature within them has reproached them with the falsehood of the assertion. There is of all the multitude not one man in ten but what will own (if he was not brought up in a slaughterhouse) that of all the trades he could never have been a butcher; and I question whether ever anybody so much as killed a chicken without reluctancy the first time. Some people are not to be persuaded to taste of any creatures they have daily seen and been acquainted with while they were alive; others extend their scruples no further than to their own poultry, and refuse to eat what they fed and took care of themselves; yet all of them will feed heartily and without remorse on beef, mutton and fowls when they are bought in the market. In this behaviour, methinks, there appears something like a consciousness of guilt; it looks as if they endeavoured to save themselves from the imputation of a crime (which they know sticks somewhere) by removing the cause of it as far as they can from themselves; and I can discover in it some strong remains of primitive pity and innocence, which all the arbitrary power of Custom, and the violence of luxury, have not yet been able to conquer.

The Fable of the Bees

It is only man, mischievous man, that can make death a sport. Nature taught your stomach to crave nothing but vegetables; but your violent fondness to change, and greater eagerness after novelties, have prompted you to the destruction of animals without justice or necessity, perverted your nature and warped your appetites which way soever your pride or luxury have called them.

The lion has a ferment within him that consumes the toughest skin and hardest bones as well as the flesh of all animals without exception; your squeamish stomach, in which the digestive heat is weak and inconsiderable, won't so much as admit of the most tender parts of them, unless above half the concoction has been performed by artificial fire beforehand; and yet what animal have you spared to satisfy the caprices of a languid appetite?

... ungrateful and perfidious man feeds on the sheep that clothes him, and spares not her innocent young ones, whom he has taken into his care and custody. If you tell me the gods made man master over all other creatures, what tyranny was it then to destroy them out of wantonness?

... when to soften the flesh of male animals, we have by castration prevented the firmness their tendons and every fibre would have come to without it, I confess I think it ought to move a human creature when he reflects upon the cruel care with which they are fattened for destruction. When a large and gentle bullock, after having resisted a ten times greater force of blows than would have killed his murderer, falls stunned at last, and his armed head is fastened to the ground with cords; as soon as the wide wound is made, and the jugulars are cut asunder, what mortal can without compassion hear the painful bellowings intercepted by his blood, the bitter sighs that speak the sharpness of his anguish, and the deep sounding groans with loud anxiety fetched from the bottom of his strong and palpitating heart; look on the trembling and violent convulsions of his limbs; see, while his reeking gore streams from him, his eyes become dim and languid, and behold his strugglings, gasps, and

293

last efforts for life, the certain signs of his approaching fate? When a creature has given such convincing and undeniable proofs of the terrors upon him, and the pains and agonies he feels, is there a follower of Descartes so inured to blood as not to refute, by his commiseration, the philosophy of that vain reasoner?

Ibid.

JAYANTILAL N. MANKAR, 1895–1977

Since all life is considered sacred, exploiting, killing and torturing animals is morally wrong and spiritually suicidal. Man as a superior being in evolution, endowed with powers of discriminating between right and wrong and conscious of his rights and responsibilities, is expected to do what is morally and spiritually right. It is in this respect that a highly evolved man differs from the less evolved lower animals. Man devoid of Dharma is nothing short of an animal. To be violent, to fight, to injure or kill animals for food, fashion, sports and science, or in the name of religion, are acts prompted by the instinct-guided behaviour of the animal, as were the acts of primitive man who was virtually an animal by his habits of life. But as man became more evolved, primitive man became more civilized and developed qualities of love, compassion and an instinctive urge for mutual aid. Man with these newly cultivated qualities developed a sense of humanity which created in him an awareness of humanism – i.e., the state of his being human – and he felt inclined to adopt a humane and natural way of life. The great Hindu law-giver Shri Manu has aptly said that 'Man is not a man merely by being born as man. He has to be Man by leading a humane life. The extent of adoption of vegetarianism is an index of humanistic evolution of man. The vegetarian way of life is a cultural medium of humanism and leads to psychological and spiritual evolution and higher ideals of life.'

The Vegetarian Way, XXIV World Vegetarian Congress, 1977

It should be realized that vegetarianism is based on the sanctity of all life. It is not merely a question of filling one's stomach with this food or that. It is a question of humane instinct and humanizing man to justify his more evolved position. Merely becoming a vegetarian, therefore, cannot achieve its basic objectives unless associated with love for all life through animal welfare. It is the love-prompted compassion and not merely love for a vegetarian diet which can alleviate the soul and develop the true image of Man.

The Vegetarian Way, XIV World Vegetarian Congress, 1967

You will know that, after all, the Government of India did not cancel the tiger hunt on the occasion of the visit of Her Majesty the Queen, though there was a good deal of opposition. We are very sorry to have to say that not only one but two tigers were shot by the Duke and his party, while many small animals were also shot by the Queen and her party. Apart from killing the innocent animals they have no doubt hit at the deep-rooted humanitarian sentiments of a large number of the people of India.

The British Vegetarian, March/April 1961

CARDINAL MANNING, 1808–1892

Vivisection is a detestable practice ... I cannot understand any civilized man committing or countenancing the continuance of such a practice. It is perfectly true that obligation and duties are between moral persons and therefore the lower animals are not susceptible of those moral obligations which we owe to one another; but we owe a seven-fold obligation to the Creator of those animals. Our obligation and moral duty is to Him who made them ... In giving a dominion over His creatures to man He gave them subject to the conditions that they should be used in conformity to His own perfections, which is His own law, and therefore our Law.

I believe the time has come, and I only wish we had the power legally, to prohibit altogether the practice of vivisection. Nothing can justify, no claim of science, no conjectural result, no hope for discovery, such horrors as these. Also, it must be remembered that whereas these torments, refined and indescribable, are certain, the result is altogether conjectural – everything about the result is uncertain, but the certain infraction of the first laws of mercy and humanity.

Speech, 21 June 1882

RANDLE MANWARING, 1912–

Nature Reserve – Dorset

Keep out – except on business –
this is their land – the lizard and the roe-deer
find here a sanctuary
and the waterfowl returning
feel peace on the Little Sea.

So come with a microscopic eye
to watch the slow-worm and the adder crawl
unhindered in the sand,
but keep out every motor-tyre,
this is a tip-toe land.

KINGSLEY MARTIN, 1897–1969

One of the remarks made by farmers at their public discussions of these problems suggest that they are rapidly ceasing to think of animals as sentient beings at all. If you handle vast numbers of creatures which are in any case going to die soon, it is, I suppose, easy to get into a state of mind in which they seem to be merely machines.

The Unlived Life

RICHARD MARTIN, 1754–1834

As to the dissection of living animals, it is in my mind too revolting to be palliated by an excuse that science may be enlarged or improved by so detestable a means.

Letter to Lewis Gompertz

JAMES MASON, 1909–1984

I don't think you should hurt or kill animals just to entertain an audience. Animals should have some rights. But there are a lot of directors, including Ingmar Bergman, who will injure animals to further a plot. I will have none of it.

Quoted late 1980, explaining why he refused to play opposite Sophia Loren in a film containing a cock-fighting sequence

JIM MASON, 1950–

The factory farm is one of the more inappropriate technologies of this century: it requires high inputs of capital and energy to carry out a simple, natural process; it causes a costly chain of problems and risks; and it does not in fact produce the results claimed by its proponents. Moreover, the animal factory pulls our society one long, dark step backward from the desirable goal of a sane, ethical relationship with other beings and the natural world.

In Defence of Animals

With PETER SINGER, 1946–

There is a final ethical cost to the animal factories. We often seem to assume that animals were put here for us to use as we please. But no good reason can be given for regarding animals as things. They are not things. They can feel pain. They can suffer frustration and boredom. They have lives of their own to lead. Much of the 'progress' in factory farming methods raises an ethical question: do we have the right to make animals live miserable lives, just to satisfy our taste for a diet so rich in animal products that it exceeds any sane nutritional requirement?

Animal Factories

Animal factories are one more sign of the extent to which our technological capacities have advanced faster than our ethics. We plow under habitats of other animals to grow hybrid corn that fattens our genetically engineered animals for slaughter. We make free species extinct and domestic species into biomachines. We build cruelty into our diet.

Ibid.

REVD GEOFFREY MATHER, 1910–

I write in sorrow [on vivisection]: as far as I can tell, no voice has been heard from the Church about this evil. The matter is forgotten for another year. It should not be. It is one of the most appalling blots on our plentifully blotted civilization.

Church Times, 20 October 1972

DR EDWARD MAYHEW, 1813–1868

What is the use of this fuss about morality when the issue only involves a horse? The first and most difficult teaching of civilization concerns man's behaviour to his inferiors. Make humanity gentle or reasonable toward animals, and strife or injustice between human beings would speedily terminate.

Illustrated Horse Management

JAYNE MEADOWS, 1926–

I feel very sad for women who continue to purchase real fur coats. They are lacking in a woman's most important requisites, heart and sensitivity.

Quoted in an animal charity advertisement

SIR PETER MEDAWAR, 1915–1987

There is a growing repugnance to the idea of killing animals for fun. Few spectacles arouse more indignant contempt than that of a modern, mechanized fisherman holidaying off the Florida coast in unequal combat with a shark or some other magnificent sea beast. The contempt is, if anything, exacerbated by an argument sometimes put forward to excuse fox hunting – that it is in the nature of such animals as foxes to enjoy being hunted and that they get as much fun out of it as the hunters.

Killing animals for fun is to be deplored for its effect on hunters as well as for the cruelty it inflicts upon animals, for one sees a coarsening of sensibilities in their manner and speech; we need not wonder that Oscar Wilde described fox hunting as 'the unspeakable in pursuit of the uneatable'.

There will, of course, always be doubts about the degree of awareness that animals enjoy. But we should behave *as if* they had a dim awareness akin to human consciousness, for humanity and equity combine to insist that animals should be given the benefit of any doubt that still persists.

Review of 'The Question of Animal Awareness'
in The Sciences, December 1981

HERMAN MELVILLE, 1819–1891

'Go to the meat market of a Saturday night, and see the crowds of live bipeds staring up at the long rows of dead quadrupeds. Does not that sight take a tooth out of the cannibal's jaw? Cannibals? Who is not a cannibal? I tell you it will be more tolerable for the Fejee that salted down a lean missionary in his cellar against a coming famine – it will be more tolerable for that provident Fejee, I say, in the day of judgment, than for thee, civilized and enlightened gourmand, who nailest geese to the ground and feastest on their bloated livers in thy *pâté de foie gras*.'

Moby Dick

YEHUDI MENUHIN, 1916–

Too long have we thought of survival only in the context of the survival of the fittest, and today this means largely the survival of the richest. But I am afraid that wealth cannot indefinitely postpone or mask the more basic determinants, the naked heart and the naked claw.

… Why is compassion not part of our established curriculum, an inherent part of our education? Compassion, awe, wonder, curiosity, exaltation, humility – these are the very foundation of any real civilization, no longer the prerogatives, the preserves of any one church, but belonging to everyone, every child in every home, in every school.

Just for Animals

For me, the [Salman] Rushdie affair highlights a basic flaw in human nature; a flaw aggravated by the intoxicating notion of man's new-found dominance, mostly destructive, over all life and all elements and a new freedom rather to debase than to ennoble.

This flaw at the very core of our thinking is the false concept which the three Mosaic religions, Judaeo-Christian-Mohammedan, despite their supreme mysticism, philosophy and wisdom, tend perversely to encourage in the baser mind – the assumption that man is both superior to and can survive isolated from all other life. Therefore he may even exploit everything for his immediate satisfaction, provided only he finds the appropriate banner.

This fatal flaw has already caused untold suffering and destruction – it may even spell our total undoing. For, by counting mankind out of the great cycle of life, in which every organism is linked in a supporting chain to every other, thus enabling a huge and continuously evolving living skin, as it were, to envelop and protect our precious planet, we break this spinning continuity and thereby risk the collapse of the entire pulsating structure, including, of course, ourselves.

May I ask if we would have been accused of blasphemy against one of the great and highly principled religions had we educated ourselves to recognize the sacredness of our continuing heritage; the sacredness of life, attendant upon the quality of air, water, food and soil; and had we cultivated our higher senses – intuitive, perceptive and meditative? I think not.

Now, time is of the essence. It demands, if we wish our children to survive, that we immediately acknowledge and correct this fatal flaw.

Letter in *The Times*, 20 March 1989

THOMAS MERTON, 1915–1968

Since factory farming exerts a violent and unnatural force upon the living organisms of animals and birds in order to increase production and profits; since it involves callous and cruel exploitation of life, with implicit contempt for nature, I must join in the protest being uttered against it. It does not seem that these methods have any really justifiable purpose, except to increase the quantity of production at the expense of quality – if that can be called a justifiable purpose.

However, this is only one aspect of a more general phenomenon: the increasingly destructive and irrational behaviour of technological man. Our society seems to be more and more oriented to over-production, to waste, and finally to *production for destruction*. Its orientation to global war is the culminating absurdity of its inner logic – or lack of logic. The mistreatment of animals in 'intensive husbandry' is, then, part of this larger picture of insensitivity to genuine values and indeed to humanity and life itself – a picture which more and more comes to display the ugly lineaments of what can only be called by its right name: barbarism.

Unlived Life

JULES MICHELET, 1798–1874

Animal Life, sombre mystery! Immense world of thoughts and of dumb sufferings. All nature protests against the barbarity of man, who misapprehends, who humiliates, who tortures his inferior brethren … Life, death! The daily murder which feeding upon animals implies – those hard and bitter problems sternly placed themselves before my mind. Miserable contradiction. Let us hope that there may be another sphere in which the base, the cruel fatalities of this may be spared to us.

La Bible de l'humanité

A revolution has taken place. We have quitted the more sober French regimen, and have adopted more and more the coarse and bloody diet of our neighbours, appropriate to their climate much more than to ours. The worst of it all is that we inflict this manner of living upon our children. Strange spectacle! To see a mother giving her daughter, whom but yesterday she was suckling at her breast, this gross aliment of bloody meats and the dangerous excitant, wine! She is astonished to see her violent, capricious, passionate; but it is herself whom she ought to accuse as the cause. What she fails to perceive, and yet what is very grave, is that with the French race, so precocious, the arousing of the passions is so directly provoked by this food. Far from strengthening, it agitates, it weakens, it unnerves. The mother thinks it fine to have a child so preternaturally mature. All this comes from herself. Unduly excitable, she wishes her child to be such another as she, and she is, without knowing it, the corruptress of her own daughter.

La Femme

An education so delicate, so varied, so complex, is it that of a machine, or a brute reduced to instinct? Who can refuse in this to acknowledge a soul?

Open your eyes to the evidence. Throw aside your prejudices, your traditional and derived opinions. Preconceived ideas and dogmatic opinions apart, you cannot offend heaven by restoring a soul to the beast. How much grander the Creator's work if He has in them created persons, souls, wills, than if He has constructed machines!

Dismiss your pride, and acknowledge a kindred in which there is nothing to make a devout mind ashamed. What are these? They are your brothers. What are they? Embryo souls – souls especially set apart for certain functions of existence, candidates for the more general and more widely harmonic life to which the human soul has attained.

When will they arrive thither? And how? God has reserved to Himself these mysteries.

All that we know is this: that He summons them – them also – to mount higher and yet higher.

The Bird

JAMES MICHENER, 1907–

… every animal that walks the earth, or swims, or flies is precious beyond description, something so rare and wonderful that it equals the stars or the ocean or the mind of man. Animals form an inalienable fragment of nature, and if we hasten the disappearance of even one species, we diminish our world and our place in it.

'Where Did the Animals Go?', *Readers' Digest* June 1976

MARY MIDGLEY, 1919–

Mourning and desolation are not our inventions. But because we can anticipate them, can think about them, and experience them widely in imagination, we have a graver problem – one, of course, which forms part of the price we pay for the joys and uses of imagination. But the way to face this problem cannot possibly be the dualist one – the way of identifying our real selves exclusively as soul or intellect, while drawing up the ladder that connects this aspect with the rest of our nature. We cannot dismiss our emotions and the rest of our non-intellectual nature, along with the body and the earth it is fitted for, as alien, contingent stuff. We have somehow to operate as a whole, to preserve the continuity of our being.

This means acknowledging our kinship with the rest of the biosphere. If we do not feel perfectly at home here, that may after all have something to do with the way in which we have treated the place. Any home can be made uninhabitable. Our culture has too often talked in terms of *conquering* nature. This is about as sensible as for a caddis worm to think of conquering the pond that supports it, or a drunk to start fighting the bed he is lying on. Our dignity arises *within* nature, not against it.

Beast and Man

People in general have perhaps thought of animal welfare as they have thought of drains – as a worthy but not particularly interesting subject. In the last few decades, however, their imagination has been struck, somewhat suddenly, by a flood of new and fascinating information about animals. Some dim conception of splendours and miseries hitherto undreamt of, of the vast range of sentient life, of the richness and complexity found in even the simplest creatures, has started to penetrate even to the least imaginative. For the first time in civilized history, people who were interested in animals because they wanted to understand them, rather than just to eat or yoke or shoot or stuff them, have been able to advance that understanding by scientific means, and to convey some of it to the inquisitive public. Animals have to some extent come off the page. With the bizarre assistance of TV, Darwin is at last getting through. Town-dwellers are beginning to notice the biosphere.

Animals and Why They Matter

... the colossal confidence which many eighteenth- and nineteenth-century intellectuals used to feel in the absoluteness of human dominion. To their minds, human dignity justified and depended on a total separation of man from all the rest of creation. That's why they got such a shock when the *Origin of Species* came out. Someone who has buttressed his sense of his own dignity by allowing no dignity at all to anybody else, naturally feels any suggestion of a relationship with those others as intolerably degrading. The separatist position.

Third Opinion, Radio Three, 26 June 1981

STANLEY MILGRAM, 1933–

We have now seen several hundred participants in the obedience experiment, and we have witnessed a level of obedience to orders that is disturbing. With numbing regularity good people were seen to knuckle under to the demands of authority and perform actions that were callous and severe. Men who are in everyday life responsible and decent were seduced by the trappings of authority, by the control of their perceptions, and by the uncritical acceptance of the experimenter's definition of the situation into performing harsh acts ... A substantial proportion of people do what they are told to do, irrespective of the content of the act and without limitations of conscience, so long as they perceive that the command comes from a legitimate authority.

Obedience to Authority

JOHN STUART MILL, 1806–1873

The reasons for legal intervention in favour of children apply not less strongly to the case of those unfortunate slaves and victims of the most brutal part of mankind – the lower animals. It is by the grossest misunderstanding of the principle of liberty that the infliction of exemplary punishment on ruffianism practised towards these defenceless creatures has been treated as a meddling by government in things beyond its province; an interference with domestic life. The domestic life of domestic tyrants is one of the things which it is the most imperative on the law to interfere with.

The Principles of Political Economy

We (the utilitarians) are perfectly willing to stake the whole question on this one issue. Granted that any practice causes more pain to animals than it gives pleasure to 'man': is that practice more moral or immoral? And if, exactly in proportion as human beings raise their heads out of the slough of selfishness, they do not with one voice answer 'immoral', let the morality of the principle of utility be forever condemned.

'Whewell on Moral Philosophy' from *Collected Works* (ed. Priestley)

SPIKE MILLIGAN, 1918–

Rage in Heaven

If a robin redbreast in a cage
Puts all heaven in a rage,
How feels heaven when
Dies the billionth battery hen?

DR WESLEY MILLS, 1847–1915

It was said that the 'brutes' cannot reason. Only persons who do not themselves reason about the subject, with the facts before them, can any longer occupy such a position. The evidence of reasoning power is overwhelming for the upper rank of animals, and yearly the downward limits are being extended the more the inferior tribes are studied.

The Nature and Development of Animal Intelligence

GIOVANNI PICO DELLA MIRANDOLA, 1463–94

Firstly there is the unity in things themselves whereby each thing is at one with itself. Secondly there is the unity whereby one creature is united with the other, and all parts of the world constitute one world.

De Hominis Dignitate

ARNOLD MONK-JONES, 1897–1965

The case against hunting is quite simple. It is that to chase and kill animals merely for pleasure is unnecessary and cruel ... But you can no more prove or disprove it than you can prove or disprove that it is wrong to torture human beings. Assertions of fact can often be proved right or wrong, but moral judgments cannot. Your attitude to hunting depends on your moral values, just as does your attitude to, say, persecution of minorities. Most of us unhesitatingly condemn both, and are surely right to condemn them, even in the face of the most eloquent pleas, by the Jew-baiter that he is championing the cause of Christianity, and by the sportsman that he is maintaining a fine old British tradition. Strip away from hunting the glamour, the picturesqueness, the sentimentality, the happy camaraderie of the human participants, and what is left? An elaborate bullying of one animal by a lot of others; and to most Englishmen such behaviour is as repulsive as any other kind of bullying.

From 'Hunting: past and present' in *Against Hunting, a Symposium*, ed. Patrick Moore

HAROLD MONRO, 1879–1932

Milk for the Cat

When the tea is brought at five o'clock,
And all the neat curtains are drawn with care,
The little black cat with bright green eyes
Is suddenly purring there.

At first she pretends, having nothing to do,
She has come in merely to blink by the grate,
But, though tea may be late or the milk may be sour,
She is never late.

And presently her agate eyes
Take a soft large milky haze,
And her independent casual glance
Becomes a stiff hard gaze.

Then she stamps her claws or lifts her ears,
Or twists her tail and begins to stir,
Till suddenly all her lithe body becomes
One breathing trembling purr.

The children eat and wriggle and laugh;
The two old ladies stroke their silk:
But the cat is grown small and thin with desire,
Transformed to a creeping lust for milk.

The white saucer like some full moon descends
At last from the clouds of the table above;
She sighs and dreams and thrills and glows,
Transfigured with love

She nestles over the shining rim,
Buries her chin in the creamy sea;
Her tail hangs loose: each drowsy paw
Is doubled under each bending knee.

A long dim ecstasy holds her life;
Her world is an infinite shapeless white,
Till her tongue has curled the last holy drop,
Then she sinks back into the night,

Draws and dips her body to heap
Her sleepy nerves in the great armchair,
Lies defeated and buried deep
Three or four hours unconscious there.

ASHLEY MONTAGU, 1905 –

To be cut off from the wilderness is to suffer a spiritual improverishment and curtailment of life which the understanding and appreciation of the wilderness and the kinship with nature and everything in it, brings. It is not the notion of the wilderness for its own sake that is of value, but the awareness of one's relatedness to it, one's unity with it, that deepens and extends the scope of human life. The aesthetic life and the enjoyment of the merely picturesque often leads to a sybaritic self-indulgence rather than to spiritual exaltation. And neither the one nor the other is enough, for what is necessary is the recognition of the simple fact that our wholeness as human beings depends upon the depth of our awareness of the fact that we are a part of the wholeness of nature, and that the standards of dominance we have erected for ourselves in relation to nature are artificial and destructive. As Immanuel Kant remarked, evolution has been anthropocentrically envis-aged as 'a very long ladder, created by man to place himself on the highest rung'. And so we have created categories of 'higher' and 'lower' animals, a kind of race prejudice from the folly of which the 'highest' so-called may justifiably do with the 'lowest' so-called whatever they opportunistically desire. It is alleged that man is made in God's image, but that the beast is made in the image of the brute. Man, it is alleged, is loving and intelligent, the most successful of all creatures, and therefore superior to all other creatures, who act from instinct and not from intelligence, from selfish appetite and not from love. These are the most entrenched beliefs of the learned as well as of the ignorant.

Wilderness in a Changing World

Man may yet restore himself to health if he will learn to understand himself in relation to the world of nature in which he evolved as an integral part, and to appreciate the nature of his relationship to the world of nature. He has for too long diminished himself by his prejudiced and false views of himself in relation to that nature, and in so doing he has diminished and devastated so much of the rest of the world. He has everything to gain from taking a fresh look at the world of nature and making it a part of life as essential to him as he is essential to it. The lessons man may learn from the study of nature are of at least as great significance as any he can learn from the purely human tradition.

Ibid.

... our relation to our fellow human beings, to other creatures, to the inanimate as well as to the animate world will undergo fundamental change in the direction of love and co-operation only when we have learned to live as if to live and love were one. I really don't think we are going to solve many of the basic problems that confront humanity today until we have made that principle a way of life, a personal life style.

Of Man, Animals and Morals

Western industrial man, the proponent of the most anthropocentric religion the world has ever seen, has become a creature who is literally alienated from the rest of nature. The church itself has as a direct result become a walled-in shrine in which its dwindling members go through their ritual motions somehow expecting that all this will make the absence of God more endurable.

What western man has seldom understood is that there is only one religion, no matter what form it may take, and that no matter what form it does take it is religion only when it is the practice of goodness.

Ibid.

The indifference, callousness and contempt that so many people exhibit toward animals is evil first because it results in great suffering in animals, and second because it results in an incalculably great improverishment of human spirit.

Ibid.

We need to understand that there is a direct relationship between man's irresponsible overmultiplication, the dehumanization of man and the callous indifference that most people display toward the unspeakably cruel conditions in which millions of animals are bred in order to feed our carnivorous appetites.

The order of mammals to which man belongs, the primates, in common with the monkeys and apes is, in every one of its almost 200 species, predominantly vegetarian. Man is the only exception to this rule ... man took to killing animals as a means of supplementing his diet from necessity. That necessity has long ceased to exist. There has long been available a complete assortment of plant foods which contain everything necessary for health and welfare, so that no one need ever eat meat or dairy products again. This is no longer a question of taste but a matter of morality. Do we have the right to rear animals in order to kill them so that we may feed appetites in which we have been artificially conditioned from childhood? The question is whether animals are to continue to be treated as if they existed for the purpose of serving as means to our ends. Does nature exist only to serve man? Shall we never learn to understand that inhumane means lead to inhumane ends? That when we demean any part of nature, because we are a part of nature, we demean ourselves? As part of it each of us has a major moral obligation towards nature, and that means that each of us must make ourselves responsible for seeing to it that the rights of nature are everywhere protected and secured against abuse and exploitation. We have the right to protest, and the responsibility to object, and when we fail to do so, we fail as human beings.

Ibid.

In the evolution of humanity love has played a highly important role. Except, however, for rare thinkers such as Charles Sanders Peirce and Petr Kropotkin, the roles of love and co-operation in human evolution have been wholly neglected. In an unloving and alienated world wracked by strife and violence, such an idea appeared both unreal and ludicrous. There can, however, be little doubt, especially when one studies the food-gathering-hunting peoples of today and other anti-violent and a-violent peoples, that no early population of human beings could have survived had it not been for the dominant role that love and co-operation played in holding them together. Indeed, it is quite evident that human beings are designed, as a consequence of their long and unique evolutionary history, to grow and develop in co-operation, and that the future development of humanity lies not with increasing conflict but with increasing love, extended to all living creatures everywhere.

Growing Young

All education should be directed toward the refinement of the individual's sensibilities in relation not only to one's fellow humans everywhere, but to all things whatsoever.

Ibid.

My reading of the evidence tells me that the directiveness, the striving, of the child is toward goodness, a longing that every human being at some time in his life experiences and that in the truly healthy human constitutes the landscape, the background of his life. What the newborn commences with by way of human nature is good. It is not neutral, or indifferent, but good – good in the sense that the child is designed to grow in the ability to love. It is human nurture that distorts and confuses. The theories of Konrad Lorenz, Robert Ardrey, and others to the effect that humans are innately aggressive, are, in the light of scientific evidence, quite untenable. It is easy to attribute the evil behaviour of some humans to 'original sin', or, as our Victorian forebears so engagingly called it, 'innate depravity'. It is even easier to saddle 'wild animals' with the evil conduct of which humans alone are capable, and then to 'trace' our allegedly evil propensities back to our animal ancestry. It all seems to make sense, for how is the unsophisticated reader to perceive the circularity in the reasoning, especially when scientists who appear to be authorities set the 'facts' before him? The answer to that question is, of course, that it isn't easy, especially when facts are wrenched out of context and are not what they seem to be. We in the Western world are part of a long tradition that has found the doctrine of original sin a congenial explanation for the horrors that have disfigured man's history. How else can one account for this bloody history, for the holocaust, for the crime, murder, sadism and brutality of so many allegedly civilized people?

Ibid.

The perfectly natural compassion and intelligence of the child is seen in its solicitude and love for younger children and especially for small animals, as well as its solicitude for suffering of any kind. Compassionate intelligence has its origins in the maternal–infant relationship, a biological reciprocity, a co-operativeness, out of which all social relations grow. Compassionate intelligence is closely related to love, but it is not quite the same thing. Compassion refers to deep sympathy and desire to help the sufferer, and if hard pressed, I would suppose it difficult in many instances to distinguish it from love; still, compassionate intelligence also implies something of pity, which is never present in love, and in addition to compassion there is the element of intelligence, the ability to make the most appropriately successful response to the particular challenge of the situation. In brief, then, compassionate intelligence is involvement in the other's plight combined with the desire to help in some practical way. Children exhibit this gift quite early, and should, of course, receive every encouragement to exercise it.

In the societies of the Western world compassionate intelligence is encouraged in girls – in boys it is taboo. The taboo on tenderness in which boys are conditioned, the emphasis on 'manliness', 'machismo', plays havoc with the male's capacity for compassionate intelligence. Tenderness is considered to be feminine, and that is sufficient to remove it from the repertoire of masculine behavior. Indeed, things have reached such a pass in the Western world that many men seem to have lost all understanding of its meaning. The masculine world would substitute for it the idea of 'justice'. The difficulty with that is that there is not much compassion in their justice, and justice without compassion is not justice at all. As Sir Thomas Noon Talfourd (1795–1854), the English jurist and dramatic poet, remarked, 'Let us have just men on our benches, but not so just that they forget human frailty.'

The world stands greatly in need of men and women who are both compassionate and intelligent.

Ibid.

As an anthropologist I have come to believe in the possibility of a universal humanity which takes the whole of animate and inanimate nature as its community, a humanity which is devoted to the encouragement of the childlike qualities with which all humans are endowed. It is in the education of those childlike traits, among them the love of animals, illumined by the inspiring knowledge we have accumulated in the world in which we live, that I see the most promising answer to the questions raised by the Conference.

> From keynote address to the International Conference on Religious Perspectives on the Use of Animals in Science, London, 25–27 July 1984

MICHEL EYQUEM DE MONTAIGNE, 1533–1592

Some mothers think it great sport to see a child wring off a chicken's necke, and strive to beat a dog or cat. And some fathers are so fond-foolish that they will construe as a good augur or foreboding of a martiall mind to see their sons misuse a poor pheasant, or tug a lackey that doth not defend himself ... yet are they the true deeds or roots of cruelty, of tyranny, and of treason. In youth they bud, and afterwards grow to strength, and come to perfection by means of custom.

> *The Essays*

After they had accustomed themselves at Rome to the spectacles of the slaughter of animals, they proceeded to those of the slaughter of men, to the gladiators.
 ... there is nevertheless a certain respect, a general duty to humanity, not only to beasts that have life and sense, but even to trees and plants. We owe justice to men, and graciousness and benignity to other creatures ... there is a certain commerce and mutual obligation betwixt them and us.

> Ibid.

Let him [who holds all other life to be brought into being for man's sole use and pleasure] show me, by the most skilful argument, upon what foundation he has built these excessive prerogatives which he supposes himself to have over other existences ... Is it possible to imagine anything so ridiculous as that this pitiful miserable creature, who is not even master of himself, exposed to injuries of every kind, should call itself master and lord of the universe, of which, so far from being lord of it, he knows but the smallest part? ... Who has given him this sealed charter? Let him show us the 'letters patent' of this grand commission. Have they been issued in favour of the wise only? They affect but the few in that case. The fools and the wicked – are they worthy of so extraordinary a favour, and being the worst part of the world, do they deserve to be preferred to all the rest?

Presumption is our natural and original disease. The most calamitous and fragile of all creatures is man, and yet the most arrogant. It is through the vanity of this same imagination that he equals himself to a god, that he attributes to himself divine conditions, that he picks himself out and separates himself from the crowd of other creatures, curtails the just shares of other animals his brethren and companions, and assigns to them only such portions of faculties and forces as seems to him good. How does he know, by the effort of his intelligence, the interior and secret movements and impulses of other animals? By what comparison between them and us does he infer the stupidity which he attributes to them?

Ibid.

Of all creatures man is the most miserable and fraile, and therewithall the proudest and disdainfullest ... How knoweth he by the vertue of his understanding the inward and secret motions of beasts? By what comparison from them to us doth he conclude the brutishnesse he ascribeth unto them? When I am playing with my Cat, who knowes whether she have more sport in dallying with me, than I have in gaming with her? We entertain one another with mutuall apish tricks. If I have my houre to begin or to refuse, so hath she hers ... It is a matter of divination to guesse in whom the fault is, that we understand not one another. For we understand them no more than they us. By the same reason may they as well esteeme us beasts, as we them.

Ibid.

For my part I have never been able to see, without displeasure, an innocent and defenseless animal, from whom we receive no offense or harm, pursued and slaughtered ... Plato, in his picture of the golden age under Saturn, reckons, among the chief advantages that a man then had, his communication with beasts, of whom, inquiring and informing himself, he knew the true qualities and differences of them all, by which he acquired a very perfect intelligence and prudence, and led his life more happily than we could do. Need we a better proof to condemn human imprudence in the concern of beasts?

An Apology of Raymond Sebond

CHARLES-LOUIS DE SECONDAT MONTESQUIEU, 1689–1755

There is something in animals beside the power of motion. They are not machines; they feel.

The Spirit of the Laws

J. HOWARD MOORE, 1862–1916

I am ashamed of the race of beings to which I belong. It is so cruel and bigoted, so hypocritical, so soulless and insane. I would rather be an insect ... a bee or a butterfly ... and float in dim dreams among the wild-flowers of summer than be a man and feel the horrible and ghastly wrongs and sufferings of this wretched world.

The New Ethics *

There is a time in the life of all of us when a thing does not have to be true in order for it to be believed. It is merely necessary for someone to say it is true, and it is accepted, and cherished just as if it were true. At the age of four or five we believe everything that other people tell us. That is why traditions are such a terrible time dying. That is why we have, mixed up with our thinking today, so many barbarous and absurd ideas. We have inherited them from the past. They were fastened upon us in our unsuspecting years – those years when, like little sightless birds, we swallowed whatever was put into our mouths. These notions are too absurd ever to have been originated by us. But we can inherit them after they have been originated, because we inherit not what is true and good and beautiful alone, but whatever is presented to us.

Ethics and Education

It is scarcely possible, according to our notions, to commit crimes upon any beings in the world except men. There are no *beings* in the universe, according to human beings, except themselves. All others are *commodities*. They are of consequence only because they have flesh and fill up the empty void of the human stomach. Human beings are *persons* and have souls, and gods, and places to go to when they die. But the hundreds of thousands of other races of terrestrial inhabitants are mere animals, mere brutes, and beasts of the field, livestock and vermin. Every crime capable of being perpetrated by one being upon another, is day by day rained upon them and with a calmness that would do honour to the managers of an inferno. Human beings preach as the cardinal rule of humanity – and they never seem to tire of its reiteration – that they should do unto others as they would that others should do unto them, but they hypocritically confine its application to the members of their own crowd, notwithstanding that there are the same reasons identically for extending it to all creatures. The happiness of the human species is assumed to be so much more precious than that of others that the most sacred interests of others are unhesitatingly sacrificed in order that human desires may all be fastidiously catered to.

The Universal Kinship

Man is not the pedestalled individual pictured by his imagination – a being glittering with prerogatives, and towering apart from and above all other beings. He is a pain-shunning, pleasure-seeking, death-dreading organism, differing in particulars, but not in kind, from the pain-shunning, pleasure-seeking, death-dreading organisms below and around him.

Ibid.

Non-human beings have, as a rule, neither the psychic variety nor the intensity of higher humans. And it is not contended that in language, science and superstition they are capable of being compared with the foremost few of civilized societies, any more than savages, especially the lowest savages, are capable of such comparison. But it *is* maintained that the non-human races of the earth are *not* the metallic and soulless lot of fixtures they are vulgarly supposed to be; that they are just as real living beings, with just as precious nerves and just as genuine feelings, rights, heartaches, capabilities and waywardnesses, as we ourselves; and that, since they are our own kith and kindred, we have no right whatever, higher than the right of main strength (which is the right of devils), to assume them to be, and to treat them as if they were, our natural and legitimate prey.

Ibid.

Cats, dogs, horses – all animals, in fact – acquire during life a fund of information as to how to act in order to avoid harm and extinction. If they did not, they would not live long. And they do it just as man does it, by memory and discrimination, by retaining impressions made upon them and acting differently when an impression is made a second, third, or thirteenth time.

Ibid.

Orphan monkeys … are often adopted by the tribe and carefully looked after by the other monkeys, both male and female. The great mass of human beings, who know about as much about the real emotional life of monkeys as wooden Indians do, are inclined to pass over lightly all displays of feeling by these people of the trees. But the poet knows, and the prophet knows, and the world will one day understand, that in the gentle bosoms of these wild woodland mothers glow the antecedents of the same impulses as those that cast that blessed radiance over the lost paradise of our own sweet childhood. The mother monkey who gathered green leaves as she fled from limb to limb, and frantically stuffed them into the wound of her dying baby in order to staunch the cruel rush of blood from its side, all the while uttering the most pitiful cries and casting reproachful glances at her human enemy, until she fell with her darling in her arms and a bullet in her heart, had in her simian soul just as genuine motherlove, and love just as sacred, as that which burns in the breast of woman.

Ibid.

Let us label beings by what they are – by the souls that are in them and the deeds they do – not by their colour, which is pigment, nor by their composition, which is clay. There are philanthropists in feathers and patricians in fur, just as there are cannibals in the pulpit and saurians among the money-changers. The golden rule may sometimes be more religiously observed in the hearts and homes of outcast quadrupeds than in the palatial lairs of bipeds. The horse, who suffers and serves and starves in silence, who endures daily wrongs of scanty and irregular meals, excessive burdens and mangled flanks, who forgets cruelty and ingratitude, and does good to them that spitefully use him, and submits to crime without resistance, misunderstanding without murmur, and insult without resentment, is a better Christian, a better exemplar of the Sermon on the Mount, than many church-goers, in spite of the creeds and interdictions of men. And the animal who goes to church on Sundays, wearing the twitching skins and plundered plumage of others, and wails long prayers and mumbles meaningless rituals, and gives unearned guineas to the missionary, and on the weekdays cheats and impoverishes his neighbours, glorifies war, and tramples under foot the most sacred principles of morality in his treatment of his non-human kindred, is a cold, hard-hearted *brute*, in spite of the fact that he is cunning and vainglorious, and towers about on his hinders.

Ibid.

Instead of the highest, man is in some respects the lowest, of the animal kingdom. Man is the most unchaste, the most drunken, the most selfish and conceited, the most miserly, the most hypocritical, and the most bloodthirsty of terrestrial creatures. Even vipers and hyenas do not exterminate for recreation. No animal, except man, habitually seeks wealth purely out of an insane impulse to accumulate. And no animal, except man, gloats over accumulations that are of no possible use to him, that are an injury and an abomination, and in whose acquisition he may have committed irreparable crimes upon others. There are no millionaires – no professional, legalized, lifelong kleptomaniacs – among the birds and quadrupeds. No animal, except man, spends so large a part of his energies striving for superiority – not superiority in usefulness, but that superiority which consists in simply getting on the heads of one's fellows. And no animal practises common, ordinary morality to the other beings of the world in which he lives so little, compared with the amount he preaches it, as man.

Ibid.

Broad as he is who can look upon all men as his brethren and countrymen – broad as he is compared with those groundlings called 'patriots', who can see nothing clearly beyond the bounds of the political unit to which they belong – he is not broad enough. He is still a *sectionalist*, a *partialist*. He represents but a *stage* in the process of ethical expansion. He is, in fact, small compared with the *universalist*, just as the savage is small compared with the philanthropist. 'Mankind', 'humanity', 'all men', 'the whole human family' these are big conceptions, too big for the poor little nubbins of brains with which most millions make the effort to think. But they are pitifully small compared with that grand conception of kinship which takes in all the races that live and move upon the earth. Smaller yet are these conceptions compared with that sublime and supreme synthesis which embraces not only the present generation of terrestrial inhabitants, but which extends longitudinally as well as laterally, extends in time as well as in space, and embraces the generations which shall grow out of the existing generation and which are yet unborn – *that conception which recognizes earth-life as a single process, world-wide and immortal, every part related and akin to every other part, and each generation linked to an unending posterity.*

Ibid.

Wherever Buddhism prevails, there will be found in greater or less purity, as one of the cardinal principles of its founder, the doctrine of the sacredness of all sentient life. But the Aryan race of the West has remained steadfastly deaf to the pleadings of its Shelleys and Tolstoys, owing to the overmastering influence of its anthropocentric religions. Not till the coming of Darwin and his school of thinkers was there a basis for hope of a reformed world. Today the planet is ripe for the old-new doctrine. Tradition is losing its power over men's conduct and conceptions as never before, and Science is growing more and more influential. A central truth of the Darwinian philosophy is the unity and consanguinity of all organic life. And during the next century or two the ethical corollary of this truth is going to receive unprecedented recognition in all departments of human thought.

Ibid.

All beings are *ends*; *no* creatures are *means*. All beings have not equal rights, neither have all men; but *all have rights*. The *Life Process* is the *End* – *not man*, nor any other animal temporarily privileged to weave a world's philosophy. Non-human beings were not made for human beings any more than human beings were made for non-human beings.

The great Law, the all inclusive gospel of social salvation, is to act toward others as you would act toward a part of your own self.

Ibid.

We think of our acts towards non-human peoples, when we think of them at all, entirely from the human point of view. We never take the time to put ourselves in the places of our victims. We never take the trouble to get over into their world and realize what is happening over there as a result of our doings toward them. It is so much more comfortable *not* to do so – so much more comfortable to be blind and deaf and insane. We go on quieting our consciences, as best we can, by the fact that everybody else nearly, is engaged in the same business as we are, and by the fact that so few ever say anything about the matter – anaesthetized, as it were, by the universality of our iniquities and the infrequency of disquieting reminders.

Ibid.

Our own happiness and that of our species are believed to be so much more important than that of others, that we sacrifice without scruple the most sacred interests of others in order that our own may be fastidiously trimmed. Even for a tooth or a feather to wear on our vanity, marauders are sent through the forests of the earth to ravage and depopulate them. Beautiful beings which fill the woods with song and beauty are compelled to sprawl, lifeless and dishevelled, on the skulls of unconscionable sillies. Criminal and inconvenient races are exterminated with eager and superfluous violence. Thousands of innocent and helpless souls are caught up and carried by unfeeling emissaries into foul dungeons, and there doomed by ghoulish clowns of science to the most protracted, useless and damning victimizations. Millions of the most sensitive and lovely organisms, all palpitating with life and full of nerves, are hourly assassinated, flayed and haggled and their twitching fragments hauled away to be ungracefully interred in the stomachic sepulchres of men and women who have the insolence to murmur intimacies to Him who in mountain thunders said: 'Thou shalt not kill!'

The very energy with which men preach peace, justice and mercy is obtained by stripping the bones and tearing out the vitals of their fellow beings. Holy days, days above all others when it seems men's minds would be bent on compassion, are farces of gluttony and ferocity. Unfeeling ruffians cowardly shoot down defenceless birds, or prowl the country in rival squads, massacring every living creature that is not able to escape them, and for no higher or humaner purpose than just to see who can kill the most!

This is egoism unparalleled on the face of the earth. No species of animal except man plunges to such depths of atrocity. It is bad enough, in all conscience, for one being to suppress another in order to tear it to pieces and swallow it; but when such outrages are perpetrated by organized packs, just for pastime, it becomes an enormity beyond characterization ... the egoism of the hominid species towards the other species is the most cruel and extravagant in the universe ... A universe is, indeed, to be pitied whose dominating inhabitants are so unconscious and so ethically embryonic that they make life a commodity, mercy a disease, and systematic massacre a pastime and a profession.

Better World Philosophy

THOMAS MOORE, 1779–1852

From *I Have a Fawn*

I have a fawn from Aden's land,
On leafy buds and berries nursed;
And you shall feed him from your hand,
Though he may start with fear at first.
And I will lead you where he lies
For shelter in the noon-day heat:

And you may touch his sleeping eyes,
and feel his little silver feet.

VICTORIA MORAN, 1950 –

... compassion in action may be the glorious possibility
that could protect our crowded, polluted planet from its
most intelligent and dangerous inhabitant, man. We have
knowledge rarely tempered with wisdom, and technological accomplishments often surpassing our sense of
responsibility regarding them ... The ultimate ethic of
compassion as a lifestyle means putting the Golden Rule
to use when that comes naturally and when it doesn't.

Compassion: the Ultimate Ethic

THOMAS MORE, 1478–1535

From thence the beasts be brought in, killed and clean
washed by the hands of their bondsmen. For they permit
not their free citizens to accustom themselves to the
killing of beasts, through the use whereof they think
clemency, the gentlest affection of our nature, by little
and little to decay and perish.

Utopia

The Utopians feel that slaughtering our fellow creatures
gradually destroys the sense of compassion, which is the
finest sentiment of which our human nature is capable.

Ibid.

What delight can there be, and not rather displeasure, in
hearing the barking and howling of dogs? Or what
greater pleasure is there to be felt when a dog followeth a
hare than when a dog followeth a dog? For one thing is
done in both, that is to say, running, if thou hast pleasure

therein. But if the hope of slaughter and the expectation of tearing in pieces the beast doth please thee, thou shouldst rather be moved with pity to see a silly innocent hare murdered by a dog: the weak of the stronger, the fearful of the fierce, the innocent of the cruel and unmerciful. Therefore all this exercise of hunting, as a thing unworthy to be used of free men, the Utopians have rejected to their butchers, to the which craft ... they appoint their bondsmen. For they count hunting the lowest, the vilest and most abject part of butchery, and the other parts of it more profitable and more honest, as bringing much more commodity, in that they kill beasts only for necessity, whereas the hunter seeketh nothing but pleasure of the silly and woeful beast's slaughter and murder. The which pleasure in beholding death they think doth rise in the very beasts, either of a cruel affection of mind or else to be changed in continuance of time into cruelty by long use of so cruel a pleasure.

Ibid.

RICHARD MORGAN, 1950 –

Animals have rights, interests, desires and needs equal, within the context of their lives, to those of humans, and we have an obligation to recognize this and to act accordingly. Animal rights is a philosophical orientation, and a practical necessity, if creatures are to be spared the systematic cruelty to which they are currently subjected.

... The same arguments which are now used by the establishment to suggest that animals should have no rights are those arguments which were used by the governing structure to maintain that women were too easily confused to be permitted to vote and that black people could not feel or think.

Millions of animals are the victims of bloody and

senseless torture in scientific laboratories. Cruelty is an integral part of our food production system; animals are increasingly raised in overcrowded and barbaric conditions and slaughtered hideously. Creatures of every kind die in leghold traps, by poison and clubbing to satisfy the desire for luxury apparel ... and countless creatures, both wild and domestic, are killed each day by cruelties for which there is not even a name or a neat category. They cannot speak. We can. Those who are articulate must be the voices of those who are voiceless.

Love and Anger

CHRISTOPHER MORLEY, 1890–1957

My prayer is that what we have gone through [World War One] will startle the world into some new realization of the sanctity of life – all life, animal as well as human.

The Haunted Bookshop

JAN MORRIS, 1926 –

It is perfectly obvious to me that the whole of animal life, from the saints to the slugs, is equal in the sight of Nature, and that our duty towards our fellow creatures is no less than it is to our fellow humans – more, perhaps, if we accept the notion of *noblesse oblige*. I find this ethical principle so self-evident that in theory I cannot see why any decent human being, with a modicum of compassion and imagination, fails to subscribe to it.

Review of *Animals' Rights: a Symposium*
in *Encounter*, September 1979

329

SIR LEWIS MORRIS, 1833–1907

Shall I Indeed Delight

Shall I indeed delight
To take you, helpless kinsman, fast and bound,
And while ye lick my hand
Lay bare your veins and nerves in one red wound,
Divide the sentient brain;
And while the raw flesh quivers with the pain,
A calm observer stand,
And drop in some keen acid, and watch it bite
The writhing life; wrench the still beating heart,
And with calm voice meanwhile discourse, and bland,
To boys who jeer or sicken as they gaze,
On the great goddess Science and her gracious ways?

LEWIS MUMFORD, 1895–1990

The very people who shudder most over the cruelty of
the hunter are apt to forget that slaughter, in the
grimmest sense of the word, is a process they entrust
daily to the butcher and that unlike the game of the
forests, even the dumbest creatures in the slaughterhouse know what lies in store for them.

The Condition of Man

AXEL MUNTHE, 1857–1949

We learn from the long history of the development of
our race that the hunter stage was the lowest of all human
conditions – the almost purely animal. The wild beast's
lust for blood has gradually evolved into an unconscious
instinct, and thousands of years of culture lie between
our savage ancestors, who slew each other with stone axes
for a piece of raw fish, and the animal hunter of today.
The method has been refined, but the principle remains

the same – the same impulse of the stronger to slay the weaker, which runs through the whole animal series. The passion for killing being an animal instinct is, as such, impossible to eradicate. But it behoves man, conscious of his high rank, to struggle against this vice of his wild childhood, the phantom from the grave where sleep the progenitors of his race. Man's right to kill animals is limited to his right of defence and his right of existence. The former can only be evoked in exceptional cases in our countries, the latter cannot be evoked by our class.

The man of culture admits his obligations towards animals in compensation for the servitude he imposes on them. The killing of animals for mere pleasure is incompatible with the fulfilment of those obligations. Sympathy extending beyond the range of humanity, i.e. kindness to animals, is one of the last moral qualities acquired by mankind; and the more this sympathy is developed by man, the greater the distance which separates him from his primitive state of savagery. The individual in which this sympathy is lacking is thus to be considered as a transitional type between the savage and the civilized man. He forms the missing link in the evolution of the human mind from brutishness to culture.

Memories and Vagaries

MUSA MURATALIYEV, 1942 –

But Zhakyp just stood staring dully at the crimson, slowly freezing patch of blood, and for the first time he thought of hunting as a perfidious act of murder. How many times, filled with excitement, he had done this very thing and never stopped to think how cruel and terrible it was.

A Man Needs a Dog

IRIS MURDOCH, 1919 –

They were shooting pigeons. What an image of our condition, the loud report, the poor flopping bundles upon the ground, trying desperately, helplessly, vainly to rise again. Through tears I saw the stricken birds tumbling over and over down the sloping roofs of warehouses. I saw and heard their sudden weight, their pitiful surrender to gravity. How hardening to the heart it must be to do this thing: to change an innocent soaring being into a bundle of struggling rags and pain.

The Black Prince

It was like hunting fish with an underwater gun, a sport which he had once been foolish enough to try. At one moment there is the fish – graceful, mysterious, desirable and free – and the next moment there is nothing but struggling and blood and confusion.

Flight from the Enchanter

'... half the world starves. What a planet. And the eating, if you're lucky enough to do any. Stuffing pieces of dead animals into a hole in your face. Then munch, munch, munch. If there's anybody watching, they must be dying of laughter.'

A Fairly Honourable Defeat

We need a moral philosophy in which the concept of love, so rarely mentioned now by philosophers, can once again be made central.

The Sovereignty of Good

GILBERT MURRAY, 1866–1957

The average beast of prey is a decent creature who merely kills for the sake of food or in a fight against an enemy. It is only man who calls killing 'sport' and kills for the pleasure of killing; not for food, not for self-defence, but just to satisfy some primitive instinct, once necessary and now perverted.

Voice of the Voiceless

The animals were not, after all, made for man's sake, so as to provide him with food by eating them, with clothes by skinning them, or with healthy amusement by trapping, hunting, shooting and tormenting them. All such anthropocentric thinking proves to have been just a part of our inordinate human conceit.

Stoic, Christian and Humanist

D.J.A.C. MUTHU, MD, MRCS, LRCP, 1864–1942

... artificial experiments made on animals in artificial surroundings cannot possibly represent what is really taking place in the animal's natural state. The experimented animals are either wild or tame. If wild, the very touch of man would fill them with fright, which would paralyse for the time being all their vital functions. The writer has seen rabbits die from sheer terror when caught alive. Using the animals for experimental purposes would cause a great shock to their system, which would interfere with their physiological functions and paralyse the efficiency of their defensive cells, thus enabling the micro-organisms to do their destructive work. Even the tame animals would suffer from disadvantages. Cooping them up in boxes and in cages and feeding them artificially, must alter their environment, which would tend to lower their vitality. Besides, the shock produced by handling them and making a wound for inoculation, or for any other operation, would still further lower their vital resistance, making them an easy prey to the onslaught of the pathogenic organisms that have been injected.

How is it possible to draw any right conclusions from experiments made under these circumstances? ... Even if it were possible to experiment on animals in their natural state, how can we reasonably infer that the results obtained from them would equally apply to man? If lives of men differ from one another, how much greater is the difference between man and animals, which are infinitely separated from the human being? If the mind controls the physiological and pathological functions of the body of man, the absence, more or less, of the operations of the mind in an animal would be likely to vitiate the experiments and the evidence drawn from them, making the conclusions at most a probability, but not a certainty when applied to man

Pulmonary Tuberculosis and Sanatorium Treatment

SIR THOMAS MYLES, CB, MD, FRCSI, 1857–1937

Vivisection, for the purpose of class demonstration as practised abroad, cannot be too severely condemned. I am quite convinced that even at the present day in these islands an immense amount of needless and absolutely purposeless suffering is caused to dumb animals by so-called scientific enquiries.

Some Medical Views on Vivisection

NATIONAL COALITION FOR ALTERNATIVES TO ANIMAL EXPERIMENTATION (US)

Animals, like people, are not mere things. People have lives that are valuable whether or not they are of use to others. Animals, too, have lives that are valuable whether or not they are of use to others. People have rights. Animals, too, therefore, have rights. To treat them as mere things, as mere tools to be used for human pleasure, profit or curiosity, is to violate their rights.

What is it about our lives that we value? Pleasure and a minimum of pain; companionship; the satisfaction of wants and needs. These, certainly, are among the things that give value to our lives.

Animals, too, have lives that are valuable to them in these ways. Animals, too, experience pleasure and pain, have needs, wants, seek companionship. In these ways at least we share a common nature with them. In these ways at least the value of animal and human life has a common basis.

Does this mean that animals have the same rights people do? Must we say that they have a right to vote because we have this right? No, we need not say this. What we must say is that there are certain rights we share based upon our common nature, especially the rights not to be made to suffer, or to be killed merely for the pleasure, profit or curiosity of another species.

Yet animals are exploited in laboratories, in zoos, in modern 'factory' farms, in schools. They are trapped and hunted, they are abused in sports and entertainment. In all these ways and more, animals are treated as mere things, as if they had no value in themselves.

Such treatments must be stopped, not only for the sake of our humanity, but because the animals in their own right are entitled to just treatment. When rights are violated justice, not kindness, is at issue. Their defenceless state, their inability to speak out for themselves, makes it our duty to speak out for them.

They will continue to suffer and be killed unless we act for them. And act we must. Respect for justice requires nothing less.

Position statement, 1979

SCOTT NEARING, 1883–1983

With vegetables, fruits, nuts and cereals we proved that
one could maintain a healthy body as an operating base
for a sane mind and purposeful harmless life.

Carnivorism involves (1) holding animals in bondage,
(2) turning them into machines for breeding and
milking, (3) slaughtering them for food, (4) preserving
and processing their dead bodies for human consumption.

We were looking for a kindly, decent, clean and simple
way of life. Long ago we decided to live in the vegetarian
way, without killing or eating animals; and lately we have
largely ceased to use dairy products and have allied
ourselves with the vegans, who use and eat no animal
products, butter, cheese, eggs or milk. This is all in line
with our philosophy of the least harm to the least number
and the greatest good to the greatest number of life
forms.

Living the Good Life (with Helen Nearing)

JOHN G. NEIHARDT, 1881–1973

Is not the sky a father and the earth a mother, and are
not all living things with feet or wings or roots their
children?

Hear me, four quarters of the world ... a relative I am!
Give me the strength to walk the soft earth, a relative to
all that is!

... all over the earth, the faces of living things are all
alike.

Black Elk Speaks

LEONARD NELSON, 1882–1927

... by virtue of its rationality a being is not only invested
with rights, but also assumes duties. A man who shirks his

duties is certainly not superior to an animal, which is not even capable of committing a wrong. Whoever takes this fact honestly into account, will hesitate before justifying an injury to an animal's interests on the sole ground that his own life is rational.

A System of Ethics

SENATOR RICHARD L. NEUBERGER, 1912–1960

People often ask me why I spend so much time protecting the welfare of animals. They refer to my active support of legislation to outlaw barbarism in packing plants ... my protesting liquidation of the famous White House squirrels ... urging a halt to the oil drilling and gas prospecting taking place all over our national wildlife and waterfowl refuges.

I have several answers. The first is that Dr Albert Schweitzer ... often said that one of the real symbols of a truly civilized person is whether or not he is kind to animals.

Also I cite one of my favourite quotations from the Bible: 'Verily I say unto you, inasmuch as ye have done it unto one of the least of these my brethren, ye have done it unto me.'

I have always believed that cruelty to beasts is a black mark in heaven ... particularly cruelty which is wanton and totally unnecessary. I realize that animals, whether of the field or of the forest, do not vote. They do not make campaign contributions to enrich the coffers of politicians running for office. But I will be their friend. I imagine that he who spoke the Sermon on the Mount would want it that way too.

Congress address

H.W. NEVINSON, 1856–1941

Cruelty is the vice most natural to dullness of mind.

Essays in Freedom and Rebellion

FRANCIS WILLIAM NEWMAN, 1805–1897

... it is a depraving tendency, sadly common with English lads, to desire to kill a beautiful animal the moment they see it. That the first thought on discovering a new creature should be 'Is it nice to eat?' is to me shocking and debasing. What is called the love of sport has become a love of killing for the display of skill, and converts man into the tyrant of all other animals; yet this rose out of a desire of eating their flesh – a desire which cannot be blamed in that state of barbarism in which little other food was to be had. But when with the growth of civilization other food is easier to get, when bread has won upon flesh-meat, it is evil to struggle for the more barbarous state. Does not the love of flesh inflame the love of killing, teach disregard for animal suffering, and prepare men for ferocity against men?

We cannot blame the butcher if he become perfectly callous to the sufferings of animals. His trade not only trains him to callousness, but even demands it of him: and this is equally true of the vivisector: hence no security whatever, in either case, is possible against any amount of wanton cruelty. The man who by practice steels his own heart *must* lose his discernment of animal suffering with his concern for it.

We must admit into our moral treatises the question of the rights of animals; and not only the limits of our rights over them, but other topics hence arising. When man must starve unless he kill a deer or a bison, no one blames the slaughter; but it does not follow that when we have plenty of wholesome food without killing, we are at liberty to kill for mere gratification of the palate. To nourish a taste for killing is morally evil; to be accustomed to inflict agony on harmless animals by wounding or maiming them without remorse, prepares men's hearts for other cruelty.

Essays on Diet

Evidently the reason why it is wicked to torture a man is not because he has an immortal soul, but because he has a highly sensitive body; and so has every vertebrate animal, especially the warm-blooded. If we have no moral right to torture a man, neither have we a moral right to torture a dog. We have to add to our morals a new chapter on the Rights of Animals.

Macaulay's Prize Essay, *Vivisection*

CARDINAL NEWMAN, 1801–1890

Now what is it moves our very heart, and sickens us so much at the cruelty shown to poor brutes? I suppose this; first, that they have done us no harm; next, that they have no power whatever of resistance; it is the cowardice and tyranny of which they are the victims which make their sufferings so especially touching ... there is something so very dreadful, so Satanic in tormenting those who have never harmed us, and who cannot defend themselves, who are utterly in our power.

Parochial and Plain Sermons

It is almost a definition of a gentleman to say he is one who never inflicts pain.

Ibid.

JOHN FRANK NEWTON, 1770–(?)1827

So long as men are compassionate to such a degree that they cannot hear a fly struggling in a spider's web without emotion, it never can be reasonably maintained that it is their natural impulse to wound and kill the dumb animals, or to butcher one another in what is called *the field of honour*.

Return to Nature

OLIVIA NEWTON-JOHN, 1948–

I would not be comfortable appearing in a country where they have permitted the destruction of such beautiful and intelligent mammals.

Newspaper interview after her 1978 cancellation of a tour to Japan because of their dolphin kill. Helen Reddy (1941–), Darrel Dragon (1942–) and others cancelled for the same reason

VASLAV NIJINSKY, 1890–1950

I do not like eating meat because I have seen lambs and pigs killed. I saw and felt their pain. They felt the approaching death. I left in order not to see their death. I could not bear it. I cried like a child. I ran up a hill and could not breathe. I felt that I was choking. I felt the death of the lamb.

Diary of Vaslav Nijinsky (ed. Romola Nijinsky) [Cape 1937]

BARBARA NOSKE, 1949–

How can those who are content to study animals totally from without whilst showing no interest whatsoever in their minds, possibly know anything about what animals feel, think or want? How do they know that animals do not strive for quality of life? Why believe that the altruism which animals show toward their animal (and human) companions just serves a genetic purpose of which the animals themselves are totally unaware?

Humans and Other Animals

The bias of human domination in *all* science, not just socio-biology, is more than a layer which can be peeled off to reveal the sound objective knowledge underneath.

... in factory farming any kind of 'unbusinesslike' behaviour is discouraged: in many cases the farmer will attempt to prevent the animals from having social contact, from engaging in post-natal parental care as well as engaging in movement and play. 'Natural political economy', alias sociobiology, claims that natural selection is working like a modern commercial farmer: any behaviour that redirects energy required for continuous reproduction and proliferation of genes will be selected against.

Ibid.

Among political ecologists especially one sometimes encounters the idea that non-human nature, including animals, is out there passively waiting for us to construct it materially and conceptually and give meaning to it. It is implied that our concept of nature is the only thing real and that it is therefore up to us humans to decide what we want nature to be. Such a view totally overlooks the possible existence of other realities apart from the human one, and the meanings that animals impose upon their world, a world which may or may not include us!

Ibid.

U NU (THAKIN NU), 1907 –

World peace, or any other kind of peace, depends greatly on the attitude of the mind. Vegetarianism can bring about the right mental attitude for peace. In this world of lusts and hatreds, greed and anger, force and violence, vegetarianism holds forth a way of life, which if practised universally, can lead to a better, juster and more peaceful community of nations.

The Vegetarian Way, XIX, 1967

HENRY L. NUNN, 1878–1972

I felt sure the chicken suffered, and could not bear to watch the process [of neck-wringing]. Why? If there was nothing wrong about it, why had God put compassion for these sentient creatures into my heart? And if this compassion made it wrong for me to kill, why was it not just as cruel to pay someone else to do it for me by purchasing flesh foods?

I began to feel there was something wrong somewhere. Could it be possible that Jesus would kill creatures that God had created with a love of life and will to live? I tried to picture Christ taking the life of a lamb and eating its body. No, it did not make sense to me ... not He who had preached the Sermon on the Mount. Not He who had said 'Blessed are the merciful, for they shall obtain mercy.'

Every sentient creature, 'even to the meanest', is endowed with the love of life and the will to live. I believe it is incumbent on man, therefore, who has developed his mentality to the highest degree and who has accepted as his most precious precept the Golden Rule, to extend and to embrace within that rule every sub-human creature.

I am not ashamed to say that it makes me uncomfortable to give others pain or to take life from them which I cannot give. It is only in self-defence that I can find justification ... Personal experience and many years of study have convinced me that it is not necessary for our life – even for our pleasure in living – to kill and feed upon the flesh of animals.

The Whole Man Goes to Work

OGONYOK*

Out of 135 criminals, including robbers and rapists, 118 admitted that when they were children they burned, hanged and stabbed domestic animals.

* A Soviet magazine campaigning for anti-cruelty laws, quoted August 1979 in *Voice of the Voiceless*

JOSIAH OLDFIELD, MA, DCL, MRCS, LRCP, 1863–1953

To say that science can harden or degrade man in his relation to animals is to malign the most sacred of all studies. The village lout may stick a cockchafer on a pin, or tie a cracker to a panting, fear-stricken cat, or throw a pup into a pond and stone it till it sinks exhausted. A cruel woman may drive or spur the tired horse till it drops, or leave a mouse to die of hunger in a trap, etc. The swell sportsman may wound and torture and kill his hundreds of beautiful pigeons, and leave a piteous leasing of wounded animals slowly dying in the hedges and in their holes – dying of acute inflammation, after he has passed on with his gun. The woman of fashion may order men to go out to the Arctic regions and flay the half-dead seal and leave it wallowing in blood and groans – a mangled mother with its little ones pitifully bleating round the frightful object hour after hour till they die of slow starvation. The butcher may perpetrate all the horrors of the slaughterhouse for gain. But to the true scientist all such atrocities are impossible … The higher science – as opposed to popular marvel hunting and self-advertising – is always reverent in the presence of the

343

mystery of life. The lowest animal must ever be treated with the respect which is its prerogative. Science elevates and does not degrade the position of the animal world, and the final point I would make is that science *increases the rights of animals by deepening the rights of man.* The higher the position in which science can place man, the nearer to the source and fount from whence the laws of the universe proceed, the greater and deeper will be the reverence for animal life, because the clearer and fuller will be the conception of the higher forces of amity over enmity in evolution. The lower the man the more cruel is he to his beast of burden, the higher the man the more nearly he approaches to those heights of scientia and gnosis, which are the crowning stamp of the true scientist, the more reverence has he for his fellow traveller – a true brother in the eyes of science – on the same spiral pathway of vitality, towards a perfection of evolution.

The Claims of Common Life

JOHN OSWALD, *fl.* 1760

The tender-hearted Hindoo would turn from our tables with abhorrence. To him our feasts are the nefarious repasts of Polyphemus; while we contemplate with surprise his absurd clemency, and regard his superstitious mercy as an object of merriment and contempt.

The Cry of Nature

OUIDA (Louise de la Ramée), 1839–1908

Should ever such an opinion as that implied in the statement for vivisection without restriction become that of mankind in general, the world will be a hell indeed. The pretensions of what are called scientists are a menace to all liberty, peace and virtue, and the doctrines thereof followed out from youth to age would make of the earth a shambles.

From Report of the American Humane Association, 1896

Those who are great or eminent in any way find the world full of parasites, toadies, liars, fawners, hypocrites; the incorruptible candour, loyalty and honor of the dog are to such like water in a barren place to a thirsty traveller.

North American Review, 1891

OVID (Publius Ovidius Naso), 43 B.C.–A.D. 17

Take not away the life you cannot give;
For all things have an equal right to live.
Kill noxious creatures where 'tis sin to save;
This only just prerogative we have;
But nourish life with vegetable food,
And shun the sacrilegious taste of blood.

Metamorphoses

Forbear, O mortals,
To spoil your bodies with such impious food!
There is corn for you, apples, whose weight bears down
The bending branches; there are grapes that swell
On the green vines, and pleasant herbs, and greens
Made mellow and soft with cooking; there is milk
And clover-honey. Earth is generous
With her provision, and her sustenance
Is very kind; she offers, for your tables,
Food that requires no bloodshed and no slaughter.

Ibid.

OVID

Oh, Ox, how great are thy desserts! A being without guile, harmless, simple, willing for work! Ungrateful and unworthy of the fruits of earth, man his own farm labourers slays and smites with the axe that toil-worn neck that had so oft renewed for him the face of the hard earth; so many harvests given!

Ibid.

Oh, impious use! to Nature's laws opposed,
Where bowels are in other bowels closed;
Where, fattened by their fellows' fat, they thrive;
Maintained by murder and by death, they live. .
'Tis then for naught that Mother Earth provides
The stores of all she shows, and all she hides,
If men with fleshy morsels must be fed,
And chaw with bloody teeth the breathing bread;
What else is this but to devour our guests,
And barb'rously renew Cyclopean feasts?
We, by destroying life, our life sustain,
And gorge the ungodly maw with meats obscene.
... Whoever was the wretch (and cursed be he)
That envied first our food's simplicity,
The essay of bloody feasts on brutes began,
And after forged the sword to murder man –
Had he the sharpened steel alone employed
On beasts of prey that other beasts destroyed,
Or man invaded with their fangs and paws,
This had been justified by Nature's laws
And self-defence: but who did feasts begin
Of flesh, he stretched necessity to sin.
To kill man-killers, man has lawful power,
But not the extended licence to devour.

Ibid. (John Dryden translation)

LADY WALBURGA PAGET, 1839–1929

I strongly condemn the practice [of slaughtering animals for food], and do not eat flesh food myself. Two or three years ago I had occasion to read up certain papers about the transport of cattle and slaughterhouses, and as I read the irresistible conviction came upon me that I must choose between giving up the eating of animal food and my peace of mind. These considerations were not the only ones that moved me. I do not think that anyone has a right to indulge in tastes which oblige others to follow a brutalizing and degrading occupation. When you call a man a butcher, it signifies that he is fond of bloodshed. Butchers often become murderers, and I have known cases where butchers have actually been hired to murder persons whom they did not even know.

Interview with Mrs S.A. Tooley, 1893

THOMAS PAINE, 1737–1809

The moral duty of man consists of imitating the moral goodness and beneficence of God manifested in the creation toward all his creatures. Everything of persecution and revenge between man and man, and everything of cruelty to animals, is a violation of moral duty.

The Age of Reason

WILLIAM PALEY, 1743–1805

Some excuse seems necessary for the pain and loss which we occasion to brutes, by restraining them of their liberty, mutilating their bodies and, at last, putting an end to their lives for our pleasure or convenience.

[It is] alleged in vindication of this practice ... that the several species of brutes being created to prey upon one another affords a kind of analogy to prove that the human species were intended to feed upon them ... [but] the analogy contended for is extremely lame; since brutes have no power to support life by any other means, and since we have, for the whole human species might subsist entirely upon fruits, pulse, herbs and roots, as many tribes of Hindoos actually do ...

It seems to me that it would be difficult to defend this right by any arguments which the light and order of nature afford; and that we are beholden for it to the permission recorded in Scripture, *Genesis* ix, 1, 2, 3.

Principles of Moral and Political Philosophy, 1785

Many ranks of people whose ordinary diet was, in the last century, prepared almost entirely from milk, roots and vegetables, now require every day a considerable portion of the flesh of animals. Hence a great part of the richest lands of the country are converted to pasturage. Much also of the bread-corn, which went directly to the nourishment of human bodies, now only contributes to it by fattening the flesh of sheep and oxen. The mass and volume of provisions are hereby diminished, and what is gained in the amelioration of the soil is lost in the quantity of the produce.

This consideration teaches us that tillage, as an object of national care and encouragement, is universally preferable to pasturage, because the kind of provision which it yields goes much farther in the sustentation of human life ... Indeed, pasturage seems to be the art of a nation, either imperfectly civilized, as are many of the tribes which cultivate it in the internal parts of Asia, or of a nation like Spain declining from its summit by luxury and inactivity.

Ibid.

CHRISTABEL PANKHURST, 1880–1958

It seems that the hunting of a creature so timorous and defenceless as the hare is at best but little calculated to foster those qualities of manliness and courage which it is so desirable to develop in the youth of our nation; but to hunt the female hare at a time when she is handicapped by the burden which Nature imposes on her would seem to be not merely contrary to the spirit of true sportsmanship, but positively demoralizing and degrading to all who consciously participate in it.

From a letter co-signed by Mrs Bramwell Booth and twenty-three other women, addressed to Canon E.L. Lyttelton, then headmaster of Eton College

HOWARD L. PARSONS, 1918–

Man may for a time deplete or erode the soil, denude the forests, pollute the streams, kill the wildlife, make numerous species extinct, spread atomic radiation, and even poison his own food with insecticides and herbicides. But what he sows he will at last reap; his *karma* will accumulate destructively. To live, and live creatively, therefore, man must deepen his sense of the holiness of nature. This is what Western man can learn from the East.

Man East and West: Essays in East-West Philosophy

DAVID A. PATERSON, 1930–

By definition, humane education aims to promote kindness and so to prevent cruelty to all forms of life: for this reason it is humane education which will provide the basic solution to almost every problem which we could discuss at this symposium.

Animals' Rights: a Symposium

Inhumane attitudes towards animals in secondary schools are sometimes 'justified' by saying that children 'need to be taught to kill' in rural science; similarly, they may be taken to hunting or coursing events 'to form a balanced opinion on the subject'. More often, though, cruelties in schools spring from ignorance or sheer thoughtlessness – killing pet animals in front of children, for instance. Direct experience of violence and cruelty must always be a cause for deep concern, but even more so where this is being inflicted, in our names, under the sacred mantle of 'education'.

Ibid.

MINNIE PEARL, 1912–

So often when you start talking about kindness to animals … someone comments that starving and mistreated children should come first. The issue can't be divided like that. It isn't a choice between animals and children. It's our duty to care for both. Kindness is the important thing. Kids and animals are our responsibility.

Quoted in North American newspapers

MARCIA C. PEARSON, 1947–

Fashion is the most frivolous, trivial reason to torture and kill animals.

Fashion With Compassion show in Seattle, 1977

Enjoy your fur; its real owner was killed in it.

Washington Living, vol.4, issue 2

This planet gives us so much – life itself – that we owe it to our earth to give something back. If we lose our reverence for any part of life, we can lose our reverence for all of life.

Ibid.

Many of us have come to the animal rights movement from the civil rights, anti-war, women's, or environmental movements, and we may well have carried our organizational skills with us from other forms of social action; but, to date, nothing has addressed itself directly to the animal rights movement. Where in the human rights struggles, the oppressed people could speak for themselves to evoke public sympathy, our oppressed non-human brothers and sisters cannot speak for themselves. Their cries are heard only by those who already know of their anguish ... we have a community of 'other nations' as Jeremy Bentham so nicely put it, that really cannot address itself in any way most humans have been able to address their problems. We must be the speakers at rallies and the voice of these non-human nations.

Agenda Magazine, July/August 1981

DR KIT PEDLER, 1928–1981

There is conditioned brutality among scientists, especially in the universities of Britain. The time has come to call a halt. The situation has got out of hand.

Evening Standard, London, 25 October 1970

... we show little recognition of the rights of other forms of life, and our attitude towards them still remains largely dominating and exploitative. The bibliography of our depredations is massive and needs no detailed repetition.

The Quest for Gaia

We need to be more fully exposed to the damage we cause. Much of present-day life shuts away the darker aspects of the comforts we take for granted. A single visit to a slaughterhouse would, I am sure, convince many people that meat eating is impossible.

Ibid.

351

ROBERT HOWELL PERKS, MD, FRCS, LRCP,
1854–1929

I condemn vivisection because:

1. It is unscientific, and its results, therefore, are misleading, contradictory, and useless. It also tends to cause neglect of the true scientific methods of clinical and pathological research.
2. It is productive of a vast amount of severe suffering to animals without any corresponding advantage to them.
3. Its effect on those who practise or who witness it, is inevitably to debase the moral and spiritual standard and to develop selfish, cruel and callous tendencies, which are a grave menace to society.
4. It is a direct infraction of the moral law – a doing of evil in the false hope that good may result.
5. It is the antithesis of the Divine Law of Love – in the observance of which lies the sole method of man's growth and upliftment – socially, morally, and spiritually.

Why I condemn Vivisection

I have always felt that the cause of Science cannot possibly be served by cruelty to animals, and especially by the barbarous practice of vivisection.

Letter to Mrs C.P. Farrell, 20 September 1913

MICHAEL PETERS, 1947–

The belief that man is essentially different from all other animals – indeed, scarcely an animal at all – is more an implicit assumption than a hypothesis. In order to understand why it has been a favourite occupation of thinkers through the ages to try to capture the essence of man in a definition, we must realize that the definition has practical consequences, since the distinction between man and the other animals has, for all practical purposes, been taken as synonymous with that between beings entitled to moral consideration and those not so entitled. An objective definition of what this unique essence is is necessary to justify a prior claim to special rights and privileges. The true significance of defining 'Man' is not to tell us what a human being is – for who could fail to recognize one? – but to rigorously bar any extension of man's rights and privileges to others. This may not have been the intention behind the definition, but it has certainly been one of its more important functions.

Animals, Men and Morals

We have come at last to the stage where both the necessity and the possibility for enforcing an absolute categorical distinction between man and animals have been exhausted.

The treatment inflicted upon animals can no longer be defended on the pretext that they are merely mechanical objects, for the same model is equally applicable to humans. With the accelerating progress of science and technology, all our traditional concepts of man are being challenged. It is no longer relevant to demarcate ourselves from the other animals and identify ourselves with those attributes such as analytical intelligence which are now much more effectively performed by machines.

Ibid.

RICHARD PHILLIPS, 1767–1840

1. Because, being mortal himself, and holding his life on the same uncertain and precarious tenure as all other sensitive beings, [man] does not find himself justified, by any supposed superiority or inequality of condition, in

destroying the enjoyment of existence of any other mortal, except in the necessary defence of his own life.

2. Because the desire of life is so paramount and so affectingly cherished in all sensitive beings, that he cannot reconcile it to his feelings to destroy or become a voluntary party in the destruction of any innocent living being, however much in his power, or apparently insignificant ...

9. Because he observes that carnivorous men, unrestrained by reflection or sentiment, even refine on the most cruel practices of the most savage animals and apply their resources of mind and art to prolong the miseries of the victims of their appetites – bleeding, skinning, roasting, and boiling animals alive, and torturing them without reservation or remorse, if they thereby add to the variety or the delicacy of their carnivorous gluttony.

10. Because the natural sentiments and sympathies of human beings, in regard to the killing of other animals, are generally so averse from the practice that few men or women could devour the animal whom they might be obliged themselves to kill; and yet they forget, or affect to forget, their living endearments or dying sufferings.

11. Because the human stomach appears to be naturally so averse from receiving the remains of the animals, that few people could partake of them if they were not disguised and flavoured by culinary preparation; yet rational beings ought to feel that the prepared substances are not the less what they truly are, and that no disguise of food, in itself loathsome, ought to denude the unsophisticated perceptions of a considerate mind.

12. Because the forty-seven millions of acres in England and Wales would maintain in abundance as many human inhabitants, if they lived wholly on grain, fruits, and vegetables; but they sustain only twelve millions [in 1811] scantily, while animal food is made the basis of human subsistence.

14. Because the practice of killing and devouring animals can be justified by no moral plea, by no physical benefit, nor by any just allegation of necessity in countries where there is abundance of vegetable food, and where the arts of gardening and husbandry are favoured by social protection, and by the genial character of the soil and climate.

Some of Sir Richard Phillips' sixteen reasons for
a vegetarian diet, *Medical Journal*, 27 July 1811

EDEN PHILLPOTS, 1862–1960

The Challenge

For you who wear our common clay with me,
Know the like uses, customs, norm of mind,
And share undying memories that bind
Man to his brother in one destiny,
Your human hearts their primal mandates find
In nature's ordinance and first decree.
A little thing it is to love our kind.

But harder far the test would any mark
The boon and bane of birds and beasts and trees,
Their hopes and fears, their obdurate mysteries
Beneath the pelt or feathers, fruit or bark;
Probe their unconscious secrets, dumb and stark;
Feel with their patient sense; see with their eyes.

The Cart-horses

Twixt two and three upon a silent night,
As earth rolled dreaming in the full moon tide,
Slow hooves came thud and thud: there hove in sight
Black horses twain, that wandered side by side.
Two great cart-horses, looming giant large,
Enjoyed their rest. Each to the other spoke,
Then bent and drank beside a streamlet's marge,

While moonlight found their lustrous eyes and woke
A glint of consciousness, a hint of mind.
Now they rubbed noses, shook their heavy manes,
Lifted their necks and neighed upon the wind,
Then fell to whispering, their little brains
Busy about shared interests, unshared
By those for whom their strenuous time was spent.
One something said, whereat the other stared,
Then started galloping, and off they went,
To vanish on the far, night-ridden heath;
And well I knew they were exchanging thought,
Uttering strange, dim things with their sweet breath
Of which we busy, daylight folk knew nought –
Views touching fate, under the still moonshine,
As near to truth, perchance, as yours, or mine.

PHILO JUDAEUS, A.D. First century

The different kinds of fish, and birds, and terrestrial animals, are not grounds for accusing nature, which invites us to pleasure by those means, but are a terrible reproach to us for our intemperate use of them ... It was not necessary that that animal, which of all others is most akin to wisdom, namely, man, should ... change his nature into something resembling the ferocity of wild beasts.

Fragments of the Lost Works

Is it not a piece of folly to imagine that we can ever avoid injuries from wild beasts which are outside, while we are continually training up the passions within ourselves to a terrible degree of savageness?

Ibid.

SIR GEORGE PICKERING, 1904–1980

The idea, as I understand it, is that fundamental truths are revealed in laboratory experimentation on lower animals and are then applied to the problem of the sick patient. Having been myself trained as a physiologist, I feel in a way competent to assess such a claim. It is plain nonsense.

British Medical Journal, 26 December 1964

BERNARDIN ST PIERRE, 1737–1814

There is one pastime, among others, which I hold to be abominable. It is that in which they seize a living goose, suspend her by the neck, and practice breaking it by throwing sticks in turns. During this long agony, which lasts entire hours, this poor animal tosses about her feet in the air, to the great satisfaction of her executioners, until the most skilful among them, ending with breaking the vertebrae, causes the body to fall to the ground mutilated and yet palpitating. He then bears it away in triumph and eats it with his companions. Thus they cause to pass into their blood the substance of an animal that has died maddened with torture. These ferocious and imbecile fêtes are frequently given in the grounds of the country houses, or close to the churches, without the owner or the priest taking the least trouble to oppose them. Often the latter forbids dancing to young girls, and permits to boys the torture of innocent birds! In the same way, in our towns priests drive from their churches women who present themselves in hats, but salute with respect men who wear swords! Very many regard as a great sin the going to operas, and yet look on with pleasure at a fight with a bull, that fellow labourer of men, torn to pieces by a pack of hounds. Everywhere barbarity is a virtue, in comparison with which pity or pardon is a crime!

Suite des Voeux d'un Solitaire

LESLIE G. PINE, 1907–1987

I think that four main classes of persons may be distinguished among the three quarters of a million in Great Britain who actively pursue blood sports. First we have those who enjoy bloodshed for its own sake, or who loving a particular form of activity, are completely indifferent as to whether or not it involves the suffering of any other creature. Fortunately these men and women – any illusions about the gentler sex are soon shattered when one takes part in blood sports – are in the minority. Still, they often carry great weight among their fellows, as obviously they are the keenest of the keen, and are most vociferous in defending their right to blood sports. It is, I have found, impossible to argue with such people. If one attempts to argue or discuss with them, they are at best brusque, and at the worst obscenely rude. They soon shout, gesticulate, swear and even proceed to blows, provided no witnesses are present. Nothing can ever be done with this minority of blood sporters; they are really ready-made subjects for the psychiatrist's couch. In days gone by they would have gone as willingly to an *auto-da-fé* as they now do (when in Spain) to a bullfight, or (surreptitiously in England) a cockfight.

In ascending order, as far as number is concerned, we come to a different class altogether. They are expert and seasoned blood sporters, but owing to their possession of finer feelings and better natures, they cannot avoid a feeling of guilt or of remorse in what they do ... had these types been taken in hand properly when young, they would have proved enthusiastic nature lovers ... Another turn in their education gave them the habit of shooting, or hunting, but nothing could entirely eradicate a gentler feeling.

A shot, indeed, which very nearly made me a right subject for enrolment in the anti-blood-sports league, for the baby bunny continued to squat where I had shot it. A tiny tongue rhythmically licked up the blood which dripped steadily from the slug-wound in its forehead; and I did not enjoy my first lesson in despatching wounded game.

'The Memory of a Boy', *The Shooting Times Anthology*, 1963

The third class is comprised of those, and they are numerous in the English social scene, who want to get on socially and financially, who are climbers, and who want to know the right thing to do. A popular newspaper some years ago ran a series of articles giving half-serious, half-facetious, advice for these aspiring Joneses. They must learn to kill and to kill fast. Consequently they take to blood sports. They know that in modern England, despite the decay of the real, old-fashioned landed gentry, enthusiasm for, and participation in, country pursuits is unchecked, and that to share these is one way to get into the swim with the best people. As far as this third class is concerned, anything would do which would get them into touch with influential persons and bring them the right social kudos. Cannibalism, or the inquisition, either would serve. They shoot pheasants, or hunt foxes, with the same zest which they would bring to rack turning or faggot gathering, had they lived some four hundred years ago. Their patron is Tony Fire the Faggot, the character in Scott's *Kenilworth*, who was equally enthusiastic to burn Protestants when Mary I sat on the throne, as he was to snuffle psalms among the godly when her half-sister had taken her place. There is no need for reformers to waste their time trying to convert this class; if blood sports can be banned, then these people will find other ways of creeping or climbing into social favour.

Lastly we come to a huge amorphous collection of men and women who cannot be accused of cruelty, for they do not really know what they are doing at sporting events. They go because it is the thing. Their type will for me at least always be personified by a nice-looking young man whom I once saw at a coursing meeting. He was nowhere near the scene of the atrocity, but was standing with two girls. The group was laughing and joking in a light-hearted way about a quarter to a half mile from where the hare was twisting and turning in a vain bid for its life against two powerful greyhounds ... They had gone to this event, simply as an event, and it could have been anything. They just did not take sides. There are multitudes like this.

After Their Blood

It is this element of having fun which damns blood sports. I would make it plain that I am not a vegetarian, nor am I opposed to the destruction of a pest, but this is a very different thing from having sport and fun from the sufferings and death of creatures.

Ibid.

I have shown that it is ludicrous to talk of fox-hunting as being necessary for the control of the fox; the fox which is hunted enjoys a measure of protection which would never be given to a creature which could not be hunted. It is preserved, indeed, through the fact that it is hunted; should fox hunting be abolished, without other measures being taken *pari passu*, then within five years the fox in the lowland country of Britain would be extinct. It is quite easy to keep down or even to exterminate the fox in country other than hill country if no hunting took place ...

As for the other blood sports, their function in keeping down or 'controlling' wild nature is even less than the corresponding value of fox-hunting control. Who can even begin to argue that pheasant shooting is necessary? Or partridge shooting, or beagling, or coursing, or falconry? These pursuits smell of blood, the love of blood. In the few moments when I have indulged in killing – and bitterly do I regret them – I have been asked by older devotees of the habit: Did I not feel bloodthirsty? The shedding of animal blood did something for these people. They loved it. On every page of their favourite magazines they must have stories and accounts of blood shedding. Not for them the interest of natural history or of animal observation. To kill is all they wanted.

In this book I have not included the half of what I have seen and heard. Incidents do, however, come back to mind with such force that they clamour for a place in the narrative. It has sometimes been my lot to travel with ardent blood sporters in their cars. They will often on observing some animal on the road accelerate in order to kill it. One young man, otherwise apparently quite human, told me – and proved it by his deeds – that he got a kick and a thrill out of running down a hare with his car, or killing birds which loitered on the road too near his vehicle. He certainly did enjoy knocking down and killing or wounding animals. Yet again, a well-known shooter accelerated so that he could knock out a cat which had got on the road. Contrast this with the distress which I have known a nature lover to feel when his car has inadvertently killed a blackbird or thrush. I recall, too, a half sentence from one sporting account, describing a boy's beginnings with a gun – '... his first thrush or blackbird'. What an attitude, so to speak, getting one's hand in with killing a songster. Again, I recall once seeing outside a keeper's cottage a trap of sorts in which a number of sparrows were chirping despondently at their inability to get out. Why, I asked, were they in this contraption? 'We don't want too many of them around.'

Faugh! These bloody sportsmen are enough to sicken

any decent person. What in the name of wonders is the matter with them? Why must their amusement be always accompanied by death for some other part of creation?

... Should we be cruel because creatures are, to our way of thinking, cruel? It is an easy step from the type of reasoning which I am criticizing, to talk of wars being sent by God. This supreme blasphemy is of a piece with the argument that cruel deeds are tolerable and just, because in the animal world we find the strong preying on the weak. We are here to rise above nature, not to imitate it in its worst aspects.

Ibid.

For many years I had been the editor of *Burke's Peerage*, for so long in fact that I began to fear lest no one should judge me capable of doing anything else. I wanted to edit a weekly paper, to see if I could manage it, and I was offered the Managing Editorship of *The Shooting Times* ...

I knew little of blood sports when I took up the appointment, beyond what is known by the general public – virtually nothing. I had done a few days' shooting in India, when I was with the R.A.F., and although I had enjoyed being out in the open in Southern India, I must admit that the sight of a dying bird, shot by myself, had made me feel uncomfortable.

When I took over the editorial management of *The Shooting Times*, I had to set myself to learn all that I could about the subject matter of the paper. To this end I visited numerous sporting events of all kinds, not only in shooting but also in hunting, and in addition to this I endeavoured to gain some insight into the important background of sport. I worked with gamekeepers in England and in Scotland, and found their knowledge of the countryside to be most impressive. I did not take much part in actual shooting, in fact I did very little, because I found that I could not rid myself of the same feeling which had attended my shooting in India, namely a repugnance to face the dying creature whose life had been cut short by myself. In due course I could not go on with the work any longer, and resigned my position.

However, I felt that my knowledge so hardly gained, and with such cost to my feelings, did enable me to speak and write with a much greater power than someone whose natural good feelings about these bloody proceedings had never passed beyond the sphere of imagination. Accordingly I have come to the writing of this book, and hope that as long as I live I shall be able to speak and write on behalf of those creatures who exist at our sufferance; who have been committed by the inscrutable will of Providence into our keeping, but of whose treatment and welfare we shall be required, I am convinced, to give account.

Ibid.

I am a Catholic and consequently for me there can be no vicarious satisfaction in the thought that a person who has behaved cruelly towards animals will pay for it in a future life, when he or she becomes a fox and is hunted by the very pack of which he (or she) was the whilom proud master. It is clear to me, however, that when, if ever, humanity lays aside its suicidal quarrels, and becomes one, the philosophical principles of Buddhism or Hinduism, in their attitude towards animals, must be integrated into the Way, the Truth and the Life of all mankind.

... The so-called acceptance of natural cruelty as something over which we should shrug our shoulders is not the view which the purest religious thinkers have taken. To them cruelty is always cruelty and a hard thing, if not impossible, to reconcile with the character of the All-Good ...

It is our duty as men and women of God's redeemed

creation to try not to increase the suffering of the world, but to lessen it. To get rid of blood sports will be a great step towards this end. I return to the pictures of nature with which I began this Introduction. Think of a golden evening, in English fields in August, when harvest is being gathered in, and when a perfect moon is sharing the light with the glorious after-glow of a splendid sunset. Part of the field has fallen; part still shields the borders, and in the slowly fading light small creatures come out from their deep hiding places. Is not the heart of man lifted up by the beauty around him? Does he not feel a benevolence which should lead him to glorify his Creator? Whatever he may be feeling he has not neglected to lift his gun from its resting place and to come out into the loveliness of evening with intent to kill. A hare is gambolling in the half-beaten-down edges of a field. Within seconds it is rolling in its death agony. Some young rabbits have incautiously come out from their burrows. One of them is bowled over, and two of its companions are so tender and inexperienced that they linger round the body.

A good evensong for the glories of that evening, as the gathering twilight sheds what should be a final radiance over God's handiwork? A last benediction, 'I think that he went into yonder wood', meaning a rabbit which has been hit but not killed. 'It's too dark now for me to follow and find him, why didn't I bring the dog?' is a poor substitute for a thanksgiving hymn.

I hope that I shall live to see the abolition within Britain of all blood sports. ... I seek to show from first-hand experience that they are unnecessary, odious and horrible, suitable only for a lower stage of civilization.

Ibid.

NIKOLAI IVANOVICH PIROGOV, 1810–1881

In my younger days I was pitiless to suffering. One day, as I remember, this indifference to the agony of animals undergoing vivisection struck me with such force that, with my knife in my hand, I involuntarily exclaimed, turning to the comrade who was assisting me: 'Why, at this rate one might cut a man's throat.'

Yes, much can be said in favour of and against vivisection. There can be no doubt that it is an important aid to science ... But science does not entirely fill the life of man; the enthusiasm of youth and the ripeness of manhood pass, and another period of life ensues, and with it an inner call for introspection; and it is then that the recollection of the violence used upon, the tortures inflicted on and the sufferings caused another creature commence to pull at one's heartstrings involuntarily. It seems to have been the same with the great Haller; so it was with me, I must confess; and in these latter years I would never be able to bring myself to perform the same cruel experiments upon animals which at one time I carried out so zealously and with such nonchalance.

Quoted by V. Smidovich, The Memoirs of a Physician

RUTH PITTER, 1897–

The Bat

> Lightless, unholy, eldritch thing,
> Whose murky and erratic wing
> Swoops so sickeningly, and whose
> Aspect to the female Muse
> Is a demon's, made of stuff
> Like tattered, sooty waterproof,
> Looking dirty, clammy, cold,
> Wicked, poisonous and old:
> I have maligned thee! ... for the Cat
> Lately caught a little bat,

Seized it softly, bore it in.
On the carpet, dark as sin
In the lamplight, painfully
It limped about, and could not fly.

Even fear must yield to love,
And Pity makes the depths to move.
Though sick with horror, I must stoop,
Grasp it gently, take it up,
And carry it, and place it where
It could resume the twilight air.

Strange revelation! warm as milk,
Clean as a flower, smooth as silk!
O what a piteous face appears,
What great fine thin translucent ears!
What chestnut down and crapy wings,
Finer than any lady's things –
And O a little one that clings!

Warm, clean, and lovely, though not fair,
And burdened with a mother's care:
Go hunt the hurtful fly, and bear
My blessing to your kind in air.

The Bush Baby

I would rather hold this creature in my hand
Than be kissed by a great king.
The love for what I do not understand
Goes from me to the slight thing.

The moth-velvet and the round nocturnal eyes
And the unchanging face
Are excellent as an image out of paradise,
As a flower in a dark place.

There is only mutual inoffensiveness
Between us, and a sense
Here in my heart, of what it is to bless
A simple immanence;

To see a glory in another kind,
To love, and not to know.
O if I could forsake this weary mind
And love my fellows so!

LORD (Robert) PLATT, MSc, MD, FRCP, 1900–1978

I think there's something more than pain in a lot of these experiments that I object to. I think there's misery. I think it's a wretched state to see an animal wasting away, perhaps with vomiting or diarrhoea, miserable in its cage.

No amount of testing can make a drug absolutely safe, if only because humans react differently from animals.

Presidential address, Royal College of Physicians

PLUTARCH, *c*. A.D. 46–*c*. 120

I, for my part, wonder of what sort of feeling, mind or reason, that man was possessed who was first to pollute his mouth with gore and to allow his lips to touch the flesh of a murdered being; who spread his table with the mangled forms of dead bodies, and claimed as daily food and dainty dishes what but now were beings endowed with movement, with perception and with voice.

Moralia

The obligations of law and equity reach only to mankind, but kindness and benevolence should be extended to the creatures of every species, and these will flow from the breast of a true man, as streams that issue from the living fountain.

Man makes use of flesh not out of want and necessity, seeing that he has the liberty to make his choice of herbs and fruits, the plenty of which is inexhaustible; but out of luxury, and being cloyed with necessaries, he seeks after impure and inconvenient diet, purchased by the slaughter of living beasts; by showing himself more cruel than the most savage of wild beasts ... were it only to learn benevolence to human kind, we should be merciful to other creatures.

Ibid.

... we eat not lions and wolves by way of revenge, but we let those go and catch the harmless and tame sort, such as have neither stings nor teeth to bite with, and slay them.
... But if you will contend that yourself were born to an inclination to such food as you have now a mind to eat, do you then yourself kill what you would eat. But do it yourself, without the help of a chopping-knife, mallet, or axe – as wolves, bears and lions do, who kill and eat at once. Rend an ox with thy teeth, worry a hog with thy mouth, tear a lamb or a hare in pieces, and fall on and eat it alive as they do. But if thou hadst rather stay until what thou eatest is to become dead, and if thou art loath to force a soul out of its body, why then dost thou against Nature eat an animate thing?

Ibid.

Why do you belie the earth, as if it were unable to feed and nourish you? Does it not shame you to mingle murder and blood with her beneficent fruits? Other carnivora you call savage and ferocious – lions and tigers and serpents – while yourselves come behind them in no species of barbarity. And yet for them murder is the only means of sustenance! Whereas to you it is superfluous luxury and crime!

Ibid.

But for the sake of some little mouthful of flesh we deprive a soul of the sun and light, and of that proportion of life and time it had been born into the world to enjoy.

Ibid.

ALEXANDER POPE, 1688–1744

Heav'n from all creatures hides the book of Fate,
All but the page prescrib'd, their present state:
From brutes what men, from men what spirits know:
Or who could suffer Being here below?
The lamb thy riot dooms to bleed today,
Had he thy Reason, would he skip and play?
Pleas'd to the last, he crops the flow'ry food,
And licks the hand just rais'd to shed his blood.

All are but parts of one stupendous whole,
Whose body Nature is, and God the soul …

Nor think, in Nature's State they blindly trod;
The state of Nature was the reign of God:
Self-love and Social at her birth began,
Union the bond of all things, and of Man.
Pride then was not; nor Arts, that Pride to aid;
Man walk'd with beast, joint tenant of the shade;
The same his table, and the same his bed;
No murder cloth'd him, and no murder fed.
In the same temple, the resounding wood,
All vocal beings hymn'd their equal God:
The shrine with gore unstain'd, with gold undrest,
Unbrib'd, unbloody, stood the blameless priest:
Heav'n's attribute was Universal Care,
And Man's prerogative to rule, but spare.
Ah! How unlike the man of times to come!
Of half that live the butcher and the tomb;
Who, foe to Nature, hears the gen'ral groan,

Murders their species, and betrays his own.
But just disease to luxury succeeds,
And ev'ry death its own avenger breeds;
The Fury-passions from that blood began,
And turn'd on Man a fiercer savage, Man.

Essay on Man

Has God, thou fool, worked solely for thy good,
Thy joy, thy pastime, thy attire, thy food?
Who for thy table feeds the wanton fawn,
For him as kindly spread the flowr'y lawn:
Is it for thee the lark ascends and sings?
Joy tunes his voice, joy elevates his wings:
Is it for thee the linnet pours his throat?
Loves of his own and raptures swell the note.
The boundling steed you pompously bestride
Shares with his lord the pleasure and the pride.
Is thine alone the seed that strews the plain?
The birds of heaven shall vindicate their grain:
Thine the full harvest of the golden year?
Part pays, and justly, the deserving steer:
The hog, that ploughs not, nor obeys thy call,
Lives on the labours of this lord of all.
    Know, Nature's children all divide her care;
The fur that warms a monarch warm'd a bear.
While man exclaims, 'See all things for my use!'
'See Man for mine!' replies a pampered goose;
And just as short of reason must he fall,
Who thinks all made for one, not one for all.

Ibid.

From *Windsor Forest*

See! From the shirring brake the pheasant springs,
And mounts exulting on triumphant wings:
Short is his joy; he feels the fiery wound,
Flutters in blood, and panting beats the ground.

370

Ah! What avail his glossy, varying dyes,
His purple crest, and scarlet-circled eyes,
The vivid green his shining plumes unfold,
His painted wings, and breast that flames with gold?

Nor yet, when moist Arcturus clouds the sky,
The woods and fields their pleasing toils deny.
To plains with well-breath'd beagles we repair,
And trace the mazes of the circling hare:
(Beasts, urg'd by us, their fellow-beasts pursue,
And learn of man each other to undo).
With slaught'ring guns th' unwearied fowler roves,
When frosts have whiten'd all the naked groves;
Where doves in flocks the leafless trees o'ershade,
And lonely woodcocks haunt the wat'ry glade.
He lifts the tube, and levels with his eye;
Straight a short thunder breaks the frozen sky:
Oft, as in airy rings they skim the heath,
The clam'rous lapwings feel the leaden death:
Oft, as the mounting larks their notes prepare,
They fall, and leave their little lives in air.

How do we know that we have a right to kill creatures
that we are so little above, as dogs, for our curiosity or
even for some use to us?

Spence's Anecdotes

It is observable of those noxious animals, that have
qualities most powerful to injure us, that they naturally
avoid mankind, and never hurt us unless provoked, or
necessitated by hunger. Man, on the other hand, seeks
out and pursues even the most inoffensive animals on
purpose to persecute and destroy them. Montaigne

371

thinks it some reflection on human nature itself that few people take delight in seeing them caress or play together; but almost everyone is pleased to see them lacerate and worry one another. I am sorry that this temper has become almost a distinguishing character of our own nation, from the observation which is made by foreigners of our favourite pastimes – bear-baiting, cock-fighting and the like.

We should find it hard to vindicate the destroying of anything that has life, merely out of sport. Yet in this principle children are bred, and one of the first pleasures we allow them is the licence of inflicting pain upon defenceless animals. Almost as soon as we are sensible what life is ourselves, we make it our sport to take it from others.

The Guardian (periodical), May 1713

I cannot think it extravagant to imagine that mankind are no less, in proportion, accountable for the ill-use of their dominion over the lower ranks of beings than for the exercise of tyranny over their own species. The more entirely the inferior creation is submitted to our power, the more answerable we must seem for the mismanagement of it.

Ibid.

PORPHYRY, 233–304

He who abstains from anything animate ... will be much more careful not to injure those of his own species. For he who loves the genus will not hate any species of animals.

On Abstinence from Animal Food

But to deliver animals to be slaughtered and cooked, and thus be filled with murder, not for the sake of nutriment and satisfying the wants of nature, but making pleasure and gluttony the end of such conduct, is transcendently iniquitous and dire.

Ibid.

And is it not absurd, since we see that many of our own species live from sense alone, but do not possess intellect and reason; and since we also see that many of them surpass the most terrible of wild beasts in cruelty, anger and rapine, being murderous of their children and their parents, and also being tyrants and the tools of kings [is it not, I say, absurd] to fancy that we ought to act justly towards these, but that no justice is due from us to the ox that ploughs, the dog that is fed with us, and the animals that nourish us with their milk and adorn our bodies with their wool? Is not such an opinion most irrational and absurd?

Ibid.

… if we depend on the argument of necessity or utility, we cannot avoid admitting by implication that we ourselves were created only for the sake of certain destructive animals, such as crocodiles and snakes and other monsters, for we are not in the least *benefited* by them. On the contrary, they seize and destroy and devour men whom they meet - in so doing acting not at all more cruelly than we. Nay, *they* act thus savagely through want and hunger; *we* from insolent wantonness and luxurious pleasure, amusing ourselves, as we do, also in the Circus and in the murderous sports of the chase. By thus acting, a barbarous and brutal nature becomes strengthened in us, which renders men insensible to the feeling of pity and compassion. Those who first perpetrated these iniquities fatally blunted the most important part of the (civilized) soul. Therefore it is that Pythagoreans consider kindness and gentleness to the lower animals to be an exercise of philanthropy and gentleness.

Ibid.

JONATHON PORRITT, 1950–

We all pay a heavy price for our alienation from the Earth. Politicians talk of human rights; jurists of justice. The churches are full of the glory of God and young people are no less hopeful or self-assured than before. Some are inspired by equity, some by liberty, some by the painful intricacies of hard-won democracy. But in all of this brave uplifting of the human spirit, it would seem that the rest of life on Earth, that preceded and may well survive the human species, remains invisible, unsung, apparently irrelevant.

JOHN COWPER POWYS, 1872–1963

The public in America has been kept in the dark, even more than the public in England, about this matter of vivisection. There has never been upon any human subject so much crafty and deliberately misleading propaganda as that which the vivisectors have used to pull wool over the eyes of the world. The 'sentimentality' in this matter is to be found, not in those who oppose themselves to this monstrous crime, but in the ridiculously emotional awe with which the average person, hypnotized by these crafty scientists and their sycophantic press, regards the whole problem. Totally unnecessary cruelty on a scale that the general public has no conception of, is going on all the while. The word 'science' covers every kind of atrocity; and the issue is perfectly clear ... This wickedness contradicts and cancels the one single advantage that our race has got from what is called Evolution, namely the development of our sense of right and wrong. If vivisection, as it is increasingly practised by these unscrupulous, pitiless, unphilosophical scientists, is allowed to go on unchecked, and it will go on unchecked until people feel as strongly about it as women did about women's suffrage – something that the mysterious forces of the universe have themselves developed in us will soon have its spiritual throat cut to the bone. In other words, certain forms of sickening and unthinkable cruelty that hitherto, when perpetrated by individuals, have been stopped at once, condemned by both moral opinion and law, are now – as long as we vaguely assume it is done for the advantage of science – tolerated as an unfortunate but inescapable necessity.

Vivisection is the new superstition, the new tyranny, the new incarnation of the powers of evil. Like all abominable wickedness that has once got into the saddle, this vivisecting science has now begun to brand as 'sentimental', as 'emotional', as 'idealistic', as 'unpractical', the deep honest realistic human instinct which it is deliberately seeking to kill. What science ... is really doing is nothing less than suggesting to the conscience of our race, this conscience that evolution itself has produced, that it is a sign of superior intellect to be completely devoid of natural goodness, of natural pity, and of all natural sensitiveness.

Autobiography

What is the importance of human lives? Is it their continuing alive for so many years like animals in a menagerie? The value of a man cannot be judged by the number of diseases from which he escapes. The value of a man is in his human qualities: in his character, in his conscience, in the nobility and magnanimity of his soul. Torturing animals to prolong human life has separated science from the most important thing that life has produced – the human conscience.

Morwyn

Let none count themselves wise who have not with the nerves of their imagination felt the pain of the vivisected.

Lecture, 4 October 1947

DR RAJENDRA PRASAD, 1884–1963

Any integrated view of life as a whole will reveal to us the connection between the individual's food and his behaviour towards others, and through a process of ratiocination which is not fantastic, we cannot but arrive at the conclusion that the only means of escaping the hydrogen bomb is to escape the [type of] mentality which has produced it, and the only way to escape that mentality is to cultivate respect for all life, life in all forms, under all conditions. It is only another name for vegetarianism.

Searchlight

JEAN BAPTISTE PRESSAVIN, 1760–1830

We cannot doubt that if Man had always limited himself to the use of the nourishment destined by nature for his organs, he would not be seen today to have become the victim of this multitude of maladies which, by a premature death, makes a harvest of the greater number of individuals before age or Nature has put bounds to the career of his life. Other animals, on the contrary, almost all arrive at that term without having experienced any infirmity. I speak of those who live free in the fields; for those whom we have subjected to our needs (real or pretended), and whom we call *domestic*, share in the penalty of our abuses, experience nearly the same alteration in their temperament, and become subject to an infinity of maladies from which wild animals are exempt.

Men, then coming from the hands of Nature, lived a long time without thinking of immolating living beings to gratify their appetite. They are, without doubt, those happy times which our ancient poets have represented to us under the agreeable allegory of the *Golden Age*. In fact Man, by natural organization, mild, nourishing himself only on vegetable foods, must have been originally of pacific disposition, quite fitted to maintain among his fellows that happy Peace which makes the delight of Society ...

But if this faculty, which is called reason, has furnished Man with so many great resources for extending his enjoyments and increasing his wellbeing, how many evils have not the multiplied abuses, which he has made of them, drawn upon him? That which regards his Food is not the one of them which has least contributed to his degradation, as well physical as moral ...

L'Art de Prolonger la Vie et de Conserver la Santé

HUMPHREY PRIMATT, DD, 18th century

Justice is a rule of universal extent and invariable obligation. We acknowledge this important truth in all matters in which Man is concerned, but then we limit it to our own species only. And though we are able to trace the most evident marks of the Creator's wisdom and goodness, in the formation and appointment of the various classes of Animals that are inferior to Men, yet the consciousness of our own dignity and excellence is apt to suggest to us, that Man alone of all terrestrial

Animals is the only proper object of Mercy and Compassion, because he is the most highly favoured and distinguished. Misled with this prejudice in our own favour, we overlook some of the Brutes, as if they were mere Excrescencies of Nature, beneath our notice, and infinitely unworthy the care and cognizance of the Almighty; and we consider others of them, as made only for our service; and so long as we can apply them to our use, we are careless and indifferent as to their happiness or misery, and can hardly bring ourselves to suppose that there is any kind of duty incumbent upon us toward them.

A Dissertation on the Duty of Mercy and Sin of Cruelty to Brute Animals

In one particular we all agree alike, from the most perfect to the most dull and deformed of men, and from him down to the vilest brute, that we are all susceptible and sensible of the misery of pain; an evil, which though necessary in itself, and wisely intended as the spur to incite us to self-preservation, and to the avoidance of destruction, we nevertheless are naturally averse to, and shrink back at the apprehension of it. Superiority of rank or station exempts no creature from the sensibility of pain, nor does inferiority render the feelings thereof the less exquisite. Pain is pain, whether it be inflicted on man or on beast; and the creature that suffers it, whether man or beast, being sensible of the misery of it whilst it lasts, suffers evil; and the sufferance of evil, umeritedly, unprovokedly, where no offence has been given, and no good end can possibly be answered by it, but merely to exhibit power or gratify malice, is cruelty and injustice in him that occasions it.

Ibid.

Now if amongst men, the differences of their powers of the mind, and of their complexion, stature, and accidents of fortune, do not give to any one man a right to abuse or insult any other man on account of these differences; for the same reason, a man can have no natural right to abuse and torment a beast, merely because a beast has not the mental powers of a man. For such as the man is, he is but as God made him; and the very same is true of the beast. Neither of them can lay claim to any intrinsic merit, for being such as they are; for before they were created, it was impossible that either of them could deserve; and at their creation, their shapes, perfections, or defects were invariably fixed, and their bounds set which they cannot pass. And being such, neither more nor less than God made them, there is no more demerit in a beast's being a beast, than there is merit in a man's being a man: that is, there is neither merit nor demerit in either of them.

A Brute is an animal no less sensible of pain than a Man. He has similar nerves and organs of sensation; and his cries and groans, in case of violent impressions upon his body, though he cannot utter his complaints by speech or human voice, are as strong indications to us of his sensibility of pain, as the cries and groans of a human being, whose language we do not understand. Now as pain is what we are all averse to, our own sensibility of pain should teach us to commiserate it in others, to alleviate it if possible, but never wantonly or unmeritedly to inflict it.

Ibid.

But there is no custom, whether barbarous or absurd; nor indeed any vice however detestable, but will find some abettors to justify or at least to palliate it; though the vindication itself is an aggravation of the crime. When we are under apprehensions that we ourselves shall be the sufferers of pain, we naturally shrink back at the very idea of it: we can then abominate it; we detest it with horror; we plead hard for mercy; and we feel that *we can feel.* But when Man is out of the question, Humanity sleeps, and the heart grows callous. We no longer consider ourselves as Creatures of sense, but as Lords of the creation. Pride, prejudice, aversion to singularity, and contracted misrepresentations of God and religion do all contribute to harden the heart against the natural impressions and soft feelings of compassion. And when the mind is thus warped and disposed to evil, a light argument will have great weight with it; and we ransack and rack all nature in her weakest and tenderest parts, to extort from her, if possible, any confession whereon to rest the appearance of an argument to defend or excuse our cruelty and oppression.

Ibid.

On allowing children to be cruel to animals, I say that such indulgence roots out from their once tender hearts every feeling of pity and compassion. So true is it that treatment of animals has an influence on our moral character.

Ibid.

The mistaken indulgence of parents; and the various instances of sportive cruelty in some shape or other daily practised by men in all ranks of life; and the many barbarous customs connived at, if not countenanced by persons in high stations or in great authority (whose conduct in other points may be truly amiable and respectable), prejudice our minds to consider the brute animals as senseless and insignificant creatures, made only for our pleasure and sport. And, when we reflect upon the most shocking barbarities, and then see the brutal rage exercised by the most worthless of men, without control of law, and without notice or reproof from the pulpit, we are almost tempted to draw this inference, that cruelty *cannot be sin*.

And, possibly, the affectation of love or hatred according to the mode of fashion; or, in other words, *Vicious Taste*, which consists in making the love or hatred of others the standard of our own love and hatred – that we must admire whatever our superiors admire, and condemn whatever they are pleased to condemn; that true politeness is to have no thought, no soul, no sentiment of our own, but a graceful resignation of the plainest dictates of truth and common sense to the follies and whims of others; that the art of pleasing is the art of flattery and base compliance; and that singularity of sentiment or practice is the mark of a mean, a vulgar, and a churlish soul; this affectation of compliance, this vicious taste, and this aversion to singularity may possibly lead us to suppose that no diversion can be cruel that has the sanction of Nobility; and that no dish can be unblessed that is served up at a great man's table, though the kitchen is covered with blood, and filled with the cries of creatures expiring in tortures.

Ibid

What should we think of a stout and strong man, that should exert his fury and barbarity on a helpless and innocent babe? Should we not abhor and detest that man, as a mean, cowardly, and savage wretch, unworthy the stature and strength of a man? No less mean, cowardly, and savage is it, to abuse and torment the innocent beast, who can neither help himself nor avenge himself; and yet has as much right to happiness in this world as a child can have: nay, more right, if this world be his only inheritance.

Ibid.

PYTHAGORAS, 6th century B.C.

Alas, what wickedness to swallow flesh into our own flesh,
to fatten our greedy bodies by cramming in other bodies,
to have one living creature fed by the death of another!
In the midst of such wealth as earth, the best of mothers,
provides, nothing forsooth satisfies you, but to behave
like the Cyclopes, inflicting sorry wounds with cruel
teeth! You cannot appease the hungry cravings of your
wicked, gluttonous stomachs except by destroying some
other life.

Depicted in Ovid: The Metamorphoses, translated Mary M. Innes

As long as man continues to be the ruthless destroyer of
lower living beings, he will never know health or peace.
For as long as men massacre animals, they will kill each
other. Indeed, he who sows the seed of murder and pain
cannot reap joy and love.

Attributed (Ovid)

Animals share with us the privilege of having a soul.

Ibid.

FRANCIS QUARLES, 1592–1644

The birds of the aire die to sustain thee;
The beasts of the field die to nourish thee;

The fishes of the sea die to feed thee.
Our stomacks are their common sepulcher.
Good God! With how many deaths are our poor lives
    patcht up!
How full of death is the life of momentary man!

Enchyridion

PRINCE RAINIER III OF MONACO, 1923–

I feel strongly about vivisection and, although scientists endeavour to explain and justify it by the research value that its practices offer, I cannot admit these arguments as really valuable in regard to one's belief and one's faith.

Statement to *The Anti-Vivisection Magazine*

JULIAN RALPH, 1853–1903

But of all the pitiful, heart-rending sights I have ever seen, none had compared to this view of hundreds upon hundreds of dead and dying horses on this 100 miles of war's promenade. The poor beasts had done no man any harm – in fact, each one had been a man's reliance – and to see them shattered by shell and then ripped open by vultures, often before they were dead, was enough to snap the tenderest chords in one's breast. They had not deserved and they could not understand their horrible ill luck. For some reason, hundreds had dragged themselves to the main road, and then had died either in the track of the wagons or by its side.

But the worst horror was to come when I approached close upon the last battlefield only twenty-four hours after the fight at Driefontein. On this field not nearly all the horses were yet dead. On the contrary, as I came up beside the prostrate body of a beautiful steed it would slowly and painfully lift its head and turn upon me a pair of the most pleading woe-stricken eyes, full of a hunger to know what I could do for it. And all I could do was to drive on, for I had no firearms – even for my own protection, deep in an enemy's country, where we had put no single armed man to guard the route of our supplies and reinforcements.

My companion used to turn back and look at these dying horses, only to find that they were still straining their sad eyes after the cart. Then he would say, 'He is looking at us yet. Oh, it makes me ill. Look! He is staring at us like a guilty conscience. What can we do? I wish we did not see such things.'

For my part, I would not look behind. Heaven knows, it was bad enough to see ahead where horses stumbled and fell from weakness while the horrible aasvogels swept in circles over them, eager to rend their living flesh. Oxen, too, were lying everywhere, with straight, stiff legs silhouetted against the veldt. They looked like the toy animals that children make out of round potatoes with wooden matches for legs.

From a despatch to the *Daily Mail*, 1900

S. SANKARANARAYARA RAO, 1923–

An overwhelming love and compassion for all living creatures, both man and beast, is the highest virtue that could be conceived of. Vegetarian food is intended not only for the cleansing of the body but also for the purification of the soul. It is a universally accepted principle that vegetarian food is conducive to a healthier and happier life among nations.

Quoted in *V.S.S.A. News Magazine*, September/October 1981

H.D. RAWNSLEY, 1851–1920

From *The Stag Impaled*

With head thrown back and heaving flank distressed
  It hears the hounds – the hunter's bugle ring;
  What hand shall save the tame unantlered thing?
What covert give the harmless creature rest?
Down the long vale and o'er the woodland crest,
  Across the flood with piteous fear for wing
  It speeds, then leaps and with a desperate spring
Hangs mute, impaled, the fence spur in its breast.

When shall the heart of gentler England prove
  Its pure compassion for all needless pain,
    When shall we learn the bond of brotherhood
    'Twixt man and these wild creatures of the wood,
  And nobler days of sport bring nobler gain
For manhood sworn to pity and to love?

TOM REGAN, 1938–

We must realize that some people will find in our speaking of a subject such as the rights of animals all the evidence they need to convict us of absurdity. Only people can have rights and animals aren't people. So, the more we speak, in a serious way, of animal rights, the more they will see us as supposing that animals are people; and since it is absurd to suppose that animals are people, it's equally absurd to think that animals have rights. That, for many, is the end of it.

Let us be honest with ourselves. There is little chance of altering the mental set of those wedded to thinking in this way. If they are content simply to spout their slogans ('Only people have rights!') as a substitute for hard thinking, we will fail to change their minds by spouting ours or by asking them to look beneath the words to the ideas themselves.

Animals' Rights: a Symposium

Cruelty is manifested in different ways. People can rightly be judged cruel either for what they do or for what they fail to do, and either for what they feel or for what they fail to feel. The central case of cruelty appears to be the case where, in Locke's apt phrase, one takes a 'seeming kind of Pleasure' in causing another to suffer. Sadistic torturers provide perhaps the clearest example of cruelty in this sense: they are cruel not just because they cause suffering (so do dentists and doctors, for example) but because they enjoy doing so. Let us term this *sadistic cruelty*.

Not all cruel people are cruel in this sense. Some cruel people do not feel pleasure in making others suffer. Indeed, they seem not to feel anything. Their cruelty is manifested by a lack of what is judged appropriate feeling, as pity or mercy, for the plight of the individual whose suffering they cause, rather than pleasure in causing it; they are, as we say, insensitive to the suffering they inflict, unmoved by it, as if they were unaware of it or failed to appreciate it as *suffering*, in the way that, for example, lions appear to be unaware of, and thus are not sensitive to, the pain they cause their prey. Indeed, precisely because one expects indifference from animals but pity or mercy from human beings, people who are cruel by being insensitive to the suffering they cause often are called 'animals' or 'brutes', and their character or behaviour 'brutal' or 'inhuman'. Thus, for example, particularly ghastly murders are said to be 'the work of animals', the implication being that these are acts that no one moved by the human feelings of pity or mercy could bring themselves to perform. The sense of cruelty that involves indifference to, rather than enjoyment of, suffering caused to others we shall call *brutal cruelty*.

Laboratory animals are not a 'resource' whose moral status in the world is to serve human interests. They are themselves the subjects-of-a-life that fares better or worse for them as individuals, logically independently of any utility they may or may not have relative to the interests of others. They share with us a distinctive kind of value – inherent value – and whatever we do to them must be respectful of this value as a matter of strict justice. To treat them *as if* their value were reducible to their utility for human interests, even important human interests, is to treat them unjustly; to utilize them so that humans might minimize the risks we voluntarily take (and that we can voluntarily decide not to take) is to violate their basic moral right to be treated with respect. That the laws require such testing, when they do, does not show that these tests are morally tolerable; what this shows is that the laws themselves are unjust and ought to be changed.

One can also anticipate charges that the rights view is anti-scientific and anti-humanity. This is rhetoric. The rights view is not anti-human. We, as humans, have an equal *prima facie* right not to be harmed, a right that the rights view seeks to illuminate and defend; but we do not have any right coercively to harm others, or to put them at risk of harm, so that we might minimize the risks we run as a result of our own voluntary decisions. That violates their rights, and that is one thing no-one has a right to do.

Nor is the rights view anti-scientific. It places the *scientific* challenge before pharmacologists and related scientists: Find scientifically valid ways that serve the public interest without violating individual rights. The overarching goal of pharmacology should be to reduce the risks of those who use drugs without harming those who don't. Those who claim that this cannot be done, in advance of making a concerted effort to do it, are the ones who are truly anti-scientific.

Perhaps the most common response to the call for elimination of animals in toxicity testing is the benefits argument:

1. Human beings and animals have benefited from toxicity tests on animals.
2. Therefore, these tests are justified.

Like all arguments with missing premises, everything turns on what that premise is. If it read: 'These tests do not violate the rights of animals,' then we would be on our way to receiving an interesting defence of toxicity testing. But, unfortunately for those who countenance these tests, and even more unfortunately for the animals used in them, that premise is not true. These tests do violate the rights of the test animals, for the reasons given. The benefits these tests have for others is irrelevant, according to the rights view, since the tests violate the rights of the individual animals. As in the case of humans, so also in the case of animals: Overriding their rights cannot be defended by appealing to 'the general welfare'. Put alternatively, the benefits *others* receive count morally only if no *individual*'s rights have been violated. Since toxicity tests of new drugs violate the rights of laboratory animals, it is morally irrelevant to appeal to how much others have benefited. Lab animals are not our Tasters. We are not their Kings.

Animals are not to be treated as mere receptacles or as renewable resources. Thus does the practice of scientific research on animals violate their rights. Thus ought it to cease, according to the rights view. It is not enough first conscientiously to look for non-animal alternatives and then, having failed to find any, to resort to using animals. Though that approach is laudable as far as it goes, and though taking it would mark significant progress, it does not go far enough. It assumes that it is all right to allow practices that use animals as if their value is reducible to their possible utility relative to the interests of others, provided that we have done our best not to do so. The rights view's position would have us go further in terms of 'doing our best'. *The best we can do in terms of not using animals is not to use them.* Their inherent value does not disappear just because we have failed to find a way to avoid harming them in pursuit of our chosen goals. Their value is independent of these goals and their possible utility in achieving them.

... The rights view ... calls upon scientists *to do science* as they redirect the traditional practice of their several disciplines away from reliance on 'animal models' toward the development and use of non-animal alternatives. All that the rights view prohibits is that science that violates individual rights. If that means that there are some things we cannot learn, then so be it. There are also some things we cannot learn by using humans, if we respect their rights. The rights view merely requires moral consistency in this regard.

Veterinarians are the closest thing society has to a role model for the morally enlightened care of animals. It is, therefore, an occasion for deep anguish to find members of this profession increasingly in the employ of, or rendering their services to, the very industries that routinely violate the rights of animals – the farm-animal industry, the lab-animal industry, etc. On the rights view, veterinarians are obliged to extricate themselves and their profession from the financial ties that bind them to these industries and to dedicate their extensive medical knowledge and skills, as *healers*, as *doctors of medicine*, to projects that are respectful of their patients' rights. The first signatures in the 'new contract' involving justice and animals would be from those who belong to the profession of veterinary medicine. To fail to lead the way in this regard will bespeak a lack of moral vision or courage (or both) that will permanently tarnish the image of this venerable profession and those who practice it.

That science that routinely harms animals in pursuit of

its goals is morally corrupt, because unjust at its core, something that no appeal to the 'contract' between society and science can alter.

The Case for Animal Rights

Both the moral right not to be caused gratuitous suffering and the right to life, I argue, are possessed by the animals we eat if they are possessed by the humans we do not. To cause animals to suffer cannot be defended merely on the grounds that we like the taste of their flesh, and even if animals were raised so that they led generally pleasant lives and were 'humanely' slaughtered, that would not ensure that their rights, including their right to life, were not violated.

I cannot help but think that each of us has been struck, at one moment or another, and in varying degrees of intensity, by the ruthlessness, the insensitivity, the (to use [I.B.] Singer's word) smugness with which man inflicts untold pain and deprivation on his fellow animals. It is, I think, a spectacle that resembles, even if it does not duplicate, the vision that Herman calls to mind – that of the Nazi in his treatment of the Jew. 'In their behaviour toward creatures,' he says, 'all men [are] Nazis.' A harsh saying, this. But on reflection it might well turn out to contain an element of ineradicable truth.

The human appetite for meat has become so great that new methods of raising animals have come into being. Called intensive rearing methods, these methods seek to ensure that the largest amount of meat can be produced in the shortest amount of time with the least possible expense. In ever increasing numbers, animals are being subjected to the rigours of these methods. Many are being forced to live in incredibly crowded conditions. Moreover, as a result of these methods, the natural desires of many animals often are being frustrated. In short, both in terms of the physical pain these animals must endure, and in terms of the psychological pain that attends the frustration of their natural inclinations, there can be no reasonable doubt that animals who are raised according to intensive rearing methods experience much non-trivial, undeserved pain. Add to this the gruesome realities of 'humane' slaughter and we have, I think, an amount and intensity of suffering that can, with propriety, be called 'great'.

To the extent, therefore, that we eat the flesh of animals that have been raised under such circumstances, we help create the demand for meat that farmers who use intensive rearing methods endeavour to satisfy. Thus, to the extent that it is known that such methods will bring about much undeserved, non-trivial pain on the part of the animals raised according to these methods, anyone who purchases meat that is a product of these methods – and almost everyone who buys meat at a typical supermarket or restaurant does this – is *causally implicated* in a practice that causes pain that is both non-trivial and undeserved for the animals in question. On this point too, I think there can be no doubt.

Contrary to the habit of thought which supposes that it is the vegetarian who is on the defensive and who must labour to show how this 'eccentric' way of life can even remotely be defended by rational means, it is the non-vegetarian whose way of life stands in need of rational justification. Indeed, the vegetarian can, if I am right, make an even stronger claim than this. For if the previous argument is sound, he can maintain that unless or until someone does succeed in showing how the undeserved, non-trivial pain animals experience as a result of intensive rearing methods is not gratuitous and does not violate the rights of the animals in question, then he (the vegetarian) is justified in believing that, and acting as if, it is wrong to eat meat, if by so doing we contribute to the intensive rearing of animals and, with this, to the great pain they must inevitably suffer. And the basis on which he can take this stand is the same one that vegetarians and non-vegetarians alike can and should take in the case of a practice that caused great undeserved pain to human beings – namely, that we are justified in believing that, and acting as if, such a practice is immoral unless or until it can be shown that it is not.

Of course, none of this, by itself, settles the question 'Do animals experience pain?' Animals ... certainly appear at times to be in pain. For us to be rationally justified in denying that they are ever in pain, therefore, we are in need of some rationally compelling argument that demonstrates that, though they may appear to suffer, they never really do so. Descartes's argument does not show this ... how animals who are physiologically similar to man behave in certain circumstances – for example, how musk-rats behave when they try to free themselves from a trap – provides us with all the evidence we *could* have that they are in pain, given that they are not able to speak; in the case of the musk-rats struggling to free themselves, that is, one wants to ask what *more* evidence could be rationally required to show that they are in pain in addition to their cries, their whimpers, the straining of their bodies, the desperate look of their eyes, and so on. For my own part, I do not know what else could be required, and if a person were of the opinion that this did not constitute enough evidence to show that the musk-rats were in pain, I cannot see how any additional evidence would (or could) dissuade him of his scepticism. My position, therefore, is the 'naive' one – namely, that animals can and do feel pain, and that, unless or until we are presented with an argument that shows that, all the appearances to the contrary, animals do not experience pain, we are rationally justified in continuing to believe that they do. And a similar line of argument can be given, I think, in support of the view that animals have experiences that are pleasant or enjoyable, experiences that, though they may be of a low level in comparison to, say, the joys of philosophy or the raptures of the beatific vision, are pleasurable nonetheless.

... Moreover, if it is unjust to cause a human being undeserved pain (and if what makes this unjust is that pain is evil and that the human is innocent and thus does not deserve the evil he receives), then it must also be unjust to cause an innocent animal undeserved pain. If it be objected that it is not possible to act unjustly toward animals, though it is possible to do so toward humans, then, once again, what we should demand is some justification of this contention; what we should want to know is just what there is that is characteristic of all human beings, and is absent from all other animals, that makes it possible to treat the former, but not the latter, unjustly. In the absence of such an explanation, I think we have every reason to suppose that restricting the concepts of just and unjust treatment to human beings is a prejudice.

All That Dwell Therein

What's wrong – fundamentally wrong – with the way animals are treated isn't the details that vary from case to case. It's the whole system. The forlornness of the veal calf is pathetic, heart-wrenching; the pulsing pain of the chimp with electrodes planted deep in her brain is repulsive; the slow, tortuous death of the racoon caught in the leg-hold trap is agonizing. But what is wrong isn't the pain, isn't the suffering, isn't the deprivation. These compound what's wrong. Sometimes – often – they make it much, much worse. But they are not the fundamental wrong.

   The fundamental wrong is the system that allows us to

view animals as *our resources*, here for *us* – to be eaten, or surgically manipulated, or exploited for sport or money. Once we accept this view of animals – as our resources – the rest is as predictable as it is regrettable. Why worry about their loneliness, their pain, their death? Since animals exist for us, to benefit us in one way or another, what harms them really doesn't matter – or matters only if it starts to bother us, makes us feel a trifle uneasy when we eat our veal escalope, for example. So, yes, let us get veal calves out of solitary confinement, give them more space, a little straw, a few companions. But let us keep our veal escalope.

In Defence of Animals

Whether and how we abolish [the use of animals] are to a large extent political questions. People must change their beliefs before they change their habits. Enough people, especially those elected to public office, must believe in change – must want it – before we will have laws that protect the rights of animals. This process of change is very complicated, very demanding, very exhausting, calling for the effort of many hands in education, publicity, political organization and activity, down to the licking of envelopes and stamps. As a trained and practising philosopher, the sort of contribution I can make is limited but, I like to think, important. The currency of philosophy is ideas – their meaning and rational foundation – not the nuts and bolts of the legislative process, say, or the mechanics of community organization.

Ibid.

That is the image of philosophy I would leave with you, not 'too cerebral' but *disciplined passion*. Of the discipline enough has been seen. As for the passion: there are times, and these not infrequent, when tears come to my eyes when I see, or read, or hear of the wretched plight of animals in the hands of humans. Their pain, their suffering, their loneliness, their innocence, their death. Anger. Rage. Pity. Sorrow. Disgust. The whole creation groans under the weight of the evil we humans visit upon these mute, powerless creatures. It *is* our hearts, not just our heads, that call for an end to it all, that demand of us that we overcome, for them, the habits and forces behind their systematic oppression. All great movements, it is written, go through three stages: ridicule, discussion, adoption. It is the realization of this third stage, adoption, that requires both our passion and our discipline, our hearts and our heads. The fate of animals is in our hands. God grant we are equal to the task.

Ibid.

LEWIS REGENSTEIN, 1943–

If we are to save the world's wildlife, we must adopt an ethic that recognizes the right of all animals to exist, places equal value on the grotesque and the spectacular, and shows as much concern for the crocodile as for the cheetah, as much for the condor as for the eagle. We must realize that it is just as important to save a species of butterfly as the elephant, that the extinction of a species of mollusc is as great a tragedy as the loss of a bird or mammal. Even endangered plants should merit our concern, for not only do they have the right to live, but also the wellbeing of a host of higher animals, including humans, may depend on their survival.

In Defence of Animals

We have done more ecological damage to the world in the last few decades than in the entire preceding period of recorded history. If we continue at the current rate, or even at a greatly reduced level, our planet will soon be unfit for habitation by most higher life forms, including our own. In wiping out the natural heritage over which we were given dominion and stewardship responsibilities, we are engaging in nothing less than the wholesale destruction of our planet and most of the living creatures on it.

Ibid.

PAUL RICHARD, 1874–1939

Hunting ... the least honourable form of war on the weak.

The Scourge of Christ

SIR BENJAMIN WARD RICHARDSON, MD, FRS, 1828–1896

Experiments on animals are not indispensable for the advancement of medicine, and the difference that exists between the organism of man and that of animals led to very contradictory results ... Of scientific pursuits vivisection is one most liable to error and is calculated to lead to intellectual and moral evil.

Biological Experimentation

Throughout all the country the land is under cultivation of the most perfect kind for cereal produce and fruit and vegetables ... A man, woman, or child who, for wanton pleasure, should hunt down or torture one of the inferior creatures would be cast out of society; while the idea of having dumb animals killed and hung up in open shops to bleed and be quartered and cooked for human beings to live on, would be treated with disgust.

Salut-land

JEAN PAUL RICHTER, 1763–1825

Love is the hemisphere of the moral heaven. Yet is the sacred being of Love little established. Love is an inborn, if differently-distributed, force and heat of the heart. There are cold and warm-blooded souls as there are animals. As for the child, so for the lower animal, love is an essential impulse; and this central fire, in the form of *compassion*, often pierces its earth-crust; but only in few cases ... The child (under proper education) learns to regard all animal life as sacred; in brief, they impart to him the feeling of a Hindu in place of the heart of a Cartesian philosopher. It is a question of something more even than compassion for other animals; but this, also, is in question. Why is it that it has so long been observed that the cruelty of the child to the lower animals presages cruelty to men, just as the Hebrew sacrifice of animals foreshadowed that of a man? It is for *himself only* that the undeveloped man can experience pain and suffering, which speak to him with the native tone of his own experience. Consequently, the inarticulate cry of a tortured animal comes to him just as some strange, amusing sound of the air; and yet he sees there life, conscious movement, which distinguish them from inanimate substances. Thus he sins against his own life, whilst he sunders it from the rest, as though it were a piece of machinery. Let life be to him sacred, even that which may be wanting in reasoning faculties. Because the heart beats under a covering of hair, feathers, or wings, is it, for that reason, to be of no account?

Levana

JEREMY RIFKIN, 1945–

Desacralization is a code word for deadening. Only after a living thing has been thoroughly deadened can it be prepared for assimilation. Unlike the other animals, human beings prefer not to tear into living flesh. We would rather separate the process of killing from the process of eating. We separate ourselves from nature, not only in the pursuit of it, but also in the consumption of it. Regardless of the stage of the assimilation process from pursuit all the way to consumption, we prefer to keep our distance. We adamantly maintain ourselves as subject and reduce everything else to object. Greater separation from nature makes it easier and easier to capture, maim and kill with impunity. Seeing the vague outline from afar is not the same as hearing the breath rush in and out of the nostrils. In Vietnam B-52 pilots dropped bombs on targets without ever witnessing the consequences. In contrast, our ground soldiers had to hear the tortured screams of the enemy soldiers and of their own comrades. The bomber pilots have far fewer nightmares today. Detachment and desacralization go together.

To sum up, desacralization is the psychic process humanity employs to drain its prey of aliveness in order to make it palatable. It is our way of convincing ourselves that there is no fundamental likeness between us and other living things. For it is always more difficult to kill and incorporate things that one identifies with. The desacralization process allows human beings to repudiate the intimate relationship and likeness that exist between ourselves and all other things that live.

Algeny

LEITCH RITCHIE, 1800(?)–1865

The Beetle-Worshipper

How com'st thou on that gentle hand, where love should
  kisses bring
For beauty's tribute? Answer me, thou foul and frightful
  thing!

Why dwell upon thy hideous form those reverent eyes
that seem
Themselves the worshipped stars that light some
youthful poet's dream?

'When bends the thick and golden grain that ripes at my
command,
From the cracked earth I creep, to bless with food the
fainting land;
And thus no foulness in my form the grateful people see,
But maids as sweet and bright as this are priestesses to
me.

'Throned in the slime of ancient Nile, I bid the earth to
bear,
And blades and blossoms at my voice, and corn and fruits
appear;
And thus upon my loathly form are showers of beauty
shed,
And peace and plenty join to fling a halo round my
head.'

Dark teacher, tell me yet again, what hidden lore doth lie
Beneath the exoteric type of thy philosophy?
'The Useful is the Beautiful; the good, and kind, and
true,
To feature and to form impart their own celestial hue.

'Learn farther, that one common chain runs through the
heavenly plan,
And links in bonds of brotherhood the beetle and the
man;
Both fair and foul alike from Him, the Lord of Love, do
spring –
And this believe, he loves not well who loves not
everything.'

JOSEPH RITSON, 1761–1830

That the use of animal food disposes man to cruel and ferocious actions is a fact to which the experience of ages gives ample testimony ... The barbarous and unfeeling 'sports' (as they are called) of the English – their horse-racing, hunting, shooting, bull- and bear-baiting, cock-fighting, prize fighting, and the like, all proceed from their immoderate addiction to animal food. Their natural temper is thereby corrupted, and they are in the habitual and hourly commission of crimes against nature, justice and humanity, from which a feeling and reflective mind, unaccustomed to such a diet, would revolt, but in which they profess to take delight.

Essay upon Abstinence

DR CATHERINE ROBERTS, 1917–

Man's increasing awareness of humaneness indicates that he has reached a new threshold in his evolution and that therefore the problem of painful animal experimentation now concerns all mankind and not just a panel of experts.

To describe the screams of tortured animals as 'high-pitched vocalization', while impeccable from the standpoint of scientific writing, only adds weight to my argument ... To inject more human feeling into the biologist's mental outlook would give him a far saner perspective than he now possesses with which to evaluate the relative importance of his own activity.

Why does any investigation which can be called 'scientific' automatically convince both the scientist and the layman that it is intrinsically valuable for the promotion of human progress?

The Scientific Conscience: Reflections on the
Modern Biologist and Humanism

... it is primarily the experimental biologists and medical scientists who regard animals as things, and that to a degree which would be wholly inconceivable to any barbarian.

There can be little hope of fundamental progress in social responsibility in science before both the means and the ends of biology are made moral. The immorality of animal experimentation must be admitted and its practice at last abandoned by the voluntary action of the biologists themselves. Whether alternative methods of research, which so many anti-vivisection societies are now actively supporting, are available or not is quite irrelevant. The crux of the matter is that a renewal of the scientific conscience must come. The biologist must at last realize that he must refuse to study life's sentient forms if it means inflicting suffering upon them and denying them their basic rights. Biological and medical knowledge attained by such immoral methods can be of no avail to evolution, since it only retards the expression of human righteousness and compassion. No more efficacious step towards restoring confidence in the ultimate aims of biology and medicine could be taken than for biologists to choose voluntarily to restrain and restrict biological progress by employing only those means which are compatible with the moral and spiritual ascent of man.

> For not to know, either awake or in a dream, the nature of justice and injustice, and good and evil, cannot in truth be otherwise than disgraceful to him, even though he have the applause of the whole world.
>
> Plato, *Phaedrus*, 277de)

Plato's view of the human conscience can hardly be bettered. All scientists and laymen alike must eventually learn to distinguish good from evil simply because it is our evolutionary responsibility to do so.

... The Greeks believed that every living organism, human and non-human, possesses a potential of supreme excellence characteristic of the group to which it belonged. They called this highest attainable good *areté*. Both wild and domestic animals often radiate an unmistakable *joie de vivre* which must have its origin in an inner life of superior excellence. If they have not reached perfection in their lives, they appear at least to be realizing their *areté* to a higher degree than is man and in doing so are helping to strengthen and sustain the whole evolutionary process. Some years ago I expressed the thought that

> A bird can strive no further than to live in complete harmony with its environment. This is to fulfil its 'rightness' and to realize its highest potentiality. But for man to live and propagate as a healthy, vigorous animal in blissful harmony with his environment represents only a fraction of human *areté*. The supreme excellence of which he is capable stretches further heavenward than that. Unique among all organisms in his awareness of the realm of the spirit, he strives to approach it, and only in the striving can he realize his potentialities and become as human as he is able.
>
> (*The Scientific Conscience*, 1974)

Although I remain convinced that human *areté* represents a higher state of reality than animal *areté* and one that is much more difficult to attain, I am no longer sure that *Homo sapiens* is the only species aware of the realm of the spirit.

If our knowledge of plants and animals depends upon our own limited sensory and intellectual equipment which precludes personal experience of their conscious and subconscious activity, can we ever hope to know whether evolving non-human lives also have immortal souls that are making an ethical ascent toward the realm of the spirit and beyond? Biology will need to consider this question. It is obviously related to the contemporary ecological view that evolving life is, in fact, an ascending whole whose human component has somehow lost its way. And since the whole of life is now threatened by ecological disaster, we can hardly afford to disregard the voices who claim that our only hope of finding again the upward path is to re-establish a closer and better relation with the rest of nature. If man is to do this, he will need to know much more about the intellectual and spiritual potentials of non-human lives than he does now. The life sciences, in other words, must concern themselves with non-human as well as human *areté*.

… man is … unique in being a species capable of sin. The reverse is equally true: animals and plants are unique by virtue of their innocence.

If they are incapable of immoral acts, then it is equally true that nature thinks no evil. This seems incontestable. When animals prey upon one another, taking their food with violence, they do so in limited measure and with self-restraint, rarely desiring more than necessary for wellbeing and survival. All their fighting and bloodshed stands no direct comparison with the egoistic acts of man. Animals do not spend their lives plotting and scheming, from minute to gigantic scales, acts of wanton destruction, greed, violence, cruelty and injustice for the sake of self-centred goals so contrary to the natural order that their very existence as human thoughts violates the concept of evolution and obstructs the evolutionary process … being himself impure, man … has spent his civilized life controlling, ravaging, and destroying his environment, and in the last five hundred years he has deliberately tried to obliterate the mutually beneficial relations that were established between nature and his ancient forebears. What is not generally recognized is that this *mésalliance* with nature has reached its monstrous culmination in the biological revolution of our times. The life sciences and medicine, proudly divesting themselves of every shred of moral aspiration and vision in order to expand their frontiers at breakneck pace, are now placing their coarse, brutal hands upon untold millions of representatives of defenceless, non-human species in defiance of all religious exhortations to compassion, love, gentleness, mercy and nonviolence. Little wonder that scientists have failed to penetrate the essential secrets of life's *areté* and its evolution. They have forgotten the reality of the spiritual realm and the divine ethic.

... However great the immediate need for abolition of painful experimentation in the laboratory, the present *mésalliance* between biologists and animals does not depend exclusively upon the infliction of pain. It depends also on the utter disregard for the basic rights of animals. Many contemporary biologists, and anti-vivisectionists as well, feel that so long as pain is banned from the laboratory, there can be no limit to the number of animals science employs or the kind of treatment it subjects them to. Ethically and evolutionally this point of view is inadequate. Just and harmonious relations with higher animals cannot be established in the belief that it is morally right to inflict on them painless mutilation or death under anesthesia, or to force them to live out their lives under the unnatural conditions of the laboratory, or to deprive them of association with their own kind. Higher animals, just as men, have need of unconfined movements, of forests, streams, hills, meadows, sun, stars and rain. Neglecting the basic interests of non-human life cannot long continue within scientific circles. A feeling of genuine repentance for having done so for so long may not be far off. The spiritual awakening is gaining theocentric momentum to strengthen and sustain evolution.

... In the course of human evolution many souls have

known that the truest and best relation man can establish with animals is but a reflection of his awareness of the human-divine relation as the central fact of his existence. In their theocentric orientation these souls sensed that the divine ethic is absolute, unchanging, and eternal in all situations. They knew, accordingly, that ethical man must treat sentient beings with love, righteousness, gentleness, mercy and compassion in order that all of us can rise to surpass ourselves.

Science, Animals and Evolution: Reflections on some
Unrealized Potentials of Biology and Medicine

With or without activism, animal advocacy is now surging ahead everywhere. Most advocates regard it as a purely secular endeavour and look to moral philosophers for guidance and to account for what is taking place. In my opinion, secular moral philosophy can no longer suffice as the basis of animal advocacy. Animal advocates do what they do because, whether conscious of it or not, they are trying to respond to a divine ethic. Working with justice and compassion for the good of suffering creation, they must sooner or later recognize that improving man's relations to animals is but a reflection of man's closer relation to deity. In this time of spiritual awakening, animal advocacy is being called upon to acknowledge its ties to the sacred. When it does, both man and beast will stand to gain immeasurably.

Spectrum Review, No.3, Spring 1988

PETER ROBERTS, 1924–

Factory farming is entering a new phase, and the time is ripe for ordinary people to make decisions – decisions which will affect the future welfare of farm animals, and which will also affect us. These animals are part of nature, part of *our* nature; they are part of an environment which will reflect back to us what we show to it – compassion or violence. It is within our power now to create for the future an environment in which we can peacefully co-exist, or to inherit a hostile environment, finding ourselves threatened on all sides by disease, hunger and pests.

Animals' Rights: a Symposium

The monks of Storrington Priory in West Sussex do not keep a fatted calf; they keep 650 which they rear for white veal in narrow and barren crates.

It may be argued that God blessed the calves, giving them each four legs and the good earth to walk upon, but the wooden crates that imprison them now do not permit the calves to walk, nor exercise, nor even so much as to turn round.

Do these monks worship the same God that made these animals ruminants, with four stomachs in order to break down fibre foods, and implanting in them a craving for fibre? On their all-milk diet the only fibre they find is hair plucked from their own bodies, or splinters from their wooden crates.

Was it not the Creator of all things that decreed that they should be sociable and playful creatures? These calves will never play, and can scarcely see one another through the bars of their crates. Their solitary confinement is a life sentence.

The monks say that the scriptures allow them to do these things and that anyway animals cannot really suffer. Yet to curse what God has blessed ...! Is that not blasphemy?

From editorial in *Agscene*, newsletter of Compassion in World Farming who in 1984 brought a case against the Canons of Storrington Priory. In April 1985 the High Court again found for the defendants.

THEODORE ROETHKE, 1908–1963

From Slug

I'm sure I've been a toad, one time or another.
With bats, weascls, worms ... I rejoice in the kinship.
Even the caterpillar I can love, and the various vermin.

ROMAIN ROLLAND, 1866–1944

In those hours when he was weak with suffering, torn
alive away from life, devoid of human egoism, he saw the
victims of men, the field of battle in which man
triumphed in the bloody slaughter of all other creatures:
and his heart was filled with pity and horror. Even in the
days when he had been happy he had always loved the
beasts: he had never been able to bear cruelty towards
them: he had always had a detestation of sport, which he
had never dared to express for fear of ridicule: perhaps
even he had never dared to admit it to himself: but his
feeling of repulsion had been the secret cause of the
apparently inexplicable feeling of dislike he had had for
certain men. He could not think of the animals without
shuddering in anguish. He looked into the eyes of the
beasts and saw there a soul like his own, a soul which
could not speak: but the eyes cried for it:

What have I done to you? Why do you hurt me?

He could not bear to see the most ordinary sights that
he had seen hundreds of times – a calf crying in a wicker
pen, with its big, protruding eyes, with their bluish whites
and pink lids, and white lashes, its curly white tufts on its
forehead, its purple snout, its knock-kneed legs: – a lamb
being carried by a peasant with its four legs tied together,
hanging head down, trying to hold its head up, moaning
like a child, bleating and lolling its grey tongue: – fowls
huddled together in a basket: – the distant squeals of a
pig being bled to death: – a fish being cleaned on the

kitchen table: ... The nameless tortures which men inflict on such innocent creatures made his heart ache. Grant animals a ray of reason, imagine what a frightful nightmare the world is to them: a dream of cold-blooded men, blind and deaf, cutting their throats, slitting them open, gutting them, cutting them into pieces, cooking them alive, sometimes laughing at them and their contortions as they writhe in agony. Is there anything more atrocious among the cannibals of Africa? To a man whose mind is free there is something even more intolerable in the suffering of animals than in the sufferings of men. For with the latter it is at least admitted that suffering is evil and that the man who causes it is a criminal. But thousands of animals are uselessly butchered every day without a shadow of remorse. If any man were to refer to it, he would be thought ridiculous. And that is the unpardonable crime. That alone is the justification of all that men may suffer. It cries vengeance upon all the human race. If God exists and tolerates it, it cries vengeance upon God. If there exists a good God, then even the most humble of living things must be saved. If God is good only to the strong, if there is no justice for the weak and lowly, for the poor creatures who are offered up as a sacrifice to humanity, then there is no such thing as goodness, no such thing as justice ...

Jean Christophe

STEVEN ROSEN, 1955–

The world of science echoes the world's religions with its own equivalent of the Golden Rule. Newton's Third Law of Motion says that 'For every action, there is an equal and opposite reaction.' While Newton's Law applies only to material nature, the implications run deeper still, extending to the most subtle levels of existence. In the East, this is called the law of *karma*.

In a very fundamental sense, too, this law relates to our treatment of animals. The violence in society is at least in part the result of our merciless diet and abuse of the natural world around us. In karmic terms, violence begets violence. In dietary terms, you are what you eat.

Food for the Spirit

CLARE ROSENFIELD, 1941– and LINDA SEGALL, 1942–

The mentality which can treat other sentient beings as if they were feelingless machines is the same as that which can conceive of dropping bombs on whole populations and sending its own sons to carry it out. What is to prevent those who close their eyes to the pain of helpless creatures from closing their eyes to the pain and loss of human lives? Once we become used to claiming no responsibility for such events, our minds become weak and spineless and we allow someone else to do the slaughtering, someone else to die for us, someone else to push the nuclear war buttons.

When blood soaks the land, we label it enemy blood or friend blood, locking up or letting loose our emotions accordingly. In the same way, when the throats of helpless creatures are cut, human minds categorize, rationalize and explain, cutting hearts off from natural compassion. Where has our human capacity for feeling and empathy gone?

Short though it is, our time on this planet can be valuable and meaningful, if we choose to discover and live by the laws of life. War, butchering and all kinds of killing are abominations, antithetical to life.

It does not make sense to be working to end discrimination against minority groups, for example, while neglecting the right to live of animals, a majority treated as a minority. We want our voices to be heard when we call out for peace; at the same time, we have no right to condone the bloody business of slaughterhouses through our eating habits.

Reverence For All Life: the Jain Way to Peace (short title)

CHRISTINA ROSSETTI, 1830–1894

From *A Nursery Rhyme Book*

Hurt no living thing:
  Ladybird, nor butterfly,
Nor moth with dusty wing,
  Nor cricket chirping cheerily,
Nor grasshopper so light of leap,
  Nor dancing gnat, nor beetle fat,
Nor harmless worms that creep.

From *To What Purpose this Waste?*

And other eyes than ours
Were made to look on flowers,
Eyes of small birds and insects small:
  The deep sun-blushing rose
  Round which the prickles close
Opens her bosom to them all.
  The tiniest living thing
  That soars on feathered wing,
Or crawls among the long grass out of sight
  Has just as good a right
To its appointed portion of delight
  As any King.

MIRIAM ROTHSCHILD, 1908–

Just as we have to depersonalize human opponents in wartime in order to kill them with indifference, so we have to create a void between ourselves and the animals on which we inflict pain and misery for profit.

The Relationship between Animals and Man,
Romanes Lecture, Oxford, 1985

I know that many experiments are performed on live animals to satisfy our thirst for knowledge. Many scientists are obsessed with the desire to get the right answer, not only to prove that their theories are correct, and to win both approbation and advancement – fame and fortune – but because the desire to 'know' is almost as compelling as the craving for a hard drug. Furthermore, to the researcher himself the answer almost inevitably seems more significant than it really is. Secondly, all too few of those in authority make it clear to their classes and their pupils or their post-doctoral students, or those planning experiments, or those applying for vivisection licences, that an increase in human knowledge is not in itself a justification for experimenting on live animals. The Medawars [*Aristotle to Zoos. A philosophical dictionary of biology*] pointed out that it is difficult for scientists to retain a sense of primary obligation to the animal rather than to the experiment and the law. Rules are not enough.

Ibid.

Looking back at the first half of my life as a zoologist, I am particularly impressed by one fact: none of the teachers, lecturers, or professors with whom I came into contact – and that includes my kindly father – none of the directors of laboratories where I worked, and none of my co-workers, ever discussed with me, or each other in my presence, *the ethics of zoology*. Nor did they ever ask me

411

what I was really trying to do, what were my zoological aims and aspirations, and in what framework I saw the life-cycles I was elucidating. No one ever suggested that one should respect the lives of animals in the laboratory or that they, and not the experiments, however fascinating and instructive, were worthy of greater consideration.

The fact is, teachers and pupils alike – quite aside from the question of earning their livings or furthering their careers as scientists – were brainwashed and self-indoctrinated. We were on the whole a rather moral group of seekers-after-truth, who loved the natural world and who were happily convinced of the importance of our subject – our research – but who were, lamentably, disinclined to think. It took me another thirty years of natural history and zoological laboratories before I, myself, began to consider the matter seriously and allowed my doubts to crystallize. This fortunate but traumatic experience I owe to my eldest daughter who, as a schoolgirl, resolutely marched out of her zoological classroom never to return. She refused to kill and then dissect an earthworm.

The penny dropped.

Ibid.

JEAN-JACQUES ROUSSEAU, 1712–1778

The animals you eat are not those who devour others; you do not eat the carnivorous beasts, you take them as your pattern. You only hunger for the sweet and gentle creatures which harm no one, which follow you, serve you, and are devoured by you as the reward of their service.

Emile

One of the proofs that the taste of flesh is not natural to man is the indifference which children exhibit for that sort of meat, and the preference they all give to vegetable foods, such as milk-porridge, pastry, fruits, etc. It is of the last importance not to de-naturalize them of this primitive taste and not to render them carnivorous, if not for health reasons, at least for the sake of their character. For, however the experience may be explained, it is certain that great eaters of flesh are, in general, more cruel and ferocious than other men. This observation is true of all places and of all times. English coarseness is well known. The Gaures, on the contrary, are the gentlest of men. All savages are cruel, and it is not their morals that urge them to be so; this cruelty proceeds from their food. They go to war as to the chase, and treat men as they do bears. Even in England the butchers are not received as legal witnesses any more than surgeons. Great criminals harden themselves to murder by drinking blood. Homer represents the Cyclopes, who were flesh-eaters, as frightful men, and the Lotophagi [lotus-eaters] as a people so amiable that as soon as one had any dealings with them, one straightway forgot everything, and one's country, to live with them.

Ibid.

I have sometimes examined those people who attach importance to good living, who thought, upon their first awakening, of what they should eat during the day, and described a dinner with more exactitude than Polybius would use in describing a battle. I have thought that all these so-called men were but children of forty years, without vigour and without consistence – *fruges* [*carnes*] *consumere nati*. Gluttony is the vice of souls that have no solidity. The soul of a gourmand is in his palate. He is brought into the world but to devour. In his stupid incapacity, he is at home only at his table. His powers of judgement are limited to his dishes.

Ibid.

413

Every animal (of the higher species) has ideas, since he has senses. He even combines his ideas up to a certain point, and man differs, in this respect, only in the *more or less*. Some philosophic writers have even advanced that there is more difference between this man and that man, than between this man and that (non-human) animal. It is not, therefore, intelligence so much as his quality of being a free agent which makes the difference.

Discourse Upon Inequality Among Men

R.F. ROWLEY, 1920–

Each time an otter is killed the pole is proudly notched by its owners as if it were a matter of personal pride that he (or she) has assisted in the inflicting of a cruel death on a wild animal which, to the shame of every Englishman, is accorded no protection by law at all.

Thus equipped, bedecked in a bizarre fashion, with twenty or more specially trained dogs, some gangs of thirty or so people set out in various parts of the country two or three times a week during the summer months for the purpose of hunting down until it is exhausted a beautiful and sensitive creature, just to provide themselves with amusement, and then brutally killing it with their pack of hunger-crazed dogs. Nothing will have been achieved, except that the children present at the hunt will have been shown how to be cruel and that the inflicting of pain and suffering on small and weaker creatures is really rather fun, and the 'grown-up' thing to do. I can think of nothing that will harm a child's mind more permanently than the deliberate killing and torture of an animal for the purpose of providing amusement. Children brought up in this atmosphere of blood-lust cannot fail to become hard and bitter, and will naturally consider that kindness, tolerance or sympathy towards the lesser creatures of creation is apparently an undesirable trait in human nature.

From 'Otter-hunting', in *Against Hunting, a Symposium*,
edited by Patrick Moore

GEOFFREY L. RUDD, 1909–

Let us consider the chain reactions of flesh eating:

1. We deliberately, for purely selfish purposes (not for necessity), cut short the life-cycle of another living being. We do this entirely on our own authority, since there is not and cannot be any authority for such an action. At the same time we are very careful to preserve our own period of incarnation and what we call our rights and freedoms.

2. In, before, and probably after, the operation of slaughter we cause fear and bewilderment, and inflict pain, on another living being. At the same time we go to considerable trouble to avoid these experiences ourselves.

3. By creating and perpetuating death centres in every small community ('abattoirs' does not sound nearly so truthful, though it comes from the French *abattre* 'to beat down') we induce other people to follow a degrading trade (butcher and slaughterer are derogatory terms). Killing cannot be of cultural value and can breed nothing but callous indifference for the sacredness of life. No sensitive person would eat flesh if he or she had to do the skull-breaking, slaughtering, strangling, shooting, bloodletting, skinning and disembowelling, and live in the stench and among the agonized cries of the victims.

We suggest that these three aspects of flesh-eating alone show the utter selfishness bred and increased by the apparently simple choice of a dish of food.

Human Nature As It is (originated as editorials in *World Forum*)

The vegetarian philosophy is not perfect. Its practice may leave something ethical to be desired. Vegetarianism is, in fact, not a philosophy but an aspect of a more perfect way of life. It is a relatively small step in a beneficial direction; a step which, if not taken, can nullify other efforts, for it is doubtful if any worthwhile system can be worked on a basis of cruelty and ruthless exploitation. In the last analysis we must be judged by what we do and not by what we believe. We are as we behave – with a very small margin of credit for our unmanifested vision of how we might behave if we could take the trouble.

Editorial, *The British Vegetarian*, September/October 1962

The basis of vegetarianism is ethical. It is a practical acknowledgement that the unnecessary killing of other creatures is barbarous. It has economic and health benefits. Being an obvious truth, the humanitarian idea is easy to grasp. No sensible person would claim that animal butchery is spiritually elevating or is anything but the opposite of all we hold beautiful and good. If it is thought that the unpleasant side is over-emphasized, a visit to the most hygienic and up-to-date slaughterhouse is recommended.

The compassionate part of Man is hardest to evoke. He seems to be ashamed of it, as though it is unmanly. Perhaps after ages of brutality the attribute has atrophied. If we try to encourage a feeling of compassion an iron curtain drops with a soulic clang to hide this embarrassing vestige.

Ibid., January/February 1964

We suppose the term 'animal-lover' has gathered to itself more than a little opprobium, but it need not imply the sentimental drooling one sees over dogs and cats, while the owner, blissfully unconscious of the fact that a cow is also an animal, gnaws part of a Friesian's rib. In its best application it might mean one who appreciates and cherishes life in all its forms.

Such appreciation is, we think, a good thing, for as Pythagoras taught, those who accustom themselves to abominate the ill-treatment and killing of animals come more easily to see that it is even more unjust and unnatural to kill human beings. We also think the opposite is true: those who ill-treat animals, as in vivisection; and kill them, as for fun; will eventually find it less distasteful to torture and kill fellow men.

Peace and humaneness are aspects of a state of being. War and viciousness are facets of non-development.

It is a complete mystery how the English acquired the epithet of 'animal-lovers' – unless it was because they loved killing them, or were keen on eating them. Bear-baiting, cock-fighting, hare-coursing, hunting, shooting, trapping, fishing, have always been the special delights of this 'other Eden', from the lowest peasant to the highest and most noble. All on holiday in Spain scramble by the bus-load to get into the bull-fights to see bulls teased with painful darts and then killed with a sword. Several efforts have recently been made to introduce the sport in England – but for the heroic few protestors we should have them with us at Belle Vue and other centres of joy.

The plight of animals is worsening with the general disintegration of standards of behaviour. Despite a growing interest in nature reserves, where people can study the beauty and habits of wild life, it is still the acme of good breeding to slaughter foxes, otters, badgers, grouse, pheasants, trout and salmon – according to the upper echelons of society whose vicious habits are copied assiduously by the lower orders. There is something wrong, surely, when guns and other weapons can be purchased cheaply at almost every street-corner; when you can hardly walk through a wood without coming across a couple of be-jeaned youths with shot-guns. It seems to us from our proletarian desk that the so-called nobility will have something to answer for in setting such a dreadful example of killing for fun.

Equally unnecessarily, more and more domestic

animals are being killed for food. Increasing numbers are produced 'scientifically' in appalling conditions. We are allowing more and more immigrants to bring their cruel and archaic method of killing to this country. It seems fantastic to us that anyone can believe his soul is put in jeopardy by the way he performs his ghastly and ungodly butchery. Goodness knows the Christian method is foul enough, but to claim that throat-cutting is painless and free from terror is pathetic. 'Animals don't have the same feelings and reactions as humans,' they say. But tread on a dog's paw and see what he says, and note the lengths to which any creature will go, humans included, to avoid pain and being killed. Both animals and men kick and writhe when their throats are cut – ask a Commando. Who dare claim that an entity is not caused great torment by a violent death? Life, emotion, and feeling, are a good deal more than brains and nerves, we think.

Editorial, *The British Vegetarian*, September/October 1966

The line of demarcation between what we refer to as human and animal, should be made, if it is made at all, much lower in the scale of creature evolution to include all sentient, thinking, reasoning and emotional beings ... Confusion on this matter is due to archaic religious ideas which assume, in an ego-inflated way, that only *Homo sapiens* has a soul (spirit or life force) and is thus different and divinely favoured to the exclusion of all other manifestations of the life principle. This is a misconception, false and utterly misleading. The result in subsequent relationships is disastrous, justifying flesh-eating, vivisection, expedient extermination, exploitation for clothing, and the indulgence of all that is lowest in human nature.

Human Nature As It Is

Having seen that we are a related part of life; that we are part matter and part spirit, and having stripped ourselves of grandiose ideas about being the special favourites of a personal God (to the exclusion of other beings in different stages of evolution), we are free to regard all other living creatures as treading the same path, and, knowing something of the difficulties, we do not cause additional and unnecessary pain and suffering.

Ibid.

We may profess to be Buddhist, a member of some obscure sect, C. of E., or Catholic, but if, say, we are eating dead animal carcasses, we are functioning on the same level as carnivorous animals and Neanderthal man. No fancy religious label will alter the level of functioning. Not that not eating dead animals has any virtue whatsoever – the vegetarian may well be Neanderthal in other relationships or may be vegetarian for purely selfish reasons. Nevertheless, the spiritual type of functioning is distinct from that of the animal type.

Ibid.

Once we see that spiritual evolution is the purpose of life (and not material acquisition or manipulation) we can begin to re-orient our lives for this specific purpose. Everything happening to us can then be regarded as the material for the operation of the faculty to make choices. In the course of time, through many experiences and lives, the ability to make good responses is recognized as wisdom – this is the only acquisition worth having; everything else is ephemeral and valueless.

Ibid.

Life is being and doing with discernment and discrimination. There is no point in being puritanical and 'good' through fear of punishment in this world or the next (or for hope of reward) – only in making the better choice for its own sake. We make our own hells and heavens and have to live in them. No other being judges or condemns us but ourselves.

We have to cultivate self-awareness without being self-regarding, which is quite different. We have to be self-critical without being morbidly introspective, and finally, be selfless. This is not a negative state but a perfected vehicle for inward and outward motion ... and the goal of human development. Evolutionary processes beyond this point need not concern us for many ages.

Ibid.

There are many political parties, from conservative to communist, using capitalism and anarchy. Good government will only follow the degree of individual self-government, which when achieved will abolish the need for physical power, armies and police forces which are symptomatic of selfishness and unwisdom. There is no solution to world problems but self-discipline and there is no point at which we can begin to govern except within ourselves. Whichever political party is in power is of no concern to the being. The only concern is how we are governing ourselves. When this is right, the outer life is right.

Ibid.

By taking part in the almost ritualistic slaughter of herded tigers, with no other purpose than for kicks, the Royal party has flouted the feelings of many millions of Indians, whose belief in Ahimsa (harmlessness) is deeply held – this after paying homage to Gandhi.

It is the burden of the leaders of our nobility, for which they are highly paid, to embody all that is finest in the nation.

This must include the human guardianship of animals, which the Queen acknowledges by being Patron of the R.S.P.C.A.

It is monstrous and nauseating that our Royal representatives should so manifestly enjoy the barbarous pastimes of shooting, hunting and killing for fun – bad even in our country where the country types are encouraged to be sadists, but to persist in a country where widespread protests have been made is as callous as it is tactless.

Letter in the *Manchester Evening News*, 27 January 1961

Consider this: after a great deal of evolutionary activity, millions of years of painful experimental experience, we have arrived at the advanced point where we need thousands of doctors, hundreds of hospitals, torrents of medicine, tons of aspirins and barbiturates, thousands of failed M.D.s in hundreds of drug research and vivisection laboratories, vast armies with weapons of destruction, and organized animal butchery on a scale at which the mind boggles – millions of deaths a day.

The vision of a perfect Man, to whose stature we might aspire, is hard to conjure up, but we can ask ourselves if his activities would include those listed. Are they, or are they not, a sorry reflexion on our spiritual development and our understanding of the human mechanism? An honest answer might be helpful.

Perhaps, if we can admit that *all* nations are underdeveloped (stark staring aborigines might be a more appropriate epithet), we might be galvanized into doing something about it, instead of being smugly satisfied with the pitiful exhibition we see all around us.

Editorial, *The British Vegetarian*, September/October 1962

HANS RUESCH, 1913–

In Dickens' day, the advocates of child labour claimed to be humanitarians, and contended that its abolition would mean the end of civilization and the starvation of the masses, and that if substitute measures existed they would have been used.

Similar arguments are being invoked by vivisectionists today, and were invoked by all those who wanted to perpetuate the slave trade, racial and sexual discrimination, and religious torture. Those who support vested interests that are responsible for severe injustice and cruelty always try to hide their crimes behind pseudo-humanitarian arguments; and many people believe them, simply because it is easier and seems safer to believe what one has been taught rather than venturing into intellectual independence. In fact conformism and inertia, not opposition, have always been the greatest obstacle to progress.

Slaughter of the Innocent

JOHN RUSKIN, 1819–1900

Without perfect sympathy with the animals around them, no gentleman's education, no Christian education, could be of any possible use.

Speech to the Society for Prevention of Cruelty to Animals

I will not kill nor hurt any living creature needlessly, nor destroy any beautiful thing, but will strive to save and comfort all gentle life, and guard and perfect all natural beauty upon the earth.

Rule 5 of Ruskin's Society of St George

It was not the question whether animals had a right to this or that in the inferiority they were placed in to mankind; it was a question of what relation they had to God, what relation mankind had to God, and what was the true sense of feeling as taught to them by Christ the Physician.

Speech at a meeting on vivisection, Oxford, 9 December 1884

These scientific pursuits were now defiantly, provokingly, insultingly separated from the science of religion; they were all carried on in defiance of what had hitherto been held to be compassion and pity, and of the great link which bound together the whole creation from its Maker to the lowest creature.

Ibid.

When I see a person indifferent to the needs and blind to the sufferings of animals, I put him down as one from whom little sympathy can be expected for the needs and sufferings of his neighbours. If he is one who abuses an animal in its dumb and pathetic helplessness, I know that the innate meanness of spirit, cruelty and cowardice of the nature so revealed would wreak itself on his fellow men.

Ibid.

The best I could do was wholly at the service of Oxford … I meant to die in my harness there, and my resignation was placed in the Vice-Chancellor's hands on the Monday following the vote endowing vivisection in the University, solely in consequence of that vote.

Letter to the *Pall Mall Gazette*, 24 April 1885

GEORGE K. RUSSELL, 1937–

The power of science without the control of compassion and admiration for life is too immense to be applied merely for the satisfaction of scientific curiosity. If Biology were taught in a manner that developed a sense of wonder and of reverence for life, these students would formulate as a lifelong goal the steadfast determination to protect and preserve all life and would bring healing to a world desperately in need of it.

American Biology Teacher

RICHARD D. RYDER, 1940–

As a scientist, I have witnessed at first hand the increasing suffering of animals here and abroad, so often doubtfully justified as being for the betterment of mankind when frequently the real motive is petty academic ambition.

Victims of Science

Unless morality is to be based entirely upon self-interest then it is high time that we based it on the logic of evolution. If we as animals respect the interests of other individuals of our so-called species – then why not extend similar considerations to the other species also?

Surely the crucial similarity that men share with other animals is the capacity to suffer? Regardless of the number of legs or the woolliness of our fur, we can all *suffer* ...

Speciesism: the Ethics of Animal Abuse

Some will take refuge in the old cliché that humans are different from other animals. *But when did a difference justify a moral prejudice?* When did those with black hair have a moral right to mistreat those with red hair – or even those with blue or purple hair?

Of course, Hitler thought this. Those with blond hair had a moral right – not to say a moral *duty* – to mistreat those with alleged Semitic features; and in case you think I am being unfair dragging in the Nazis, listen to what Professor Rose had to say about his researches into typhus:

'We know today how many of the subjects of experiments perished; but we cannot, naturally, prove how many lives were saved.'

Dr Fisher, too, said the basic motive for his research 'was my desire to help the wounded'.

I refer, of course, to what Professor Rose and Dr

Fisher said as they stood trial at Nuremberg; as they attempted to justify their experiments upon the human inmates of concentration camps – the Jewish men at Buchenwald, the women at Ravensbruck.

These men were well-established scientists before the Second World War. Yet now they are totally condemned and blasted by civilized opinion. But what exactly is the logic in this? Their justifications are perennial. We hear them still today.

What, logically speaking, makes them so contemptible while the scientist who experiments on rats, dogs, cats, monkeys and chimps, is lauded and applauded and covered in honours?

What exactly is the difference, logically or biologically?

Where is the magic line to be drawn between what is good and bad? Is the species gap different in *quality* from the race gap? There are marked physical differences between the races. Does that justify a Hottentot surgeon experimenting on an unwilling Englishman? Did that justify slavery?

To say one species has a *right* to exploit the others is to be guilty of the prejudice of *speciesism*, just as to argue that one race has a right to subordinate another race is *racism*. Racism and speciesism stand together as two similar forms of selfishness and discrimination – and together, in my opinion, they stand condemned. The words 'race' and 'species' have, after all, been used interchangeably and some geneticists have questioned whether the races of mankind could not better be called species or sub-species.

What does the word 'species' signify other than a degree of physical difference? It used to be said that the species could not interbreed. But how about lions and tigers? They have interbred and produced viable offspring which are themselves able to reproduce. It was only a question of bringing together two geographically separated groups, and hey presto!

There are scores of examples of Primate species interbreeding – and men share the Primate order with the other apes and monkeys. When a professor of genetics fathers an orang-utang hybrid, what will he do with it? Send it to Eton? Or perhaps just vivisect it? Will he put it in a cradle or a cage?

The biological distinction between species is flimsy, to say the least. So is the moral distinction ...

Superior intelligence gives not greater rights but greater responsibilities. Surely the more intelligent or educated a man, the greater his responsibility towards the less intelligent and less educated?

Because one species is more clever than another, does it give it the right to imprison or to torture the less clever species? Does one exceptionally clever individual have a right to exploit the less clever individuals of his own species? To say that he does is to say with the Fascists that the strong have a right to abuse and exploit the weak – might is right, and the strong and the ruthless shall inherit the Earth.

We recognize, I hope, our special responsibilities towards the aged and infirm, towards the sick, the mentally subnormal and the physically handicapped. We say that such sentient creatures that are less able to fend for themselves deserve our special care and support. The same argument applies to children – and we as adults claim to recognize our special duties towards them. If this is so, then why do we not also recognize our special duties towards individuals from less clever species? John Stuart Mill wrote in 1848 in *The Principles of Political Economy*:

> The reasons for legal intervention in favour of children apply not less strongly to the case of those unfortunate slaves and victims of the most brutal part of mankind – the lower animals. It is by the grossest misunderstanding of the principle of liberty that the infliction of exemplary punishment on ruffianism

practised towards these defenceless creatures has been treated as a meddling by government in things beyond its province; an interference with domestic life. The domestic life of domestic tyrants is one of the things which it is the most imperative on the law to interfere with.

The implication of this would seem to be that those of us who count ourselves as Socialists or Liberals, Humanists or Christians, should extend our ideologies to include the other species. The welfare of animal citizens is as much our concern as is that of other humans.

Surely if we are all God's creatures, if all animal species are capable of feeling, if we are all evolutionary relatives, if all animals are on the same biological continuum, then also we should all be on the same *moral* continuum – and if it is wrong to inflict suffering upon an innocent and unwilling human, then it is wrong to so treat another species. To ignore this logic is to risk being guilty of the prejudice of Speciesism.

Ibid.

Speciesism clogs and constrains and distorts our outlook just as tenaciously as racism and sexism. There is a widespread tendency for people to wish to regard others as subordinate to themselves. Partly, this is a reflection of their own insecurity, often the insecurity of the sawdust Caesar. The fascist is a very weak person pretending that he is very strong; he wants to convince himself (as well as others) that he is not the inferior creature that he fears himself to be. Such psychological cripples need crutches and they often use racism or sexism or indeed speciesism for this purpose. For example, those who choose to become lion-tamers or big-game shots, as well as some herdmen and hunters – a proportion follow these occupations because they like to play god with other creatures. By subjugating Jews or women or 'vermin' into an inferior position such people manage to make themselves feel a little bit more superior and more secure.

From the Proceedings of the Symposium held by the Human Education Council at Sussex University, 1980

I have worked with adolescents for more than ten years as a clinical psychologist and I can state categorically that the child's experience of dissection in schools, and his or her attitude towards it, can correlate with the child's whole attitude towards society. A child who has acquired a professional indifference to dissection is likely to have a high score on the P scale of Eysenck's Personality Questionnaire – itself a feature of teenage delinquents and criminals.

What are we doing when we brainwash children in schools to cut open their fellow animals? Are we dangerously desensitizing them? Some of the most warped and blunted people I know are those who have gone through prolonged trainings of this sort.

Ibid.

Animal sacrifice is a widespread feature of primitive religions and, in my opinion, precisely because it shocks and excites those who observe it. The killing of an animal is used as a psychological device to raise arousal, stimulate interest, and stir deep and sometimes dangerous feelings.

Ibid.

My thesis is that children often see other animals as friends or colleagues, or as brothers and sisters. Yet, so I contend, adults systematically erode this attitude, replacing it by the mentality of speciesism, teaching children to regard animals as inferior beings, at best to be treated with the patronizing kindness of a medieval lord to his serf, or at worst to be mercilessly exploited. I have welcomed Science Fiction insofar as it shakes our arrogant assumption that man is central in the universe.

Ibid.

Charles Darwin died in 1882 and his theory of Evolution was roundly condemned by many churchmen during his lifetime. But one of its moral implications is only now being realized. If man is *biologically* related to other animals, then it seems to me that we should also be *morally* related. Since Darwin, the alleged gap between man and the rest of creation can no longer be taken so seriously. Nor can any excuse be accepted for giving to man privileges and rights which are entirely withheld from the other sentient species. We are *all* animals and we are all cousins.

Ibid.

To be true to the logic of Animal Liberation entails considerable alteration to the structure of human society. Not only should we stop eating animals and experimenting upon them, cease shutting them in zoos or hunting and trapping them in the wild, we should also, perhaps, put them on an equal footing with children and the mentally handicapped in the eyes of the law.

Ibid.

The idea of 'natural sympathy' or 'natural compassion' was frequently expressed by eighteenth-century writers. In the twentieth century there appeared the assumption that kindness is motivated only by acquired cultural values, and the conception of man as innately aggressive has been over-emphasized. Man is both naturally aggressive and naturally sympathetic; certain stimuli (e.g. frustration or the pathetic cries of an injured child or animal, respectively) may trigger aggression or compassion. In addition, of course, such behaviour may also be acquired, and in any event will inevitably be modified through learning.

It is incredible that modern psychology (one of the century's most uncreative as well as cruellest sciences) has ignored the very powerful phenomenon of squeamishness – that is to say the emotional reaction to the sight of blood, injury, etc. Those attending a surgical operation for the first time very often experience feelings that are strange and strong; some faint, some feel nausea, few are unmoved. In a small sample of adolescent female biology students, 55 per cent disliked dissecting a mouse and a third found such procedures made them feel sick or ill (R.D. Ryder, Paper read to the British Psychological Society, A.G.M., Exeter, 1977). Such natural aversion to the sight of injury has had survival value for the species and counter-balances the argument that 'man is naturally a hunter/killer/exploiter of animals'. It would seem that man is only the latter when he overcomes, through hunger, fear, anger or custom, his natural fellow feeling for other sentients.

Animals' Rights: a Symposium

Often before and occasionally after these experiences (if they survive them, that is to say) the research animals are kept in the laboratories for months and even years. Sometimes captured from the great aboreal freedom of their jungle homes, monkeys are closely confined in cages only three or four feet square. Usually they receive no variety of diet but only approved proprietary pellets. They may see no other living creatures except a white-coated technician on a brief daily visit. Very often the animal room is without windows, being artificially ventilated by a machine which produces a constant unvarying drone. In order to facilitate cleaning, the animals live upon wire-mesh. They can never sit or lie down on a flat, soft or yielding surface. Little wonder that by the time they are needed for the knife or the needle they are so crazed or inert that they are no longer representative examples of animal life. Psychologists who study the behaviour of thousands of such creatures annually, rarely make allowances for the fact that their pathetic subjects have been so deprived that they have become more like monsters than animals.

Animals, Men and Morals

It is a sorry comment upon the international legal situation that although the British Cruelty to Animals Act 1876 is so outdated, it is nevertheless still one of the most enlightened laws in the world which deals with the issue ...

The present Act seems to presuppose that all animal experiments are necessary. There is no record of the Home Office refusing a licence on the grounds that a proposed experiment is pointless, badly designed, repetitive or wasteful; the inspector's function has been merely to establish that the application is for a class or purpose permitted by the Act; he is not required to evaluate the potential benefit likely to accrue from it (Littlewood Report, p. 36). In other words, the principal loophole in this law, as in all equivalent laws in other countries, is simply that, although painful experiments are technically only allowed if they are 'necessary', *the necessity itself is rarely, if ever, questioned.* Only a small proportion of experiments can have more than an infinitesimal chance of being necessary in the sense that they will prolong human life. A slightly larger proportion may be necessary in as much as they will be published and so may perhaps increase human knowledge, however academic and trivial. For the vast bulk of experiments, however, the only necessities are curiosity, commercial

profit, and ambition. Any experienced animal exper-
menter will know in his heart that for many workers in
this field the suffering of animals is not a price too much
to pay for enhanced academic prestige or a better job.
The layman is too easily overawed by science and its
apparently high-minded aims. The law and the
Littlewood Report are similarly gullible and obsequious
in these respects.

Ibid.

The cruel experimenter cannot be allowed to have it both
ways. He cannot, in the same breath, defend the scientific
validity of vivisection on the grounds of the physical
similarities between man and the other animals, and then
defend the morality of vivisection on the grounds that
men and animals are physically different. The only
logical alternatives for him are to admit that he is either
pre-Darwinian or immoral.

Ibid.

Whatever are the *causes* of consciousness, its moral
importance is clearly paramount. It matters not if an
animal, whether human or non-human, is intelligent or
communicative, or has an immortal soul. All that matters
is that it is conscious: in particular that it can be conscious
of pain and pleasure. This should be the bedrock of our
morality. Pain is pain, regardless of the species suffering
it.

Animal Revolution; Changing Attitudes towards Speciesism

SADI (Sheikh Muslih Addin), *c.*1184–1263; or 1213–1292

Crush not yonder ant as it draggeth along its grain; for it
too liveth, and its life is sweet to it.

A shadow there must be, and a stone upon that heart,
that could wish to sorrow the heart even of an ant!

Strike not with the hand of violence the head of the
feeble; for one day, like the ant, thou mayest fall under
the foot thyself!

Bustan (Garden of Perfume)

CARL SAGAN, 1934–

If chimpanzees have consciousness, if they are capable of
abstractions, do they not have what until now has been
described as 'human rights'? How smart does a
chimpanzee have to be before killing him constitutes
murder?

The Dragons of Eden

There is no right to life in any society on Earth today, nor
has there been at any former time. We raise farm animals
for slaughter; destroy forests; pollute rivers and lakes
until no fish can live there; hunt deer and elk for sport,
leopards for their pelts, and whales for dog food; entwine
dolphins, gasping and writhing, in great tuna nets; and
club seal pups to death for 'population management'. All
these beasts and vegetables are as alive as we. What is
protected in many human societies is not life, but human
life.

Ibid.

DMITRII SAKHAROV, 1921–1989

We know that the little brain of animals can suffer as much
as ours. But again and again the scalpel cuts into the bodies
of quadruped sufferers in order to get a piece of tissue,
and sometimes – and this is shameful – to fulfil a plan.

It has become clear now that the wellbeing of living
nature is very vital to us. Pretending to be the king of

nature, man has only brought it to poverty. The time has come for man to become an 'elder brother' in the family of Nature.

Japan Times, 3 November 1971

CONNIE SALAMONE, 1940–

Just as it is not possible to lay claim to a non-violent life while ignoring or co-operating with a militaristic or racist institution, neither is it possible to be genuinely non-violent while ignoring the violence done to the myriad varieties of life with which we share this planet.

From *Reweaving the Web of Life*, ed. Pam McAllister

There is something strangely queer about walking into a feminist collective where women are busy munching on the greasy bones of little murdered birds, dressed in animal skins that will never be theirs no matter how much they paid for them. A shocking thought passed through my mind the other day – if a feminist and the macho who called her names in the street sat down together over a steak dinner and discussed their views on animals, they would be exactly the same: animals are to be used, eaten, worn and experimented upon for the benefit of humans. Neither has separated their position from the other. Feminists have spent too much time writing papers on our relationships to men. Let's begin to make stronger bonds with our sisters, children, and especially those who have never harmed us, the non-humans. We must develop a feminist society where the production of goods for human living should come about by the most frugal, essential means, squandering neither land nor animals; indeed, it must be one of our goals.

Majority Report 73

Veganism is an advanced way of living in accordance with total reverence for the rights of all living creatures. Veganism excludes all forms of cruelty to, and exploitation of, the living kingdom. Veganism believes that the responsibility for keeping this order lies within human beings who have the power. Now, it is this power, my sisters, that we already have, to help all oppressed creatures; or we can continue to support the production and use of animal foods and other commodities of cruelty and death. The unnatural conditions of animal slavery are a shortened life span, forced breeding, disruption of hormonal balance (as when a steer is injected with steroids to make muscle meat plumper), and separation of mother animals from their young. These should outrage the consciousness of any sensitive feminist.

Majority Report 72

HENRY S. SALT, 1851–1939

Mr Facing Both Ways

When the Huntsman claims praise for the killing of foxes,
Which else would bring ruin to farmer and land,
Yet so kindly imports them, preserves them, assorts them,
There's a discrepance I'd fain understand

When the Butcher makes boast of the killing of cattle,
That would multiply fast and the world overrun,
Yet so carefully breeds them, rears, fattens and feeds
    them –
Here also, methinks, a fine cobweb is spun.

Hark you, then, whose profession or pastime is killing!
To dispel your benignant illusions I'm loth;
But be one or the other, my double-faced brother,
Be slayer or saviour – you cannot be both.

Dumb Animals

The air was full of summer sounds;
    The lambs were gaily bleating;
Small birds were gossiping around,
    Their joyful news repeating.

In tones vociferously clear
    Rooks chattered overhead.
'*Sweet creatures! How I love to hear*
    Dumb animals,' she said.

And as they parleyed each with each
    Their thoughts and fancies showing,
It seemed as though a flood of speech
    This earth were overflowing.

Methought with every breath that moved,
    A gift of tongues was shed.
'*How beautiful! I've always loved*
    Dumb animals,' she said.

The difference between the earlier 'barbarism' and the later so-called 'civilization' is, in the main, a mere matter of the absence or presence of certain intellectual refinements and mechanical sciences, which, while largely altering and complicating the outward conditions of life, leave its essentially savage spirit almost entirely untouched …

But it is when we turn to their treatment of the non-human races that we find the surest evidences of barbarism; yet their savagery, even here, is not wholly 'naked and unashamed', for, strange to say, these curious people delight to mask their rudeness in a cloak of fallacies and sophisms, and to represent themselves as 'lovers' of those very creatures whom they habitually torture for 'sport', 'science' and the 'table'. They actually have a law for the prevention of cruelty to animals, under which certain privileged species, classed as 'domestic', are protected from some specified wrongs, though all the time they may, under certain conditions, be subjected with impunity to other and worse injuries at the hands of the slaughterman or the vivisector; while the wild species, though presumably not less sensitive to pain, are regarded as almost entirely outside the pale of protection, and as legitimate subjects for those brutalities of 'fashion' and 'sport' which are characteristic of the savage mind.

... almost every conceivable form of cowardly slaughter is practised as 'sportsmanlike' and commended as 'manly'. All this, moreover, is done before the eyes and for the example of mere youths and children, who are thus from their tenderest years instructed in the habit of being pitiless and cruel.

... in spite of their boasted progress in sciences and arts, my countrymen are still practically ignorant of the real kinship which exists between mankind and the other races, and of the duties which this kinship implies. They are still the victims of that old anthropocentric superstition which pictures man as the centre of the universe, and separated from the inferior animals – mere playthings made for his august pleasure and amusement – by a deep intervening gulf.

What appeal *can* be made to people whose first instinct, on seeing a beautiful animal, full of joyousness and vitality, is to hunt or eat it?

Seventy Years Among Savages

The emancipation of men from cruelty and injustice will bring with it in due course the emancipation of animals also. The two reforms are inseparably connected, and neither can be fully realized alone.

... the Humanitarian League always looked with disfavour on the expression 'dumb animals', because, to begin with, animals are not dumb, and secondly, nothing more surely tends to their depreciation than thus to attribute to them an unreal deficiency or imperfection: such a term may be meant to increase our pity, but in the long run it lessens what is more important, our respect.

Ibid.

... in spite of all the barriers and divisions that prejudice and superstition have heaped up between the human and the non-human, we may take it as certain that, in the long run, as we treat our fellow beings, 'the animals', so shall we treat our fellow men.

Ibid.

... it does not so greatly matter whether this or that particular form of cruelty is prohibited; what matters is that all forms of cruelty should be shown to be incompatible with progress.

Religion has never befriended the cause of humaneness. Its monstrous doctrine of eternal punishment and the torture of the damned underlies much of the barbarity with which man has treated man; and the deep division imagined by the Church between the human being, with his immortal soul, and the soulless 'beasts', has been responsible for an incalculable sum of cruelty.

Ibid.

... the moral of the war for social reformers will perhaps be this: that it is not sufficient to condemn the barbarities of warfare alone, as our pacifists have too often done. The civilized spirit can only be developed by a consistent protest against all forms of cruelty and oppression; it is only by cultivating a whole-minded reverence for the rights of all our fellow beings that we shall rid ourselves of that inheritance of selfish callousness of which the militarist and imperialist mania is a part.

Ibid.

To what sort of comfort can a person of sensibility hope to attain, in sight of the immense sum of wretchedness and suffering that is everywhere visible, and audible, around us? I know not a few humanitarians whose lives are permanently saddened by the thought of the awful destitution that afflicts large masses of mankind, and of the not less awful cruelties inflicted on the lower animals in the name of sport and science and fashion.

No League of Nations, or of individuals, can avail, without a change of heart. Reformers of all classes must recognize that it is useless to preach peace by itself, or socialism by itself, or anti-vivisection by itself, or vegetarianism by itself, or kindness to animals by itself. The cause of each and all of the evils that afflict the world is the same – the general lack of humanity, the lack of the knowledge that all sentient life is akin, and that he who injures a fellow being is in fact doing injury to himself. The prospects of a happier society are wrapped up in this despised and neglected truth, the very statement of which, at the present time, must (I well know) appear ridiculous to the accepted instructors of the people.

It is useless to hope that warfare, which is but one of many savage survivals, can be abolished, until the mind of man is humanized in other respects also – until all savage survivals are at least seen in their true light. As long as man kills the lower races for food or sport, he will be ready to kill his own race for enmity. It is not *this* bloodshed, or *that* bloodshed, that must cease, but *all* needless bloodshed – all wanton infliction of pain or death upon our fellow beings. Only when the great sense of the universal kinship has been realized among us, will love cast out hatred, and will it become impossible for the world to witness anew the senseless horrors that disgrace Europe today.

Ibid.

Grace

To pray for animals, the Bishop vows,
Is not canonical. Who prays for cows?
But prey upon them – that's the road to take.
Behold the Bishop blessing his beefsteak!

Humaneness is not a dead external precept, but a living impulse from within; not self-sacrifice, but self-fulfilment.

The Creed of Kinship

Homo Sapiens

What mocking elf, on impish mischief bent,
Called Man, this barbarous Man, the Sapient;
Man, who, disdainful of the nobler way,
Still lives by rapine, a dull beast of prey,
Nor spares, if so a savage gust he win,
To rob his fellows or devour his kin?
Yet nearer than he knew that jester came
To give rapacious Man the fitting name;
For change one single letter, and behold –
In 'Homo Rapiens' the true tale is told!

Cum Grano

In an unpublished letter dated 17 February 1927, the poet Ralph Hodgson suggested to Salt a few additional lines to the above verse:

Or if that's not a civil thing to do –
Though every Pytchley gatepost knows it's true,
And every stick of Altcar proves it, too –
Why – still to rob the jester of his joke –
Drop *off* the R – but drop it with a pang
Of shame at foisting him on better folk:
Gorilla, Gibbon, Chimpanzee, Orang!

I cannot see how there can be any real and full recognition of Kinship as long as men continue either to cheat or to eat their fellow beings.

In a letter to Gandhi, 1932

... in proportion as man is truly 'humanized', not by schools of cookery but by schools of thought, he will abandon the barbarous habit of his flesh-eating ancestors, and will make gradual progress towards a purer, simpler, more humane, and therefore more civilized diet-system.

The Humanities of Diet

Vegetarianism is the diet of the future, as flesh-food is the diet of the past. In that striking and common contrast, a fruit shop side by side with a butcher's, we have a most significant object lesson. There, on the one hand, are the barbarities of a savage custom – the headless carcasses, stiffened into a ghastly semblance of life, the joints and steaks and gobbets with their sickening odour, the harsh grating of the bone-saw, and the dull thud of the chopper – a perpetual crying protest against the horrors of flesh-eating. And as if this were not witness sufficient, here close alongside is a wealth of golden fruit, a sight to make a poet happy, the only food that is entirely congenial to the physical structure and the natural instincts of mankind, that can entirely satisfy the highest human aspirations. Can we doubt, as we gaze at this contrast, that whatever intermediate steps may need to be gradually taken, whatever difficulties to be overcome, the path of progression from the barbarities to the humanities of diet lies clear and unmistakable before us?

Ibid.

The logic of the larder is the very negation of a true reverence for life, for it implies that the real lover of animals is he whose larder is fullest of them:

> He prayeth best, who eateth best
> All things both great and small.

It is the philosophy of the wolf, the shark, the cannibal.

Ibid.

It is grievous to see or hear, and almost to hear of, any man, or even any animal whatever, in torture. For example, when a man turns aside to avoid crushing an insect, why does he do so? Certainly not because of any reasoned conviction as to the sufferings of the 'poor beetle that we tread upon', but for the simple fact that, consciously or unconsciously, he is humane; the sight of suffering, however slight, is distasteful to him as being human. Of all mistaken notions concerning humanitarianism, the most mistaken is that which regards it as some extraneous artificial cult, forced on human nature from without; whereas in truth it is founded on an instinctive conviction from within, a very part of human development. When we talk of a man 'becoming a humanitarian', what we really mean is that he has recognized a fact that was already within his consciousness – the kinship of all sentient life – of which humanitarianism is the avowed and definite proclamation.

The Encyclopaedia of Religion and Ethics

… the principle of humaneness is based on the broad ground of universal sympathy, not with mankind only, but with all sentient beings, such sympathy being, of course, duly proportioned to the sensibility of its object. Humanitarianism is not to be confused with philanthropy – love of mankind – on the one side, or with zoophily – kindness to animals – on the other; it includes and comprehends them both.

Ibid.

Again, when we turn to the protection of animals, we **sometimes hear it said that we ought to help men first** and animals afterwards. But if the principle which prompts the humane treatment of men is the same essentially as that which prompts the humane treatment of animals, how can we successfully safeguard it in one direction while we violate it in another? By condoning cruelty to animals we perpetuate the very spirit which condones cruelty to men. Humanitarians do not say that the lower forms of life must be treated in the same way as the higher forms, but that in both cases alike we must be careful to inflict no unnecessary, no avoidable, suffering.

Ibid.

We have to decide, not whether the practice of fox-hunting, for example, is more, or less, cruel than vivisection, but whether *all* practices which inflict unnecessary pain on sentient beings are not incompatible with the higher instincts of humanity.

From Preface to Animals' Rights Considered in Relation
to Social Progress*

The wise scientist and the wise humanist are identical. A true science cannot possibly ignore the incontrovertible fact that the practice of vivisection is revolting to the human conscience, even among the ordinary members of a not oversensitive society. The so-called 'science' which overlooks this vital fact, and confines its view to the material aspects of the problem, is not science at all, but a

---

* *Editor's Note*: These brief extracts from Salt's most important book must serve for introduction to one of the least-known but most outstanding champions of animals' rights. A scholar, and then a master, at Eton College, Salt was a friend of Shaw, Gandhi and William Morris. A vegetarian and pacifist, he was also an early environmentalist with considerable botanical knowledge. Civilized and witty, he chose a life of great simplicity. He wrote nearly forty books, most of them urging humane reforms in prison conditions, schools, in the economic organization of society, and in the treatment of animals. Biographical notes and a full bibliography are to be found in the 1980 edition of *Animals' Rights*.

443

one-sided assertion of the views which find favour with a particular class of specialists.

Nothing is necessary which is abhorrent, revolting, intolerable, to the general instincts of humanity. Better a thousand times that science should forgo or postpone the questionable advantage of certain problematical discoveries, than that the moral conscience of the community should be unmistakably outraged by the confusion of right and wrong. The short cut is not always the right path; and to perpetrate a cruel injustice to the lower animals, and then attempt to excuse it on the ground that it will benefit posterity, is an argument which is as irrelevant as it is immoral. Ingenious it may be (in the way of hoodwinking the unwary), but it is certainly in no true sense scientific.

Ibid.

The Sending of the Animals

The Animals, you say, were 'sent'
For man's free use and nutriment.
Pray, then, inform me, and be candid,
Why came they aeons before Man did,
To spend long centuries on earth
Awaiting their Devourer's birth?
Those ill-timed chattels, sent from Heaven,
Were, sure, the maddest gift e'er given –
'Sent' for man's use (can man believe it?)
When there was no man to receive it!

Cum Grano

Of all the fictions with which mankind has allowed itself to be fooled, none is vainer than the belief that the 'instinct' of animals is absolutely different from the 'reason' of men, and that the lower races are dumb and soulless automata, separated from the human by a deep and impassable gulf.

The Story of My Cousins

Of all death-bed sayings perhaps the wisest was Thoreau's 'One world at a time'. When we have grasped the great central fact about animals, that they are in the full sense our fellow beings, all else will follow for them; and we shall know, and act upon the knowledge, that in the words of Howard Moore, author of that memorable book *The Universal Kinship*: 'They are not conveniences but cousins.'

Ibid.

SALVATION ARMY

It is a great delusion to suppose that flesh-meat of any kind is essential to health. Considerably more than three parts of the work of the world is done by men who never taste anything but vegetables, farinaceous food, and that of the simplest kind. There are far more strength-producing properties in wholewheat flour, peas, beans, lentils, oatmeal, roots, and other vegetables of the same class, than there are in beef or mutton, poultry or fish, or animal food of any description whatever.

Orders and Regulations of the Officers of the Salvation Army

JACK SANDERSON, 1912–1983

Our adversaries and those who ill-treat others and other kingdoms have need of us – and we have need of all of them. If we express the 'caring-for' principle with wisdom and gentleness, we shall join with hosts of other positive beings and become co-creators of the new order. Let us be inspired by the thoughts and lives of other men and women, but let us not forget that our own unique experience and inner guidance can express to us the way forward – the way in which the Infinite Benevolence wishes us to go. Truth is revealed to each according to his present understanding, and that is why we should be neither unduly critical of our own thoughts and experiences, nor of our brother's which may differ from our own. If we truly adopt a vegan way of life with balance between head and heart development, we shall become aware of a gradual transformation within ourselves, from loneliness in a cold universe to a sense of belonging in a caring-for, living, developing cosmos; from a fractional, segmented life to becoming a vital part of a creative whole; from life as a predator to life as a server.

The Vegan, Winter 1977

STEVE F. SAPONTZIS, 1945–

The slaves bore all the burdens, while the masters reaped all the benefits of slave labour, and that is the rankest form of exploitation, no matter how benign the masters were to their slaves. And that is the way things remain with animals today.

Between the Species, Vol. 3, No.2, 1987

Just as our basic moral concepts are colour blind and sex blind, so they are species blind. There is nothing in the logic of the Golden Rule to treat others as we would like to be treated by them which restricts it to people.

Ibid.

Perhaps what most sharply separates the new animal rights movement from the traditional animal welfare movement is the new movement's insistence that no matter how humanely we do it, our continuing routinely to sacrifice animals' interests for our benefit is unfair. That claim has still to be rebutted, if it can be.

Ibid., Vol.3, No.3, 1987

All other Copernican revolutions notwithstanding, we have remained securely at the centre of the moral universe. Animal liberation now claims that even this claim to distinction is erroneous. Morally, we are on all fours with them.

Morals, Reason and Animals

The liberating of animals from human exploitation is the next logical step in the progress of our everyday, Western moral concepts.

Between the Species, Vol.3, No.2, 1987

PHILIP HENRY SAVAGE, 1868–1899

This poor silver fish…

This is thy brother, this poor silver fish,
Close to the surface, dying in his dish;
　　Thy flesh, thy beating heart, thy very life;
All this, I say, art thou, against thy wish.

Thou may'st not turn away, thou shalt allow
The truth, nor shalt thou dare to question how:
　　There is but one great heart in nature beating,
And this is thy heart – this, I say, art thou.

In all thy power and all thy pettiness,
With this and that poor selfish purpose, this
　　And that high-climbing fancy, and a heart
Caught into heaven or cast in the abyss.

Thou art the same with all the little earth,
A little part; and sympathy of birth
　　Shall tell thee, and thine openness of soul,
What fear is death and what a life is worth.

VERNON SCANNELL, 1922–

A Couple of Heavyweights

i

Marine

This huge and sawn-off airship of the ocean,
This floating zeppelin, blunt-nosed, with eyes

447

Conspiratorial which – should emotion
Or the weather order tears – weep wax, he lies
And flaps his swallow-tail in waves, his skin
Polished like a stove, blue-black. A bright
And glittering plume of spray has source within
The great box of his head. Sometimes, at night,
He sighs mysterious music in his sleep.
No wonder, through the ages, many tales
Have flowered about this mammoth of the deep
Who grazes in the green and heaving dales
Among the flowers of foam, and one of these,
That we all know has been preserved among
The frail leaves of a holy book – to tease
And tempt our disbelief – of someone flung
In raging seas to live three nights and days
Inside the dungeon of the fish's gut.
The story might invite a sneer, or praise,
From pious folk, of God's great mercy; but
I see the creature now, just as he is,
As evidence of something else; by this
I mean a proof of God's inventive wit
To think up such a poem and publish it.

ii
Terrestrial

He is a mobile country or
A jungly part of one with four
Great trunks of trees instead
Of ordinary legs. His head,
Domed like a cupola, appears
To sprout, like rhubarb leaves, huge ears,
And where most creatures have a snout
This hose-like nose is stretched way out;
It waves and snakes in air, and then
Goes plunging down to suck things in –
Food or water – like a Hoover,

And though he's not a rapid mover
He can work. Those horn-shaped teeth
Are tools for him, can dig beneath
The soil for tasty roots, for he
Is vegetarian: a tree
May offer him a three-course dinner
Of fruit and leaves and of the inner
Bark he loves to masticate;
Each day he eats four hundredweight.
I like this chap. He has a kind
Of dignity you rarely find
In clumsy creatures, and I'm not
Excluding any of *our* lot.

Postscript

And what – you may quite reasonably ask –
Prompted me to link these two together,
The great sea-heaver who will roll and bask
In depthless waters in all kinds of weather
And this vast dusty tonnage of the earth
Who weights about two hundred pounds at birth.

I only know I like them both, and they
Are preyed on by a certain kind of beast,
One ruthlessly resolved to hurt and slay,
Not because it must do, not to feast
Upon the carcass, but for selfish trade –
This pallid biped, in *whose* image made?

Ruminant

The leather belly shades the buttercups.
Her horns are the yellow of old piano keys.
Hopelessly the tail flicks at the humming heat;
Flies crawl to the pools of her eyes.
She slowly turns her head and watches me
As I approach; her gaze is a silent moo.

I stop and we swap stares. I smoke. She chews.

How do I view her then? As pastoral furniture,
Solid in the green and fluid summer?
A brooding factory of milk and sausages,
Or something to be chopped to bits and sold
In wounded paper parcels? No, as none of these.
My view is otherwise and infantile,
But it survives my own sour sneers.
It is the anthropomorphic fallacy
Which puts brown speculation in those eyes.
But I am taken in: that gentleness endears,
As do the massive patience and submission
Huge among buttercups and flies.
But, in the end, it is those plushy eyes,
The slow and meditative jaws, that hold
Me to this most untenable of views:
Almost, it seems, she might be contemplating
Composing a long poem about Ted Hughes.

VICTOR B. SCHEFFER, 1906–

I sometimes wonder about the language of hunting. I question whether 'game' or 'sport' should be used to describe an activity in which one of the players has only his pure wildness to call on for defence, while the other has weapons of shocking power, lures and decoys, a hunting dog, telescopic vision, the automobile or boat, the ambush or blind, and a coloured map of the migratory path of the prey. It is a game in which the stakes are life and death, but for only one of the players. It is a game in which courage is rarely called upon.

... I do not understand why anyone should want to shoot an eight ounce mourning dove or a clapper rail simply because the bird is a moving target and the test of a man's quickness on the draw. I do not understand how anyone, for pleasure, should want to take particles of life from the common good, the common trust.

An argument often presented is that the hunter is playing a predestined role ... the predatory instinct still runs in our blood – or so the argument goes. Never mind that modern hunting with the help of man's technology is very different from primitive hunting. Never mind that behaviourists discredit the inheritance of aggressiveness and that human teeth are not the teeth of a carnivore. A sense of rightness about hunting is for some hunters equivalent to religion, and for a non-hunter to challenge that faith is a waste of time. Yet, for too many hunters, the metallic feel of a gun – a solid extension of personal power – is a temptation to kill carelessly.

... As a hunter grows older, his vision of the man-wildlife relationship often changes in a way that foreshadows a similar change in American thought as it too matures. The American author Robert F. Leslie, after a hunter killed an orphan cub which he was mothering, wrote bitterly: 'All hunting, except for survival, is a shabby postponement of growing up.'

A Voice for Wildlife

HARRIET SCHLEIFER, 1952–

The animal liberation ethic demands a basic shift in moral consciousness, a repudiation of human superiority over other species through force. Our way of viewing the world becomes more compassionate, more respectful of the needs of other living beings. The vegetarian lifestyle is both a fundamental and a personal means of affirming such a shift. Confronting the oppression of food animals through vegetarianism lies at the heart of the animal liberation ethic and offers the greatest potential for the radical transformation of our society.

In Defence of Animals

Furthermore, the attitude that allows us to raise animals for food colours our treatment of all other creatures, from pets to laboratory animals and wildlife. Once we have accepted that we may utilize animals for so trivial a reason as our enjoyment of the taste of their flesh, it is easy to use them for any purpose which is equally frivolous, such as domesticating them as pets or confining them in zoos to amuse us, or for those which are more serious, such as using them in medical experiments that we believe will save human lives.

Ibid.

ARTUR SCHOPENHAUER, 1788–1860

The unpardonable forgetfulness in which the lower animals have hitherto been left by the moralists of Europe is well known. It is pretended that the beasts have no rights. They persuade themselves that our conduct in regard to them has nothing to do with morals or (to speak the language of their morality) that we have no duties towards animals; a doctrine revolting, gross and barbarous ...

On the Basis of Morality

The assumption that animals are without rights, and the illusion that our treatment of them has no moral significance, is a positively outrageous example of Western crudity and barbarity. Universal compassion is the only guarantee of morality.

Ibid.

A pity without limits, which unites us with all living beings – in that we have the most solid, the surest guarantee of morality. Whoso possesses it will be quite incapable of causing harm or loss to any one, of doing violence to any one, or doing ill in any way. But rather he will have for all, long-suffering; he will aid the helpless with all his powers, and each one of his actions will be marked with the stamp of justice and of love ... I know of no more beautiful prayer than that which the Hindus of old used in closing their public spectacles. It was: 'May all that have life be delivered from suffering!'

Ibid.

European priestcraft knows no limits to its disavowal and blasphemy against the Eternal Reality that lives in every animal. Thus was laid the foundation of that harshness and cruelty towards beasts which is customary in Europe, and on which a native of the Asiatic uplands could not look without righteous horror ... The fact that Christian morality takes no thought for beasts is a defect in the system which is better admitted than perpetuated ... Boundless compassion for all living beings is the surest and most certain guarantee of pure moral conduct.

Ibid.

... it is expressly stated in the *Metaphysical Principles of the Doctrine of Virtue*, § 16, that 'man can have no duty to any beings except human'; and then it says in § 17 that 'cruelty to animals is contrary to man's duty *to himself*, because it deadens in him the feeling of sympathy for their sufferings, and thus a natural tendency that is very useful to morality in relation to *other human beings* is weakened.' Thus only for practice are we to have sympathy for animals, and they are, so to speak, the pathological phantom for the purpose of practising sympathy for human beings. In common with the whole of Asia not tainted with Islam (that is, Judaism), I regard such propositions as revolting and abominable. At the same time, we see here once more how entirely this philosophical morality, which as previously shown is only a theological one in disguise, depends in reality on the biblical one. Thus, because Christian morality leaves animals out of account ... they are at once outlawed in philosophical morals; they are mere 'things', mere *means* to any ends whatsoever. They can therefore be used for vivisection, hunting, coursing, bullfights and horse racing, and can be whipped to death as they struggle along with heavy carts of stone. Shame on such a morality that is worthy of pariahs, chandalas and mlechchhas, and that fails to recognize the eternal essence that exists in every living thing, and shines forth with inscrutable significance from all eyes that see the sun! But that morality knows and respects only its own worthy species, whose characteristic *reason* [Vernunft] is the condition on which a being can be an object of moral consideration and respect.

Ibid.

Boundless compassion for all living things is the surest and most certain guarantee of pure moral conduct, and needs no casuistry. Whoever is filled with it will assuredly injure no one, do harm to no one, encroach on no man's rights; he will rather have regard for every one, forgive every one, help every one as far as he can, and all his actions will bear the stamp of justice and loving-kindness.

Ibid.

Between pity towards 'beasts' and goodness of soul there is a very close connexion. One might say without hesitation, when an individual is wicked in regard to them, that he cannot be a good man. One might, also, demonstrate that this pity and the social virtues have the same source.

Ibid.

Man is the only animal which causes pain to others without any further purpose than just to cause it. Other animals never do it except to satisfy their hunger, or in the rage of combat ... No animal ever torments another for the mere purpose of tormenting, but man does it, and it is this that constitutes that diabolical feature in his character which is so much worse than the merely animal.

On Human Nature

OLIVE SCHREINER, 1855–1920

I have been watching a little ant this morning for more than half an hour ... It was trundling along a dried ball from a mimosa tree three times in bulk as large as itself. I followed it for nearly 100 yards, being blown over and over by the wind, regaining its feet, never leaving hold of its ball, climbing over stones and sticks and through grasses till it got to the hole. I never knew one's heart could go out in such a curious way to such a small speck of matter.

I don't know how people can endure unending physical anguish if they can't fall back on the thought that they've not caused any wilful physical or mental pain to human beings or animals. If all the world is permeated by injustice and suffering forced by sentient creatures on each other, one clings to the thought one hasn't willingly consented to it, or tried to increase it, as a drowning man clings to a straw. If I could be cured tomorrow by torturing animals, I wouldn't have it.

I've had too much physical suffering to rejoice in the suffering of any sentient creature; if a lion had torn my arm off, I wouldn't want it to have cancer. There would be *its* physical suffering added to *my* physical suffering, to make the terrible sum total of suffering bigger! I think I can understand most things in human nature, but *delight* in human suffering (or animal) I *cannot* understand.

The Letters of Olive Schreiner

BILL SCHUL, 1928–

The issue is greater than this [human suffering]. Our treatment of animals is important to our own internal state. If we are to expand our horizons, to grow to understand what the relatedness of each and every thing means, then our love and appreciation of all life is essential. Our respect and reverence for all living things will be reflected in our own living.

The Psychic Power of Animals

E.F. SCHUMACHER, 1911–1977

… If I have an animal – be it only a calf or a hen – a living, sensitive creature, am I allowed to treat it as nothing but a utility? Am I allowed to run it to ruin?

It is no use trying to answer such questions scientifically. They are metaphysical, not scientific, questions. It is a metaphysical error, likely to produce the gravest practical consequences, to equate 'car' and 'animal' on account of their utility, while failing to recognize the most fundamental difference between them, that of 'level of being'.

Small is Beautiful

Man, the highest of his creatures, was given 'dominion', not the right to tyrannize, to ruin and exterminate. It is no use talking about the dignity of man without accepting that *noblesse oblige*. For man to put himself into a wrongful relationship with animals, and particularly those long domesticated by him, has always, in all traditions, been considered a horrible and infinitely dangerous thing to do. There have been no sages or holy men in our or anybody else's history who were cruel to animals or who looked upon them as *nothing but* utilities, and innumerable are the legends and stories which link sanctity as well as happiness with a loving kindness towards lower creation.

Ibid.

The extraordinary thing about the modern 'life sciences' is that they hardly ever deal with *life as such*, the factor *x*, but devote infinite attention to the study and analysis of the physico-chemical body that is life's carrier ... there is no excuse for the pretence that life is nothing but physics and chemistry.

Nor is there any excuse for the pretence that consciousness is nothing but a property of life. To describe an animal as a physico-chemical system of extreme complexity is no doubt perfectly correct, except that it misses out on the 'animal-ness' of the animal. Some zoologists, at least, have advanced beyond this level of crudite absurdity and have developed an ability to see animals as more than complex machines. Their influence, however, is as yet deplorably small, and with the increasing 'rationalization' of the modern life-style, more and more animals are being treated as if they really were nothing but 'animal machines'.

A Guide for the Perplexed

... it is impossible for any civilization to survive without a faith in meanings and values transcending the utilitarianism of comfort and survival – in other words, without a religious faith.

Ibid.

MAGNUS SCHWANTJE, 1877–1959

It is amazing that most people who are horrified at the atrocities committed in wartime do little or nothing to prevent children having their compassion desensitized and their cruelty aroused.

They are given picture books showing sheep, cattle, goats, hares, roe-deer, poultry and other animals with captions such as 'Our Dear Friends'. When children meet a lamb, a kid-goat, or a calf, they are encouraged to pet the creature, and everyone is pleased at the display of love for animals which awakens in every good-natured child at the sight of such creatures.

But a few hours later, the children may see the same animals they have petted and played with, now hanging on a hook with bloody throats, dead eyes and bodies disembowelled. And then the children are encouraged to eat pieces of their 'dear friends', their playmates. Is this not an education in treachery?

Reverence for Life, Brotherhood and Vegetarianism

Wars and concentration camps exist for several years and may be followed by some decades of peace. But the atrocities against animals, as hideous as the worst committed on battlefields and in concentration camps, are being committed incessantly. We can do little to improve the conduct of humans toward their fellow humans if we do not radically change our conduct toward defenceless animals and fight the main cause of animal persecution and torture – meat-eating.

Ibid.

DR ALBERT SCHWEITZER, 1875–1965

As long as I can remember, I have suffered because of the great misery I saw in the world. I never really knew the artless, youthful joy of living, and I believe that many children feel this way, even when outwardly they seem to be wholly happy and without a single care.

I used to suffer particularly because the poor animals must endure so much pain and want. The sight of an old, limping horse being dragged along by one man while another man struck him with a stick – he was being driven to the Colmar slaughterhouse – haunted me for weeks.

Memoirs of Childhood and Youth

This was a horrible proposal [that the eight-year-old Albert join a friend in killing birds with a sling] ... but I dared not refuse for fear he would laugh at me. So we came to a tree which was still bare, and on which the birds were singing out gaily in the morning, without any fear of us. Then stooping over like an Indian on the hunt, my companion placed a pebble in the leather of his sling and stretched it. Obeying his peremptory glance I did the same, with frightful twinges of conscience, vowing firmly that I would shoot when he did. At that very moment the church bells began to sound, mingling with the song of the birds in the sunshine. It was the warning bell that came a half-hour before the main bell. For me it was a voice from heaven. I threw the sling down, scaring the birds away, so that they were safe from my companion's sling, and fled home. And ever afterwards when the bells of Holy Week ring out amidst the leafless trees in the sunshine I remember with moving gratitude how they rang into my heart at that time the commandment: Thou shalt not kill.

Ibid.

In modern European thought a tragedy is occurring in that the original bonds uniting the affirmative attitude toward the world with ethics are, by a slow but irresistible process, loosening and finally parting.

Out of My Life and Thought

What is the nature of this degeneration in our civilization and why has it come about? ... The disastrous feature of our civilization is that it is far more developed materially than spiritually. Its balance is disturbed ... Now come the facts to summon us to reflect. They tell us in terribly harsh language that a civilization which develops only on its material side, and not in the sphere of the spirit ... heads for disaster.

Civilization and Ethics

The ethic of Reverence for Life prompts us to keep each other alert to what troubles us and to speak and act dauntlessly together in discharging the responsibility that we feel. It keeps us watching together for opportunities to bring some sort of help to animals in recompense for the great misery that men inflict upon them, and thus for a moment we escape from the incomprehensible horror of existence.

Ibid.

I must interpret the life about me as I interpret the life that is my own. My life is full of meaning to me. The life around me must be full of significance to itself. If I am to expect others to respect my life, then I must respect the other life I see, however strange it may be to mine. And not only other human life, but all kinds of life: life above mine, if there be such life; life below mine, as I know it to exist. Ethics in our Western world has hitherto been largely limited to the relations of man to man. But that is a limited ethics. We need a boundless ethics which will include the animals also.

Ibid.

A man is really ethical only when he obeys the constraint laid on him to aid all life which he is able to help, and when he goes out of his way to avoid injuring anything living. He does not ask how far this or that life deserves sympathy as valuable in itself, nor how far it is capable of feeling. To him life as such is sacred.

... If he goes out into the street after a rainstorm and sees a worm which has strayed there, he reflects that it will certainly dry up in the sunshine if it does not quickly regain the damp soil into which it can creep, and so he helps it back from the deadly paving stone into the lush grass. Should he pass by an insect which has fallen into a pool, he spares the time to reach a leaf or stalk on which it may clamber and save itself.

Ibid.

The man who has become a thinking being feels a compulsion to give every will-to-live the same reverence for life that he gives to his own. He experiences that other life in his own.

Ibid.

The thinking man must oppose all cruel customs no matter how deeply rooted in tradition and surrounded by a halo. When we have a choice, we must avoid bringing torment and injury into the life of another, even the lowliest creature; to do so is to renounce our manhood and shoulder a guilt which nothing justifies.

Ibid.

The human spirit is not dead. It lives on in secret ... It has come to believe that compassion, in which all ethics must take root, can only attain its full breadth and depth if it embraces all living creatures and does not limit itself to mankind.

Nobel Peace Prize address: *The Problem of Peace in the World Today*

Our civilization lacks humane feeling. We are humans who are insufficiently humane! We must realize that and seek to find a new spirit. We have lost sight of this ideal because we are solely occupied with thoughts of men instead of remembering that our goodness and compassion should extend to all creatures. Religion and philosophy have not insisted as much as they should on the fact that our kindness should include all living creatures.

Letter to Aida Flemming, 1959

461

SCHWEITZER

Any religion or philosophy which is not based on a respect for life is not a true religion or philosophy.

Letter to Japanese Animal Welfare Society, 1961

It is the fate of every truth to be an object of ridicule when it is first acclaimed. It was once considered foolish to suppose that black men were really human beings and ought to be treated as such. What was once foolish has now become a recognized truth. Today it is considered as exaggeration to proclaim constant respect for every form of life as being the serious demand of a rational ethic. But the time is coming when people will be amazed that the human race existed so long before it recognized that thoughtless injury to life is incompatible with real ethics. Ethics is in its unqualified form extended responsibility to everything that has life.

Civilization and Ethics

Very little of the great cruelty shown by men can really be attributed to cruel instinct. Most of it comes from thoughtlessness or inherited habit. The roots of cruelty, therefore, are not so much strong as widespread. But the time must come when inhumanity protected by custom and thoughtlessness will succumb before humanity championed by thought. Let us work that this time may come.

Memoirs of Childhood and Youth

The quiet conscience is an invention of the devil.

The Philosophy of Civilization

Until he extends the circle of his compassion to all living things, man will not himself find peace.

Ibid.

It is our duty to share and maintain life. Reverence concerning all life is the greatest commandment in its most elementary form. Or expressed in negative terms: 'Thou shalt not kill'. We take this prohibition so lightly, thoughtlessly plucking a flower, thoughtlessly stepping on a poor insect, thoughtlessly, in terrible blindness because everything takes its revenge, disregarding the suffering and lives of our fellow men, sacrificing them to trivial earthly goals.

Reverence for Life

To affirm life is to deepen, to make more inward, and to exalt the will-to-live.

At the same time, the man who has become a thinking being feels a compulsion to give to every will-to-live the same reverence for life that he gives to his own. He experiences that other life as his own. He accepts as being good: to preserve life, to raise to its highest value life which is capable of development; and as being evil: to destroy life, to injure life, to repress life which is capable of development. This is the absolute, fundamental principle of the moral, and it is a necessity of thought.

Quoted in *A Treasury of Albert Schweitzer*, ed. Kiernan

SIR PETER SCOTT, 1909–1989

What we have done to the great whales in the sacred name of commerce is an affront to human dignity, a debasement of human values and sensibility.

In the light of present knowledge of these intelligent mammals no civilized person can contemplate the whaling industry without revulsion and shame at the insensitivity of our own species.

From address to the International Whaling Commission, London, July 1979

CHIEF SEALTH (Chief Seattle), *c.* 1786–1866

We are part of the earth and it is part of us.
The perfumed flowers are our sisters; the deer, the horse, the great eagle, these are our brothers.
The rocky crests, the juices of the meadows, the body heat of the pony, and man
– all belong to the same family.

So, when the Great Chief in Washington sends word that he wishes to buy our land, he asks much of us.

… we will consider your offer to buy our land.
If we decide to accept, I will make one condition: the white man must treat the beasts of this land as his brothers.

I am a savage and I do not understand any other way.
I have seen a thousand rotting buffalos on the prairie, left by the white man who shot them from a passing train.
I am a savage and I do not understand how the smoking iron horse can be more important than the buffalo that we kill only to stay alive.

What is man without the beasts?
If the beasts were gone, men would die from a great loneliness of spirit. For whatever happens to the beasts, soon happens to man. All things are connected.

This we know. The earth does not belong to man; man belongs to the earth.
This we know. All things are connected like the blood which unites one family.
All things are connected.

Whatever befalls the earth befalls the sons of the earth.
Man did not weave the web of life, he is merely a strand of it.
Whatever he does to the web, he does to himself.

Chief Seattle's Testimony, an 1854 oration

SENECA, *c.* 5 B.C.–A.D. 65

How long shall we weary heaven with petitions for superfluous luxuries, as though we had not at hand wherewithal to feed ourselves? How long shall we fill our plains with huge cities? How long shall the people slave for us unnecessarily? How long shall countless numbers of ships from every sea bring us provisions for the consumption of a single mouth? An ox is satisfied with the pasture of an acre or two; one wood suffices for several elephants. Man alone supports himself by the pillage of the whole earth and sea. What! Has Nature indeed given us so insatiable a stomach, while she has given us such insignificant bodies? No, it is not the hunger of our stomachs, but insatiable covetousness which costs so much.

Epistola, lx

In the simpler times there was no need of so large a supernumerary force of medical men, nor of so many surgical instruments or of so many boxes of drugs. Health was simple for a simple reason. Many dishes have induced many diseases. Note how vast a quantity of lives one stomach absorbs ... Insatiable, unfathomable, gluttony searches every land and every sea. Some animals it persecutes with snares and traps, with hunting nets, with hooks, sparing no sort of toil to obtain them ... There is no peace allowed to any species of being ... No wonder that with so discordant a diet disease is ever varying ... Count the cooks: you will no longer wonder at the innumerable number of human maladies.

Ibid., xcv

If these maxims are true, the Pythagorean principles as to abstaining from flesh foster innocence; if ill-founded they at least teach us frugality, and what loss have you in losing your cruelty? I merely deprive you of the food of lions and vultures ... We shall recover our sound reason only if we shall separate ourselves from the herd – the very fact of the approbation of the multitude is a proof of the unsoundness of the opinion or practice. Let us ask what is best, not what is customary. Let us love temperance – let us be just – let us refrain from bloodshed. None is so near the gods as he who shows kindness.

Ibid., cviii

RICHARD SERJEANT (William Van Essen), 1910–

Every particle of factual evidence supports the contention that the higher mammalian vertebrates experience pain sensations at least as acute as our own. To say that they feel less because they are lower animals is an absurdity; it can easily be shown that many of their senses arc far more acute than ours – visual acuity in certain birds, hearing in most wild animals and touch in others; these animals depend more than we do today on the sharpest possible awareness of a hostile environment. Apart from the complexity of the cerebral cortex (which does not directly perceive pain) their nervous systems are almost identical to ours and their reactions to pain remarkably similar, though lacking (so far as we know) the philosophical and moral overtones. The emotional element is all too evident, mainly in the form of fear and anger.

The Spectrum of Pain

JAMES SERPELL, 1952–

People who, for whatever reason, kill or harm animals regularly and frequently, become progressively desensitized to the experience. The first few episodes are generally disquieting, but after a period of time the person tends to habituate, and the act becomes a reflex, virtually devoid of emotional content.

In the Company of Animals

Detachment and unnecessary brutality seem to be universal components of intensive animal husbandry ... Modern livestock producers are generally unwilling to consider the welfare of their animals, because this would entail thinking about them as subjects rather than objects; as persons, rather than things; and this would raise imponderable questions about the morality of their treatment. Far easier and less painful to treat them as Cartesian automata that can be slaughtered and exploited according to the dictates of market forces and nothing more.

Ibid.

Instead of promoting a more honest and responsible attitude to animal exploitation and slaughter, Christianity gave rise to the ultimate expression of blame-shifting with the idea of a God-given human supremacy over the rest of creation. In the religions of antiquity animals that were sacrificed were generally treated with respect, and were sometimes pampered and fêted for a year before dying under the sacrificial knife. Their deaths were seen as necessary but, at the same time, sufficiently culpable to warrant some form of preliminary recompense. Under Christianity, this sort of respect for the animal's feelings became entirely superfluous. Animals had only one purpose in life and that was to serve human beings. They owed their existence to God and God had ordained that they should suffer under the yoke of human domination. If anyone was to blame, it was God, but of course God was Almighty and therefore beyond reproach.

Ibid.

... we have created an artificial distinction between us and [the animals], and have constructed a defensive screen of lies, myths, distortions and evasions, the sole purpose of which has been to reconcile or nullify the conflict between economic self-interest, on the one hand, and sympathy and affection on the other.

Ibid.

Instead of questioning our supposedly objective, utilitarian attitudes to other species, or the morality that governs our callous exploitation of animals and nature, we tend to ridicule or denigrate those who take the opposite view. People who display emotional concern for animal suffering, or the destruction of the environment, or the extinction of wild species, are often treated as misguided idealists ... [they] are damned with the accusation of sentimentality, as if having sentiments or feelings for other species were a sign of weakness, intellectual flabbiness or mental disturbance ... The truth is that it is normal and natural for people to empathize and identify with other life forms, and to feel guilt and remorse about harming them. It is the essence of our humanity. The sooner we come to terms with this novel idea, the better, since our future on this planet may depend on it.

Ibid.

ERNEST THOMPSON SETON (Ernest Seton-Thompson), 1860–1946

We and the beasts are kin. Man has nothing that the animals have not at least a vestige of; the animals have nothing that man does not in some degree share. Since, then, the animals are creatures with wants and feelings differing in degree only from our own, they surely have their rights.

Wild Animals I Have Known

ANNA SEWELL, 1820–1878

There is no religion without love, and people may talk as much as they like about their religion, but if it does not teach them to be good and kind to beasts as well as man it is all a sham.

Black Beauty

... he said that cruelty was the Devil's own trade mark, and if we saw anyone who took pleasure in cruelty we might know whom he belonged to, for the Devil was a murderer from the beginning, and a tormentor to the end.

My doctrine is this, that if we see cruelty or wrong that we have the power to stop, and do nothing, we make ourselves sharers in the guilt.

Ibid.

LORD SHAFTESBURY (Anthony Ashley Cooper), 1801–1885

England had prohibited bull-baiting, cock-fighting, prize fighting, all of which had in their day, no end of logic and sentiment in their favour; and why should she not hold her place among the nations of the earth, and be the first to reduce, within the closest possible limits, the sufferings inflicted by man on the whole animal kingdom?

Speech on the second reading of the Cruelty to Animals Bill, 26 May 1876

These ill-used and tortured animals are as much His creatures as we are; and to say the truth, I had, in some instances, rather been the animal tortured than the man who tortured it. I should believe myself to have higher hopes, and a happier future.

Ibid.

469

… to delight in torture and pain of other creatures indifferently, natives or foreigners, of our own or of another species, kindred or no kindred, known or unknown; to feed as it were on death, and to be entertained with dying agonies; this has nothing in it accountable in the way of self-interest or private good … but is wholly and absolutely unnatural, as it is horrid and miserable.

Ibid.

No physical pain can possibly equal the injury caused by the moral degradation of the feelings which such barbarous experiments must naturally induce.

Ibid.

We are bound in duty, I think, to leap over all limitations, and go in for the total abolition of this vile and cruel form of Idolatry [vivisection]; for idolatry it is, and like all idolatry, brutal, degrading, and deceptive.

Letter to Frances Power Cobbe, 3 September 1878

The thought of this diabolical system disturbs me night and day …

Diary, vol. III

WILLIAM SHAKESPEARE, 1564–1616

SIR ANDREW AGUECHEEK:
  Methinks sometimes I have no more wit than a Christian or an ordinary man has: but I am a great eater of beef, and I believe that does harm to my wit.
SIR TOBY:
  No question.

Twelfth Night, Act I, Scene 3

ISABELLA:
>   Dar'st thou die?
> The sense of death is most in apprehension,
> And the poor beetle, that we tread upon,
> In corporal sufferance finds a pang as great
> As when a giant dies.

Measure for Measure, Act III, Scene 1

PORTIA:
>   Then must the Jew be merciful.

SHYLOCK:
> On what compulsion must I? tell me that.

PORTIA:
> The quality of mercy is not strain'd,
> It droppeth as the gentle rain from heaven
> Upon the place beneath: it is twice bless'd;
> It blesseth him that gives and him that takes:
> 'Tis mightiest in the mightiest; it becomes
> The throned monarch better than his crown;
> His sceptre shows the force of temporal power,
> The attribute to awe and majesty,
> Wherein doth sit the dread and fear of kings;
> But mercy is above this sceptred sway,
> It is enthroned in the hearts of kings,
> It is an attribute to God himself,
> And earthly power doth then show likest God's
> When mercy seasons justice.

Merchant of Venice, Act IV, Scene I

DUKE SENIOR:
> Come, shall we go and kill us venison?
> And yet it irks me, the poor dappled fools,
> Being native burghers of this desert city,
> Should in their own confines with forked heads
> Have their round haunches gor'd.

FIRST LORD:
>   Indeed, my lord,

The melancholy Jaques grieves at that;
And, in that kind, swears you do more usurp
Than doth your brother that hath banish'd you.
Today my Lord of Amiens and myself
Did steal behind him as he lay along
Under an oak whose antique root peeps out
Upon the brook that brawls along this wood;
To the which place a poor sequester'd stag,
That from the hunters' aim had ta'en a hurt,
Did come to languish; and, indeed, my lord,
The wretched animal heav'd forth such groans
That their discharge did stretch his leathern coat
Almost to bursting, and the big round tears
Cours'd one another down his innocent nose
In piteous chase; and thus the hairy fool,
Much marked of the melancholy Jaques,
Stood on the extremest verge of the swift brook,
Augmenting it with tears.

As You Like It, Act II, Scene 1

KING HENRY:
Thou never did'st them wrong, nor no man wrong:
And, as the butcher takes away the Calf,
And binds the wretch, and beats it when it strays,
Bearing it to the bloody slaughterhouse;
Even so, remorseless, have they borne him hence:
And, as the Dam runs lowing up and down,
Looking the way her harmless young one went,
And can do naught but wail her darling's loss,
Even so myself bewail good Gloster's case,
With sad unhelpful tears; and with dimmed eyes
Look after him, and cannot do him good.

King Henry the Sixth, Part 2, Act III, Scene 1

QUEEN:
I will try the forces
Of these thy compounds on such creatures as

We count not worth the hanging – but none human –
To try the vigour of them, and apply
Allayments to their act, and by them gather
Their several virtues and effects.

CORNELIUS:
　　　　　　　Your Highness
Shall from this practice but make hard your heart;
Besides, the seeing these effects will be
Both noisome and infectious.
QUEEN:
　　　　　　　O! Content thee.
CORNELIUS (Aside):
　I do suspect you, madam;
But you shall do no harm.

Cymbeline, Act I, Scene 5

KARL SHAPIRO, 1913–

Interlude III

Writing, I crushed an insect with my nail
And thought nothing at all. A bit of wing
Caught my eye then, a gossamer so frail

And exquisite, I saw in it a thing
That scorned the grossness of the thing I wrote.
It hung upon my finger like a sting.

A leg I noticed next, fine as a mote,
'And on this frail eyelash he walked,' I said,
'And climbed and walked like any mountain-goat.'

And in this mood I sought the little head,
But it was lost; then in my heart a fear
Cried out, 'A life – why, beautiful, why dead!'

It was a mite that held itself most dear,
So small I could have drowned it with a tear.

GEORGE BERNARD SHAW, 1856–1950

Once grant the ethics of the vivisectionists and you not only sanction the experiment on the human subject, but make it the first duty of the vivisector. If a guinea pig may be sacrificed for the sake of the very little that can be learnt from it, shall not a man be sacrificed for the sake of the great deal that can be learnt from him?

Preface to *Doctor's Dilemma*

We are, as a matter of fact, a cruel nation; and our habit of disguising our vices by giving polite names to the offences we are determined to commit, does not, unfortunately for my own comfort, impose on me. Vivisectors can hardly pretend to be better than the classes from which they are drawn, or those above them; and if these classes are capable of sacrificing animals in various cruel ways under cover of sport, fashion, education, discipline and even, when the cruel sacrifices are human sacrifices, of political economy, it is idle for the vivisector to pretend that he is incapable of practising cruelty for pleasure or profit or both under the cloak of science. We are all tarred with the same brush.

Ibid.

Public support of vivisection is founded almost wholly on the assurances of the vivisectors that great public benefits may be expected from the practice. Not for a moment do I suggest that such a defence would be valid even if proved. But when the witnesses begin by alleging that in the cause of science all the customary ethical obligations (which include the obligation to tell the truth) are suspended, what weight can any reasonable person give to their testimony? I would rather swear fifty lies than take an animal which had licked my hand in good fellowship and torture it. If I did torture the dog, I should certainly not have the face to turn round and ask how any person dare suspect an honourable man like myself of telling lies. Most sensible and humane people would, I hope, flatly reply that honourable men do not behave dishonourably even to dogs.

... If you cannot attain to knowledge without torturing a dog, you must do without knowledge.

Ibid.

The only knowledge we lose by forbidding cruelty is knowledge at first hand of cruelty itself, which is precisely the knowledge humane people wish to be spared.

... You do not settle whether an experiment is justified or not by merely showing that it is of some use. The distinction is not between useful and useless experiments, but between barbarous and civilized behaviour. Vivisection is a social evil because if it advances human knowledge, it does so at the expense of human character.

Ibid.

Vivisection is now a routine, like butchering or hanging or flogging; and many of the men who practise it do so only because it has been established as part of the profession they have adopted. Far from enjoying it, they have simply overcome their natural repugnance and become indifferent to it, as men inevitably become indifferent to anything they do often enough. It is this dangerous power of custom that makes it so difficult to convince the common sense of mankind that any established commercial or professional practice has its root in passion. Let a routine once spring from passion, and you will presently find thousands of routineers following it passionlessly for a livelihood. In the same way many people do cruel and vile things without being in the least cruel or vile, because the routine to which they have been brought up is superstitiously cruel and vile.

Ibid.

SHAW

The natural abhorrence of sane mankind for the vivisector's cruelty, and the contempt of able thinkers for his imbecile casuistry, have been expressed by the most popular spokesmen of humanity. If the medical profession were to outdo the anti-vivisection societies in a general professional protest against the practice and principles of the vivisectors, every doctor in the kingdom would gain substantially by the immense relief and reconciliation which would follow such a reassurance of the humanity of the doctor.

Ibid.

The worst sin towards our fellow creatures is not to hate them, but to be indifferent to them. That's the essence of inhumanity.

The Devil's Disciple

Custom will reconcile people to any atrocity; and fashion will drive them to acquire any custom.

'Killing for Sport' (*Prefaces*)

When a man wants to murder a tiger, it's called sport; when the tiger wants to murder him, it's called ferocity.

The Revolutionist's Handbook

I have to admit, if we look facts in the face, that the English nation is not in the habit of allowing considerations of humanity to interfere either with its interests or with its pleasures.

From address at the annual meeting of the National
Anti-Vivisection Society, Queen's Large Hall,
Langham Place, London, 22 May 1900

Let us, then, taking the question on the utilitarian ground, admit that vivisections either have added or at some future time may add to our knowledge of disease

476

and to our knowledge of the secrets of nature. But the next step in the argument is that experiments upon dogs and guinea pigs and creatures equally unlike men and women can never be as conclusive as experiments on men and women. On the one hand, you are asked, are you going to set a few moments' pain to a rabbit against the hygienic salvation of the human race? Well, are you going to set a few moments' anguish on the part of your baby against it? Are you going to set a few moments' anguish to anybody on earth against it? If you once begin to balance the thing in that way, you will soon prove that you are justified not only in vivisecting dogs and guinea pigs, but in dissecting every human being you can get into your power.

We are all in the doctor's power when we are ill. I myself have been vivisected. And why? Because I had to accept the doctor's word that it was necessary. He had me as much as any doctor ever had a guinea pig in his power. I submitted, and the sole ground for my submission was my faith in that man's dealing with me honestly and mercifully. But if he had begun to argue in my presence in the way I have been describing, I could not have helped asking, 'Why should not this man sacrifice me if he thinks he can confer a benefit on humanity or advance science by doing so? I suggest to you, ladies and gentlemen, that if you bring this home to the ordinary man he will see that it will lead him much further than he desires to go. He will see that even if he takes the most sordid view of it; if he puts aside all questions of sympathy or compassion; if he shares the view – not altogether so rare in England as I could desire – that there is something manly and characteristically British in not being too sentimental about those things, yet he must draw the line somewhere; and if he draws it in such a way as to include quadrupeds only, the doctor may draw it a little higher up. He may say, quite logically, 'Here is a person who will never be missed. If I perform an experiment on him in the interest of science, and anything comes of it, that man by his death under my scalpel will have done more for the world than he would if I merely cured him.'

... There are hundreds of paths to scientific knowledge. The cruel ones can teach us only what we ought not to know.

Ibid.

We have it at last from Mr Wells. The vivisector experiments because he wants to know. On the question whether it is right to hurt any living creature for the sake of knowledge, his answer is that knowledge is so supremely important that for its sake there is nothing that it is not right to do.

Thus we learn from Mr Wells that the vivisector is distinguished from the ordinary run of limited scoundrels by being an infinite scoundrel. The common scoundrel who does not care what pain he (or she) inflicts as long as he can get money by it can be satiated. With public opinion and a stiff criminal code against him he can be brought to a point at which he does not consider another five-pound note worth the risk of garrotting or sandbagging or swindling anybody to get it. But the vivisector-scoundrel has no limit at all except that of his own physical capacity for committing atrocities and his own mental capacity for devising them. No matter how much he knows there is always, as Newton confessed, an infinitude of things still unknown, many of them still discoverable by experiment. When he has discovered what boiled baby tastes like, and what effect it has on the digestion, he has still to ascertain the gustatory and metabolic peculiarities of roast baby and fried baby, with, in each case, the exact age at which the baby should, to produce such and such results, be boiled, roast, fried, or fricasseed. You remonstrate with him, especially if you are the mother of one or two of the babies. You say, 'What good is all this? You do not eat babies.' He replies contemptuously, 'Do you think, then, that I have any practical end in view? Not at all. My object is to learn something I do not know at present. Like Cleopatra I have immortal longings in me. When I know all these things about babies I shall know more than Einstein, more than Solomon. I shall have eaten one more apple from the tree of knowledge of good and evil. I ...'

'You will have eaten your own damnation, as Paul said to the Corinthians' is as good a reply as another to such a claim. The proper place in organized human society for a scoundrel who seeks knowledge or anything else without conscience is the lethal chamber.

From reply to H.G. Wells in *The Sunday Express*, August 1927

The Anti-Vivisector does not deny that physiologists must make experiments and even take chances with new methods. He says that they must not seek knowledge by criminal methods, just as they must not make money by criminal methods. He does not object to Galileo dropping cannon balls from the top of the leaning tower of Pisa; but he would object to shoving off two dogs or American tourists. He knows that there are fifty ways of ascertaining any fact; that only the two or three worst of them are wicked ways; that those who deliberately choose them are not only morally but intellectually imbecile; that it is ridiculous to expect that an experimeter who commits acts of diabolical cruelty for the sake of what he calls Science can be trusted to tell the truth about the results; that no vivisector ever accepts another vivisector's conclusions nor refrains from undertaking a fresh set of vivisections to upset them; that as any fool can vivisect and gain kudos by writing a paper describing what happened, the laboratories are infested with kudos hunters who have nothing to tell that they could not have ascertained by asking a policeman, except when it is something that they should not know (like the sensations of a murderer); and that as these vivisectors crowd humane research workers out of the schools and discredit them, they use up all the available endowments and bequests, leaving nothing for serious research.

Ibid.

... Darwin popularized Evolution generally, as well as making his own special contribution to it. Now the general conception of Evolution provides the humanitarian with a scientific basis, because it establishes the fundamental equality of all living things. It makes the killing of an animal murder in exactly the same sense as the killing of a man is murder.

... this sense of the kinship of all forms of life is all that is needed to make Evolution not only a conceivable theory, but an inspiring one. St Anthony was ripe for the Evolution theory when he preached to the fishes, and St Francis when he called the birds his little brothers. Our vanity, and our snobbish conception of Godhead as being, like earthly kingship, a supreme class distinction instead of the rock on which Equality is built, has led us to insist on God offering us special terms by placing us apart from and above all the rest of his creatures. Evolution took that conceit out of us; and now, though we may kill a flea without the smallest remorse, we at all events know that we are killing our cousin. No doubt it shocks the flea when the creature that an almighty Celestial Flea created expressly for the food of fleas, destroys the jumping lord of creation with his sharp and enormous thumbnail; but no flea will ever be so foolish as to preach that in slaying fleas Man is applying a method of Natural Selection which will finally evolve a flea so swift that no man can catch him, and so hardy of constitution that Insect

Powder will have no more effect on him than strychnine on an elephant.

Preface to Back to Methuselah

A dinner!

How horrible!

I am to be made the pretext for killing all those wretched animals and birds, and fish! Thank you for nothing.

Now if it were to be a fast instead of a feast; say a solemn three days' abstention from corpses in my honour, I could at least pretend to believe that it was disinterested.

Blood sacrifices are not in my line.

Letter 30 December 1929

THE YOUNG WOMAN: You know, to me this is a funny sort of lunch. You begin with the dessert. We begin with the entrées. I suppose it's all right: but I have eaten so much fruit and bread and stuff, that I don't feel I want any meat.

THE PRIEST: We shall not offer you any. We don't eat it.

THE YOUNG WOMAN: Then how do you keep up your strength?

THE PRIEST: It keeps itself up.

The Simpleton of the Unexpected Isles, Prologue, Sc. III

On being asked why he was a vegetarian

Oh, come! That boot is on the other leg. Why should you call *me* to account for eating decently? If I battened on the scorched corpses of animals, you might well ask me why I did that.

The Vegetarian, 15 January 1898

I do not eat flesh, fish or fowl. I drink neither the narcotics which are used as stimulants (alcohol mostly) nor the true stimulants like tea ... It does not greatly

matter what most people eat or drink because they are
not working to the limit of their capacity either in quality
or quantity. To the few who are working on the finest
edge of their utmost powers it matters a great deal. You
can be a Sancho Panza on any food provided there is
enough of it. If you want to be a Pythagoras, you have to
be more careful …

Letter to Thomas Demetrius O'Bolger, 16 March 1920,
quoted in *Bernard Shaw, Collected Letters 1911–1925*
edited by Dan H. Laurence

PERCY BYSSHE SHELLEY, 1792–1822

Never again may blood of bird or beast
Stain with its venomous stream a human feast,
To the pure skies in accusation steaming.

Revolt of Islam

Earth, ocean, air, beloved brotherhood!
If our great Mother has imbued my soul
With aught of natural piety to feel
Your love, and recompense the boon with mine;
If dewy morn, and odorous noon, and even,
With sunset and its gorgeous ministers,
And solemn midnight's tingling silentness;
If autumn's hollow sighs in the sere wood,
And winter robing with pure snow and crowns
Of starry ice the gray grass and bare boughs;
If spring's voluptuous pantings, when she breathes
Her first sweet kisses, have been dear to me;
If no bright bird, insect, or gentle beast
I consciously have injured, but still loved
And cherished these my kindred – then forgive
This boast, beloved brethren, and withdraw
No portion of your wonted favour now!

Alastor or *The Spirit of Solitude*

How strange is human pride!
I tell thee that those living things,
To whom the fragile blade of grass,
That springeth in the morn
And perisheth ere noon
Is an unbounded world;
I tell thee that those viewless beings,
Whose mansion is the smallest particle
Of the impassive atmosphere,
Think, feel and live like man;
That their affections and antipathies,
Like his, produce the laws
Ruling their moral state;
And the minutest throb
That through their frame diffuses
The slightest, faintest motion,
Is fixed and indispensable
As the majestic laws
That rule yon rolling orbs.

Queen Mab

I wish no living thing to suffer pain.

Prometheus Unbound

No longer now
He slays the lamb that looks him in the face,
And horribly devours his mangled flesh;
Which, still avenging nature's broken law,
Kindled all putrid humours in his frame,
All evil passions, and all vain belief,
Hatred, despair, and loathing in his mind,
The germs of misery, death, disease, and crime.
No longer now the winged habitants,
That in the woods their sweet lives sing away,
Flee from the form of man; but gather round,
And prune their sunny feathers on the hands
Which little children stretch in friendly sport
Towards these dreadless partners of their play.

Ibid.

Man, and the other animals whom he has afflicted with his malady or depraved by his dominion, are *alone diseased*. The Bison, the wild Hog, the Wolf, are perfectly exempt from malady, and invariably die either from external violence or from mature old age. But the domestic Hog, the Sheep, the Cow, the Dog, are subject to an incredible variety of distempers, and, like the corruptors of their nature, have physicians who thrive upon their miseries. The super-eminence of man is, like Satan's, the super-eminence of pain; and the majority of his species doomed to poverty, disease and crime, have reason to curse the untoward event that, by enabling him to communicate his sensations, raised him above the level of his fellow animals. But the steps that have been taken are irrevocable. The whole of human science is comprised in one question: How can the advantages of intellect and civilization be reconciled with the liberty and pure pleasures of natural life? How can we take the benefits and reject the evils of the system which is now interwoven with the fibre of our being? I believe that abstinence from animal food and spiritous liquors would, in a great measure, capacitate us for the solution of this important question.

A Vindication of Natural Diet

I address myself not to the young enthusiast only, but to the ardent devotee of truth and virtue – the pure and passionate moralist yet unvitiated by the contagion of the world. He will embrace a pure system from its abstract truth, its beauty, its simplicity, and its promise of wide extended benefit. Unless custom has turned poison into food, he will hate the brutal pleasures of the chase by instinct. It will be a contemplation full of horror and disappointment to the mind that beings, capable of the gentlest and most admirable sympathies, should take delight in the death pangs and last convulsions of dying animals.

Ibid.

It is evident that those who are necessitated by their profession to trifle with the sacredness of life, and think lightly of the agonies of living beings, are unfit for the benevolence and justice which is required for the performance of the offices of civilized society. They are by necessity brutal, coarse, turbulent and sanguinary. Their habits form an admirable apprenticeship to the more wasting wickedness of war, in which men are hired to mangle and murder their fellow beings by thousands, that tyrants and countries may profit. How can he be expected to preserve a vivid sensibility to the benevolent sympathies of our nature, who is familiar with carnage, agony and groans? The very sight of animals in the fields who are destined to the axe must encourage obduracy if it fails to awaken compassion. The butchering of harmless animals cannot fail to produce much of that spirit of insane and hideous exultation in which news of a victory is related altho' purchased by the massacre of a hundred thousand men. If the use of animal food be, in consequence, subversive to the peace of human society, how unwarrantable is the injustice and barbarity which is exercised towards these miserable victims. They are called into existence by human artifice that they may drag out a short and miserable existence of slavery and disease, that their bodies may be mutilated, their social feelings outraged. It were much better that a sentient being should never have existed, than that it should have existed only to endure unmitigated misery. (The attachment of animals to their young is very strong. The monstrous sophism that beasts are pure unfeeling machines, and do not reason, scarcely requires a confutation.)

On the Vegetable System of Diet

DR HERBERT SHELTON, 1895 – 1985

The cannibal goes out and hunts, pursues and kills another man and proceeds to cook and eat him precisely as he would any other game. There is not a single argument nor a single fact that can be offered in favour of flesh eating that cannot be offered, with equal strength, in favour of cannibalism.

Superior Nutrition

It is certainly more in harmony with the facts of comparative anatomy to regard man's love of fruit as normal and proper and his taste for flesh as an acquired taste than to regard him as a carnivore that has adopted non-carnivorous habits. We must regard man's frugivorous tendencies as normal and proper, and his carnivorous practices as something acquired under pressure of circumstance and discard the view that man is either a carnivore or an omnivore. The argument for human carnivorism, when based on man's capacity for adaptation, is based on the unconscious assumption that it is desirable for man to take a step backward.

The laws governing man's life cannot be annulled or suspended by the artifices of civilization and every effort to do so can only result in injury. His true position is one in harmony with nature, and in proportion as he conforms in his eating habits to the foods for which he is constitutionally adapted, the better must his life become.

Man's Dietetic Character

WILLIAM SHENSTONE, 1714–1763

Tenderness

I have found out a gift for my fair,
I have found where the wood-pigeons breed:
But let me that plunder forbear,
She will say 'twas a barbarous deed.

For he ne'er could be true, she averr'd,
Who could rob a poor bird of its young:
And I loved her the more when I heard
Such tenderness fall from her tongue.

UPTON SINCLAIR, 1878–1968

At the same instant the ear was assailed by a most terrifying shriek; the visitors started in alarm, the women turned pale and shrank back. The shriek was followed by another, louder and yet more agonizing – for once started upon that journey, the hog never came back; at the top of the wheel he was shunted off upon a trolley, and went sailing down the room. And meantime another was swung up, and then another, and another, until there was a double line of them, each dangling by a foot and kicking in frenzy – and squealing. The uproar was appalling, perilous to the ear-drums; one feared there was too much sound for the room to hold – that the walls must give way or the ceiling crack. There were high squeals and low squeals, grunts, and wails of agony; there would come a momentary lull, and then a fresh outburst, louder than ever, surging up to a deafening climax. It was too much for some of the visitors – the men would look at each other, laughing nervously, and the women would stand with hands clenched and the blood rushing to their faces, and the tears starting in their eyes.

The Jungle

ISAAC BASHEVIS SINGER, 1904–

As often as Herman had witnessed the slaughter of animals and fish, he always had the same thought: in

487

their behaviour toward creatures, all men were Nazis. The smugness with which man could do with other species as he pleased exemplified the most extreme racist theories, the principle that might is right.

Enemies, A Love Story

In his thoughts, Herman spoke a eulogy for the mouse who had shared a portion of her life with him and who, because of him, had left this earth. 'What do they know – all these scholars, all these philosophers, all the leaders of the world – about such as you? They have convinced themselves that man, the worst transgressor of all the species, is the crown of creation. All other creatures were created merely to provide him with food, pelts, to be tormented, exterminated. In relation to them, all people are Nazis; for the animals it is an eternal Treblinka.'

'The Letter Writer' from *The Seance and Other Stories*

The same questions are bothering me today as they did fifty years ago. Why is one born? Why does one suffer? In my case, the suffering of animals also makes me very sad. I'm a vegetarian, you know. When I see how little attention people pay to animals, and how easily they make peace with man being allowed to do with animals whatever he wants because he keeps a knife or a gun, it gives me a feeling of misery and sometimes anger with the Almighty. I say 'Do you need your glory to be connected with so much suffering of creatures without glory, just innocent creatures who would like to pass a few years in peace?' I feel that animals are as bewildered as we are except that they have no words for it. I would say that all life is asking: 'What am I doing here?'

Newsweek interview, 16 October 1978, after winning the Nobel Prize in literature

Even though the number of people who commit suicide is quite small, there are few people who have never thought about suicide at one time or another. The same is true about vegetarianism. We find very few people who have never thought that killing animals is actually murder, founded on the premise that might is right ... I will call it the eternal question: What gives man the right to kill an animal, often torture it, so that he can fill his belly with its flesh? We know now, as we have always known instinctively, that animals can suffer as much as human beings. Their emotions and their sensitivity are often stronger than those of a human being. Various philosophers and religious leaders tried to convince their disciples and followers that animals are nothing more than machines without a soul, without feelings. However, anyone who has ever lived with an animal – be it a dog, a bird or even a mouse – knows that this theory is a brazen lie, invented to justify cruelty.

The only justification for killing animals is the fact that man can keep a knife or an axe in his hands and is shrewd enough and selfish enough to do slaughter for what he thinks is his own good. The Old Testament has many passages where the passion for meat is considered to be evil. According to the Bible, it was only a compromise with so-called human nature that God had allowed people to eat meat. I'm often astonished when I read about highly sensitive poets, preachers of morality, humanists and do-gooders of all kinds who found pleasure in hunting – chasing after some poor, weak hare or fox and teaching dogs to do likewise. I often read of people who say that when they retire they will go fishing. They say this with an understanding that from then on they won't do any damage to anybody. An epoch of charity and tranquillity will begin in their life. It never occurs to them for a moment that innocent beings will suffer and die from this innocent little sport.

... I personally am very pessimistic about the hope that humanity's disregard for animals will end soon. I'm sometimes afraid that we are approaching an epoch when the hunting of human beings may become a sport. But it is good that there are some people who express a deep protest against the killing and torturing of the helpless, playing with their fear of death, enjoying their misery. Even if God or nature sides with the killers, the vegetarian is saying: I protest the ways of God and man. We may admire God's wisdom but we are not obliged to praise what seems to us His lack of mercy. It may be that somewhere the Almighty has an answer for what He is doing. It may be that one day we shall grasp His answer. But as long as we don't understand it, we shouldn't agree and we shouldn't flatter Him.

... as long as human beings will go on shedding the blood of animals, there will never be any peace. There is only one little step from killing animals to creating gas chambers *à la* Hitler and concentration camps *à la* Stalin ... all such deeds are done in the name of 'social justice'. There will be no justice as long as man will stand with a knife or with a gun and destroy those who are weaker than he is.

From foreword to *Vegetarianism, a Way of Life*,
by Dudley Giehl

There reposed within me an ascetic who reminded me constantly of death and that others suffered in hospitals, in prisons, or were tortured by various political sadists. Only a few years ago millions of Russian peasants starved to death just because Stalin decided to establish collectives. I could never forget the cruelties perpetrated upon God's creatures in slaughterhouses, on hunts, and in various scientific laboratories.

Lost in America

PETER SINGER, 1946–

Why do we lock up chimpanzees in appalling primate research centres and use them in experiments that range from the uncomfortable to the agonizing and lethal, yet would never think of doing the same to a retarded human being at a much *lower* mental level? The only possible answer is that the chimpanzee, no matter how bright, is not human, while the retarded human, no matter how dull, is.

This is speciesism, pure and simple, and it is as indefensible as the most blatant racism. There is no ethical basis for elevating membership of one particular species into a morally crucial characteristic. From an ethical point of view, we all stand on an equal footing – whether we stand on two feet, or four, or none at all.

In Defence of Animals

The animal liberation movement ... is not saying that all lives are of equal worth or that all interests of humans and other animals are to be given equal weight, no matter what those interests may be. It *is* saying that where animals and humans have similar interests – we might take the interest in avoiding physical pain as an example, for it is an interest that humans clearly share with other animals – those interests are to be counted equally, with no automatic discount just because one of the beings is not human. A simple point, no doubt, but nevertheless part of a far-reaching ethical revolution.

Ibid.

The sphere of altruism has broadened from the family and tribe to the nation, race and now to all human beings. The process should be extended ... to include all beings with interests, of whatever species. But we cannot simply propose this as the ultimate ethical standard and then expect everyone to act accordingly. We must begin to design our culture so that it encourages broader concerns without frustrating important and relatively permanent human desires.

The Expanding Circle

This book is about the tyranny of human over non-human animals. This tyranny has caused and today is still causing an amount of pain and suffering that can only be compared with that which resulted from the centuries of tyranny by white humans over black humans. The struggle against this tyranny is a struggle as important as any of the moral and social issues that have been fought over in recent years.

Animal Liberation

If a being suffers there can be no moral justification for refusing to take that suffering into consideration. No matter what the nature of the being, the principle of equality requires that its suffering be counted equally with the like suffering – in so far as rough comparisons can be made – of any other being. If a being is not capable of suffering, or of experiencing enjoyment or happiness, there is nothing to be taken into account. So the limit of sentience (using the term as a convenient if not strictly accurate shorthand for the capacity to suffer and/or experience enjoyment) is the only defensible boundary of concern for the interests of others. To mark this boundary by some other characteristic like intelligence or rationality would be to mark it in an arbitrary manner. Why not choose some other characteristic, like skin colour?

The racist violates the principle of equality by giving greater weight to the interests of members of his own race when there is a clash between their interests and the interests of those of another race. The sexist violates the principle of equality by favouring the interests of his own sex. Similarly the speciesist allows the interests of his own species to override the greater interests of members of other species. The pattern is identical in each case.

Ibid.

The practices discussed ... involve ... in one case tens of millions of animals, and in the other case, literally billions of animals every year ... we cannot pretend that we have nothing to do with these practices. One of them – experimentation on animals – is promoted by the government we elect, and largely paid for out of the taxes we pay. The other – rearing animals for food – is possible only because most people buy and eat the products of this practice. That is why I have chosen to discuss these particular forms of speciesism. They are the central ones. They cause more suffering to a greater number of animals than anything else that humans do. To stop them we must change the policies of our government, and we must change our own lives, to the extent of changing our diet. If these officially promoted and almost universally accepted forms of speciesism can be abolished, abolition of the other speciesist practices cannot be far behind.

Ibid.

How can a man who is not a sadist spend his working day heating an unanaesthetized dog to death, or driving a monkey into a lifelong depression, and then remove his white coat, wash his hands and go home to dinner with his wife and children? How can taxpayers allow their money to be used to support experiments of this kind? And how can students go through a turbulent era of protest against injustice, discrimination, and oppression of all kinds, no matter how far from home, while ignoring the cruelties that are being carried out on their own campuses?

The answers to these questions stem from the

unquestioned acceptance of speciesism. We tolerate cruelties inflicted on members of other species that would outrage us if performed on members of our own species. Speciesism allows researchers to regard the animals they experiment on as items of equipment, laboratory tools rather than living, suffering creatures. Sometimes they even refer to the animals in this way. Robert White of the Cleveland Metropolitan General Hospital, who has performed numerous experiments involving the transplanting of heads of monkeys, and the keeping alive of monkey brains in fluid, outside the body, has said in an interview that:

> Our main purpose here is to offer a laboratory tool: a monkey 'model' in which and by which we can design new operative techniques for the brain.

And the reporter who conducted the interview and observed White's experiments found his experience

> a rare and chilling glimpse into the cold, clinical world of the scientist, where the life of an animal has no meaning beyond the immediate purpose of experimentation. (Scope, Durban, S.A., 30.3.1973)

This 'scientific' attitude to animals was exhibited to a large audience in December 1974 when the American public television network brought together Harvard philosopher Robert Nozick and three scientists whose work involves animals. The programme was a follow-up to Fred Wiseman's controversial film *Primate*, which had taken viewers inside the Yerkes Primate Center, a research centre in Atlanta, Georgia. Nozick asked the scientists whether the fact that an experiment will kill hundreds of animals is ever regarded, by scientists, as a reason for not performing it. One of the scientists answered: 'Not that I know of.' Nozick pressed his question: 'Don't the animals count at all?' Dr A. Perachio, of the Yerkes Center, replied: 'Why should they?' While Dr D. Baltimore, of the Massachusetts Institute of Technology, added that he did not think that experimenting on animals raised a moral issue at all. ('The Price of Knowledge' broadcast in New York, 12 December 1974.)

Ibid.

When are experiments on animals justified? Upon learning of the nature of many contemporary experiments, many people react by saying that all experiments on animals should be prohibited immediately. But if we make our demands as absolute as this, the experimenters have a ready reply: Would we be prepared to let thousands of humans die if they could be saved by a single experiment on a single animal?

This question is, of course, purely hypothetical. There never has been and there never could be a single experiment that saves thousands of lives. The way to reply to this hypothetical question is to pose another: Would the experimenter be prepared to carry out his experiment on a human orphan under six months old if that were the only way to save thousands of lives?

If the experimenter would not be prepared to use a human infant, then his readiness to use non-human animals reveals an unjustifiable form of discrimination on the basis of species, since adult apes, monkeys, dogs, cats, rats and other mammals are more aware of what is happening to them, more self-directing, and, so far as we can tell, at least as sensitive to pain as a human infant.

Ibid.

At present scientists do not look for alternatives simply because they do not care enough about the animals they are using.

Ibid.

495

For most humans, especially those in modern urban and suburban communities, the most direct form of contact with non-human animals is at meal time: we eat them. This simple fact is the key to our attitudes to other animals, and also the key to what each one of us can do about changing these attitudes. The use and abuse of animals raised for food far exceeds, in sheer numbers of animals affected, any other kind of mistreatment. Hundreds of millions of cattle, pigs, and sheep are raised and slaughtered in the United States alone each year; and for poultry the figure is a staggering three *billion*. (That means that about 5000 birds – mostly chickens – will have been slaughtered in the time it takes you to read this page.) It is here, on our dinner table and in our neighbourhood supermarket or butcher's shop, that we are brought into direct touch with the most extensive exploitation of other species that has ever existed.

Ibid.

As a matter of strict logic, perhaps, there is no contradiction in taking an interest in animals on both compassionate and gastronomic grounds. If a person is opposed to the infliction of suffering on animals, but not to the painless killing of animals, he could consistently eat animals that had lived free of all suffering and been instantly, painlessly slaughtered. Yet practically and psychologically it is impossible to be consistent in one's concern for non-human animals while continuing to dine on them. If we are prepared to take the life of another being merely in order to satisfy our taste for a particular type of food, then that being is no more than a means to our end. In time we will come to regard pigs, cattle, and chickens as things for us to use, no matter how strong our compassion may be; and when we find that to continue to obtain supplies of the bodies of these animals at a price we are able to pay it is necessary to change their living conditions a little, we will be unlikely to regard these changes too critically. The factory farm is nothing more than the application of technology to the idea that animals are means to our ends. Our eating habits are dear to us and not easily altered. We have a strong interest in convincing ourselves that our concern for other animals does not require us to stop eating them. No one in the habit of eating an animal can be completely without bias in judging whether the conditions in which that animal is reared caused suffering.

Ibid.

The people who profit by exploiting large numbers of animals do not need our approval. They need our money. The purchase of the corpses of the animals they rear is the only support the factory farmers ask from the public. They will use intensive methods as long as they continue to receive this support; they will have the resources needed to fight reform politically; and they will be able to defend themselves against criticism with the reply that they are only providing the public with what it wants.

Hence the need for each one of us to stop buying the produce of modern animal farming – even if we are not convinced that it would be wrong to eat animals that have lived pleasantly and died painlessly. Vegetarianism is a form of boycott. For most vegetarians the boycott is a permanent one, since once they have broken away from flesh-eating habits they can no longer approve of slaughtering animals in order to satisfy the trivial desires of their palates. But the moral obligation to boycott the meat available in butcher shops and supermarkets is just as inescapable for those who disapprove only of inflicting suffering, and not of killing. In recent years Americans have boycotted lettuce and grapes because the system under which those particular lettuces and grapes had been produced exploited farm labourers, not because lettuce and grapes can never be produced without exploitation. The same line of reasoning leads to boycotting meat. Until we boycott meat we are, each one of us, contributing to the continued existence, prosperity and growth of factory farming and all the other cruel practices used in rearing animals for food.

It is at this point that the consequences of speciesism intrude directly into our lives and we are forced to attest personally to the sincerity of our concern for non-human animals. Here we have an opportunity to *do* something, instead of merely talking and wishing the politicians would do something. It is easy to take a stand about a remote issue, but the speciesist, like the racist, reveals his true nature when the issue comes nearer home. To protest about bull-fighting in Spain or the slaughter of baby seals in Canada while continuing to eat chickens that have spent their lives crammed into cages, or veal from calves that have been deprived of their mothers, their proper diet, and the freedom to lie down with their legs extended, is like denouncing apartheid in South Africa while asking your neighbors not to sell their houses to blacks.

Ibid.

Vegetarianism brings with it a new relationship to food, plants and nature. Flesh taints our meals. Disguise it as we may, the fact remains that the centrepiece of our dinner has come to us from the slaughterhouse, dripping blood. Untreated and unrefrigerated, it soon begins to putrefy and stink. When we eat it, it sits heavily in our stomachs, blocking our digestive processes until, days later, we struggle to excrete it. When we eat plants, food takes on a different quality. We take from the earth food that is ready for us and does not fight against us as we take it. Without meat to deaden the palate there is an extra delight in fresh vegetables taken straight from the ground. Personally, I found the idea of picking my own dinner so satisfying that shortly after becoming a vegetarian I began digging up part of our backyard and growing some of my own vegetables – something that I had never thought of doing previously, but which several of my vegetarian friends were also doing. In this way dropping flesh-meat from my diet brought me into closer contacts with plants, the soil, and the seasons.

Ibid.

All the arguments to prove man's superiority cannot shatter this hard fact: in suffering the animals are our equals.

Ibid.

Animal Liberation will require greater altruism on the part of human beings than any other liberation movement. The animals themselves are incapable of demanding their own liberation, or of protesting against their condition with votes, demonstrations, or bombs. Human beings have the power to continue to oppress other species forever, or until we make this planet unsuitable for living beings. Will our tyranny continue, proving that we really are the selfish tyrants that the most cynical of poets and philosophers have always said we are? Or will we rise to the challenge and prove our capacity for genuine altruism by ending our ruthless exploitation of the species in our power, not because we are forced to do so by rebels or terrorists, but because we recognize that our position is morally indefensible?

The way in which we answer this question depends on the way in which each one of us, individually, answers it.

Ibid.

To disrupt a hunt so as to make it possible for the intended victim to escape is one thing; to seek 'retribution' on the benighted hunters is another thing altogether and morally far more dubious. (If we consider the unfortunate social background and childhood experiences of most hunters, their atrocious behaviour becomes readily explicable, and more a matter for pity than retribution.)

The Animal Liberation Movement

The animal liberation movement must do its part to avoid the vicious spiral of violence. Animal Liberation activists must set themselves irrevocably against the use of violence, even when their opponents use violence against them. By violence I mean any action which causes direct physical harm to any human or animal; and I would go beyond physical harm to acts which cause psychological harm like fear or terror. It is easy to believe that because some experimenters make animals suffer, it is all right to make the experimenters suffer. This attitude is mistaken. We may be convinced that a person who is abusing animals is totally callous and insensitive; but we lower ourselves to their level and put ourselves in the wrong if we harm or threaten to harm that person. The entire animal liberation movement is based on the strength of its ethical concern. It must not abandon the high moral ground.

Instead of going down the path of increasing violence, the animal liberation movement will do far better to follow the examples of the two greatest – and, not coincidentally, most successful – leaders of liberation movements in modern times: Gandhi and Martin Luther King. With immense courage and resolution, they stuck to the principle of non-violence despite the provocations, and often violent attacks, of their opponents. In the end they succeeded because the justice of their cause could not be denied, and their behaviour touched the consciences even of those who had opposed them. The struggle to extend the sphere of moral concern to non-human animals may be even harder and longer, but if it is pursued with the same determination and moral resolve, it will surely also succeed.

Ibid.

SACHEVERELL SITWELL, 1897–1988

There comes a surge or thrill of excitement which is indescribable; a thing, not of the brain, but of the blood; while flourishes of trumpets sound from the interior of the bull ring. Not the herald's fanfare; not the tirralirra of the hunting horn. Death and torture are in its tones. For the dumb animals who have no souls. In their sufferings they are to give pleasure to the men and women of the audience. That is the secret in this shedding of blood. It is the raping of the virgins and sentence of death upon the male, which is carried out upon the spot; only the virgins are old, worn out horses, nags or mares, it does not matter, but they are the spinsters of the comedy, thin and comic, ludicrous in their torments, while the bulls are lusty young males tasting blood for the first and last time. The punishment for that is death. Tonight, not an animal will come alive out of the bullring.

Splendours and Miseries

JOSHUA SLOCUM, 1844–*c*.1910

In the loneliness of the dreary country about Cape Horn I found myself in no mood to make one life less in the world, except in self-defence and, as I sailed, this trait of the hermit character grew till the mention of killing food animals was revolting to me.

Sailing Alone Around the World

GEORGE SMALL, 1924 –

What is the nature of a species that knowingly and without good reason exterminates another? How long will man persist in the belief that he is the master of this Earth rather than one of its guests? When will he learn that he is but one form of life among thousands, each one of which is in some way related to and dependent on all the others? How long will he survive if he does not? Whatever the nature of the creator, he surely did not intend that the forms on which he bestowed the gift of life should be exterminated by man. The only homage we can now pay to the blue whale is to learn the lessons of dependence on and kinship with all life. If we do not learn them, the great blue whale will have died in vain, having taught nothing to his only mortal enemy.

The Blue Whale

WILLIAM SMELLIE, 1740?–1795

Vulgar and uninformed men, when pampered with a variety of animal food, are much more choleric, fierce and cruel in their tempers than those who live chiefly on vegetables.

The Philosophy of Natural History

COLIN SMITH, 1941–

There is no moral justification for using animals in cruel experimental procedures, also no evidence whatever to suggest that an increase in the number of animal tests brings a corresponding increase in the understanding of human health and disease.

Inaugural address to the International Association
Against Painful Experiments on Animals, 1969

SIR JAMES EDWARD SMITH, 1759–1828

It is only pride and imbecility in man to imagine all things made for his sole use. There exist millions of suns and their revolving orbs which the eye of man has never perceived. Myriads of animals enjoy their pastime unheeded and unseen by him – many are injurious and destructive to him. All exist for purposes but partially known. Yet we must believe, in general, that all were created for their own enjoyment, for mutual advantage, and for the preservation of universal harmony in nature. If, merely because we can eat sheep pleasantly, we are to believe that they exist only to supply us with food, we may as well say that man was created solely for the various parasitical animals to feed on, because they do feed on him.

Fruits and Farinacea

JILL SMITH, 1935–

This is not a sentimental issue. It goes to the very heart of our morality and humanity. It defines our values and describes our concept of power. Do we hold power and dominion over others for exploitation or for their care? The responsibility of power extends to all forms of life. Is private power at public expense above morality? Is scientific experimentation that sacrifices all human and humane standards above morality? Is the daily killing of thousands and thousands of innocent animals above legislative responsibility? Mercy is not weakness; it is the expression of ultimate strength. We should not be embarrassed by the feelings that force us to stop the daily massacre and torture of helpless life.

Coalition for Animal Welfare *Bulletin*, 1978

HERBERT SNOW, MD, MRCS, 1847–1930

Those who endeavour to pierce to the core of things, regard vivisection as not only an outrage on morality but a gross hindrance to the progress of science properly so called, and an insurmountable impediment to the higher evolution of the race. Held forth for men's admiration and adoration as an adjunct and aid to the healing art, it is no more than a colossal sham. As such, without any question of the cruelties it may involve, it should be totally abolished.

On the Utter Futility of Vivisection

ALEXANDER SOLZHENITSYN, 1918–

Nowadays we don't think much of a man's love for an animal; we laugh at people who are attached to cats. But if we stop loving animals, aren't we bound to stop loving humans too?

Cancer Ward

THE REVD THE LORD (Donald) SOPER, 1903–

I could say in a very few words what I have believed, and come to believe with greater fervour, as the years have gone by. Dr Schweitzer called it 'reverence for life', Jesus called it the Love of God. Put into modern terms it is the obligation and joy of caring. I have lived in one of the most violent ages that the world has known and have seen so much contempt for the value of human and animal life. If my experience has anything of value to pass on to others, it has been the increasing conviction that only a non-violent love will be sufficient to make the world a happier place for God's creatures to live in without fear and without privation; and if I could leave the world with the confidence that at long last man was beginning to turn from the foolishness and waste of violence and war, then I should have an added reason for looking into the future with tranquillity and hope.

Just for Animals

The reasons which finally persuaded me to become a vegetarian were reached at two levels, one much more superficial than the other.

What triggered off the decision was a sense of exasperation at being repeatedly asked in the open air on Tower Hill how I could reconcile the pacifism which I advocated with a carnivorous diet. I made up my mind one day to put an end to the somewhat evasive answers which I had been making by becoming a vegetarian.

The deeper-seated reason, of course, is that I felt vegetarianism to be more consistent with the Christian faith I hold, and in particular with the repudiation of violence, which for me is an integral part of that faith.

I would not pretend for a moment that Christians can be completely consistent in this imperfect world, but aesthetically as well as ethically I have felt a strong sense of satisfaction – a peace of mind, if you like since I took this decision ... Godliness with contentment is great gain.

The British Vegetarian, March/April 1959

ROBERT SOUTHEY, 1774–1843

From *The Dancing Bear*

Alas, poor Bruin! How he foots the pole,
And waddles round it with unwieldy steps! ...
But we are told all things were made for Man;
And I'll be sworn there's not a fellow here
Who would not swear 'twere hanging blasphemy
To doubt that truth. Therefore as thou'wert born,
Bruin, for Man, and Man makes nothing of thee
In any other way – most logically

It follows thou wert born to make him sport;
That that great snout of thine was form'd on purpose
To hold a ring; and that thy fat was given thee
For an approved pomatum! To demur
Were heresy. And politicians say
(Wise men who in the scale of reason give
No foolish feelings weight) that thou art here
Far happier than thy brother bears who roam
O'er trackless snow for food ... Besides
'Tis wholesome for thy morals to be brought
From savage climes into a civilized state,
Into the decencies of Christendom.
Bear, Bear! It passes in the Parliament
For excellent logic, this!

COLIN SPENCER, 1933–

The manner in which we treat all living creatures upon this planet is an aspect of our respect for all minorities. If we exploit animals, we blunt our sensibilities and are prepared to maim, unjustly imprison and kill each other.

BUAV Cruelty-Free campaign, 1987

HERBERT SPENCER, 1820–1903

The behaviour of men to the lower animals, and their behaviour to each other, bear a constant relationship.

Social Statics

HENRY SPIRA, 1927–

Animal liberation is also human liberation. Animal liberationists care about the quality of life for all. We recognize our kinship with all feeling beings. We identify with the powerless and the vulnerable – the victims, all those dominated, oppressed and exploited. And it is the non-human animals whose suffering is the most intense, widespread, expanding, systematic and socially sanctioned of all.

'Fighting for Animal Rights', in *Ethics and Animals*

Society programmes us into inconsistency, into being kind to household pets while other animals suffer from birth to death. And society also programmes us into not focusing on the true levers of power. We therefore need to study the realities consciously, in a detached way, as a guide to action. Who is profiting and who is calling the tune? And how does the rest of the world perceive our powers?

The majority of people would certainly prefer that animals not suffer, were the matter brought to their attention. Yet the intense pain of billions of animals continues unabated.

To fight successfully for the rights of animals, we need priorities, programmes, effective organization, imagination, tenacity, expertise, and a good sense of strategy and tactics as we create bridges with the public's current awareness and move forward.

And we need to remember the words of the Abolitionist leader Frederick Douglas – 'If there is no struggle, there is no progress. Those who profess to favour freedom, and yet deprecate agitation, are people who want rain without thunder and lightning. They want the ocean without the roar of its many waters. Power concedes nothing without a demand. It never did and it never will.'

Ibid.

MARGARET STANLEY-WRENCH, 1916–1974

The Hare at Harvest

The hare in the harvest field
Crouches, a small, recumbent sphinx, burnt red
As earthenware, as sand,
Sheltered by her world of sun-bleached grain.
Forgotten the days when she danced
Across the furrows laced by the green corn.
Forgotten the leaping lovers,
And the leverets hidden when the first poppies lolled
Their knopped and mouse-grey bud.
And unforeseen
The day of doom ahead, when hissing blades
Shall level the soughing, rustling waves of grain,
And naked to the arid stubble, she
Will run her labyrinthine course, and find
The friendly acres now her enemy.

GERTRUDE STEIN, 1874–1946

… money … is really the difference between men and animals; most of the things men feel, animals feel, and vice versa, but animals do not know about money.

Everybody's Autobiography

JOHN STEINBECK, 1902–1968

We have never understood why men mount the heads of animals and hang them up to look down on their conquerors. Possibly it feels good to these men to be superior to animals, but does it not seem that if they were sure of it they would not have to prove it? Often a man who is afraid must constantly demonstrate his courage and, in the case of the hunter, must keep a tangible record of his courage.

The Sea of Cortez

JAMES STEPHENS, 1882–1950

Student Taper

When
— at the mid of noon,
at end of day —
my lamp is lit,
grant me a boon,
I pray,
and do
so order it

— that the small creatures,
terrified and blind:
the gold and silvern moths
of lovely kind,
do not whirl to my taper,
nor, therein,
die, painfully,
and bring my light
to sin.

My light
is innocent!
Grant
— that it may be
harmless,
and helpful,
and remarked
of Thee.

The Snare

I hear a sudden cry of pain!
There is a rabbit in a snare:
Now I hear the cry again,
But I cannot tell from where.

But I cannot tell from where

He is calling out for aid!
Crying on the frightened air,
Making everything afraid!

Making everything afraid!
Wrinkling up his little face!
And he cries again for aid;
– And I cannot find the place!

And I cannot find the place
Where his paw is in the snare!
Little One! Oh, Little One!
I am searching everywhere!

The Cage

It tried to get from out the cage;
Here and there it ran, and tried
At the edges and the side,
In a busy, timid rage.

Trying yet to find the key
Into freedom, trying yet,
In a timid rage, to get
To its old tranquillity.

It did not know, it did not see,
It did not turn an eye, or care
That a man was watching there
While it raged so timidly.

It ran without a sound, it tried,
In a busy, timid rage,
To escape from out the cage
By the edges and the side.

Little Things

Little things that run and quail,
And die, in silence and despair!

Little things, that fight, and fail,
And fall, on sea, and earth, and air!

All trapped and frightened little things,
The mouse, the coney, hear our prayer!

As we forgive those done to us –
The lamb, the linnet, and the hare –

Forgive us all our trespasses,
Little creatures, everywhere!

LAURENCE STERNE, 1713–1768

'I'll not hurt thee,' says Uncle Toby, rising with the fly in
his hand. 'Go,' he says, opening the window to let it
escape. 'Why should I hurt thee? This world is surely
wide enough to hold both thee and me.'

Tristram Shandy

HENRY BAILEY STEVENS, 1891–1976

The Bull Calf

Well, sonny! Come along,
Swinging your little tail!
This is the price you have to pay
For being born a male.

Moo, moo, old cow!
And start a hunger-strike.
Lots of us have to do
Things that we don't like.

Lots of us have to suffer;
Don't let it spoil your meal.
This is the price you have to pay;
Somebody wants some veal.

Don't take it too hard, old cow;
I'm sorry you've got so wild;
But somebody's got an appetite
And wants to eat your child.

Lines to be Said after Soup

With lentils, tomatoes and rice,
Olives and nuts and bread,
Why do I have to gnaw on a slice
Of something bloody and dead?

With honey, banana and pear,
Orange and corn and beet,
Why do I feel I must tear
Into some carcass-meat?

How does my nose go astray?
What in my instinct warps,
That I have to ravish and slay
In order to feed on a corpse?

A region where olives, oranges, grapes, figs, apricots, melons, dates, cereals, cottonseed, sesame and many vegetables could flourish has been grazed for three thousand years by sheep and goats, and made in large part into a desert. To this day the nomad tribes which roam over the vast interior of the Middle East pick their scanty living principally from meat, dairy products, skins, casings, wool, hair and furs.

Thus from a long-time viewpoint it was Cain, the gardener, the older son of Adam, who was struck down. Abel, the keeper of livestock, slew him, initiating the business of murder in its present wholesale fashion. His is the name that should be blackened.

It was *breeding* the animals that made the difference. So long as man hunted them, he was simply another beast of prey – a part of the natural balance keeping animal life in check. But when he bred and protected vast hordes of livestock, he threw an intolerable burden upon the soil resources of the earth and has been paying for it with war ever since. It is as though the screw of the carnivorous habit during the hunting period has been going through the primary board; now during the period of animal domestication it has been biting into a secondary board and pulling together human life with that of the beasts.

So man fell – below the level of the ape, of the monkey, of the entire primary family. He fell back beyond the level of the last sixty million years into the class of the carnivores – the snarling cats, the scavenging birds, the beasts of prey. Actually he has set up as emblems the serpent, the dragon, the eagle, the lion, the bear, as if they were his models. And he has trained his own children into a belief that this is their heritage.

The Recovery of Culture

Centuries before these modern prophets, Francis of Assisi promoted a religious programme of brotherhood toward both animals and man. His thoughts, which were collected and called flowers, brought a fragrance like Easter lilies and balm into the stone cathedrals that depict the various agonies of Christ. Since his time the conscience of the primitive Christians, stirring again in stalwart bosoms, caused the Protestants to revolt against the unholy alliance of the Church with the violence of the State; caused George Fox to organize the Society of Friends and other leaders to form similar sects which were sworn to non-participation in mass murder; and in our own day has caused many powerful voices even in orthodox pulpits to cry out in horror at man's inhumanity to man. The failure of these leaders to connect the butchery of war with that of the animal slaughterhouse has no doubt been due largely to their instinctive dread of the very weight of propaganda which they have had to carry in their attack against militarism. They have shrunk from visualizing the full extent of the dominance of the blight of bloodshed.

Now in the last two decades Gerald Heard has keenly traced the thin line of sensitivity running back through man's entire development like a spinal cord; and Albert Schweitzer, writing full-bloodedly out of his African service station, has asked religion to identify itself with reverence for all life.

The foregoing are a few of the more significant eruptions of Primate Culture in recent centuries. They have usually been considered separately and not related. The conclusions of leaders like Tolstoy, Wagner, Shelley, Gandhi and Bernard Shaw have thus been treated as if they were aberrations. Critics have bemoaned the fact that a great novelist should have left his fiction or that a great composer should have deserted his music to express himself upon ethics or diet, as if a man should not be concerned with the implications of his own actions or the nature of his daily bread! The truth is that these leaders have risen out of their specialized arts to speak of Total Culture.

Ibid.

With 2000 A.D. in the offing, we are coming to the crisis of the race, when man must turn the corner and recover his primate tradition, renouncing war and the slaughter-house, which are historically and inexorably tied together. The very fact that most meat-eaters do not dare face the abattoir and set up a built-in taboo against thought of it, is symptomatic. A psychiatrist would have to say: 'If there is such fear in you, you had better face it. Otherwise, you will be living with an unhealthy mind.'

World Forum, April/June 1967

ADLAI STEVENSON, 1900–1965

... it is difficult to picture the great Creator conceiving of a programme of one creature (which He has made) using another living creature for purposes of experimentation. There must be other, less cruel ways of obtaining knowledge.

Putting First Things First

ROBERT LOUIS STEVENSON, 1850–1894

We consume the carcasses of creatures of like appetites, passions and organs with our own, and fill the slaughterhouses daily with screams of pain and fear.

Quoted in *The Vegetarian Way*, 1967

Nothing more strongly arouses our disgust than cannibalism, yet we make the same impression on Buddhists and vegetarians, for we feed on babies, though not on our own.

Familiar Studies of Men and Books

You think those dogs will not be in Heaven!
I tell you they will be there long before any of us.

Ibid.

JIMMY STEWART, 1908–

Animals give me more pleasure through the viewfinder of a camera than they ever did in the crosshairs of a gunsight. And after I've finished 'shooting', my unharmed victims are still around for others to enjoy. I have developed a deep respect for animals. I consider them fellow living creatures with certain rights that should not be violated any more than those of humans.

The Reader's Digest, 1975

W.J. STILLMAN, 1828–1901

I bought him and named him Billy. From the first moment that he became my companion he gave me his entire confidence, and accepted his domestication without the least indication that he considered it captivity … he came to me for his bread and milk, and slept in my pocket, from the first, and enjoyed being caressed as completely as if he had been born under my roof. No other animal is so clean in its personal habits as the squirrel, when in health; and Billy soon left the basket which cradled his infancy, and habitually slept under a fold of my bed-cover, sometimes making his way to my pillow and sleeping by my cheek …

The Farewell. Billy signed to go into my pocket and lay there, still, even in his apathy, grasping my forefinger with his paws, and licking it as if in his approaching dissolution he still wished to show me his love for me …

The dear little creature had been to me not merely a pet to amuse my vacant hours, though many of those most vacant which the tired brain passes in its sleepless nights had been diverted by his pretty ways as he shared my bed, and by his singular devotion to me; but he had been as a door open into the world of God's lesser creatures, an apostle of pity and tenderness for all living things, and his memory stands on the eternal threshold, nodding and beckoning to me to enter in and make part of the creation I had ignored till he taught it to me, so that while life lasts I can no longer idly inflict pain upon the least of God's creatures.

Billy and Hans

DR ALAN STODDARD, MB, BS, 1915–

Man's population explosion is a disaster because we are rapidly using up irreplaceable resources and causing irreversible changes in our environment. The demands of each human being for an area to live in and the basic needs of food, clothing and shelter are invading the habitat of the animal kingdom.

Quite apart from any humanitarian considerations which enlightened people foster, the sheer weight of demand creates excessive claims on, and privation to, animal life. The shortage of arable land has led to factory farming which perpetuates and extends cruelty. Some animals and birds do not even have room enough to turn round in their cages, let alone respond to their instinctive need to be free. Even the harshest treatment of our worst criminals is less cruel than this, and yet the animals are innocent of any crime.

Many animals are brought into this world artificially by insemination forcing them to reproduce against all their natural instincts. Cruel as is the slaughter of animals for food (and my lifelong vegetarianism was reinforced when as a child I witnessed the throat-slitting of some twenty sheep in a field near our home), the practices of factory farming are even worse. Yet such practices are condoned or ignored. These crimes against animals are the greater because they are unable to protest or fend for themselves. Our ill treatment of the weak and inarticulate seems especially contemptible.

In a press interview, 1985

HARRIET BEECHER STOWE, 1811–1896

It's a matter of taking the side of the weak against the strong, something the best people have always done.

The Minister's Wooing

I and my daughters and husband have been regarded as almost fanatical in our care of animals wherever we have been, and in Florida we have seen much to affect us; not so much in the oppression of useful working animals, as in the starving of dogs and cats and other creatures which people keep and will not feed. Again, we have been distressed by the wholesale barbarity of tourists who seem to make Florida animals mere marks for unskilful hunters to practise upon, and who go everywhere maiming, wounding and killing poor birds and beasts that they do not even stop to pick up, and shoot in mere wantonness. Last year we exerted ourselves to get a law passed protecting the birds of Florida which were being trapped and carried off by thousands to die in little miserable cages ... veritable slave ships. I never happen to have seen any instances of cruelty to working animals, but presume there is much need of attention. I for my part am ready to do anything that can benefit the cause. I am glad of this opportunity to say with what wholehearted delight we have watched your noble course, in pleading for the dumb and helping the helpless. May God bless you.

From a letter to Henry Bergh dated 6 November 1877, eleven years after the founding of America's first humane society

DAVID FRIEDRICH STRAUSS, 1808–1874

Criminal history shows us how many torturers of men, and murderers, have first been torturers of the lower animals. The manner in which a nation in the aggregate treats animals, is one chief measure of its civilization. The Latin races, as we know, come forth badly from this examination, we Germans not half well enough. Buddhism has done more in this direction than Christianity.

The Old and the New Faith

GUSTAV VON STRUVE, 1805–1870

Every step from the lower conditions to a higher is bound up with certain difficulties. This is especially the case when it is a question of shaking off habits strengthened by numbers and length of time. Had the human race, however, not the power to do so, then the step from Paganism to Christianity, from predatory life to tillage; in particular, from savage barbarousness to a certain stage in civilization, would have been impossible. All these steps brought many struggles in their train, which to many thousands produced some hardships; to untold millions, however, incalculable benefits. So, also, the steps onward from the flesh diet cannot be established without some disturbances. The great majority of men hold fast to old prejudices. They struggle, not seldom with senseless rage, against enlightenment and reason, and a century often passes away before a new idea has forced the way for the spread of new blessings ...

All barbarians, or semi-barbarians, will struggle desperately against this with their selfish coarseness. But the result will be that the soil which, under the influence of the flesh regime supported one man only, will, with the unfettered advantages of the vegetable diet, support five human beings. Liebig, even, recognized so much as this – that the flesh diet is twelve times more costly than the non-flesh.

Pflanzenkost

They tell children, perhaps, that they must not be cruel either to 'animals' or to human beings weaker than themselves. But when the child goes into the kitchen, he sees pigeons, hens and geese slaughtered and plucked; when he goes into the streets, he sees animals hung up, with bodies besmeared with blood, feet cut off, and heads twisted back. If the child proceeds still further, he comes upon the slaughterhouse, in which harmless or useful beings of all kinds are being slaughtered or strangled. We shall not here dwell upon all the barbarisms bound up in the butchery of animals; but in the same degree, in which men abuse their superior power, in regard to the weaker species, do they usually cause their tyranny to be felt by weaker human beings in their power.

What avails all the fine talk about morality, in contrast with acts of barbarism and immorality presented to them on all sides?

It is no proof of an exalted morality when a man acts justly towards a person as strong as himself, who can injure him. He alone acts justly who fulfils his obligatory duties in regard to the weaker … He, who has no human persons under him, at least can strike his horse, barbarously drive his calf and cudgel his dog. The relations of men to the other species are so full of significance, and exercise so mighty an influence upon the development of human character, that Morality wants a wider province that shall embrace all within it.

Das Seelenleben

BHIKKHUNI MIAO KWANG SUDHARMA, 1928–

All beings hold themselves dear. Just as we want to live, so do our fellow creatures. How can we feel peaceful and happy about taking another's life, in order to sustain our own? Even a dog or a tiger has Buddha nature. Rabbits, birds, turtles – all are potential Buddhas. How can we kill and eat potential and future Buddhas? Living on the flesh of others cuts our seed of compassion. Do we really want to cause fear, pain, suffering and death, in order to satisfy a taste desire that vanishes as soon as it goes beyond our tongues?

As we – and all creatures – may have been each other's mothers, fathers, brothers, sisters, husbands, wives, sons and daughters, for countless lifetimes, how can we feast upon our past relatives? As we must maintain the body in order to realize our 'pure mind', vegetables, fruit and grains can supply our needs, and even for these we can feel deep gratitude. Give your seed of compassion a chance to sprout and grow by living in as harmless a manner as possible. You will begin to experience something wonderful – a oneness with all life!

The Source

EMANUEL SWEDENBORG, 1688–1772

A relation to man in each and all things of the animal kingdom is plain from these considerations: Animals of every kind have limbs by which they move, organs by which they feel and viscera by which these are put in motion. These they have in common with man. They have also appetites and affections similar to those natural to man. At birth they have knowledge corresponding to their affections, in some of which appears something like the spiritual. This is more or less plain to the eye in the case of beasts, birds, bees, silkworm, ants, etc. From these facts it is that altogether natural men assert that living creatures of this kingdom are like them, apart from speech.

Angelic Wisdom Concerning The Divine Love and The Divine Wisdom (short title: *Divine Love and Wisdom*), trans. from Latin by H. Goyder Smith from the author's original edition published Amsterdam 1763.

Eating the flesh of animals, considered in itself, is
somewhat profane; for in the most ancient times they
never ate the flesh of any beast or bird, but only grain ...
especially bread made of wheat ... the fruits of trees,
vegetables, milks and such things as are made from them,
as butter, etc. To kill animals and eat their flesh was to
them unlawful, being regarded as something bestial.
They only took from them uses and services, as is evident
from Genesis I, 29–30. But in the course of time, when
mankind became cruel like wild beasts, yea, more cruel,
then first they began to kill animals and eat their flesh.
And because man had acquired such a nature, the killing
and eating of animals was permitted and is permitted at
the present day.

Heavenly Arcana

J.M. SYNGE, 1871–1909

Today when I went down to the slip I found a pig-jobber
from Kilronan with about twenty pigs that were to be
shipped for the English market.

When the steamer was getting near, the whole drove
was moved down on the slip and the curraghs were
carried out close to the sea. Then each beast was caught
in its turn and thrown on its side, while its legs were
hitched together in a single knot, with a tag of rope
remaining, by which it could be carried.

Probably the pain inflicted was not great, yet the
animals shut their eyes and shrieked with almost human
intonations, till the suggestion of the noise became so
intense that the men and women who were merely
looking on grew wild with excitement, and the pigs
waiting their turn foamed at the mouth and tore each
other with their teeth.

After a while there was a pause. The whole slip was covered with a mass of sobbing animals, with here and there a terrified woman crouching among the bodies, and patting some special favourite to keep it quiet while the curraghs were being launched.

Then the screaming began again while the pigs were carried out and laid in their places, with a waistcoat tied round their feet to keep them from damaging the canvas. They seemed to know where they were going, and looked up at me over the gunwale with an ignoble desperation that made me shudder to think that I had eaten of this whimpering flesh. When the last curragh went out I was left on the slip with a band of women and children, and one old boar who sat looking out over the sea.

The Aran Islands

DR ALBERT SZENT-GYORGYI, 1893–1986

The desire to alleviate suffering is of small value in research – such a person should be advised to work for a charity. Research wants egotists, damn egotists, who seek their own pleasure and satisfaction, but find it in solving the puzzles of nature.

Lancet, 1961

GLADYS TABER, 1899–

My own species, unfortunately, is the greatest predator on the planet. We have the distinction of killing our own kind as well as other living creatures. But mankind is relatively new and may develop beyond this in time.

... when people reach out to relate to animals, life is richer for both ... Shooting or trapping may give a momentary sense of triumph – man the powerful. But the limp body is only another victim; no more experience can come of it. Life has more to give than death.

Conversations with Amber

ROBERT LAWSON TAIT, FRCS, 1845–1899

Admitting the so-called lower animals are part of ourselves, in being of one scheme and differing from us only in degree, no matter how they be considered, is to admit they have equal rights. These rights are in no case to be hastily and unfairly set aside, but should be all the more tenderly dealt with ...

The Uselessness of Vivisection as a Method of Scientific Research,
a paper read before the Birmingham Philosophical Society,
20 April 1882

Some day I shall have a tombstone put over me and an inscription upon it. I want only one thing recorded on it, and that to the effect that 'he laboured to divert his profession from the blundering which has resulted from the performance of experiments on the sub-human groups of animal life, in the hope that they would shed light on the aberrant physiology of the human groups'. Such experiments never have succeeded, and never can, and they have, as in the cases of Koch, Pasteur and Lister, not only hindered true progress, but have covered our profession with ridicule.

Letter in the *Medical Press and Circular*, 10 May 1899

TAOISM

Mr T'ien, of the State of Ch'i, was holding an ancestral banquet in his hall, to which a thousand guests had been invited. As he sat in their midst, many came up to him with presents of fish and game. Eyeing them approvingly, he exclaimed with unction: 'How generous is Heaven to man! Heaven makes the five kinds of grain to grow, and brings forth the finny and the feathered tribes, especially for our benefit.' All Mr T'ien's guests applauded this sentiment to the echo, except the twelve-year-old son of a Mr Pao who, regardless of seniority, came forward and said: 'It is not as my Lord says. The ten thousand creatures [in the universe] and we ourselves belong to the same category, that of living things, and in this category there is nothing noble and nothing mean. It is only by reason of size, strength, or cunning, that one particular species gains the mastery over another, or that one feeds upon another. None is produced in order to subserve the uses of others. Man catches and eats those that are fit for [his] food, but how [could it be maintained that] Heaven produced them just for him? Mosquitoes and gnats suck [blood through] his skin; tigers and wolves devour his flesh – but we do not therefore assert that Heaven produced man for the benefit of mosquitoes and gnats, or to provide food for tigers and wolves.'

Taoist Teachings from the Book of Lieh Tzu, trans. R. Wilhelm

CHARLES BELL TAYLOR, MD, FRCS, 1830–1909

The public would not tolerate vivisection for a day if they did not believe that the animals were rendered insensible, and the plain fact is that they are not rendered insensible ... It is the public who are anaesthetized – it must be so, for in many experiments, to render the animal insensible would be to defeat the object of the operator ...

Never mind what physiologists say, as Ouida has

remarked, the arrogance, the conceit, the sophisms of the so-called scientists of today are as like the arrogance, the conceit, and the sophisms of the Bidas and Torquemadas of old, as the Physiological Laboratory is like the Torture Chamber of the Inquisition. We have got rid of one, and we shall get rid of the other. Meantime, never let it be said that we as a profession were on the side of wrong, of cruelty, of injustice and oppression. The main task of civilization has ever been the vindication of the rights of the weak. Animals have rights (so much is conceded by our laws), and men have duties towards them; and for us to ignore the one, or counsel neglect of the other, is simply to proclaim ourselves enemies of the human race and foes to its destined progress.

If anything could exceed the hideous cruelty of the whole business, it would be the childish absurdity of the claims to benefit which are being constantly put forth by the advocates and promoters of the system ... No good ever came out of vivisection since the world began; and, in my humble opinion, no good ever can.

From an address, 'Vivisection: Is it Justifiable?'
Nottingham, 16 November 1892

D.M. THOMAS, 1935–

Sun Valley*

It was the first time they had seen the light,
    and gazing, they were too dazed by the sun's
    radiance to murmur when their legs were caught

from under them: with a clean snap of bones
    as they were lifted out, reminding me
    of Yule feasts, or the faint click of a stone's

---

* Allegedly the largest chicken factory in Europe

fall down a chasm. One, that had dropped free,
   was frightened by a ground so fathomless;
   its wings flapped and its legs flopped uselessly.

More fathomless to my vision was the place
   where they were hung up on the hooks that bore
   them swiftly onwards, upside-down in space;

the cause I know not, but all as they hung there
   let fall a rain of excrement, whence came
   the gross miasma everyone must bear.

How weak are words, and how unfit to frame
   my concept – which lags after what was shown
   so far, it flatters it to call it lame!

And it might be ten thousand fowl or one
   went smoothly past the imperceptible
   electric impulse where they had begun

their afterlife, wings fluttering the while;
   and even after they had been thrust through
   the cutter, headless they were fluttering still.

But swiftly after that their power to move
   compassion vanished – as when, journeying far
   down through Inferno, one's own power to love

Vanishes like the sun and the other stars.

EDWARD THOMAS, 1878–1917
Suddenly a pheasant is hurled out of a neighbouring
copse: something crosses the road: and out over a large

and shining meadow goes a fox, tall and red, going easily as if he sailed in the wind. He crosses that meadow, then another, and he is half a mile away before a loud halloo sounds in the third field, and a mile away before the first hound crosses the road upon his scent.

Run hard, hounds, and drown the jackdaws' calling with their concerted voices. It is good to see your long swift train across the meadow and away, away; on such a day a man would give everything to run like that. Run hard, fox, and may you escape, for it would not be well to die on such a day, unless you could perchance first set your teeth into the throats of the foolish ones who now break through the hedge on great horses and pursue you – I know not why – ignorant of the command that has gone forth from the heart of this high blue heaven, 'Be beautiful, and enjoy and live!'

The Heart of England

KEITH THOMAS, 1933–

By the late seventeenth century the anthropocentric tradition itself was being eroded. The explicit acceptance of the view that the world does not exist for man alone can be fairly regarded as one of the great revolutions in modern Western thought, though it is one to which historians have scarcely done justice.

Man and the Natural World

But the most powerful argument for the Cartesian position was that it was the best possible rationalization for the way man actually treated animals. The alternative view had left room for human guilt by conceding that animals could and did suffer; and it aroused worries about the motives of a God who could allow beasts to undergo undeserved miseries on such a scale. Cartesianism, by contrast, absolved God from the charge of unjustly causing pain to innocent beasts by permitting humans to ill-treat them; it also justified the ascendancy of men, by freeing them, as Descartes put it, from 'any suspicion of crime however often they may eat or kill animals'. By denying the immortality of beasts, it removed any lingering doubts about the human right to exploit the brute creation. For, as the Cartesians observed, if animals really had an immortal element, the liberties men took with them would be impossible to justify; and to concede that animals had sensation was to make human behaviour seem intolerably cruel. The suggestion that a beast could feel or possess an immaterial soul, commented John Locke, had so worried some men that they 'had rather thought fit to conclude all beasts perfect machines rather than allow their souls immortality'. Descartes's explicit aim had been to make men 'lords and possessors of nature'. It fitted in well with his intention that he should have portrayed other species as inert and lacking any spiritual dimension. In so doing he created an absolute break between man and the rest of nature, thus clearing the way very satisfactorily for the uninhibited exercise of human rule.

Ibid.

The embarrassment about meat-eating thus provides a final example of the way in which, by the end of the eighteenth century, a growing number of people had come to find man's ascendancy over nature increasingly abhorrent to their moral and aesthetic sensibilities. This was the human dilemma: how to reconcile the physical requirements of civilization with the new feelings and values which that same civilization had generated. It is too often assumed that sensibilities and morals are mere ideology: a convenient rationalization of the world as it is. But in the early modern period the truth was almost the reverse, for, by an inexorable logic, there had gradually emerged attitudes to the natural world which were essentially incompatible with the direction in which English society was moving. The growth of towns had led to a new longing for the countryside. The progress of cultivation had fostered a taste for weeds, mountains and unsubdued nature. The new-found security from wild animals had generated an increasing concern to protect birds and preserve wild creatures in their natural state. Economic independence of animal power and urban isolation from animal farming had nourished emotional attitudes which were hard, if not impossible, to reconcile with the exploitation of animals by which most people lived. Henceforth an increasingly sentimental view of animals as pets and objects of contemplation would jostle uneasily alongside the harsh facts of a world in which the elimination of 'pests' and the breeding of animals for slaughter grew every day more efficient. Oliver Goldsmith wrote of his contemporaries that 'they pity and they eat the objects of their compassion'. The same might be said of the children of today who, nourished by a meat diet and protected by a medicine developed by animal experiments, nevertheless take toy animals to bed and lavish their affection on lambs and ponies. For adults, nature parks and conservation areas serve a function not unlike that which toy animals have for children; they are fantasies which enshrine the values by which society as a whole cannot afford to live.

Ibid.

As [G.M.] Trevelyan implies [*Must England's Beauty Perish?*], it was not for the sake of the creatures themselves, but for the sake of men, that birds and animals would be protected in sanctuaries and wild-life parks. In 1969 the United Nations and the International Union for the Conservation of Nature defined 'conservation' as 'the rational use of the environment to achieve the highest quality of living for mankind' ...

There was thus a growing conflict between the new sensibilities and the material foundations of human society. A mixture of compromise and concealment has so far prevented this conflict from having to be fully resolved. But the issue cannot be completely evaded and it can be relied upon to recur. It is one of the contradictions upon which modern civilization may be said to rest. About its ultimate consequences we can only speculate.

Ibid.

DOROTHY THOMPSON, 1894–1961

Among psychopaths the most readily observable trait is lack of sympathy and affection. Sight of pain and suffering does not move them. Anything, whatever, therefore, that develops callousness to the sufferings of others during childhood and adolescence is psychologically injurious. Callousness is not a symbol for bravery; if it were, criminals would make the best soldiers, instead of being immediately classified as unfit for service.

Ladies' Home Journal, February 1960

The case histories of delinquents of brutal and homicidal tendencies often reveal that cruelties and brutalities were first performed on dogs, cats or other animals.

This spiritual universe is responsive to feelings rather than intellect. The unfeeling man, no matter how brilliant, is a thoroughly sick soul. And I submit that in education of children and adolescent youth, nothing should enter the curriculum that tends to produce unfeeling callousness.

Ibid.

EDWARD THOMPSON, 1886–1946

To my mind we'll no get a decent God that's guid and fair-minded to fash himself to make wars and slaughter to cease so long as he sees we think pain to ourselves verra, verra hard, and pain to helpless ither creatures something we can inflict and think no mair about.

Burmese Silver

SIR HENRY THOMPSON, FRCS, MB, 1820–1904

It is a vulgar error to regard meat in any form as necessary to life. All that is necessary to the human body can be supplied by the vegetable kingdom ... The vegetarian can extract from his food all the principles necessary for the growth and support of the body, as well as for the production of heat and force. It must be admitted as a fact beyond all question that some persons are stronger and more healthy who live on that food. I know how much of the prevailing meat diet is not merely a wasteful extravagance, but a source of serious evil to the consumer.

Diet in Relation to Age and Activity

... flesh-eating ... appears to be by no means a natural taste with the young. Few children like that part of the meal which consists of meat, but prefer the pudding, and fruit, or the vegetables, if well-dressed, which unhappily is not often the case. Many children manifest great repugnance to meat at first, and are coaxed and even scolded by anxious mothers until the habit of eating it is acquired. Adopting the insular creed, which regards beef and mutton as necessary to health, the mother suffers from groundless forebodings about the future of a child who rejects flesh, and manifests what is regarded as an unfortunate partiality for bread and butter and pudding.

Nevertheless, I am satisfied, if the children followed their own instincts in this matter, the result would be a gain in more ways than one. Certainly if meat did not appear in the nursery until the children sent for it, it would rarely be seen there, and the young ones would thrive better on milk and eggs, with the varied produce of the vegetable kingdom.

Ibid.

I have been compelled by facts to accept the conclusion that more physical evil accrues to man from erroneous habits of diet than from even alcoholic drink. I suspect this also to be the case with moral evil.

Ibid.

JAMES THOMSON, 1700–1748

From *The Seasons*

… The wolf, who from the nightly fold
Fierce drags the bleating prey, ne'er drunk her milk,
Nor wore her warming fleece: nor has the steer,
At whose strong chest the deadly tiger hangs,
E'er ploughed for him. They too are temper'd high,
With hunger stung and wild necessity;
Nor lodges pity in their shaggy breast.
But man, whom nature form'd of milder clay,
With every kind emotion in his heart,
And taught alone to weep; while from her lap
She pours ten thousand delicacies, herbs,
And fruits, as numerous as the drops of rain
Or beams that give them birth; shall he, fair form,
Who wears sweet smiles, and looks erect on Heaven,
E'er stoop to mingle with the prowling herd,
And dip his tongue in gore?

Poor is the triumph o'er the timid hare!
Scar'd from the corn, and now to some lone seat
Retir'd: the rushy fen; the ragged furze,
Stretch'd o'er the stony heath; the stubble chapt;
The thistly lawn; the thick-entangled broom;
Of the same friendly hue, the withered fern;
The fallow ground laid open to the sun,
Concoctive; and the nodding sandy bank,
Hung o'er the mazes of the mountain brook.
  Vain is her best precaution; tho' she sits
Conceal'd, with folded ears; unsleeping eyes,
By Nature made to take th'horizon in;
And head couch'd close betwixt her hairy feet
In act to spring away. The scented dew
Betrays her early labyrinth; and deep,
In scattered, sullen openings, far behind,
With every breeze she hears the coming storm.
But nearer, and more frequent, as it loads
The sighing gale, she springs amaz'd, and all
The savage soul of game is up at once;
The pack full opening, various; the shrill horn
Resounding from the hills; the neighing steed,
Wild for the chase; and the loud hunter's shout;
O'er a weak, harmless, flying creature, all
Mix'd in mad tumult, and discordant joy.

The stag too, singled from the herd, where long
He rang'd, the branching monarch of the shades,
Before the tempest drives. At first, in speed
He, sprightly, puts his faith; and, rous'd by fear,
Gives all his swift aerial soul to flight …

He bursts the thickets, glances through the glades,
And plunges deep into the wildest wood;
If slow, yet sure, adhesive to the track
Hot-steaming, up behind him come again
Th'inhuman rout, and from the shady depth
Expel him circling thro' his very shift.
He sweeps the forest oft, and sobbing sees
The glades, mild opening to the golden day;
Where, in kind contest with his butting friends
He wont to struggle, or his loves enjoy.
Oft in the full descending flood he tries
To lose the scent, and lave his burning sides;
Oft seeks the herd; the watchful herd, alarm'd
With selfish care avoid a brother's woe.
What shall he do? His once so vivid nerves,
So full of buoyant spirit, now no more
Inspire the course; but fainting breathless toil,
Sick, seizes on his heart; he stands at bay
And puts his last weak refuge in despair.
The big round tears run down his dappled face;
He groans in anguish; while the growling pack
Blood-happy, hang at his fair jutting chest,
And mark his beauteous chequered sides with gore.

SIR J. ARTHUR THOMSON, MA, LLD, 1861–1933

It must be kept clearly in view that the mental aspect in animal life is not restricted to control of activities and the like; it may manifest itself in feelings, in concrete purposes, in music and artistry.

The Minds of Animals

HENRY D. THOREAU, 1817–1862

I have found repeatedly, of late years, that I cannot fish without falling a little in self-respect. I have tried it again

535

and again. I have skill at it, and, like many of my fellows, a certain instinct for it, which revives from time to time, but always when I have done I feel it would have been better if I had not fished. I think that I do not mistake. It is a faint intimation, yet so are the first streaks of morning.

Walden

The practical objection to animal food in my case was its uncleanness; and, besides, when I had caught, and cleaned, and cooked, and eaten my fish, they seemed not to have fed me essentially. It was insignificant and unnecessary, and cost more than it came to. A little bread or a few potatoes would have done as well, with less trouble and filth. Like many of my contemporaries, I had rarely for many years used animal food, or tea, or coffee, etc.: not so much because of any ill effects which I had traced to them, as because they were not agreeable to my imagination. The repugnance to animal food is not the effect of experience, but is an instinct. It appears more beautiful to live low and fare hard in many respects; and though I never did so, I went far enough to please my imagination. I believe that every man who has ever been earnest to preserve his higher or poetic faculties in the best condition has been particularly inclined to abstain from animal food, and from much food of any kind.

Ibid.

It may be vain to ask why the imagination will not be reconciled to flesh and fat. I am satisfied that it is not. Is it not a reproach that man is a carnivorous animal? True, he can and does live, in a great measure, by preying on other animals; but this is a miserable way – as anyone who will go to snaring rabbits, or slaughtering lambs, may learn – and he will be regarded as a benefactor of his race who shall teach man to confine himself to a more innocent and wholesome diet. Whatever my own practice may be, I have no doubt that it is a part of the destiny of the human race, in its gradual improvement, to leave off eating animals, as surely as the savage tribes have left off eating each other when they came in contact with the more civilized.

Ibid.

No humane being, past the thoughtless age of boyhood, will wantonly murder any creature which holds its life by the same tenure that he does.

Ibid.

I once had a sparrow alight on my shoulder for a moment while I was hoeing in a village garden, and I felt that I was more distinguished by that circumstance than I should have been by any epaulet I could have worn.

Ibid.

Our science, so called, is always more barren and mixed with error than our sympathies.

Familiar Letters

The squirrel that you kill in jest, dies in earnest.

Ibid.

I do not consider the other animals brutes in the common sense. I am attracted toward them undoubtedly because I never heard any nonsense from them. I have not convicted them of folly or vanity or pomposity or stupidity in dealing with me. Their vices, at any rate, do not interfere with me.

Ibid.

I have just been through the process of killing the cistudo for the sake of science; but I cannot excuse myself for this murder, and see that such actions are inconsistent with the poetic perception, however they may serve science, and will affect the quality of my observations. I pray that I may walk more innocently and serenely through nature. No reasoning whatever reconciles me to this act. It affects my day injuriously. I have lost some self-respect. I have a murderer's experience to a degree.

The Heart of Thoreau's Journals

I saw a musk-rat come out of a hole in the ice ... While I am looking at him, I am thinking what he is thinking of me. He is a different sort of man, that is all.

Journal

SURGEON-GENERAL SIR JAMES HOWARD THORNTON, KCB, BA, MB, MRCS, 1834–1919

The advocates of experiments on living creatures are continually asserting that the great majority of these experiments are almost painless inoculations – mere pinpricks – which ought not to be called vivisection. But they carefully refrain from noticing the consequences of these inoculations, so that a general impression is likely to be produced on the public that such experiments are not in any degree cruel or otherwise objectionable. This involves a suppression of the truth and a suggestion which is entirely false ... Such experiments are a very large part of the daily work done in all bacteriological institutes, and it is impossible to estimate the amount of animal suffering which is caused by them.

National Canine Defence League paper No.297

There is no doubt that vivisection is an immoral practice and can only be defended on the principle that the end justifies the means – a principle which has been used in past times for the defence and justification of all kinds of cruelty ... This principle undermines mortality itself, and opens the door to crimes of every description, all of

which can be defended if we once admit that it is right to
do evil that good may come.

The Principal Claims on Behalf of Vivisection

In my judgement, we should lose nothing worth having
by the abolition of vivisection, but were it otherwise, I am
convinced that the promotion of justice, mercy and
humanity among the human race would be well worth
the sacrifice.

The Anti-Vivisection Review, London, October 1910

TIRUVALLUVAN, 9th century

Prayer

May my soul always find fulfilment
In friendship towards all beings,
In happiness, in the goodness of men,
In compassion towards all suffering creatures.
May my feelings be neutral towards those hostile.
This is my prayer.

How can he be possessed of kindness, who to
increase his own flesh, eats the flesh of creatures?

Like the [murderous] mind of him who carries a
weapon [in his hand], the mind of him who feasts
with pleasure on the body of another [creature], has
no regard for goodness.

Is it asked what is kindness and its opposite? It is the
preservation of life, and its destruction.

Is it asked, what is the sum of all virtuous conduct? It is, never to destroy life. On the contrary, [the destruction of life] leads to every evil deed.

The chief of all [the virtues] which authors have summoned up, is to eat of food that has been shared with others, and to preserve the manifold life of other creatures.

Not to destroy life is the one [great] good; next in goodness to that is freedom from falsehood.

Is it asked what is the good way? It is the path which considers how it may avoid killing any creature.

> Aphorisms from *Tirukkural: On Non-Killing*
> (The Tirukkural was part of a Tamil poetic
> anthology of the 6th to 9th centuries)

LEO NIKOLAYEVICH TOLSTOY, 1828–1910

If a man's aspirations toward right living be serious, they will inevitably follow one definite sequence; in this sequence the first virtue a man will strive after will be self-control, self-restraint. And in seeking for self-control a man will inevitably follow one definite sequence, and in this sequence the first thing will be self-control in food-fasting. And in fasting, if he be really and seriously seeking to live a good life, the first thing from which he will abstain will always be the use of animal food, because, to say nothing of the excitation of the passions caused by such food, its use is simply immoral, as it involves the performance of an act which is contrary to moral feeling – killing; and is called forth only by greediness and the desire for tasty food ...

> *The First Step*

Not long ago I also had a talk with a retired soldier, a butcher, and he too was surprised by my assertion that it was a pity to kill, and said the usual things about its being ordained; but afterwards he agreed with me: 'Especially when they are quiet, tame cattle. They come, poor things, trusting you. It is very pitiful.'

This is dreadful! Not the suffering and death of the animals, but that man suppresses in himself, unnecessarily, the highest spiritual capacity – that of sympathy and pity toward living creatures like himself – and by violating his own feelings becomes cruel. And how deeply seated in the human heart is the injunction not to take life! But by the assertion that God ordained the slaughter of animals, and above all as a result of habit, people entirely lose their natural feeling.

Ibid.

If a man aspires towards a righteous life, his first act of abstinence is from injury to animals.

Ibid.

What I think about vivisection is that if people admit that they have the right to take or endanger the life of living beings for the benefit of many, there will be no limit for their cruelty.

Letter to Mrs C.P. Farrell, July 1909

The Vegetarian movement ought to fill with gladness the souls of those who have at heart the realization of God's kingdom upon earth, not because Vegetarianism itself is such an important step towards the realization of this kingdom (all real steps are equally important or unimportant), but because it serves as a criterion by which we know that the pursuit of moral perfection on the part of man is genuine and sincere.

News Review, 1892

A man can live and be healthy without killing animals for food; therefore, if he eats meat, he participates in taking animal life merely for the sake of his appetite. And to act so is immoral.

On Civil Disobedience

CHRISTINE TOWNEND, 1944–

There should not be one set of morals for farm animals, and a different superior set for animals which are sharing our living quarters, and our daily activities. When it is recognized that the animals we eat have the same sort of needs and feelings as the animals we use for amusement and companionship, then a big step forward will have been taken, and people will find it as repugnant to eat a sheep as to eat their pet puppy.

Pulling the Wool

Sheep are treated as walking wool bales, rather than as sentient, feeling individuals. The Bureau of Rural Economics figures tell us that out of a flock of 151.4 million sheep in 1988, approximately 7.8 million sheep and 11.4 million lambs died 'on the farm'.

They died from lack of nutrition, from lack of proper veterinary care and from lack of shelter. They died because managers did not have the time to get off their horses as they rode past. One Department of Agriculture study showed that in the month following shearing alone, one million sheep died from exposure due to lack of shelter.

If I had to say what is wrong with agriculture, I would not say it is because one million sheep die in the month following shearing. It is not because something like 6 per cent of the national flock die on the farm from lack of proper attention. It is not because one in every four or five lambs that are born dies. It is not even because there are 100 million stock mutilations performed without any anaesthetic. It is because there is no love. There is no love of the soil, which is beaten and flattened and stained and poisoned. There is no love of the trees, which are felled and burnt. And there is no love of the animals.

Taken from a speech on the wool industry given
to a WSPA conference in Melbourne in 1987

SIR GEORGE TREVELYAN, 1906–

The whole of evolution is a lifting of the levels of consciousness ... But ... in our time human beings are appearing with acutely developed intellect and powerful will and ego drive, but with no heart to hold the balance. These are the horrible creatures who can torture their fellow men in concentration camps, or the animals in the vivisection laboratory. Here we sense a soul drive towards coarsening of human feeling and destruction of tenderness, brutalizing the human species.

So let us return to the concept of Oneness and acknowledge now that such use of will and intelligence for cruelty is dragging down the whole human race ... We are each part of the whole and are all tarnished by the dark impulses which flow through our world ...

... mankind is loading upon itself a karmic debt of enormous weight and proportions by its collective treatment of the animal kingdom. Much of this cruelty, as in the blood sports, may be due to sheer lack of thought or rudimentary imagination. We all share the responsibility and the degrading effects of cruelty. Ours is a violent society in which greed and desire lead to rivalry, hate, fear and finally war as an accepted way of gaining our ends. The constant stressing of violence and cruelty by the media impregnates it ever deeper into the human psyche. The redemption of mankind turns on individual and collective acceptance of an impulse to greater compassion, a 'gentling' of human nature. And this impulse is very apparent in our generation and, it may be, brings with it a power which can transform and cleanse our world ...

... the task of becoming human is gradually to transmute the brutalizing and violent impulses.

Operation Redemption

RALPH WALDO TRINE, 1866–1958

Let them [children] be taught to have pity for the aimals that are at our mercy, that cannot protect themselves, that cannot explain their weakness, their pain or their suffering. Soon this will bring to their attention that higher law, the moral obligation of man as a superior being to protect and care for the weak and defenceless. Nor will it stop there, for this in turn will lead them to the highest law – man's duty to man.

Every Living Creature

The Golden Rule must be applied in our relations with the animal world, just as it must be applied in our relations with our fellow men, and no one can be a Christian until this finds embodiment in his or her life.

Ibid.

The strongest and noblest types of men and women are never devoid of this tender, humane sympathy, which is ever quick to manifest itself in kindness and care for the innocent creatures.

'If I were an Educator', reprinted *Voice of the Voiceless*, June 1978

PRINCE PAUL TROUBETZKOY, 1866–1938

As I cannot kill, I cannot authorize others to kill. Do you see? If you are buying from a butcher you are authorizing him to kill – to kill helpless, dumb creatures which neither you nor I could kill ourselves.

A 'Morning Leader' interview, reported in
Vegetarian Messenger, 1907

THOMAS TRYON, 1634–1703

Refrain at all times from such Foods as cannot be procured without violence and oppression. For know that all the inferior Creatures when hurt do cry and send forth their complaints to their Maker or grand Fountain whence they proceeded. Be not insensible that every Creature doth bear the Image of the great Creator according to the Nature of each, and that He is the Vital Power in all things. Therefore let none take pleasure to offer violence to that life, lest he awaken the fierce wrath and bring danger to his own soul.

Wisdom's Dictates

The inferior creatures groan under your cruelties. You hunt them for your pleasure, and overwork them for your covetousness, and kill them for your gluttony, and set them to fight one with another till they die, and count it a sport and a pleasure to behold them worry one another.

*Friendly Advice to the Gentlemen-Planters
of the East and West Indies*

TU FU, 712–770

I see shining fish struggling within tight nets, while I hear orioles singing carefree tunes. Even trivial creatures know the difference between freedom and bondage. Sympathy and compassion should be but natural to the human heart.

Hsin yüeh-fu shih

AGNES SLIGH TURNBULL, 1888–1979

Dogs' lives are too short. Their only fault, really.

The Flowering

CHARLES TENNYSON TURNER, 1808–1879

On Shooting a Swallow in Early Youth

I hoard a little spring of secret tears
For thee, poor bird; thy death-blow was my crime:
From the far past it has flow'd on for years;
It never dries; it brims at swallow-time.
No kindly voice within me took thy part,
Till I stood o'er thy last faint flutterings;
Since then, methinks, I have a gentler heart,
And gaze with pity on all wounded things.
Full oft the vision of thy fallen head,
Twittering in highway dust, appeals to me;
Thy helpless form, as when I struck thee dead,
Drops out from every swallow-flight I see.
I would not have thine airy spirit laid,
I seem to love the little ghost I made.

Julius Caesar and the Honey-bee

Poring on Caesar's death with earnest eye,
I heard a fretful buzzing in the pane:
'Poor-bee!' I cried, 'I'll help thee by-and-by;'
Then dropp'd mine eyes upon the page again.
Alas! I did not rise; I help'd him not:
In the great voice of Roman history
I lost the pleading of the window-bee,
And all his woes and troubles were forgot.
In pity for the mighty chief, who bled

Beside his rival's statue, I delay'd
To serve the little insect's present need;
And so he died for lack of human aid.
I could not change the Roman's destiny;
I might have set the honey-maker free.

On Finding a Small Fly Crushed in a Book

Some hand, that never meant to do thee hurt,
Has crush'd thee here between these pages pent;
But thou has left thine own fair monument,
The wings gleam out and tell me what thou wert:
Oh! that the memories, which survive us here,
Were half as lovely as these wings of thine!
Pure relics of a blameless life, that shine
Now thou art gone. Our doom is ever near;
The peril is beside us day by day;
The book will close upon us, it may be,
Just as we lift ourselves to soar away
Upon the summer airs. But, unlike thee,
The closing book may stop our vital breath,
Yet leave no lustre on our page of death.

E.S. TURNER, 1909–

In our attitudes to animals we are hopelessly, perversely inconsistent. There have been fox-hunters who revolted at the idea of performing animals. Game shots who litter the ground with cripples denounce deer-hunters as barbarians. Old ladies assault men who try to kill pigeons, but keep cats which destroy birds. Women wearing 'cruel furs' used to criticize women who wore 'cruel feathers'. People send cheques to the RSPCA and next day eat *pâté de foie gras*, which the Society begs them not to do. All of us applaud the trouble taken to tranquillize and lift hippos from the sites of dams, but none of us cares

whether rats are killed humanely or cruelly. Nobody has
ever started a Society for the Prevention of Cruelty to
Fish. The law is riddled with illogicality. A dogs' home is
awarded damages against an author who said that its
dogs were sent for scientific experiments; yet experimentation is not only legal but, in some contexts, compulsory.
In a sentimental moment the law exempted stray dogs
from being sent to the laboratory, while leaving the
householders free to sell their unwanted pets for this
purpose. A clergyman has to pay damages for saying that
a fox was dug out and thrown live to the hounds, but if
the hounds catch a live fox and kill it, well, that is the
purpose of hunting.

... The sporting Englishman refuses to worry
over-much about these things. 'This amiable man', wrote
Miss Victoria Sackville-West, 'to whom organized cruelty
would be abhorrent should he once recognize it as such,
is enabled by his peculiar national and racial capacity for
the avoidance of lucid thinking to esteem himself rather a
fine fellow under cover of that good totem name of
sportsman.'

All Heaven in a Rage

The Renaissance brought a quickening of men's minds
but no immediate quickening of their compassion. Old
superstitions were replaced by new. The humanists, who
saw man as the measure of all things, had as little charity
for the animal kingdom as had the theologians. Reviving
science picked on animals as something to be carved and
taken apart, in search of the secret of life. Only the
feeblest flame of humanitarianism stirred in the cold
wind of humanism.

Ibid.

The Enquiring Child

'Daddy, tell me why they drip
Acid on that puppy's lip,
Also in that monkey's eye.
Tell me, Daddy, why oh why?'
'Hush, my little son, be brave –
They are testing after-shave.'

MARGARET WHEATON TUTTLE, 1909–

To understand fully the concepts of the world of animal research, one must understand that to researchers, humans are more important than animals. The acquisition of knowledge is of paramount importance. Scientific search transcends morality. The noble end justifies the hideous means. And what the public doesn't know, doesn't hurt them.

Over the whole earth, there is one subject on which all sane people agree: cruelty to children is an abomination. How could there be such a cleavage between the agreement regarding cruelty to children, and the disagreement regarding cruelty to animals?

They (animals) have brains and hearts and feelings! And they're used like metal, to be bent and twisted, like canvas to be cut and stitched. And because they can't defend themselves, nobody seems to care!

The Crimson Cage

'Some-a these researchers swear animals don't feel pain. Feature that one! But seeing as most animals hear better than you or me, and smell better, how about feel better?

'What do you do with the animals that get forgotten? Live and die in a cage when everyone thinks someone else is using 'em? What do you do when the paperwork, based on a buncha animals, gets mixed up, lost, thrown out? What do you do with the experiment that's been done over and over, but along comes someone else who does it over again? They got such a big thing going, I'm telling you, they don't know who's done what.

'Know what Clare Boothe Luce called vivisection laboratories? The Buchenwalds, Auschwitzes and Dachaus of the animal world. And it's the truth, believe me ... It's just big business and the animal is so much waste-paper.'

Ibid.

MARK TWAIN, 1835–1910

In studying the traits and dispositions of the so-called lower animals, and contrasting them with man's, I find the result humiliating to me.

Man is the only animal that blushes, or needs to.

Following the Equator

The vast majority of the race, whether savage or civilized, are secretly kind-hearted and shrink from inflicting pain, but in the presence of the aggressive and pitiless minority they don't dare to assert themselves ... Some day a handful will rise up on the other side and make the most noise ... perhaps even a single daring man with a big voice and determined front will do it ... and in a week all the sheep will wheel and follow him and witch-hunting will come to a sudden end.

The Mysterious Stranger

It is just like man's vanity and impertinence to call an animal dumb because it is dumb to his dull perceptions.

What is Man?

Heaven is by favour; if it were by merit your dog would go in and you would stay out.

Ibid.

I believe I am not interested to know whether vivisection produces results that are profitable to the human race or doesn't. To know that the results are profitable to the race would not remove my hostility to it. THE PAIN WHICH IT INFLICTS UPON UNCONSENTING ANIMALS is the basis of my enmity toward it, and it is to me sufficient justification of the enmity without looking further.

Ibid.

Of all the creatures ever made he (man) is the most detestable. Of the entire brood, he is the only one ... that possesses malice. He is the only creature that inflicts pain for sport, knowing it to be pain.

Autobiography

The fact that man knows right from wrong proves his *intellectual* superiority to the other creatures; but the fact that he can *do* wrong proves his *moral* inferiority to any creature that cannot.

What is man?

Loyalty to petrified opinion never yet broke a chain or freed a human soul.

Inscription beneath his bust in the Hall of Fame

JOHN UPDIKE, 1932–

I'm somewhat shy about the brutal facts of being a carnivore. I don't like meat to look like animals. I prefer it in the form of sausages, hamburger and meat loaf, far removed from the living thing.

Interview for the New York Times News Service, 1982

DR ROBERT VAN CITTERS, 1926–

I think I would be remiss if I did not express my concern over the absence of sensitivity for the welfare of experimental animals which has been shown by the animal research community.

Painful Experiments Upon Animals

SRI T.L. VASWANI, 1879–1966

I regard all life as sacred, and it seems to me that in ethics we are concerned not alone with mankind but also with animals. The ethical ideal as I understand it is: help all life; have sympathy with all life; avoid injuring anything living ...

I believe all education is defective which does not teach sympathy with birds and beasts. I believe, too, that without teaching our students to do their best for God's creatures, all efforts at character-building must fail. In training your children in acts of kindness to animals, you teach them effectively the one great lesson of life: 'Be ye kind to one another!'

The Vegetarian Way, XXIV World Vegetarian Congress, 1977

To defend the weak, to guard those that are below us in the scale of evolution, is to grow in the nobility and strength of life.

The beast and the bird cannot speak to us in the language we understand; they cannot protect themselves; for centuries they have suffered for our sins against them.

The Blessed Buddha said: 'When wisdom came to me, I resolved to defend the weak, and to all living things I gave the compassion of my heart.'

... with wisdom grows *Maitri* or the feeling of kinship with all life, and *Maitri* (compassion) will be the basis of a new morality, a new culture, and new civilization in the coming days.

From 'Fruit Gatherings' in *Steps Unto Him*, March 1963

The nations are wandering, today, in a 'jungle' of 'civilization'. The nations love the violent. They trample upon the great vision of the One-Life-in-all. Modern civilization is baptized in blood. Even India is forgetting her ancient vision of reverence for life.

The soul of India has never countenanced the killing of creatures. When the great scriptures of India speak of 'yagna', they refer to 'internal sacrifice', the sacrifice of the senses and egotistic self-speaking impulse, the sacrifice of the animal within us.

'Let us be modern,' said an 'educated' man to me. Are we modern, I ask, when we torture the animals and shoot the birds? Wilberforce was a modern of moderns, and he said: 'The horrors of slaughterhouses, cattle trucks, and transport steamers confound and sicken us. I suppose, if we really knew a hundredth part of the agony, we should rather starve than profit by it.'

I have heard 'educated' Indians speak, echoing the words of some western books, of 'humane' slaughter! As well might we speak of 'humane' murder! Stop all slaughter!

Modern civilization has gone astray, for it thinks from the head, not the heart. If, indeed, life is one, is not the animal, too, my brother? And am I not his keeper?

Again and again, I have felt within me that when the life of man becomes purer, and nobler, will not man realize that he must have reverence for life, for all forms of life? And growing daily in reverence, must I not grow in the thought that my life is linked up with all life, and the life of bird and beast is linked with me? Must I not grow in sympathy and helpfulness, in devotion and love? And must I not in this sympathy and love, receive the call to union with the Divine Will that is the creative will of the cosmos!

Steps Unto Him, March 1965

The world is waiting to listen to simple things and simple men. Humanitarianism stands for the gospel of simple life and the spirit of creative sympathy. Humanitarianism is inspired by an intuition of the kinship of all sentient life, a vision of the fellowship and brotherhood of life.

All Life is Sacred

THORSTEIN VEBLEN, 1857–1929

Sportsmen ... are more or less in the habit of assigning a love of nature, the need of recreation and the like, as the incentives for their favourite pastime ... These ostensible needs could be more readily and fully satisfied without the accompaniment of a systematic effort to take the life of those creatures that make up an essential feature of that 'nature' that is beloved by the sportsman. It is, indeed, the most noticeable effect of the sportsman's activity to keep nature in a state of chronic desolation by killing off all the living things whose destruction he can encompass.

Theory of the Leisure Class

VIKENTY VERESSAYEV (Vikentii Vikentevich Smidovich), 1867–1945

We ought not to ridicule the pretensions of the anti-vivisectionists – the sufferings of animals are truly horrible; and sympathy with them is not sentimentality.

The Memoirs of a Physician, trans. Simeon Linden

QUEEN VICTORIA, 1819–1901

The Queen has done all she could on the dreadful subject of vivisection, and hopes that Mr Gladstone will speak strongly against a practice which is a disgrace to humanity and Christianity.

Letter to Mr Gladstone, 1881

The Queen hears and reads with horror of the sufferings which the brute creation often undergo from the thoughtlessness of the ignorant, and she fears also sometimes from experiments in the pursuit of science.

Letter to Lord Harrowby, 19 June 1874

There is, however, another subject on which the Queen feels *most* strongly, and that is this horrible, brutalizing, *unchristian-like vivisection*.

That poor dumb animals should be kept alive as described in this trial [of Prof. David Ferrier on 17 November 1881] is *revolting and horrible*. This *must* be stopped. Monkeys and dogs – two of the most intelligent amongst these poor animals who cannot complain ... Dogs, 'man's best friend', possessed of more than instinct, to be treated in this fearful way is *awful*. She directs Sir William Harcourt's attention *most strongly to it*.

It must really not be permitted. It is a disgrace to a civilized country.

Letter to Sir William Harcourt, then Home Secretary,
published in *Life of Sir William Harcourt*

ELIZABETH GRAY VINING, 1902–

I had been scolded one day – I felt, scolded unjustly. Hot with resentment and humiliation, I went out into the yard, my kitten in my arms. No doubt, in the grip of my emotions, I held her too tightly; she struggled to escape, digging her claws into me. My anger flared. I slapped my kitten on the head. She laid back her head and cowered in my arms. The next instant, overwhelmed with remorse, I cried over her, kissed her again and again, and at last succeeded in soothing her. I saw quite clearly what I had done: I had passed on to a small helpless creature that I loved an injury done to me. I was bitterly ashamed; for years I could not think of the incident without wincing inwardly.

... For me, religion was, in Fosdick's phrase, 'a total response to life's meaning'. I felt a firm conviction of the unity of all life, a kinship with all living things, even to the invisible busy atom, a sense that we all were made of the same stuff and moved to the same patterns, from the atoms to the universes, the macrocosm repeating the microcosm, that love and truth and goodness in a single life were interpenetrated by the infinite love and truth and goodness which we might call God.

Quiet Pilgrimage

VIVEKANANDA, 1862–1902

The highest truth is this: God is present in all beings. They are his multiple form. There is no other god to seek ... everywhere His feet, everywhere His ears. He covers everything. The first of all worships is the worship of those around us. He alone serves God who serves all other beings.

Quoted by Willand Ariel Durant in *Our Oriental Heritage*

CONSTANTIN FRANCOIS CHASSEBOEUF (Comte de Volney), 1757–1820

The habit of shedding blood, or even of seeing it shed, corrupts all sentiment of humanity.

Voyages

VOLTAIRE (Francois Marie Arouet de), 1694–1778

How pitiful, and what poverty of mind, to have said that the animals are machines deprived of understanding and feeling ...

Judge (in the same way as you would judge your own) the behaviour of a dog who has lost his master, who has searched for him in the road barking miserably, who has come back to the house restless and anxious, who has run upstairs and down, from room to room, and who has found the beloved master at last in his study, and then shown his joy by barks, bounds and caresses. There are some barbarians who will take this dog, that so greatly excels man in capacity for friendshiip, who will nail him to a table and dissect him alive, in order to show you his veins and nerves. And what you then discover in him are *all the same organs of sensation that you have in yourself.* Answer me, mechanist, has Nature arranged all the springs of feeling in this animal *to the end that he might not feel?* Has he nerves that he may be incapable of suffering?

Philosophical Dictionary

Men fed upon carnage, and drinking strong drinks, have all an impoisoned and acrid blood which drives them mad in a hundred different ways.

Ibid.

The treatise of Porphyry is addressed to one of his old disciples named Firmus, who became a Christian, it is said, to recover his liberty to eat flesh and drink wine.

He remonstrates with Firmus, that in abstaining from flesh and from strong liquors the health of the soul and the body is preserved — that one lives longer, and with more innocence. All his reflections are those of a scrupulous theologian, of a true philosopher, and of a gentle and sensitive spirit. One might believe in reading him that this great enemy of the Church is a Father of the Church. He does not speak of the metempsychosis, but he regards other animals as our brothers — because they are endowed with life as we are, because they have the same principles of life, the same feelings, the same ideas, memory, industry – as we. [Human] speech alone is wanting to them. If they had it, should we dare to kill and eat them? Should we dare to commit these fratricides? What barbarian is there, who would cause a lamb to be butchered and roasted, if that lamb conjured him, in an affecting appeal, not to be at once assassin and cannibal?

Ibid.

There is in man a disposition to compassion as generally diffused as his other instincts. Newton had cultivated this sentiment of humanity, and he extended it to the lower animals. With Locke he was strongly convinced that God has given to them a proportion of ideas, and the same feelings, which he has to us ... In truth, without humanity, a virtue which comprehends all virtues, the name of philosopher is little deserved.

Eléments de la Philosophie de Newton

It may be inferred from these and several other passages [in the Mosaic account of the alliance made between deity and men and the rest of the animal world], what all antiquity has always thought, that animals have intelligence and knowledge. The deity does not make a pact with trees and with stones, which have no feeling, but he makes it with animals whom he has endowed with feeling often more exquisite than ours, and with some ideas necessarily attached to it. This is why he will not allow [to men] the barbarity of feeding upon their blood, because, in reality, blood is the source of life, consequently of feeling ...

Traité sur la Tolérance

People must have renounced, it seems to me, all natural intelligence to dare to advance that animals are but animated machines ... It appears to me, besides, that [such people] can never have observed with attention the character of animals, not to have distinguished among them the different voices of need, of suffering, of joy, of pain, of love, of anger and of all their affections. It would be very strange that they should express so well what they could not feel ... We know neither how these organs were formed, nor how they are developed, nor how they receive life, nor by what laws, feelings, ideas, memory, will, they are attached to life. And, in this profound and eternal ignorance inherent to our nature, we dispute without ceasing, we persecute one another, like bulls who butt against each other with their horns, without knowing *why* or *how* they have horns.

Ibid.

ALEXANDER VON HUMBOLDT, 1769–1859

Cruelty to animals is one of the most characteristic vices of a base and mean people. Wherever it is to be found, it is an unmistakable sign of ignorance and callousness, which cannot be concealed by any superficial appearance of glory.

Cosmos

JOHN VYVYAN, 1908–1975

Knowledge without pity may well be the greatest danger that besets the world.

Vivisection – a social evil that advances human knowledge at the expense of human character.

The Dark Face of Science

The humane acquisition of knowledge is indispensible to a civilized society.

Science ... has established a new set of values, which amounts to the pitiless exploitation of the rest of nature for the physical benefit of man.

559

If knowledge were the highest of all values, it would be proper to apply rigorous scientific method to everything – including, of course, ourselves. The fact that we instantly make a reservation about ourselves shows that we do not consider knowledge to be the highest value.

In Pity and in Anger

By confining his morality to his own species, man has become the most immoral of all animals; and in so far as the Earth is the Great Mother, and he himself one of her children, man is a matricide. His urgent need, for his own salvation, is a conviction of this sin.

We have failed to understand ourselves and our place in nature because we have been blinded by conceit. Our virtues are real, but they are not exclusive to ourselves. In societies far older than our own, the natural activities of mating, care of the young, and group-defence had already led to an expansion of the sense of self to include others, so that the female would give her life for her young and the male would give his life for the group ... When our dogs show these qualities habitually, we call them instinctive; when we ourselves display them now and then, we call them divine. And this is absolutely typical of the instinctive arrogance of man ... man is a far more dangerous and unpredictable animal than was the extinct tyrannosaur, and may devastate the Earth by knowledge without love. The study of life without sympathy with it leads at best to a husk of learning and at worst to disastrous results. If we are to be creators and not destroyers, we need knowledge with love, taking from the one a new world-picture and from the other a new ethic.

Sketch for a World-Picture

RICHARD WAGNER, 1813–1883

Human dignity begins to assert itself only at the point where man is distinguishable from the beast by pity for it.

The Regeneration of Mankind

This teaching [of the sinfulness of murdering and living upon our fellow beings] was the result of a deep metaphysical recognition of a truth; and, if the Brahman has brought to us the consciousness of the most manifold phenomena of the living world, with it is awakened the consciousness that the sacrifice of one of our near kin is, in a manner, the slaughter of one of ourselves; that the non-human animal is separated from man only by the *degree* of its mental endowment, that it has the faculties of pleasure and of pain, has the same desire for life as the most reason-endowed portion of mankind.

Art and Religion

The thought of their sufferings penetrates with horror and dismay into my soul, and in the sympathy evoked I recognize the strongest impulse of my moral being, and also the probable source of all my art. The total abolition of the horror we fight against must be our real aim. In order to attain this our opponents, the vivisectors, must be frightened, thoroughly frightened, into seeing the people rise up against them with stocks and cudgels. Difficulties and costs must not discourage us ... If experiments on animals were abandoned on grounds of compassion, mankind would have made a fundamental advance.

Letter to Ernst von Weber, 19 October 1879

Everyone who revolts at the sight of an animal's torment, is prompted solely by compassion, and he who joins with others to protect dumb animals, is moved by naught save pity, of its very nature entirely indifferent to all calculations of utility or the reverse. But, that we have not the courage to set this motive of pity in the forefront of our appeals and admonitions to the folk, is the curse of our civilization.

'Against Vivisection', reprinted in *Selections from Three Essays by Richard Wagner* (ed. M.R.L. Freshel)

ALFRED RUSSEL WALLACE, 1823–1913

I have a fundamental disgust of vivisection for its brutalizing and immoral effects.

The moral argument against vivisection remains whether the animals suffer as much as we do or only half as much. The bad effect on the operator and on the students and spectators remains; the undoubted fact that the practice tends to produce callousness and a passion for experiment, which leads to unauthorized experiments in hospitals on unprotected patients, remains; the horrible callousness of binding the sufferers in the operating trough, so that they cannot express their pain by sound or motion, remains; their treatment after the experiment by careless attendants, brutalized by custom, remains; the argument of the uselessness of a large proportion of the experiments, repeated again and again on scores and hundreds of animals, remains; and finally, the iniquity of its use, to demonstrate already established facts to physiological students of hundreds of colleges and schools all over the world, remains.

World of Life

I have for some years come to the conclusion that nothing but total abolition will meet the case of vivisection. I am quite disgusted at the frequency of the most horrible experiments to determine the most trivial facts recorded in the publications of scientific societies month by month, evidently carried on for the interest of the 'research' and the reputation it gives.

Letter to Dr W.R. Hadwen, September 1905

DR GEORGE FREDERICK WALKER, 1896–1963

I believe vivisection, overwhelmingly on the whole, has misdirected research, misled research workers, and, by absorbing energy, money, intellect and time in the pursuit of frequently barren investigation, has incalculably delayed and impeded medical progress.

From a lecture

REVD DR WALTER WALSH, 1857–1931

Many excellent people deplore the sufferings of sentient creatures on this planet without perceiving that they themselves are morally responsible for the greater part of such sufferings ... They cling to the barbaric dietary of less civilized times ...

If those benevolent-minded people could but visualize the agonies connected with the breeding, raising, railing, shipping, driving and slaughtering of the defenceless victims of human voracity they would abhor the bloody morsel they now pick so daintily from their dinner plates.

From a lecture

ISAAK WALTON, 1593–1683

VENATOR: Gentleman Huntsman, where found you this otter?

HUNTSMAN: Marry, Sir, we found her a mile from this place ... and have given her no rest since we came; sure she will hardly escape all these dogs and men. I am to have the skin of her if we kill her ... Now we have at him with Killbuck, for he vents again.

VENATOR: Marry, so he does, for look, he vents in that corner. Now, now, Ringwood has him: now he's gone again, and has bit the poor dog. Now Sweetlips has her; hold her, Sweetlips! Now all the dogs have her, some above, some under water; but now, now, she's tired, and past losing: come, bring her to me, Sweetlips. Look, 'tis a Bitch-Otter, and she has lately whelped; let's go to the place where she has put down, and not far from it you will find all her young ones, I dare warrant you, and kill them all too.

HUNTSMAN: Come, Gentlemen! Come all! Let's go to the place where we put down the Otter. Look you, hereabouts it was that she kennelled; look you, here it was indeed, for here's her young ones, no less than five: come, let's kill them all.

The Compleat Angler

SIR WILLIAM WATSON, 1858–1935

From *Vivisection*

Thou noble hound, with thy immortal gift
Of loving whom thou servest …
If none entitled is to bind me down …
None hath a title so to ravage you.

ARTHUR WAUGH, 1866–1943

Can it be pretended that the ordinary relations between men and animals have been generally dictated by a sense of proportion, or a passion for common justice? Goldfish in a tiny bowl: a captive coon in a wooden box: a lark in a cage: pigeons in a trap: rabbits on the course: are not these poor suffering creatures the helpless victims of man's obtuse and unbalanced cruelty?

Galaxy

FRANCIS WAYLAND, 1796–1856

We are forbidden to treat [animals] unkindly on any pretence, or for any reason.

The Elements of Moral Science

BERNARD WEATHERILL, PC, MP, 1920–

I became a vegetarian as a result of seeing the famine of 1942 in Bengal.

The consumption of meat is not just a question of cruelty to animals, but of cruelty to people. It is the duty of politicians to look ahead, and the world's hungry could be fed if 10 per cent of the grain now given to animals were used for human consumption. We grow twice as much food on this planet each year as is necessary to give everyone an adequate diet, and we are obsessed with animal protein.

In Britain we spend a ridiculous £100 million a year on slimming aids to avoid the consequences of over-eating. That cannot be right. But I have a great hope for the future. There is now even a vegetarian chef in the House of Commons. I have not managed to convert my wife yet, although she never eats meat when we are alone.

It is strange. 150 years ago they abolished slavery, and I'll bet that 150 years from now people will say with horror that in 1984 they used to eat meat. The image has changed; once vegetarians all wore sandals and went looking for fairies. We really need a new name.

The Times, 2 April 1984

DENNIS WEAVER, 1924–

Man is innately a creature of love. That love is the most powerful force in the universe, and eventually – it's a very slow process – it will conquer. I think there will come a time, and this is down the road a great many years, when civilized people will look back in horror on our generation and the ones that have preceded it: the idea that we should eat other living things running around on four legs, that we should raise them just for the purpose of killing them! The people of the future will say

565

'meat-eaters!' in disgust and regard us in the same way that we regard cannibals and cannibalism.

The Vegetarians

MARY WEBB, 1881–1927

Beauty was everywhere, except in the meat market. There, slow bluebottles, swollen and unwholesome, crawled and buzzed; men of a like complexion shouted strenuously, brandishing stained carving knives; an unbearable stench arose from the offal, and women with pretty clothes and refined manners bought the guts of animals under such names as 'sweetbreads' or 'prime fat kidneys', and thrust their hands into the disembowelled bodies of rabbits to test their freshness.

The Golden Arrow

ROBERT F. WELBORN, 1919–

Early this century Gandhi said: 'If the beast had intelligent language at its command, it would state a case against mankind that would stagger humanity.' This poignantly tells us of the silent voices of the animals and asks us to consider what they would say of the subject before us. This is our duty when we deliberate in terms of the substance and life and beauty of God's creation, and we must ask – by what moral right does the human species presume to use other species in unnatural ways for mankind's physical comfort and pleasure?

I have heard these voices at night after a session of an animal care committee, the most emotionally and mentally draining experience I have ever had, except for the war. I see in my mind's eye the monkeys used for psychological experiments, separation of mother and child, forced drug addiction. I see the lonely dogs in cages, after experimental operations, craving love.

There is no moral justification for this under God. The human species brings on itself illnesses and other maladies and then, in despicable self-righteousness, uses poor innocent animals, inflicting misery for days or months or years.

I have been in slaughterhouses, kosher slaughterhouses, veal calf structures, steer-roping arenas where the poor creatures are thrown to the ground over and over again all day long, chicken factories and other places of animal abuse, sordid reflections on the human race, and I hear the voices of these animals as I see misery in their eyes.

The state of mind which is indifferent to or justifies the massive man-made suffering of animals is the state of mind that will manipulate the genes and alter the species. The rationalization is, if they bother to rationalize at all, that whatever benefits or pleases mankind is right. This is not the teaching of God's common law and it is not the teaching of compassion and reason in God's service.

From address given at the International Network for Religion and Animals' first major conference 'Respect for Life and the Environment: Ethical and Theological Aspects of Genetic Engineering and Biotechnology', held at Airlie, Virginia, 23–25 April 1988

DOROTHY WELLESLEY (Duchess of Wellington), 1889–1956

Slaughter of Seals

I know the smallest islands of the seas;
They have their Everests and Niagara Falls,
And the seal nurseries.
There laid on ledges in a flying spume
Seals lie; or suckle in blonde estuaries
Where the sea-lavenders bloom.

I know the inlets where they breed,
The mothers, like sea-worn stones and wisely grey –
Smooth stones between sharp rocks so likely drifted –
Rocks jellied with the bubbles of the weed
Rising to summer swells,
Weeds living a dancing lifetime, lowered and lifted,
Slung fine with opal and pale purple shells,
Holding the light of that deep-driven day,
Where tides ring in and out with the sea bells.

Shadowy lighted seals, small difference ours:
Seals lie on daisies, mother's milk they love.
They trust, they doze to sound of woodland dove
Among sea-poppies and the long-shore flowers.
Their lives are but a dying even as ours
Upon haphazard frontiers of life and death,
Which ever uncertain faintly discerned we see
Upon the nightfall on the boundaries wide;
When foamy beaches make a night of stars
On pebbles after-tide.

When all seems love that lives
And all the shore's a plenitude of sighs
That breathe around the Isles,
Then we may know that seals
Follow the green bubble of boat-keels,
That April puppies hurry to the bars
To leap the lamp-lit foam,
To follow the silvery bells, wide-eyed from home,
And men with clubs.

Men manage better now, being fur-wise.
They spare the skin of scars
And shoot the seals close up between the eyes;
Or stalking drowsy nurseries they lash
The awaiting mother to a rock, and flay

Her skin like some rich fruit before she dies;
Then, ripping up her stomach with one gash,
Tear out the unborn puppy where it cries,
The skins of these being jet, or golden ash.

H.G. WELLS, 1866–1946

In all the round world of Utopia there is no meat. There used to be. But now we cannot stand the thought of slaughterhouses. And in a population that is all educated and at about the same level of physical refinement, it is practically impossible to find anyone who will hew a dead ox or pig. We never settled the hygienic aspect of meat-eating at all. This other aspect decided us. I can still remember as a boy the rejoicings over the closing of the last slaughterhouse.

A Modern Utopia

DR FREDRIC WERTHAM, 1895–

Children have an inborn capacity for sympathy. But that sympathy has to be cultivated ... And it is this point that the mass media trample on. Even before the natural feelings of compassion have a chance to develop, the fascination of overpowering and hurting others is displayed in endless profusion. Before the soil is prepared for sympathy, the seeds of sadism are planted.

A Sign for Cain

JESSAMYN WEST, 1907–1984

Abel was a dog poisoner. It sometimes works out that way. A man wants to have some direct connection with life. If he can't bring life into being, he'll put an end to it.

In that way he's not completely powerless. Some men can start it. Others can end it.

You see this in hunters. The most avid hunters are grizzled old bucks who are past the age of creating. Their substitute for the thrill they've lost is another thrill; for the life they can't make, they substitute the life they can take. They can still get a gun up and put a bullet into something warm and living and see it crumple.

The Life I Really Lived

He takes great pleasure in walking among those square-headed, stiff-legged, rollicking Black Angus calves. I can't do it myself. I may not eat *them*, but I will eat their brothers. Is it sentimental to refuse to enjoy the life of those whose death you plan and whose flesh you will ingest? If I think flesh-eating wrong, why not give it up? Would I be able to touch those velvet muzzles then? I doubt it. Little Black Angus, I know where you are going. I am one of those sending you there. For this reason I don't go out with Max to look at the cattle.

Hide and Seek

BROOKE FOSS WESTCOTT, DD (Bishop of Durham), 1825–1901

If He Who made us made all the other creatures also: if they find a place in His providential plan: if His tender mercies reach to them – and this we most certainly believe – then I find it absolutely inconceivable that He should so arrange the avenues of knowledge that we can attain to truth only through the unutterable agonies of beings who trust in us. Life is more than a bundle of physical facts. Life in each distinct form is a sacred gift to be dealt with reverently ... Better than any increase in our acquaintance with phenomena, better than any fresh increase in vital force drawn for man from mutilated animals, better than a brief span possibly added to our earthly sojourn – better than all this is the pure consciousness that we have not broken down the barriers of a holy reverence, nor sought relief from our own pain by inflicting it on some weaker beings.

From a sermon preached in Westminster Abbey

EDWARD WESTERMARCK, 1862–1939

According to Brahmanism, tenderness towards all creatures is a duty incumbent upon the four castes. It is said that 'he who injures innoxious beings from a wish to give himself pleasure, never finds happiness, neither living nor dead' (*Laws of Manu*, v. 45) ... In Buddhism, Jainism and Taoism the respect for animal life is extreme. A disciple of Buddha may not knowingly deprive any creature of life, not even a worm or an ant ... The Jain is stricter still in his regard for animal life. He sweeps the ground before him as he goes, lest animate things be destroyed; he walks veiled, lest he inhale a living organism; he considers that the evening and night are not times for eating, since one might then swallow a live thing by mistake; and he rejects not only meat but even honey, together with various fruits that are supposed to contain worms, not because of his distaste for worms but because of his regard for life ... According to *Thâi-Shang*, one of the books of Taoism, a good man will feel kindly towards all creatures, and refrain from hurting even the insect tribes, grass and trees ... In the book called *Merits and Errors Scrutinized*, which enjoys great popularity in China, it is said to be meritorious to save animals from death – even insects if the number

amounts to a hundred – to relieve a brute that is greatly
wearied with work, to purchase and set at liberty animals
intended to be slaughtered. On the other hand, to
confine birds in a cage, to kill ten insects, to be unsparing
of the strength of tired animals, to disturb insects in their
holes, to destroy the nests of birds, without great reason
to kill and dress animals for food, are all errors of various
degrees. And 'to be the foremost to encourage the
slaughter of animals, or to hinder persons from setting
them at liberty', is regarded as an error of the same
magnitude as the crime of devising a person's death or of
drowning or murdering a child.

The Origin and Development of Moral Ideas

No creed in Christendom teaches kindness to animals as
a dogma of religion ... Nor is there any such allusion in
most treatises on ethics which base their teachings upon
distinctly Christian tenets.

Ibid.

EDITH WHARTON, 1862–1937

From A Lyrical Epigram

My little old dog;
A heart-beat at my feet.

MICHAEL WHARTON ('Peter Simple'), 1931–

The rapidly developing science of genetic engineering
has been described by scientists as the greatest advance
since the splitting of the atom. New life forms are already
being produced by the manipulation of genes in the
laboratory: carp that grow more quickly than natural
carp; chickens resistant to certain kinds of disease; sheep
which by the insertion of human genes can produce
drugs to deal with human ailments.

But the greatest triumph (if that is the right word) so far is a mouse carrying a human cancer gene which will guarantee that it develops cancer. This mouse, produced in America, has already been 'patented' and will be marketed for medical research.

There is much talk of ethical objections to these developments, balanced against their benefits to the human race; much talk, too, of the danger of releasing laboratory-made organisms into the outer world, where they may get out of control with unpredictable consequences.

There will be much talk, no doubt, of setting up commissions, advisory boards and what have you to decide how genetic engineering should be regulated and controlled by the licensing of experiments and other measures. We have heard all this before. It will not make an atom of difference. Genetic engineering will go on advancing just the same; even as you read this, scientists are busy with their disgusting experiments on the sole principle – not a truly scientific one, either – which they obey: that if a thing can be done, it will be done.

There is no stopping runaway experimental science. All we can do is not to applaud it; denounce it even though we know our denunciations are in vain. We do not need experts to tell us it is wicked to bring into the world a living creature which has been deliberately infected with a cruel disease – wicked and mad. We know it, if not from ordinary decent feeling then from ordinary human common sense, that common sense which, if all else fails, may in the end bring down those proud laboratories in ruin.

'Way of the World', The Daily Telegraph, 20 July 1989

RT REVD JOHN CHANDLER WHITE, 1867–1956

As a Bishop of the Church of God, I am ashamed to say that the Church as an organization has never made any official pronouncement on the subject of the care and treatment of animals that I am able to find. I am more and more amazed as I have studied the matter to find that the Church has almost completely ignored the animal kingdom ...

It is time, fully time, that all Christian people awake to the necessity of taking an active part in the fight against what I dare to call the Crime of Animal Cruelty. Everyone who loves God and animals should help bear the burden of the fight against this insidious evil.

The evil practice of vivisection is damnable in its effect on human character.

Voice of the Voiceless

LYNN WHITE, 1907–

Christianity in absolute contrast to ancient paganism ... not only established a dualism of man and nature but also insisted that it is God's will that man exploit nature for his proper ends ... In antiquity every tree, every spring, every stream, every hill, had its own *genius loci*, its guardian spirit ... By destroying pagan animism, Christianity made it possible to exploit nature in a mood of indifference to the feeling of natural objects.

Science

WALT WHITMAN, 1819–1892

From *Song of Myself*

I think I could turn and live with animals, they are so
    placid and self-contain'd,
I stand and look at them long and long.
They do not sweat and whine about their condition,

They do not lie awake in the dark and weep for their
   sins,
They do not make me sick discussing their duty to God;
Not one is dissatisfied, not one is demented with the
   mania of owning things,
Not one kneels to another, nor to his kind that lived
   thousands of years ago,
Not one is respectable or unhappy over the whole earth.

DR J.D. WHITTALL, 1912–

The question must be asked whether scientists, now able
to alter man's environment, body and mind in sinister
ways, should be allowed to construct their brave new
world regardless of what people think. This question is
relevant to animal experimentation.

If there had been no vivisection and reliance had been
placed on clinical research and observation for finding
out about the human body; and if there had been a real
study of the human being as a person rather than as a
machine, we would doubtless not now be threatened by
science with such monstrous scientific goals as head
transplants, deep freezing of human beings and
indefinite prolongation of life, radical alteration of the
human mind by drugs and other means, remote control
of humans by means of electrodes implanted in the brain,
the creation of man-animal chimeras, etc.

The untold miseries of animals extending worldwide
for decades would not now be the subject of controversy
between pro and anti-vivisectionists, and the world would
not be saddened and threatened by the increasing
number of scientists and technologists who are being
conditioned by their laboratory employment to callous
disregard of animal suffering, leading inevitably to
callous disregard of human suffering. There would not

now be a growing number of people greatly distressed by the appalling cruelties which they know go on in laboratories.

There would not now be a worldwide epidemic of torture where techniques are used similar to those that have been used on animals for many years.

There would not now be a predominantly experimental medicine in the western world instead of a clinical medicine. There would be less disease and greater happiness.

And perhaps this planet would not now be in greater danger of destruction due to cruel and greedy exploitation of its treasures by its human inhabitants than at any time since the world began.

People and Animals

The psychological effects upon the personality of the individual cannot be over-emphasized. In no way does vivisection make a man better, more capable, or more humane. Every time a person kills an animal he becomes increasingly insensitive, callous and cruel ... An individual able to inflict suffering on defenceless animals will certainly be capable of doing the same to his fellow human beings.

Ibid.

ARCHDEACON (Basil) WILBERFORCE, 1841–1916

For myself, I believe that no greater cruelty is perpetrated on this earth than that which is committed in the name of science in some physiological laboratories. I gratefully allow that there is less cruelty in English laboratories than in many laboratories abroad. But in many of these Daitain hells on the Continent there prevails a prying into the movements of life by cutting open and torturing living animals, which, if the general public once realized the truth, would be swept away in the torrent of indignation that would pour forth ... The popular superstition that vivisection produces benefit to the human race – a superstition which degrades humanity by exalting physical above moral interest – is breaking down ... The cause which we are championing is no fanatical protest based on ignorant sentimentality, but a claim of simple justice not only on the transcendent truth of the immanence of the divine truth in all that lives, but also upon the irrefutable logic of ascertained fact.

... I believe that this practice panders to the very lowest part of human nature, which is our selfishness engendered by fear. There is nothing on God's earth that is so brutally cruel as fear. And when they excite our terrors, and then pander to this fear that they have excited, and tell us by the exhibition of a certain amount of necessary cruelty they will be able to relieve us, they are degrading the human race.

From a sermon, Westminster Abbey, 11 July 1909

ELLA WHEELER WILCOX, 1850–1919

Many times I am asked why the suffering of animals should call forth more sympathy from me than the suffering of human beings; why I work in this direction of charitable work more than toward any other. My answer is that because I believe that this work includes all the education and lines of reform which are needed to make a perfect circle of peace and goodwill about the earth ...

The Worlds and I

So Many Gods

So many gods, so many creeds,
So many paths that wind and wind,
While just the art of being kind
Is all the sad world needs.

Voice of the Voiceless

Oh, never a brute in the forest and never a snake in the
    fen
Or ravening bird, starvation stirred, has hunted its prey
    like men.

For hunger and fear and passion alone drive beasts to
    slay.
But wonderful man, the crown of the plan, tortures and
    kills for play.

Kinship

I am the voice of the voiceless;
    Through me the dumb shall speak,
Till the deaf world's ear be made to hear
    The wrongs of the wordless weak.

From street, from cage and from kennel,
    From stable and zoo, the wail
Of my tortured kin proclaims the sin
    Of the mighty against the frail.

Oh, shame on the mothers of mortals,
    Who have not stooped to teach
Of the sorrow that lies in dear, dumb eyes,
    The sorrow that has no speech.

The same force formed the sparrow
    That fashioned man the king;
The God of the whole gave a spark of soul
    To furred and to feathered thing.

And I am my brother's keeper,
    And I will fight his fight,
And speak the word for beast and bird,
    Till the world shall set things right.

OSCAR WILDE, 1854–1900

The unspeakable in full pursuit of the uneatable.

A Woman of No Importance

JAMES JOHN GARTH WILKINSON, 1812–1899

We have seen that there are wicked facts and sciences, innumerable ones, in the moral and social world. Cruelty to others, self-seeking at the cost of others – in a word, aggressive selfishness – is one expression of them all. Exactly parallel with these are the wicked facts and sciences elicited by cruelty to the lower animals; by cutting them up alive; by poisoning them and noting the symptoms of the poisoning; by burning them with hot irons; by injecting corruption into their veins, and filling them with animalcules; and by countless other ways inherited from ancient, and aggravated by modern science; i.e., wicked science. Whatever benefits might accrue, whatever seeming property of knowledge might accrue, from such deeds, they are unnatural, abominable and, save for legal repression, not to be named among Christians ... Mankind has no right to them. They are hellish facts; and they belong not to life and nature, but to imposture, death, and destruction; not to organization, but to ruin; not to order, but to the chaos of sin.

On Human Science and Divine Revelation

For vivisection lives by destructions, and is the record of isolated agonies and spasms, whereas the correspondence indicated, between social and organic truths, is the result of a high philosophy, directed by adequate genius,

579

and regards living organs in their places in the economy of the human form.

Ibid.

True analysis stands indeed on another track; but in the organic sciences it is hard to find its face at present. It results from the course and antecedents of the worse analysis, that a time should come when it brings itself face to face with all life, Divine and human, attempts to bind it hand and foot, to muzzle it, to cast it into the scientific trough, and to violate it by every instrument that the fruitful dreaming selfhood can invent and excogitate. We live in that age now, in the consummation of this analysis. There is no love of truth in it, there is no love of good in it, there is no love of use in it, but only the rights of science, and the glory of the individual, which taken together form the last pretexts of the infernal man.

Ibid.

The lust of extorting the secrets of life by invading it from without; the lust of destroying the animal world to batten the selfhood of science; the lust of crucifying nature as Christ was crucified; the altruism which wields the instruments of the scientific inquisition; the foolishness of believing in an insight into the human body, the image of the temple of the Holy Ghost, by the violation of beasts; the madness of attempting to build the heart of healing out of the bricks of cruelty; these and many more elements must contribute to the terrible blazon of physiology coiling on the spiritual walls. Whatever the shape may be, it is sufficient to know that the end is mental destruction ...

Ibid.

A corollary is that cruelty on earth, done under any pretext, opens the unhappy abodes, and draws forth their inhabitants; and very especially, cruelty done in the name of the love of truth, for that profanes truth; and cruelty done in the name of the love of serving mankind, for that adulterates good. It is better to be cruel with no pretexts, than to defile all holy virtue by claiming it as an ally of devilish practice.

Ibid.

HOWARD WILLIAMS, 1837–1931

In the general constitution of life on our globe, suffering and slaughter, it is objected, are the normal and constant condition of things – the strong relentlessly preying upon the weak in endless succession – and it is asked, why then should the human species form an exception to the general rule, and hopelessly fight against Nature? ... But Man, in order to be the highest of all the series of living beings, is in that proportion bound to prove his right to the supreme place and power of his asserted claims to moral and mental superiority, by his conduct. In brief, in so far only as he proves himself to be the beneficient ruler and pacificator, and not the selfish tyrant of the world, can he have any just title to moral pre-eminence.

The Ethics of Diet

Humanitarianism – the extension of the sublime principles of justice and of compassion to all harmless sentient existence, irrespective of nationality, creed, or species – is a very modern, and even now very inadequately recognized, principle of morals.

Ibid.

Upon the extinction of the last remains of Hellenic and Latin thought, in the fifth century, profound darkness settled upon Western Civilization; and a few brilliant names excepted, mental torpor or (worse) cruel superstition everywhere prevailed. That the humaner spirit of the better pre-christian thinkers was very far from inspiring orthodox Mediaeval Christianity – whether in respect of the human or of the non-human species – history political, social and religious, super-abundantly witnesses, in almost every page of its horri-fying annals. Every incipient movement, which showed sign of revolt from the established ecclesiastical or political order, was ruthlessly crushed. Every symptom of dissent from the orthodox morality (or immorality) and every struggle, however feeble, for the establishment of a less barbarous mode of life, was regarded by the Western Christian Church, in particular, with undisguised hosti-lity. *Heresy* was the always successful accusation, with which the ecclesiastical authorities branded every opinion or practice which might seem to endanger their authority or to encroach upon their prerogatives.

Ibid.

HENRY WILLIAMSON, 1895–1977

She came upon him kneeling in the snow with the dog beside him, holding a rabbit he had taken from a gin, with both its forepaws broken.

'Do you mind if I kill it? It's no good releasing it with both forepaws gone, is it?'

She shook her head, and calmly he grasped the kicking hind legs in his left hand and the head in his right, and stretched the body across his thigh, so that the neck was broken. He dropped it beside the gin, over which its head rolled.

'As though in a caress of forgiveness,' he said, and her lips moved in a small smile.

'Are there many traps here? I suppose there are?'

'They trap ten thousand every year on the Burrows. And the trapping rent just keeps Ronnie at school. Ten thousand screams in the darkness every year. I hear them sometimes.' She spoke very gently.

'The story of the Burrows is the story of all the world,' he said.

The Pathway

LORD (Edward Henry) WILLIS, 1918–

Why do you gentlemen think for one moment that people are screaming out, year after year, about cruelty to animals if there is no basis of truth in it? Why do you arrogate to yourselves all the moral judgements, all the rights? Why do you say: 'We, and we alone, know what goes on, because we, and we alone, can understand what an experiment is for'? I beg you, gentlemen, to come down from that great big pyramid on which you place yourselves and listen occasionally to the humble voice of the amateur. Think sometimes that the man in the street could be right.

House of Lords debate, December 1973

FRANK AVRAY WILSON, 1914–

Although a preoccupation with the mystical and the occult is a normal human interest, an expression of man's defiance of matter and time, the magical is clearly anti-human, in its relish of the macabre, the sordid, and the ugly. While mystical experience is invariably associated with beauty, the magical purposefully excludes beauty and obliges a relish in the obscene and the excremental. Today, there is a discernible arousal of the magical mind. Indeed magic has never been fully quenched by the rise of reason; many aspects of so-called civilized life reveal it. Eating habits are not without their magical asides.

If the mark of the human is a need for the beautiful, and if the magical shows itself by a relish of the hideous, it is simple enough to pick out the features of the diet which are magical – the bloody joint, the dripping steak, organs like the kidney concerned with filth elimination, foul-smelling foods, the desecration of living things which the killing and cooking of any animal entails. This magical relish can go to extremes, which then acquire a gruesome twist, as in the chewing of eyeballs and the gobbling of brains, the sucking of marrow and the savouring of testicles.

The point is that once the magical mind is aroused, such practices are felt to be exciting, strength-giving, indispensable, and in fact become supported by a corrupted reason, by science itself. Just as the politician uses his reason to justify an atomic overkill, entailing the murder of millions, so the nutritionist assures one that fried brains are a good source of protein. This is the frailty of reason – its easy misuse for human ends by minds no longer sufficiently irradiated by the humanizing resources.

There is a sinister ally to such humanly debasing habits. Protein products foreign to the normal physiology of the body provoke chaotic reactions when eaten. In a wild attempt to allay the intruding substances, the body produces too much of the allaying chemicals, an excess which has the malicious result of demanding more, and ever more, of the foreign substances. The essential abnormality of all animal foods is shown by the habituation and craving they provoke, a demand which can come to defy all sense and economy.

In this manner, eating habits which comply with the secret desires of a disturbed mind are fortified by an insidious biochemistry.

Food habits also reflect the life-hatred which goes with a hardening of the heart to a hardened existence, as in the barely believable hideousness of the death-dealing industries supporting every civilized table. This life-hatred, and the hatred of nature which accompanies it, goes back to the onset of the Ice Ages, which chased the earliest humans from their earthly paradise. No longer guided by instinct, but by cortical conditioning, human beings are able to adopt virtually any ruse in order to survive, no matter how unbiological. But the fact that humanization occurred in idyllic conditions, left humans badly equipped for the periodical geological and climatic cataclysms of earth history. While in all other animals, instinct would insist that the normal habits were reverted to as soon as conditions returned to normal, in the case of man, cortical conditioning, revived in each succeeding generation by social customs, tend to persist. Animal foods, and the vast machinery of suffering their eating entails, have become one of the most entrenched of social customs, defended by science as natural and beneficial, and ardently insisted upon by the public.

Admittedly, attempts are made to give such horrible habits a veneer of aesthetic appeal. Cooking of animal foods removes the reek of raw flesh, and sauces help to smother the sheer animality of the ingredients. Here and there, vegetables, fruits, and even flowers come into the decoration of some recipe as if to humanize the offence, sometimes ludicrously, as the ears of roast pork stuffed with flowers. But the underlying ugliness is scarcely covered, as most children show in their initial protests.

One is entitled to enquire how it is that science, which claims to operate on impartial reasoning, has failed to point out the unbiological and irrational features in such patently human habits. The environmental crisis is proof enough that science is no impartial observer to the follies of an age, of a culture, and indeed serves them faithfully. Most scientists, and science as a whole, show the same spirit of aggressiveness and inconsideration regarding nature which dominated Palaeolithic existence.

Food Fit for Humans

Those coming the closest to the ideal human diet are the vegans, and, somewhat less close, the vegetarians. These people are usually above average in sensitivity, in an awareness of self and of others, of things and creatures, which is one reason why many of them come to differ from the common patterns in the first place. There can be no doubt that the subjective rewards are considerable, providing a sense of compassion and purpose, a zeal for what is whole and natural, and a delight in simplicities, rarely met in the general modern confusion. It is this cleansing of the doors of perception which no doubt accounts for the fact that many of the more sensitive people in the arts are attracted to vegetarianism, while the more tough-minded tend to go in an opposite dionysian direction of booze and beef.

One does find in the ranks of vegetarians, persons with a tendency to anxiety neurosis above the usual, as one does in any sensitivity-demanding pursuit. Their condition is usually improved or cured, thanks to the sense of purpose and an effective life-pattern and idealism which vegetarianism can provide. But there are the few health-kick vegetarians who may not rise beyond a self-centred preoccupation. If that was all there was to vegetarianism, it would be a shallow concern, even if the pursuit of health is a primordial duty.

The great advantage of vegetarianism today is not only its practice, but the philosophy it offers regarding other human beings, living creatures and nature generally. As the help in these directions which past religions could provide is now minimal, vegetarianism is particularly well suited to offer a life-pattern ideally adapted to modern conditions, restoring a sense of purpose and participation in the natural world, without which human beings are only too obviously alienated and distraught, the reason probably why an increasing number of young are being attracted to the vegetarian ideology.

Ibid.

No wonder all living things are so fussy about their foods. Many animals will rather die than eat food which is very different from their accustomed diet. The lucky fools! They have an unanswerable instinct to guide them and no intelligence to interfere. That is our doubtful privilege.

... In general, nations that have eaten the most unnatural foods have been historically the most restless and disturbing. The hordes of Genghis Khan were nomads that lived chiefly on their animals ... The four-legged John Bull came into prominence on the pastures of England a little before the Elizabethans. Before that, the people of England had been relatively quiet peasants, living on their coarse bread and beer and only a very little meat. The Germans are another restless people who gorge on all sorts of abominations made from meat, and the extraordinary pillage of the continent of Europe by the French after the Revolution coincided with the adoption of the foods which had been previously reserved for the aristocracy ... Man pays for the sin of unnecessary slaughter by the slaughter of his own kin; the revenge for the horror of the slaughter-house is the battlefield.

Food for the Golden Age

Science, like all human activity, has a traditionalist lobby, resistant to fundamental change. Working scientists, not concerned with original research or discovery, are probably better as traditionalists. Others are traditionalists because it pays them to be so. In the field of scientific popularization, for example, it is the ideas of a former generation which are popular, ideas regarding the animal nature of man, natural aggressiveness, innate sexual promiscuity, ideas of 'nature red in tooth and claw' current in Darwin's time. The emergent ideas in physics and biology are much more difficult to popularize because they do not suppose most people's own notions of human nature or reality.

There is also among scientists and scientific populrizers an unmistakable element of mischief. Dr Desmond Morris, of chimpanzee-painting fame, wrote a book on the biology of art which reduces the subject to animalistic analogies, which are not only misleading, but incomplete, for the emotional nature of art, in the fantastic activity of birds, is barely mentioned. But the applause which this and his other books have received shows what kind of biology people want.

Art as Revelation

The attitudes necessary, and the sensitivities to be nurtured, have to be practised not only through a revised aesthetic and appreciation of the arts, but through a new relationship to nature, matter, object, work and entertainment. A course in natural philosophy, so popular with the Victorians, should once again have a place in every curriculum, so reconciling art, aesthetics and science. Virtually any subject pursued with an awakened awareness of its aesthetic potential can serve as a guide. The study of botany, mineralogy or geology – all within the grasp of the average educated person – is full of potential instruction along the lines of a reconciled intellect and intuition. Although it is not fashionable to praise them, I believe personally that the Victorians with their sense of wonder at the strange urban and industrial world they were making, came close to finding the solution from which we have strayed so far.

Ecology is a particularly relevant subject, for in it the interrelatedness of art, science, nature and cosmos can be clearly perceived. The unravelling of the ecological web provides a high level of aesthetic and intellectual satisfaction, making one aware, as no other subject can, of the relevance of the forces at work in Creation, and of the role of the humanized mind in this great work. The dynamic integration of creatures and environments is widespread and, as knowledge increases, it is beginning to be understood that this extends to the stars.

In this book I have tried to demonstrate how the process of humanization is intrinsically tied to aesthetic sensitivity. It is my belief that people cannot properly be human unless this activity is manifest, and the measure of de-humanization in any society, in any age, can be fairly accurately measured by the level of aesthetic sensitivity. The great social value of art is that even as a minority preoccupation it has a radiative influence, and there is no doubt that if even a few people truly accept the relevance of art and put it into practice, the present drift to the trivial, insensitive and increasingly inhuman, can be reversed, and the long work of healing and recovery can begin.

Ibid.

DR GEORGE WILSON, LLD (Edinburgh), CPH (Cantab), 1848–1921

... the indiscriminate maiming and slaughtering of animal life with which these bacteriological methods of research and experimentation have been inseparably associated, cannot be proved to have saved one single human life, or lessened in any appreciable degree the load of human suffering ...

... I accuse my profession of misleading the public as to the cruelties and horrors which are perpetrated on animal life. When it is stated that the actual pain involved in these experiments is commonly of the most trifling description, there is a suppression of the truth, of the most palpable kind, which could only be accounted for at the time by ignorance of the actual facts. I admit that in

the mere operation of injecting a virus, whether
cultivated or not, there may be little or no pain, but the
cruelty does not lie in the operation itself, which is
permitted to be performed without anaesthetics, but in
the after-effects. Whether so-called toxins are injected
under the skin into the peritoneum, into the cranium
under the dura mater, into the pleural cavity, into the
veins, eyes or other organs – and all these methods are
ruthlessly practised – there is long-drawn-out agony. The
animal so innocently operated on may have to live days,
weeks, or months, with no anaesthetic to assuage its
sufferings, and nothing but death to relieve.

From his Presidential Address to the British Medical
Association, Portsmouth, 5 August 1899

L. FORBES WINSLOW, DCL, MB, LL D, MRCP,
1844–1913

Vivisection is against all the principles of medicine, and it
is against all the principles of religion … As a result of
forty years' experience, I say that vivisection should not
be tolerated, and I should be sorry to see as
representative of any university or any constituency a
man who is a vivisector.

From address given at Caxton Hall, 5 December 1910

There are many more eminent men in my profession
who are adverse to vivisection than who are in favour of
it.

Animals' Guardian, October 1911

JOHN WOLCOT ('Peter Pindar'), 1738–1819
Susan and the Spider

'Come down, you toad,' cry'd Susan to a Spider
High on the gilded cornice a proud rider,

And wanton swinging by his silken rope;
'I'll teach thee to spin cobwebs round the room;
You're now upon some murder, I presume:
  I'll bless thee – if I don't, say I'm no Pope.'

The Spider, blest with oratory grace,
Slipp'd down, and staring Susan in the face,
  'Fie, Susan! Lurks there murder in that heart?
O barbarous, lovely Susan, I'm amazed!
O, can that form, on which so oft I've gazed,
  Possess of cruelty the slightest part?'

'Aren't you a murderer?' gravely Susan cries;
'Aren't you for ever busy with that claw,
Killing poor unoffending little flies,
  Merely to satisfy your nasty maw?'

'But, Susan, don't *you* feed on gentle lamb?
Don't *you* on pretty little pigeons cram?
  Don't you on harmless fishes often dine?'
'That's very true,' quoth Susan, 'true indeed;
Lord! With what eloquence these spiders plead!
  This little rascal beats a grave Divine.'

To a Fish of the Brook

Why fliest thou away with fear?
Trust me there's naught of danger near,
  I have no wicked hook
All covered with a snaring bait,
Alas, to tempt thee to thy fate,
  And drag thee from the brook.

O harmless tenant of the flood,
I do not wish to spill thy blood,
   For nature unto thee
Perchance hath given a tender wife,
And children dear, to charm thy life,
   As she hath done for me.

Enjoy thy stream, O harmless fish;
And when an angler for his dish,
   Through gluttony's vile sin,
Attempts, a wretch, to pull thee out,
God give thee strength, O gentle trout,
   To pull the rascal in!

WILLIAM WOLLASTON, 1659–1724

There is something in human nature, resulting from our very make and constitution, which renders us obnoxious to the pains of others, causes us to sympathize with them, and almost comprehends us in their case. It is grievous to see or hear (and almost to hear of) any man, or even any animal whatever, in torture.

Religion of Nature

DAVID WOOD, 1946–

My special concern is with a particular sort of intellectual clot that forms soon after the initial exposure to the arguments and facts we present. This clot can be described in the language of psychology as the result of a clash of motives or in the language of psychoanalysis as a reaction-formation. I hope to have avoided these languages because, whatever scientific truth they hold, both tend to reinforce an increasingly object-like view of the person as controlled from within by forces out of his power. A description that emphasizes freedom actually re-establishes a conception of oneself that makes it possible.

The reaction with which I am concerned is not absolutely defined in real life, but its standard range of variation covers the following set of responses:

'Well, I agree with some/much/all of what you say, *but —*

(a) I don't care;
(b) I'm too weak-willed/too old/too much a creature of habit to change;
(c) What difference would it make if *I* were to change my habits (it's a social problem, not an individual one);
(d) It strikes me as a very complex question. I really can't commit myself to do anything about it.'

These reactions can be characterized as follows:

(a) *The cynic or the hypocrite*

The cynic adopts a patronizing attitude to any argument that appeals to motives beyond self-interest (narrowly conceived) and while, as in this case, he may agree that they are plausible, he insists that one can after all make any argument *sound* plausible. The hypocrite clearly recognizes in some sense the truth of what is being said, but will not bring himself to take this recognition seriously, for a number of reasons. Most likely, he will elevate one of the causes we mentioned earlier to the status of a reason. A *true* hypocrite, of course, would dispense with any defensive apparatus. He would just say one thing (and even 'believe' it) and do another.

(b) *The pathetic/defensive reaction*

This is a form of self-degradation the achievement of which absolves one from significance as a moral agent. What is claimed to be a description of oneself (e.g., 'I'm too weak') is made into a reason or an excuse. But that immediately lays the whole self open to the same criticism. One does not get absolution from an evil act by saying that one is an evil person.

(c) *The moral straggler*

Knowing what he should do, he thinks 'realistically', claiming that the consequences of any personal reform would not be very great (and therefore worthless). If a movement got going, he would join in. He has no conception of the value or importance of his own actions, seeing himself as an insignificant part of great social processes thoroughly beyond his control or responsibility.

(d) *The evasive intellectual*

Naturally at home in the realm of ideas, he uses his 'puzzlement' at what is a quite straightforward argument as a subtle sign that he has the intelligence to complicate any question to a point beyond solution. This task becomes especially important to him, when, to his horror, he finds himself having to decide on the correctness of a position that actually has practical consequences. He initiates a fully-blown 'holding operation'. I am not denying that he may be able to offer plausible-sounding objections, but claiming that rather than finally coming to a rational conclusion on the issue, he will simply pile up a sheaf of objections on the other scale-plan until the two balance. Utterly lost in the complications he will then postpone proceedings indefinitely, and go on acting as before.

Each of these reactions is very common, often overlapping in particular individuals.

… But the case we are discussing is not just an internal problem for a self-concerned being, for upon it rests the quality of life and the very lives of other beings equally worthy of respect in their own right. One's freedom of conscience must take into account those beings dependent on its deliberations. When all the arguments are over, if one has not been convinced by the weight of reason, one's nightmares and day dreams should still be filled, if one's actual experience is not, with the vision of countless other animals dying and dead in the misconceived interests of man.

Animals, Men and Morals

G.F. WOODS, 1907–1966

The quest for moral perfection is far more than a quest for private excellence. It involves the attainment of right relationships with God and with our fellow men. And it includes a right relation of re-created humanity to the natural world.

A Defence of Theological Ethics

JOHN WOOLMAN, 1720–1772

I was early convinced that true religion consisted in an inward life wherein the heart doth love and reverence God the creator and learn to exercise true justice and goodness not only toward men but also toward the brute creation ... To say we love God as unseen and at the same time exercise cruelty toward the least creature moving by his life or by life derived from him, was a contradiction in itself.

Quoted in *John Woolman, Quaker Saint,* by Elizabeth Gray Vining

Be careful that the love of gain draw us not into any business which may weaken our love of our Heavenly Father, or bring unnecessary trouble to any of his creatures.

On the Right Use of the Lord's Outward Gifts

Our gracious Creator cares and provides for all his Creatures. His tender mercies are over all his works; and so far as his love influences our minds, so far we become interested in his workmanship, and feel a desire to take hold of every opportunity to lessen the distress of the afflicted and increase the happiness of the Creation. Here we have a prospect of one common interest, from which our own is inseparable, that to turn all the treasures we possess into the channel of Universal Love is the business of our lives.

John Woolman's Journal

Some fowls yet remained of those the passengers took for their sea-store. I believe about fourteen perished in the storms at sea, by the waves breaking over the quarter-deck, and a considerable number with sickness at different times ... In observing their dull appearance at sea, and the pining sickness of some of them, I often remembered the Fountain of goodness, who gave being to all creatures, and whose love extends to caring for the sparrows. I believe where the love of God is verily perfected, and the true spirit of government watchfully attended to, a tenderness towards all creatures made subject to us will be experienced, and a care felt in us that we do not lessen that sweetness of life in the animal creation which the great Creator intends for them under our government.

Ibid.

WILLIAM WORDSWORTH, 1770–1850

From *The Tables Turned*

... Let Nature be your teacher.
Sweet is the Lore which Nature brings;
Our meddling intellect
Mis-shapes the beauteous forms of things:
We murder to dissect.
Enough of Science and of Art;
Close up those barren leaves;
Come forth, and bring with you a heart
That watches and receives.

From *The Excursion*

Then, too, this song of mine once more could please,
Where anguish, strange as dreams of restless sleep,
Is tempered and allayed by sympathies
Aloft descending, and descending deep,
Even to the inferior Kinds; whom forest trees
Protect from beating sunbeams and the sweep
Of the sharp winds: fair Creatures! – to whom Heaven
A calm and sinless life, with love, has given.
          ... Birds and beasts,
And the mute fish that glances in the stream
And harmless reptile coiling in the sun,
And gorgeous insect hovering in the air,
The fowl domestic and the household dog –
In his capacious mind, he loved them all:
Their rights acknowledging he felt for all.

From *Hartleap Well*

For thirteen hours he ran a desperate race;
And in my simple mind we cannot tell
What cause the Hart might have to love this place,
And come and make his death-bed near the well.

Here on the grass perhaps asleep he sank,
Lulled by the fountain in the summer-tide;

This water was perhaps the first he drank
When he had wandered from his mother's side.

In April here beneath the flowering thorn
He heard the birds their morning carols sing;
And he, perhaps, for aught we know, was born
Not half a furlong from that self-same spring.

Now, here is neither grass nor pleasant shade;
The sun on drearier hollow never shone;
So will it be, as I have often said,
Till trees, and stones, and fountain, all are gone.

Grey-headed Shepherd, thou has spoken well;
Small difference lies between thy creed and mine:
This Beast not unobserved by Nature fell;
His death was mourned by sympathy divine.

The Being, that is in the clouds and air,
That is in the green leaves among the groves,
Maintains a deep and reverential care
For the unoffending creatures whom he loves.

The pleasure-house is dust: – behind, before,
This is no common waste, no common gloom;
But Nature, in due course of time, once more
Shall here put on her beauty and her bloom.

She leaves these objects to a slow decay,
That what we are, and have been, may be known;
But at the coming of the milder day,
These monuments shall all be overgrown.

One lesson, Shepherd, let us two divide,
Taught both by what she shows and what conceals;
Never to blend our pleasure or our pride
With sorrow of the meanest thing that feels.

Humanity

… If Power could live at ease with self-restraint! …
Then would …
Love ebb and flow untroubled by caprice;
And not alone harsh tyranny would cease.
But unoffending creatures find release
From *qualified* oppression, whose defence
Rests on a hollow plea of recompense.

To a Butterfly

I've watched you now a full half-hour,
Self-poised upon that yellow flower;
And, little Butterfly! indeed
I know not if you sleep or feed.
How motionless! not frozen seas
More motionless! and then
What joy awaits you when the breeze
Hath found you out among the trees,
And calls you forth again.

This plot of orchard-ground is ours;
My trees they are, my Sister's flowers;
Here rest your wings when they are weary;
Here lodge as in a sanctuary!
Come often to us, fear no wrong;
Sit near us on the bough!
We'll talk of sunshine and of song,
And summer days, when we were young;
Sweet childish days that were as long
As twenty days are now.

BASIL WRIGHTON, 1900–1988

We can by-pass the question of 'rights' as a legal irrelevancy, since there can hardly be a juridical relation between beings of different species. But we cannot blind ourselves to the affinity of nature between man and the higher animals which share his sensitive qualities.

The Ark

RICHARD OF WYCHE (Bishop of Chichester), 1197–1253

On seeing animals being killed for food

You, who are innocent, what have you done worthy of death!

The Life of Richard of Wyche

ESMÉ WYNNE-TYSON, 1898–1972

Looking back from the beginning of this century when animal victims in the experimental laboratories numbered only a few hundreds, we find that, despite the ever-increasing setting up of societies for the prevention of animal exploitation, the amount of experiments has risen steadily from hundreds to millions per annum; and it is all too obvious that the scientific hierarchy is now so firmly entrenched that unless something infinitely more powerful is put into action than the present humanitarian efforts, there will soon be no limits to the 'freedom' of the experimentalists, which is precisely what they have aimed at from the first.

... although the way of *ahimsa* is undeniably right, spiritually, morally and ethically, the present methods of advocating it are like straws in a raging river. We have been drifting optimistically for too long. Today, we must face the situation as it is and deal with it at a deeper level than has ever before been attempted. Our foe is primarily not the experimentalist, the scientist, the Communist, but their religion – the Gospel of Utilitarianism; the doctrine that utility is all; that the termitary state and not the individual workers is what matters; that science can solve all the problems of life.

We must cease trying to combat this view of life piecemeal, as we have been doing, fighting this or that aspect of cruelty or exploitation. Instead we must confront it with the diametrically opposite viewpoint – that of philosophical idealism which so enraged Lenin when Tolstoy advocated it, because he knew it offered a practical and superior alternative to Marxism.

To utility it opposes idealism; to domination and power-lust it opposes compassion and non-violence. It argues that only the individual by his own efforts can evolve to a higher species and that therefore it is the individual and not the termitary that counts. It insists that materialistic science cannot solve a single problem relating to man's only worthwhile aim in life – evolution; for it cannot make him spiritually or morally better than he is. It cannot conquer for him such failings as fear, lust, hate and greed. It can only provide *things*.

World Forum editorial, April/June 1964

It so obviously rests with women, who even in these days of dual work in and out of the home, still have the care of the children in their earliest and most impressionable years, to train them into that understanding of the oneness of life with its resultant compassion for all living things that is so essential if the world is ever to be a better place than the jungle it is today, and will remain until we return to the humane philosophy advocated by the rejected wise men of antiquity.

World Forum, April/June 1966

601

... ecclesiastical teaching has kept humanity from evolving to a more harmless species. By entirely ignoring the necessity for compassion, and quoting certain discreditable utterances ascribed to Jehovah in the Old Testament, it has been possible to argue that flesh-eating is morally right and according to the will of God.

The Philosophy of Compassion

Far from being unrealistic, Plotinus' system is the most practical measure so far conceived for ensuring the evolution of man to a higher, better and more harmless species, which is the fundamental need of the world today. Unless this policy is adopted, and this step taken, there is a very real danger of humanity finding itself on the cosmic scrapheap as a failure of evolution, not by the decree of a punishing God but by reason of mankind's inability or unwillingness to outgrow its animalism and the self-destroying violence of the jungle, which today can be expressed in terms of nuclear deterrents with their potentiality for deterring the continuance of the human race.

Man can never be better, never be himself, unless he understands his relationship to God and the universe; unless he realizes the unity and oneness of being, and therefore understands what his conduct should be towards all other forms of sentient life. In the eyes of tame and harmless beasts, we cannot fail to recognize the brightness of the life-stimulating Soul such as we find in those we love, shining from these lesser manifestations of Mind. The scientific man exploits this likeness; the understanding man has compassion on it.

Ibid.

When the late Professor Einstein, who may be presumed to have known the potentialities of materialistic science for ensuring an improved way of life, was asked: 'What can we do to get a better world?' he made the classic reply, 'You have to have better people.' And this is precisely what Plotinus' system aims to produce.

Ibid.

The Golden Rule is a natural consequence of the recognition of the unity of being. The sufferings of other living creatures then evoke the tenderness and care that we should wish for ourselves in like circumstances, and a determination to do nothing that will add to the general misery of sentient life, but instead to live harmlessly and lovingly as expressions of the God towards which all things are so painfully striving.

Ibid.

... dazzled by the prospect of turning the desert of Non-Being into an earthly paradise by mental means, Descartes apparently forgot that we cannot arrive at a destination by walking in the reverse direction. With his natural concern for health, he could not foresee the present scientific civilization in which a mighty army of medical men strive to conquer sickness in man by torturing and killing annually millions of other sentient beings, and by injecting into the pure bloodstream of children concoctions made from diseased matter induced in a calf or the kidneys of monkeys. Nor could he know that after nearly a century of ever-increasing 'scientific' experimentation on animals, such ailments as cancer would be steadily on the increase, and that, as a direct result of trying to be 'lords and possessors of nature', the whole atmosphere of the earth would be in danger of becoming poisoned with death-and-disease-bringing substances, in order that man could achieve the ultimate triumph of being able to blast all sentient beings from the face of the globe.

Living nearer to a time when men still strove for moral

perfection, Descartes could not foresee that when this striving gave place to the philosophy of utilitarianism, perfection would recede ever farther from humanity's horizon, and the Lords of nature, having ceased to exercise their spiritual energies owing to the demands made on the physical variety, would become unregenerate, irresponsible power-addicts.

Ibid.

... apart from the fallacy of the argument as to the emotions of animals and men being wholly dissimilar, a fallacy obvious to anyone who has had personal experience of the lesser creatures, the idea that one may kill and ill-treat helpless sentient creatures because their emotions are different from our own, is not only utterly inhumane but verges on the ridiculous. Remembering the treachery, violence, lust and cruelty of many human beings, the 'difference' in the comparatively mild emotions of most animals points to their superiority.

Ibid.

... in a masculine world, torn by strife, nationalistic ambition, cruelty, greed and hate, what is needed beyond all else are the civilizing and harmonizing 'feminine' qualities of pacific, tender, protective, compassionate Love. Instead of which, the human symbols of these divine qualities – women – have, since their liberation, been heaping fuel on the fire; not only, in many cases, encouraging men in their policies of violence, but actually joining in the fray, going into uniform, marching with machine guns, entering into competition with men even in occupations that are most obviously suitable for men only; taking part in masculine sports, attending bull and prize fights, flaunting their sexual promiscuity and indulgence in narcotics and stimulants, and in every way aping the toughness, callousness and downright bestial stupidity of the unredeemed, or unbalanced, male nature. By such misguided emulation she is rapidly eliminating in herself all the qualities of her higher nature which are precisely what she should be contributing to the world in order to adjust the balance of psychological power.

Ibid.

It was perfectly in keeping with his creed of compassion that [Jesus] should endeavour to put an end to the cruelty of animal sacrifices; but that he used violence in his attempt to do so is neither indicated in John's version of the incident, nor is credible in view of what we know of his outlook and customary behaviour.

Mithras

We have only to imagine Jesus of Nazareth slaughtering a bull or a fellow creature to understand the immense, impassable gulf existing between Mithraism and true Christianity, and the folly and peril of ignoring that gulf and trying to reconcile the irreconcilable.

Ibid.

JON WYNNE-TYSON, 1924–

Cruelty, like kindness, is indivisible. Children and men cannot safely be taught to take delight in cruelty to some living things and to abhor cruelty to others ... once we accept the obscenities of cruelty, in whatever form, we must also accept the impossibility of arguing degrees.

Man cannot claim an instinct for aggression if many of his species show no such instinct and manage to live normal and unfrustrated lives without killing their fellows, hunting, fighting, persecuting minorities, thrashing their wives and dogs or tormenting their children. Indeed, if only one member of the human race displayed no urge to indulge in violent aggression while being in normal health, it would be enough to disprove the assumption of *Homo sapiens*' ineradicable instinct of violence.

Western man is schooled in violence and greed from the moment he is born. The society into which he arrives is incessantly concerned to persuade him of the merits of violence. From the moment that his scarcely co-ordinated fingers try to push away the 'nice beef stew' and the small gobbets of flesh that most anxious and deluded mothers try to push into his system (all those battles of the high-chair would hardly be necessary if man was naturally the carnivore that some still claim), the Western baby is learning that his society rests squarely on the credo of 'I kill, therefore I am'.

The Civilized Alternative: a Pattern for Protest

The case against vivisection is the same as that against war and all other forms of cruelty – that violence does not produce long-term solutions.

Ibid.

... it takes no great degree of education to detect the monstrous and callous absurdity of a society that chooses to over-indulge and pollute its way into physical and mental ill-health, and then tortures millions of animals in order to find answers to diseases that could so often be prevented by a change of habit. Perhaps the twenty-first century's symbol of contemporary insanity will be the twitching tail-ends of a dozen imprisoned white mice being compelled to inhale tobacco smoke until they develop the cancers that human beings invite in preference to the rejection of an addiction no self-respecting mouse would give skirting room to.

Ibid.

... the only argument against vivisection that will be seen to have lasting power — that we do not improve human society by means that debase human character.

Ibid.

We must develop a better sense of responsibility towards our total environment ... this better sense cannot any longer exclude from revision the staples of our diet.

Food for a Future: the Ecological Priority of a Humane Diet

... not only have other creatures a right to live ... they have the even more critical right not to be born at all at the whim of man ... in our half-baked thinking and incessant ferocity towards the countless creatures whom, alive, we imprison, mutilate, maim, trap, strangle, shoot, hook, chase, snare, de-limb, behead, suffocate, flay, disembowel, stab, crush, over-feed, burn, drown, boil, freeze, cut up, make sick, terrorize and by numerous other means mercilessly exploit day in and day out for no better reason than that we wish to devour them, we are shamefully forsaking that one obligation which above all others we should recognize — to put our unique knowledge of the difference between good and evil, between mercy and cruelty, before our heart-hardening greed.

Unless one subscribes to the primitive and shocking belief that animals, being without souls, are fair game for whatever treatment humans wish to inflict on them, the obligation to show pity towards all sentient life is universally recognized as religious in the widest and best sense of that all too often narrow word. There are few religious beliefs that fail to emphasize the need for compassion. Unfortunately there are few scientific specialisms which grant it the least attention. While no theist who conceives of his god as aligned to the smallest degree of mercy can logically dismiss the right of all sentient beings to expect from man more than from the other members of creation evidence of the divine values of pity and love, the scientific mind has as yet shown little sign of awakening to this realization. Yet without it mere knowledge is nothing more than contaminated dust.

Here, in the wide field of our treatment of other living beings, religion and science are capable of finding a unity on the very highest level of their separate specialisms. Here the balance born of humane eclecticism can bring about a vital and applicable ethic ... But it is vitally important, if there is a shred of reason for believing that mankind is working out some evolutionary pattern and accepting an obligation or profound need to grow spiritually, that we do the right things for the right reasons rather than for expediency or lack of alternative.

Ibid.

Dietethics – that is, the study of the ethics of diet – relate not only to the animals we eat, but also to the world's malnourished and starving human millions ... if we abandoned the grossly wasteful habit of eating our plants via the bodies of animals, there need be no starving people in the world today.

I see no realistic long-term alternative to a world whose natural resources are regarded as factors with which we have to collaborate – not dominate – in order to take our proper place in the scheme of things. I suggest the reasons for this are not only expedient, but evolutionary ... it is surely our role to envisage and work toward a world which is sanely and humanely controlled, not exploited, by those with the vision and humility to question established *mores*. I say 'humility' because it is the arrogance born of long habit and entrenched prejudice that seeks to defend behavioural patterns that have long been a matter of comfortable acceptance for a privileged minority at the expense of the rest of the world.

Animals' Rights: a Symposium

Flying fish would land on board, sometimes being caught by the sails and dropping on deck, sometimes hitting the coach-roof or stanchions. He retrieved them, sharing the sea's gift with Seamew. But one day he found himself studying a fish that landed by the forward hatch. He noted the helpless lifting of its strange 'wings' as it sought to return to the life-giving sea. He picked it up, feeling the tremulous proof of its humble being, the vibrating will to survive, and in what might have been idle curiosity he held it over the side, watching the eager response of its fins to the dousing of a passing crest.

So Say Banana Bird

Vegetarianism is a step in the right direction, but the logic of the vegan case is absolute. No one – whether nutritionist, physician, sociologist or churchman – can refute the veganic argument in any important respect. Veganism is part of the most civilized concept of life man has been able to envisage. More than lacto-vegetarianism, veganism 'speaks to the condition' of our modern world. That still only a minute number of Western people put its principles into practice is evidence of nothing but our reluctance to break with habit and to place conscience before social inconvenience.

From a speech at Animals' Rights Symposium given at the Commonwealth Institute, London, May 1980

Of the animal rights issue, some would say it is a minor, irrelevant, even ridiculous concern. 'Man must come first' is the cry, as though it was an either/or matter.

What they really mean is that man must come first and last and that nothing must be done in the animals' cause apart from the occasional cover-up job where the evidence of our abuse of other sentient life is too painful for more sensitive humans to tolerate.

I believe such diehards to be wrong on every count. Wrong not only to be indifferent to our treatment of animals, for those animals' sakes, but wrong because such callousness helps substantially to prolong the worst aspects of the human predicament. Cruelty is indivisible. Violence is indivisible. What has variously been called karma, the Golden Rule, and so forth, cannot be side-stepped by our tricky minds. It is something that just happens, just 'works', like night following day.

Until we establish a felt sense of kinship between our own species and those fellow mortals – those 'other nations', as Henry Beston put it – who share with us the sun and shadow of life on this agonized planet, there is no hope for other species, there is no hope for our environment, and there is no hope for ourselves. The writing is on the wall – large and clear.

Talk for Writers Against Experiments on Animals at
St James's, Piccadilly, London, 24 April 1985

WILLIAM YOUATT, 1776–1847

But to what degree are [the claims of humanity] recognized and obeyed? To what extent are they inculcated, not only in many excellent treatises on moral philosophy, but by the great majority of the expounders of the scriptures? We answer with shame, and with an astonishment that increases upon us in proportion as we think of the subject: the duties of humanity are represented as extending to our fellow men, to the victim of oppression or misfortune, the deaf, the dumb, the blind, the slave, the beggared prodigal, and even the convicted felon – all these receive more or less sympathy. But, with exceptions, few and far between, not a writer pleads for the innocent and serviceable creatures – brutes, as they are termed – that minister to our wants, natural or artificial.

Nevertheless, the claims of the lower animals to humane treatment, or, at least, to exemption from abuse, are as good as any that man can urge upon man. Although less intelligent, and not immortal, they are susceptible of pain: but because they cannot remonstrate, nor associate with their fellows in defence of their rights, our best theologians and philosophers have not condescended to plead their cause, or even to make mention of them; although, as just asserted, they have as much right to protection from ill usage as the best of their masters have.

Nay! the matter has been carried further than this. At no very distant period, the right of wantonly torturing the inferior animals, as caprice or passion dictated, was unblushingly claimed; and it was asserted that the prevention of this was an interference with the rights and liberties of man! Strange that, at the beginning of the nineteenth century, this should have been the avowed opinion of some of the British legislators; and that the advocate of the claims of the brute should have been regarded as a fool or a madman, or a compound of both.

Humanity to Brutes

Imagination is a faculty of the mind by which we recall parts and portions of former impressions, and combine them in different ways; forming new images, fanciful, or sublime, or ridiculous …

No one can doubt the existence of imagination in the brute. We perceive it in his dreams; he runs, he hunts, he fights while the external senses are asleep. When the sportsman is preparing for his excursion, what is it but the anticipation of the pleasures of the field that animates his dog, and produces the most boisterous ebullitions of joy? When the hunter starts at a distant cry of the hounds – every motion and every attitude telling how eager he is to break away – what is this but the vivid recollection of past, and the anticipation of future pleasure?

The brutes, then, are evidently possessed of attention,

and memory, and association, and imagination. The difference between the biped and his quadruped slave is in degree, and not in kind. Then how stands the account as to the result of these preparatives for the exercise of the reasoning principle? By means of one of the senses an impression is made on the mind – attention fixes it there – memory frequently recurs to it – association and imagination combine it rightly or erroneously with many another – and judgement determines the value of it and the conclusions which may be drawn. This is the process of animal reasoning.

... I wanted one day to go through a tall iron gate, from one part of my premises to another; but, just within it, lay a poor lame puppy, and I could not get in without rolling the little fellow over, and perhaps seriously injuring him. I stood for awhile hesitating, and at length determined to go round, through another gate; when a fine Newfoundland dog, who had been waiting patiently for his wonted caresses, and wondering why I did not come in, looked accidentally down at the invalid. He comprehended the whole business in a moment; he put down his great paw; and as quickly and as gently as possible rolled the invalid out of the way, and then drew himself back in order to leave room for the opening of the gate. Here was a plain and palpable act of reasoning.

Ibid.

Dr Darwin used to tell a curious story of a wasp. As he was walking one day in his garden he perceived a wasp upon the gravel walk with a fly almost as large as itself, which it had just caught. Kneeling down in order to observe the manoeuvres of the murderer, he saw him distinctly cut off the head and the body; and then, taking up the trunk, to which the wings still remained attached, he attempted to fly away. A breeze of wind, however, acting upon the wings of the fly, turned the wasp round, and impeded or forbad his progress. Upon this, he alighted again on the gravel, deliberately sawed off one wing, and then the other, and, having thus removed the cause of his embarrassment, he flew off with his booty.

Can any process of reasoning be more perfect than this? ... Instinct has, and can have, nothing to do with it. The attempt was made to carry off the insect with the wings on; this was found to be impossible; the cause why it was impossible was ascertained; that cause was removed, and the task was accomplished. Here is a perfect course of reasoning.

Ibid.

I pass to another division of our subject – the moral qualities. What, of brutes? Ay! and strongly developed, and beautifully displayed, and often putting the biped to shame ... The social affections are as necessary in the little republics of the brutes as among any of the associations of men. They are the cement which binds together the different parts of the fabric.

'But,' say some, 'they are mere instincts!' We care not for that. These instincts or propensities are the foundation of every virtue in the human being; and in the quadruped they cannot escape our regard and admiration.

The parental affection, the hallowed basis of the whole! Let it be an instinct! What character is so attractive as the wisely indulgent father – the devoted mother? Is it instinct only in the brute, and associated with every virtue in the human being? Is it not instinct and virtue in both?

FRANCIS BRETT YOUNG, 1884–1954

Bête Humaine

Riding through Ruwu swamp, about sunrise,
I saw the world awake; and as the ray

Touched the tall grasses where they sleeping lay,
Lo, the bright air alive with dragonflies:
With brittle wings aquiver, and great eyes
Piloting crimson bodies – slender and gay.
I aimed at one, and struck it, and it lay
Broken and lifeless, with fast-fading dyes ...
Then my soul sickened with a sudden pain
And horror, at my own careless cruelty,
That in an idle moment I had slain
A creature whose sweet life it is to fly:
Like beasts that prey with tooth and claw ...
                     Nay, they
Must slay to live, but what excuse had I?

MARGUERITE YOURCENAR, 1903–

Cruelty is the luxury of those who have nothing to do,
like drugs or racing stables.

Coup de Grace

EMILE ZOLA, 1840–1902

The fate of animals is of greater importance to me than
the fear of appearing ridiculous; it is indissolubly
connected with the fate of men.

Correspondance

SELECT BIBLIOGRAPHY
(last known editions)

Keith Akers: *A Vegetarian Sourcebook*, Putnam, 1983

Nathaniel Altman: *Ahimsa*, Theosophical Publishing House, 1980; *The Nonviolent Revolution*, Element Books, 1988

Brigid Brophy: *The Rights of Animals*, Sunday Times/Vegetarian Society, 1965

Gerald Carson: *Men, Beasts and Gods*, Scribners, 1972

Stephen R.L. Clark: *The Moral Status of Animals*, Clarendon Press, 1984; *The Nature of the Beast*, Oxford U.P., 1984; *From Athens to Jerusalem*, Clarendon Press, 1984

Michael Cox: *The New Vegetarian*, Thorsons, 1985

Daniel A. Dombrowski: *Vegetarianism: the Philosophy Behind the Ethical Diet*, Thorsons, 1985

Maureen Duffy: *Men and Beasts: an Animal Rights Handbook*, Paladin, 1984

Michael F. Fox: *Returning to Eden: Animal Rights and Human Liberation*, Viking, 1979; *One Earth, One Mind*, Coward McCann, 1980

Dudley Giehl: *Vegetarianism, a Way of Life*, Harper & Row, 1979

Mark Gold: *Living Without Cruelty*, Green Print, 1988

Rebecca Hall: *Animals are Equal*, Wildwood House, 1980

George and Willene Hendrick: *The Savour of Salt: a Henry Salt Anthology*, Centaur Press, 1989

Philip Kapleau: *To Cherish All Life*, Harper & Row, 1982

Clay Lancaster: *The Incredible World's Parliament of Religions*, Centaur Press, 1987

Andrew Linzey: *Christianity and the Rights of Animals*, SPCK, 1987

Andrew Linzey and Tom Regan (eds.): *Animals and Christianity: a Book of Readings*, SPCK, 1989; *Compassion for Animals: Prayers and Readings*, SPCK, 1988; *Song of Creation: Poetry in Celebration of Animals*, Marshall Pickering, 1988

Charles Magel: *Keyguide to Information Sources in Animal Rights*, Mansell, 1989

BIBLIOGRAPHY

Jim Mason and Peter Singer: *Animal Factories*, Crown, 1980

Mary Midgley: *Beast and Man*, Harvester Press, 1979, Cornell U.P., 1978; *Animals and Why They Matter*, Penguin, 1983

Ashley Montagu: *Of Men, Animals and Morals*, National Association for the Advancement of Humane Education, 1974; *The Nature of Human Aggression*, Oxford, 1976

Victoria Moran: *Compassion: the Ultimate Ethic*, Thorsons, 1985

Charles D. Niven: *History of the Humane Movement*, Johnson, 1967

David Paterson and Richard D. Ryder (eds.): *Animals' Rights: a Symposium*, Centaur Press, 1979

Porphyry: *On Abstinence from Animal Food*, Centaur Press, 1965

Tom Regan: *Animal Rights and Human Obligations* (with P. Singer), Prentice-Hall, 1976; *Matters of Life and Death*, Random House, 1979; *All That Dwell Therein*, University of California Press, 1982; *The Case for Animal Rights*, University of California Press and Routledge, Kegan Paul, 1984

Tom Regan (ed.): *Animal Sacrifices: Religious Perspectives on the Use of Animals in Science*, Temple University Press, 1986; *The Struggle for Animal Rights*, International Society for Animal Rights, 1987

Lewis Regenstein: *The Politics of Extinction*, Macmillan (NY), 1975

Catherine Roberts: *The Scientific Conscience*, George Braziller, 1967, and Centaur Press, 1974; *Science, Animals and Evolution*, Greenwood Press, 1980

Rosen, Steven: *Food for the Spirit: Vegetarianism and the World Religions*, Bala Books, 1987

Hans Ruesch: *Slaughter of the Innocent*, Futura, 1979

Richard D. Ryder: *Speciesism: the Ethics of Vivisection*, Scottish Society for the Prevention of Vivisection, 1974; *Victims of Science*, National Anti-Vivisection Society (UK)/Centaur Press, 1983; *The Animal Revolution*, Blackwell, 1989

Henry S. Salt: *Animals' Rights Considered in Relation to Social Progress*, International Society of Animal Rights and Centaur Press, 1980; *see* G. and W. Hendrick

James Serpell: *In the Company of Animals*, Blackwell, 1986

Peter Singer: *Animal Liberation*, Avon Books, 1977, and Thorsons, 1983; *In Defence of Animals* (editor), Blackwell, 1985; *See also* under Mason and Regan

Keith Thomas: *Man and the Natural World*, Penguin, 1984

E.S. Turner: *All Heaven in a Rage*, Michael Joseph, 1964

James Turner: *Reckoning with the Beast*, Johns Hopkins University Press, 1980

John Vyvyan: *In Pity and in Anger*, Michael Joseph, 1969; *The Dark Face of Science*, Michael Joseph, 1971, Transatlantic Arts, 1972

Esmé Wynne-Tyson: *The Philosophy of Compassion*, Centaur Press, 1970

Jon Wynne-Tyson: *The Civilized Alternative*, Centaur Press, 1972; *Food for a Future: How World Hunger could be Ended by the Twenty-first Century*, Thorsons, 1988

SOME ADDITIONAL READING

As mentioned in the Introduction, the purpose of this dictionary has been not to select quotations whose main effect is to shock or depress with evidence of mankind's capacity for cruelty, which has been well documented, but to quote those who have spoken out against it and who seek a better pattern.

The media give daily proof of our tolerance of almost any injustice toward humans or non-humans that may bring pleasure or profit. Our worst excesses are those we permit by default – those we may safely leave in others' hands. Increasingly, urban and technological values are eclipsing the empathy we might otherwise feel toward non-human species. Brainwashed into an uncritical tolerance of science (a much misused designation), we too readily take as evidence of practitioners' infallibility and integrity their badges of office and the support they receive from government and industry for their contributions to the end products of a consumer society.

It is sometimes said that the plight of other species has improved over the years. Anyone wishing to examine this claim in the cold light of the facts can do so in greater depth by reading the literature produced by anti-vivisection and other animal rights organizations, and the many books now on the general market. A short list of the latter (not all in print) follows:

M. Beddow Bayly, MRCS, LRCP, *The Futility of Experiments on Living Animals* (and other works)
John Bryant, *Fettered Kingdoms*, Remous, 1983
Gerald Carson, *Men, Beasts and Gods*
Marie Dreyfus, *Crimes Against Creation*
Martyn Ford, *Towards Animal Rights*
Mark Gold, *Assault and Battery*, Pluto Press, 1983; *Living Without Cruelty*, Green Print, 1988
Rebecca Hall, *Voiceless Victims*

Ruth Harrison, *Animal Machines*
André Launay, *Caviare and After*
Albert Leffingwell, MD, *An Ethical Problem*
Jim Mason and Peter Singer, *Animal Factories*
Leslie Pine, *After Their Blood*
Hans Ruesch, *Slaughter of the Innocent*
Richard D. Ryder, *Victims of Science*
Robert Sharpe, *The Cruel Deception*, Green Print, 1988
Peter Singer, *Animal Liberation* (chapter 'Tools for Research')
E.S. Turner, *All Heaven in a Rage*
John Vyvyan, *In Pity and in Anger* and *The Dark Face of Science*.
E. Westacott, *A Century of Vivisection and Anti-Vivisection* and *Spotlights on Performing Animals*

PLANET EARTH IS 4,600 MILLION YEARS OLD

If we condense this inconceivable time-span into an understandable concept, we can liken Earth to a person of 46 years of age.

Nothing is known about the first 7 years of this person's life, and whilst only scattered information exists about the middle span, we know that only at the age of 42 did the Earth begin to flower.

Dinosaurs and the great reptiles did not appear until 1 year ago, when the planet was 45. Mammals arrived only 8 months ago; in the middle of last week man-like apes evolved into ape-like men, and at the weekend the last ice age enveloped the Earth.

Modern man has been around for 4 hours. During the last hour, Man discovered agriculture. The industrial revolution began a minute ago.

During those sixty seconds of biological time, Modern Man has made a rubbish tip of Paradise.

He has multiplied his numbers to plague proportions, caused the extinction of 500 species of animals, ransacked the planet for fuels and now stands like a brutish infant, gloating over this meteoric rise to ascendancy, on the brink of a war to end all wars and of effectively destroying this oasis of life in the solar system.

GREENPEACE

SEX IN HISTORY

Reay Tannahill

Sex in History chronicles the pleasures – and the perils –
of the flesh from the time of mankind's distant ancestors
to the modern day; from a sexual act which was brief,
crude and purposeful, to the myriad varieties of
contemporary sexual mores.

Reay Tannahill's scholarly, yet accessible study ranges
from the earliest forms of contraception (one Egyptian
concoction included crocodile dung) to some latter-day
misconceptions about it – like the men who joined their
lovers in taking the Pill 'just to be on the safe side.' It
surveys all manner of sexual practice, preference and
position (the acrobatic 'wheelbarrow' position, the
strenuous 'hovering butterflies' position . . .) and draws
on sources as diverse as the *Admirable Discourses of the
Plain Girl*, the *Exhibition of Female Flagellants*, *Important
Matters of the Jade Chamber* and *The Romance of
Chastisement*.

Whether writing on androgyny, courtly love,
flagellation or zoophilia, Turkish eunuchs, Greek
dildoes, Taoist sex manuals or Japanese geisha girls,
Reay Tannahill is consistently enlightening and
entertaining.

First published in 1980, this edition has been updated to
consider AIDS and the shifting landscape of recent
sexual attitudes.

'Level-headed . . . diligent, provocative and fascinating.
The book is the most complete of its kind ever written'
Time

'Sanity on the subject of sex is all too rare; wit is in even
shorter supply; and an engaging style is about as
commonplace as eyebrows on an egg. Three cheers,
therefore, for Reay Tannahill' *Washington Post*

NON-FICTION
0 7474 0522 0

GOODWIN WHARTON

J Kent Clark

This is the story of a quest – the attempt of a
seventeenth-century aristocrat to transmute arcane
knowledge into wealth, power and salvation. Goodwin
Wharton was the most unfortunate member of the
politically powerful and influential Wharton family.
Overshadowed by his elder brother, he was desperate
for love, sympathy and recognition.

When Goodwin met Mary Parish in 1683 he was
consumed by debt and close to despair. He had tried his
hand at any number of money-making enterprises –
deep-sea diving, alchemy, an early form of fire engine –
all of which had proved calamitous failures. Mary, he
decided, would change all this.

She had a peerless knowledge of the arcane; she could
converse with angels; she enjoyed a close acquaintance
with the fairy inhabitants of the 'lowlands' – situated
somewhere beneath Hounslow Heath. Her skills ran to
the manufacture of 'magic purses' – which mysteriously
generated money – the location of buried treasure, and
match-making Goodwin with Penelope, the Queen of
the Fairies.

So was born the remarkable partnership of a desperate
young man and a con-woman nonpareil, one which was
to last the twenty years until her death. In all that time
none of Mary's promises were realised. She failed even
to keep her promise to revisit Goodwin after her death.

Goodwin's political fortunes had changed, however,
with the Glorious Revolution of 1688 – he entered the
Commons and rose to the Lord of the Admiralty – but
wealth and fame were of little consequence to him
beside the huge spiritual adventure he had embarked
upon with Mary, and to his dying day he was to keep
faith with the bizarre world he had glimpsed through
her eyes.

NON-FICTION
0 7474 0550 6

CARDUS ON MUSIC:
A CENTENARY COLLECTION

Neville Cardus

Sir Neville Cardus, whose formal training in music was
virtually non-existent, joined the *Manchester Guardian* in
1917, where he wrote on cricket and music until his
death in 1975. In that time he wrote over 2000 pieces of
music criticism and established an unassailable
reputation as one of the subject's most eloquent critics
this century. *Cardus on Music* is a collection of his finest
essays, and shows Cardus at his best; the last critic from
a more generous era, where criticism was an art and not
a technical evaluation. Shafts of wisdom illuminate
composers, conductors and performers equally.
Whether rhapsodising over Wagner or cutting Karajan
down to size, delivering bouquets to Du Pré or brickbats
to Webern, his unique wit and perception captures the
essence of his subjects in a manner that is a joy to expert
and layperson alike.

NON-FICTION
0 7474 0687 1

THE MEMOIRS OF HECTOR BERLIOZ

Ed David Cairns

Writing with unreserved candour and emotion, sparing no one's feelings – least of all his own – Hector Berlioz began, when he was forty-four (in 1848) to set down a memoir of his musical and personal life. Twenty-one years later, the work was completed. It is regarded to this day, as one of the greatest of all biographies.

David Cairns, renowned Berlioz scholar and author of the definitive biography, has further updated and revised his original translation of 1969.

'By some alchemy, the unmistakable voice of Berlioz himself, passionate, witty, enraged, high-spirited, sardonic, tormented and infinitely proud, speaks from these pages. An overwhelming sense of identity unites life, book and translation . . . Of the composers of the nineteenth century only Berlioz was a genius in the use of words. His *Memoirs* are more than a great musician's vivid account of his life. They are a crucial document of their age, for they illuminate as little else the early romantic temperament and its relations with the outside world' *Observer*

BIOGRAPHY
0 7474 0582 4

CAPTAIN BLIGH
AND HIS MUTINIES

Gavin Kennedy

'Everyone, Professor Kennedy begins, knows the truth
about William Bligh. He was the tyrannical Captain of
HMS Bounty who drove his crew to mutiny in the
South Seas and was turned adrift by the noble Fletcher
Christian. Surviving by a miracle, he then mobilised the
power of the Royal Navy to have his revenge, from
which Christian escaped only by leading his men to the
remote fastness of Pitcairn, where he, they and their
Tahitian wives created an island paradise.

Almost everything in this story, as the author goes on to
show, is false. Christian was not a hero. Pitcairn was not
a paradise. Bligh's escape was not a miracle but an
extraordinary feat of seamanship. And he was certainly
not a tyrant, not at least in a navy where the
qualification to the title was set fairly high. He was,
nevertheless, a very peculiar man . . .' *Sunday Telegraph*

'Gavin Kennedy's book is based on an extraordinary
range of primary sources which build up three well-told
narratives; Bligh's career leading up to the mutiny, the
mutiny itself and the fate of the mutineers, and Bligh's
career – which included two further mutinies – from the
moment he was cast adrift in an open boat. This is
history on the human scale, depicting a reality of
squalid motivation and psychological inadequacy . . .
takes us as close to the reality of Bligh as we are ever
likely to get' *Scotsman*

'The background causes and aftermath of the 1789
mutiny on the Bounty make compulsive reading; a
shattering tale that highlights the hellish conditions of
life in the 18th century Royal Navy . . . A vast amount
of meticulous research has come to rest in these pages, a
true summation of the current state of Bligh scholarship'
The Times

BIOGRAPHY/HISTORY
0 7474 0679 0

READS

Brigid Brophy

Brigid Brophy: novelist, critic, biographer, journalist
and promoter of – amongst much else – animal rights,
Mozart, Firbank, and the Baroque. Her writing is
inimitable and incomparable. *Reads* captures her spirit
in a collection of reviews and essays spanning the whole
period of her writing career.

'We read therefore we are. The idea is suggested to me
by Brigid Brophy's essays, which constitute one of the
strongest proofs of personal identity I have ever come
across. If a real person is not here, where is a person to
be found? She writes therefore she is, and to receive
such an impression, so clearly, is very uncommon
indeed'   John Bayley, *London Review of Books*

NON-FICTION
0 7474 0275 2